WE are MANY

REFLECTIONS ON
MOVEMENT STRATEGY
FROM OCCUPATION
TO LIBERATION

EDITED BY
KATE KHATIB, MARGARET KILLJOY, AND MIKE MCGUIRE

We Are Many: Reflections on Movement Strategy From Occupation to Liberation
Edited by Kate Khatib, Margaret Killjoy, and Mike McGuire

All essays © 2012 by their respective authors.

This edition © 2012 AK Press (Oakland, Edinburgh, Baltimore)
ISBN: 978-1-84935-116-4 | e-ISBN: 978-1-84935-117-1
Library of Congress Control Number: 2012914345

AK Press	AK Press
674-A 23rd Street	PO Box 12766
Oakland, CA 94612	Edinburgh, EH8 9YE
USA	Scotland
www.akpress.org	www.akuk.com
akpress@akpress.org	ak@akedin.demon.co.uk

The above addresses would be delighted to provide you with the latest AK Press distribution catalog, which features the several thousand books, pamphlets, zines, audio and video products, and stylish apparel published and/or distributed by AK Press. Alternatively, visit our websites for the complete catalog, latest news, and secure ordering.

Visit us at:
www.akpress.org | www.akuk.com | www.revolutionbythebook.akpress.org

Printed in the USA on acid-free, recycled paper.

Cover and interior design by Margaret Killjoy | www.birdsbeforethestorm.net
Cover image based on a sign painted by Erin Barry-Dutro

TABLE OF CONTENTS

Introduction: Kate Khatib. 1

Vijay Prashad: This Concerns Everyone 9
Movement Story: Molly Crabapple 20
Josh MacPhee: A Qualitative Quilt Born of Pizzatopia 23
Movement Story: Annie Cockrell 36
George Ciccariello-Maher: From Oscar Grant to Occupy. 39

Joel Olson: Whiteness and the 99%. **46**
Lester Spence & Mike McGuire: Occupy and the 99% 53
Movement Story: Brendan Maslauskas Dunn 66
Occupy Research and DataCenter: Research By
and For the Movement. 69
Yvonne Yen Liu: Where Is the Color in Occupy? 75
Croatoan: Who is Oakland?. 81

Research & Destroy: Plaza-Riot-Commune **88**
Joshua Clover: The Coming Occupation .95
Immanuel Wallerstein: Upsurge in Movements Around the Globe . . 105
Janaina Stronzake: People Make the Occupation,
and the Occupation Makes the People. 115
Ryan Harvey: Occupy Before and Beyond. 123
Movement Story: Gabriella *134*
Morrigan Phillips: Room for the Poor 137
Movement Story: Yotam Marom *146*

Declaration of the Occupation of the City of New York **148**

Marisa Holmes: The Center Cannot Hold 151

Andy Cornell: Consensus: What it Is, What it is Not,
Where it Came From, and Where it Must Go 163

Movement Story: Manissa McCleave Maharawal *174*

Manissa McCleave Maharawal:
Reflections from the People of Color Caucus at Occupy Wall Street 177

Max Rameau: Occupy to Liberate 185

RANT: Solidarity in Practice for the Street Demonstrations **188**

Movement Story: Paul Dalton *190*

Mike King and Emily Brissette: Overcoming Internal Pacification. . . 193

Kristian Williams: Cops and the 99%. 205

Rachel Herzing and Isaac Ontiveros:
Reflections From the Fight Against Policing. 217

CrimethInc. Ex-Worker's Collective:
Bounty Hunters and Child Predators. 229

**Occupy Oakland: Statement
of Solidarity Against Police Repression** **237**

Michael Andrews: Taking the Streets 239

Jonathan Matthew Smucker: Radicals and the 99% 247

Nathan Schneider: No Revolution Without Religion 255

Rose Bookbinder & Michael Belt:
OWS and Labor Attempting the Possible 263

John Duda: Where Was the Social Forum in Occupy? 275

Movement Story: Chris Dixon *284*

Occupy Wall Street Community Agreement **286**

Cindy Milstein: Occupy Anarchism 291

Movement Story: Koala Largess. *306*

Movement Story: Anonymous. *308*

Movement Story: Sophie Whittemore *310*

Movement Story: Unwoman. *312*

Michael Premo: Unlocking the Radical Imagination 315

Janelle Treibitz: The Art of Cultural Resistance 325

Nadine Bloch: Shine a Light on It 337

Movement Story: Mattilda Bernstein Sycamore 344

Jaime Omar Yassin: Farmers, Cloud Communities,
and Issue-Driven Occupations. 351

Gabriel Hetland: Occupying Democracy 361

Occupy Wall Street: Statement of Autonomy 369

Movement Story: Mark Bray 370

Frances Fox Piven: Is Occupy Over? 373

Lisa Fithian: Strategic Directions for the Occupy Movement. 381

George Caffentzis: In Desert Cities 389

Team Colors Collective: Messy Hearts Made of Thunder. 399

Some Oakland Antagonists:
Occupy Oakland Is Dead—Long Live the Oakland Commune 409

Yotam Marom: Rome Wasn't Sacked In a Day. 417

Afterword: David Graeber 425

YOU CANNOT
EVICT AN IDEA
WHOSE TIME
HAS COME

WE ARE THE 99%

WE ARE
EVERYWHERE

Gan Golan
2011

Kate Khatib
for the editors

THE PRODUCTIVE LIFE OF CHAOS: AN INTRODUCTION TO *WE ARE MANY*

THIS BOOK IS DIFFERENT. LIKE THE MOVEMENT FROM WHENCE IT CAME, IT refuses to acquiesce to our traditional notions of analysis and action, shuns the antiquated idea that there is a single right answer to any problem, scoffs in the face of a single set of demands. Our demand? We want everything and nothing. Our perspective? We are all a little bit right, and we are all a little bit wrong. What matters is that we are *doing something*.

We Are Many started with a simple question: what have we learned over the course of the past year, since Zuccotti Park and the city of New York was "occupied" on September 17, 2011? And subsequently: What do we wish we had known then? What do we know now? What lessons do we want to leave for future social movement actors as this movement shifts and grows? As readers, we longed for a book that would give space to the voices of on-the-ground activists, that would shine a light on the inner workings of Occupy in different cities around the country. As activists, we longed for a resource guide we could use in our organizing work, something to show us that the problems we had in our Assemblies and affinity groups were far from unique, and something to point us towards strategies for overcoming our roadblocks. As historical actors, we wanted to be responsible towards future generations of movements and document our innovations and mistakes, to answer the questions that Janaina Stronzake sets out in her essay on the MST—"Why are we doing this? What do we want in the future? Where do we want to go and how do we want get there? Is there anyone else in history who wanted the same, or something similar? What did they do, and what happened?"—so that next time, and for generations to come, we can build stronger, better, and more agile movements for social change.

In reality, we didn't manage to do any of that. Or rather, what we managed to do is *start* that process. It will take more work, more analysis, more conversations, and crucially more *action* to finish the story. In the nine months since we began this project, so many things have changed, grown, developed. Every time we sat down to look at the pieces we'd amassed, we found a new hole, a new element that had presented itself as *central* to any account of the Occupy movement. After a while, we lost count. We accepted pieces that brought something new to the table (of contents), pieces that seemed to be an invitation to conversation—our primary criteria. We wanted this book to feel like a General Assembly: many voices, multiple perspectives, some in conversation with each other, some at odds with each other, jumbled, exciting, frustrating, at times painful and at times joyful. A reflection of the actual experience of Occupy, written by those who lived it. Productive chaos.

In the process of putting this collection together, we learned a few things as editors. The first is that you don't have to agree with everything in an essay to see the value in it. As editors, we don't all agree politically on every aspect of Occupy, or really on anything else. And that's a good thing. Throughout the process, we challenged each other to think critically about our own strengths and weaknesses as movement actors, and learned to recognize our own blind-spots. That wasn't always an easy thing to do, and it sometimes felt schizophrenic. Just like Occupy itself, which brought together so many different and disparate worldviews from so many different parts of society.

We also learned that social movements have geographical differences. For many east coasters, the issues at stake tended to be largely those of process and structure. For west coasters, especially folks in Oakland, the conversation tended towards actions and tactics. As a close friend from Oakland pointed out to us, what made Occupy different from so many social movements of the past several decades was that it started out with a radical act, it started out by *doing* something—occupying territory—and, especially in cities like Oakland, it continued to *do things* and refused to settle solely for marches and statements. Indeed, Occupy managed, for a time at least, to balance both the need for symbolic acts and tangible acts. As we read through the pieces that eventually came together to form this book, we realized these differences of geography are important to underscore—but that process and tactics are equally important as parts of a larger movement analysis.

In terms of *what* the book covers, and *who* covers it, we each solicited pieces and encouraged submissions from the parts of the movement and the perspectives that we felt closest to—although we tried desperately to strike a balance and bring as many new voices into the mix as we possibly could. Of the countless activists and organizers I could have reached out to as co-editors, I chose Mike and Margaret because they both bring a very different set of skills and perspectives to the table—and neither one of them is wholly in line with my own perspective, either. I also chose to ask these two unique humans because they are people I *trust*—and trust has been in short supply this past year, perhaps wrongly so, and perhaps rightly so, as CrimethInc point out in their discussion of state repression included in this collection. At the end of the day, trust is what carried us through this process, and allowed us to see past the immediate conflict of *what* and *who*, and focus on the larger project of creating a lasting, productive movement document, albeit one with the same rough edges as Occupy itself.

For my part, one of the things I like about this book is the way it addresses complex and charged issues. Take race, for example: the race question—is Occupy a white movement?—is one that comes up again and again, in so many different contexts, in this book, and in our everyday discussions about Occupy. We can't ignore the question of race when we discuss social, political, and economic inequality, but increasingly we are learning, as a movement, that race isn't entirely black and white. As an Arab-American, I largely don't figure into most of the discussions that rage in social movement circles around this question—I'm neither white, nor black, nor what we traditionally think of as brown. Equally accepted and equally *not* accepted by both the white folks and the not-white folks. Hated at various points by everyone, when anti-Arab sentiment in this country has been at its

We wanted this book to feel like a General Assembly: many voices, multiple perspectives, some in conversation with each other, some at odds with each other, jumbled, exciting, frustrating, at times painful and at times joyful. A reflection of the actual experience of Occupy, written by those who lived it. Productive chaos.

peak. It doesn't bother me—I'm a project-based organizer, and I tend to be resistant to identity politics, mostly because it's not a framework that I find personally useful for organizing the way I see the world, even though I know that so many of my fellow activists find great solace in it. For me, everything is a mixture—fluid shades of gray, rather than the stark contrast of black and white.

Yet over the course of the past year, I found myself drawn more and more into conversations about the question of color in the movement. And, I found the dominant narrative about Occupy as a "white movement" less and less representative of my own everyday experiences as an organizer. But none of this really dawned on me in a way that I could vocalize (more like a dull confusion or a blind rage, depending on the day) until I read Croatoan's piece included in this anthology, which was originally published as a much larger pamphlet and circulated in Oakland: in the debates that have raged around race and Occupy, in the portrayal of this movement as a "largely white" movement, the roles and actions of people of color *in* the movement have largely been erased.

At Occupy Baltimore, I watched the facilitation team transform from a group comprised predominantly of white men (and me) into a group predominantly populated with women and folks of color. When I looked around me at the camp, I saw a mixture of people, from all walks of life: yes, there were young, idealistic white folks and lots of them! But there were aging Black veterans, transgender folks, anarchists, communists, immigrants of all walks of life, the houseless, the unstable, the raver kids, and more and more and more. Occupy Baltimore, like all Occupies, had its problems—it replicated the "isms" of society at large, and three months of working on those issues was never going to be enough to solve the problems of a society gone mad with inequity and imbalance. But, it was a start.

Reality is never a simple thing. It is true, as essays in this book argue, that Occupy will have to overcome its whiteness, will have to own that whiteness and organize in solidarity with communities of color, that we don't know whether we will ever be able to escape the trap that is "left white colorblindness," as Lester Spence and Mike McGuire frame it in their excellent essay included here. It is also true, as other essays in this book argue, that, despite the very real shortcomings of the movement unfolding around us, people of color kept on going. We kept meeting, facilitating, thinking, dreaming, and occupying, as individuals, as people of color, as active participants, despite the attempt to erase our presence from the movement, and we learned a lot. We learned *so much*. This book, and these voices of color writing *as participants* of Occupy, is, in a tiny way, a testament to that presence within the movement, a reminder that when we define a movement as having a specific identity, we erase the participation of those who identify otherwise.

And, the same narrative exists for so many other "marginal" groups who participated in Occupy. The media would like to tell a story about our movement that casts it as a white middle-class uprising of moderate folks pissed off at the economic crisis and the big banks. And it was that. But it was so much more. Anarchists, those black-clad bogeymen cast as "troublemakers" and "bad elements" by media and moderates alike, paid a heavy social price, finding themselves pariahs of the movement, "convenient strawmen," as Cindy Milstein writes, while still being expected to contribute organizational skills to keeping the camps running. Apparently, it's okay to be an anarchist when that involves building a mobile kitchen and feeding hundreds of people on the basis of skills learned through years of Food Not Bombs and mass mobilizations. But it's not okay to be an anarchist when that involves militant street action. I cannot help but think of one General Assembly early on in Occupy Baltimore's life when a well-meaning Occupier stood up to very earnestly warn the rest of the group about a threat we needed to be resistant to: the anarchists were out there, and we needed to be sure to not allow our camp to be co-opted by them. Apparently his fears had already been realized—I saw my anarchist friends, cheerful participants from day one, wearing medical badges, working at the kitchen, organizing supplies, and standing next to me on the facilitation team, and as I caught each of their eyes, I knew we were all thinking the same thing: "Too late!"

There are countless stories like these, and one of my regrets is that this book

Each of these pieces defies simple categorization—they don't fit into neat little boxes, and the great thing about Occupy is that it reminded us that we don't either. Essays about race are also about class; essays about class are also about struggle; essays about struggle are also about solidarity; essays about solidarity are also history lessons; and history lessons are also suggestions of how to move forward.

didn't manage to collect more of them. In the final analysis, though, *We Are Many* presents only a tiny fraction of the mass movement that is Occupy. This project is a jumping off point to a larger conversation about tactics and strategies, about the past and the future, and about how and why we can work together in the struggles to come.

A note on structure

WITH OVER FIFTY unique contributions to this book, the logical thing to do would be to arrange the pieces into nicely-defined sections oriented around subject categories, issues, chronology, geography, or some other schema. We tried. It didn't work. The fact of the matter is that each of these pieces defies simple categorization—they don't fit into neat little boxes, and the great thing about Occupy is that it reminded us that we don't either. Essays about race are also about class; essays about class are also about struggle; essays about struggle are also about solidarity; essays about solidarity are also history lessons; and history lessons are also suggestions of how to move forward.

Instead, we chose to group these pieces into *conversations*—sometimes literal ones, sometimes figurative ones—centered around what we call "movement documents." *We Are Many* is, and was always intended to be, a collection of interventions into movement discourse. We tried, as much as possible, to avoid using pieces that had already appeared elsewhere, because there are so many books already out that are collections of articles that have appeared online, or that collect "primary source" documents from within the movement. We wanted to contribute something different, since those bases are well covered. Yet we found that there were documents—resolutions, analyses, manifestos, essays—that people referenced, or that seemed to us to be magnetic poles around which these conversations revolved. So, we include them here not as section markers, but as punctuation in the paragraph that is this book. They indicate the places where one thought trails off and another begins, and they help the book to loop back on itself thematically and geographically over the course of the narrative. The movement documents appear here with black backgrounds.

We also included what we call "Movement Stories": short first-person narratives that also do the work of punctuating and anchoring the longer analytical pieces. The movement stories largely came to us through an open submission process announced in February 2012; most of the longer essays were either solicited by one of the editors, or came to us through a series of movement connections. The movement stories appear here with black margins.

Images also punctuate this book. Like so many social movements, Occupy has produced a wealth of graphics, as well as incredible documentary photographs and films. We tried to include a range of images in this book, some illustrations by folks involved with the Occupy movement, some photographs by on-the-ground parrticipants, and some photos mined from the wealth of content that is the Internet. They provide a beautiful and sometimes haunting accompaniment to the words in this collection.

There are few people in the book that all three of the editors know, and there are many people in the book that *none* of the editors know. I haven't asked my co-editors (and I suspect I never will) but I'd doubt that there is a single piece in this book that we all agree with equally. This seems fitting.

There are so many aspects to the Occupy movement that this book does not explore: the role of the media (both mass and social); gender dynamics in Occupy spaces; the usefulness or not of property destruction; the mechanics of foreclosure defense, and the stories of those whose homes have been taken away; the role of Anonymous; militarism; and countless other elements that make Occupy what it is. While we, as editors, take responsibility for perceived slights or misconstruals caused by what we did and did not include, these omissions are not intentional. They are an indicator of the massive spread of what Occupy has taken on during the past year. No one book will be able to tell the definitive story of Occupy, because there is no definitive story, and, one hopes, there never will be. Therein lies our great power. We must use it well.

THE BEGINNING IS NEAR

OCCUPY
WALL STREET

Alexandra Clotfelter
"The Beginning Is Near," 2011
HTTP://WWW.LADYFAWN.COM

Vijay Prashad

THIS CONCERNS EVERYONE

My heart makes my head swim.
                    —Frantz Fanon, *Black Skin, White Masks*

part i: bare life

In the old days, a zombie was a figure whose life and work had been captured by magical means. Old zombies were expected to work around the clock with no relief. The new zombie cannot expect work of any kind—the new zombie just waits around to die.

                    — Junot Diaz

REPORTS AND RUMORS FILTER OUT OF GOVERNMENT DOCUMENTS AND FAMily distress signals to locate precisely the ongoing devastation of social life in the United States. Unemployment rates linger at perilously high levels, with the effective rate in some cities, such as Detroit, stumbling on with half the population without waged work. Home foreclosures fail to slow down, and sheriffs and debt-recovery paramilitaries scour the landscape for the delinquents. Personal debt has escalated as ordinary people with uneven means of earning their livings turn to banks and to the shady world of personal loan agencies to take them to the other side of starvation. Researchers at the RAND Corporation tell us that, absent of family support, poverty rates among the elderly will be about double what they are now: economist Nancy Folbre's "invisible heart" is trying its best to hold back the noxious effects of the "invisible hand."

Swathes of the American landscape are now given over to desolation: abandoned factories make room for chimney swallows and the heroin trade, as old farmhouses become homes for methamphetamine labs and the sorrows of broken, rural dreams. Returning to his native Indiana, Jeffrey St. Clair writes, "My grandfather's farm is now a shopping mall. The black soil, milled to such fine fertility by the Wisconsin glaciation, is now buried under a black sea of asphalt. The old Boatenwright pig farm is now a quick lube, specializing in servicing SUVs." Into this bleak landscape, St. Clair moans, "We are a hollow nation, a poisonous shell of our former selves."

What growth comes to the economy is premised upon the inventions and discoveries of a fortunate few, those who were either raised with all the advantages of the modern world or who were too gifted to be held back by centuries of hierarchies. Biochemists and computer engineers, as well as musical impresarios and film producers—they devise a product, patent it, and then mass-produce it elsewhere, in Mexico or China, Malaysia or India. These few collect rent off their inventions, and hire lawyers and bankers to protect their patents and grow their money. Around them, in their gated communities, exist a ring of service providers, from those who tend to their lawns to those who teach their children, from those who cook their food to those who protect them.

Those many in the United States who would once have been employed in mass industrial production to actually make the commodities that are invented by the few are now no longer needed. Production has slipped the national leash; it now takes place in pockets of the world that are "export processing" or "free trade," geographies of wage arbitrage that benefit Finance. The US working class has been rendered disposable—unnecessary to the political economy of accumulation. These many survive in the interstices of the economy, either with part time jobs, or crowded into family shops, either with off-the-books legal activity or off-the-books illegal activity: the struggle for survival is acute. Only 37% of unemployed Americans received jobless benefits, which amounts to $293 per week, and only 40% of very poor families who qualify for public assistance actually are able to claim it. Strikingly, the new recession has hit hard against low-wage service jobs with no benefits, which are mainly held by women. In times of recession, these women, with those jobs, stretched their invisible hearts across their families; now, even this love-fueled glue is no longer available.

The few luxuriate, the many vegetate: this is the social effect of high rates of inequality, the trick of jobless growth.

The political class has no effective answer to this malaise. It has drawn the country in the opposite direction from a solution. Rather than raise the funds to build a foundation for the vast mass, it continues to offer tax cuts to the wealthy: the average tax cut this year to the top 1% of the population was larger than the average income of the bottom 99%. Furthermore, the political class has diverted $7.6 trillion to the military for the wars, the overseas bases, the homeland security ensemble, and for the healthcare of the veterans of these endless wars. There is no attempt to draw down the personal debt that now stands at $2.4 trillion, and none whatsoever to tend to the $1 trillion in student debt that remains even after a declaration of bankruptcy. Our students are headed into the wilderness, carrying debt that constrains their imagination.

Zombie capitalism has made the heartland of the United States silent, reliant upon goods from elsewhere and credit from elsewhere to buy those goods. This is unsustainable madness. It is unrealistic to live within the confines of Zombie Capitalism. Another system is necessary.

part 2: dates

By 2042, the country is going to become majority minority, or, to put it bluntly, more people who claim their descent from outside Europe would populate the country. This worried Harvard political scientist Samuel Huntington, who wrote in an influential *Foreign Policy* article in 2004, "The persistent inflow of Hispanic immigrants threatens to divide the United States into two peoples, two cultures, and two languages. Unlike past immigrant groups, Mexicans and other Latinos have not assimilated into mainstream US culture, forming instead their own political and linguistic enclaves—from Los Angeles to Miami—and rejecting the Anglo-Protestant values that built the American dream. The United States ignores this challenge at its peril."

Globalization hollows out the core of the nation's manufacturing, devastates the social basis of its culture, and threatens the integrity of its people, and yet, it is the Migrant who bears the cross. Illusions about the social glue of Anglo-Protestantism, which whips between the Declaration of Independence and Chattel Slavery, provide the only outlet for Huntington's frustrations. There is no authentic cultural project to attract the new migrants, to encourage them to find shelter in these Anglo-Protestant values. Huntington knows that these have run their course, or they were never such strong magnets in the first place. Huntington's fearful panic can only be mollified by the prison-house of border walls, the Minutemen, the Border Patrol agents, SB-170, English-Only ordinances, and so on. Force alone can govern Huntington's vision. It no longer can breed mass consent.

2042 is far off. Closer still is 2016. It is the date chosen by the International Monetary Fund in its *World Economic Outlook* report from 2011 to signal the shift for the world's largest economy: from the United States to China. We are within a decade of that monumental turn, with the US having to surrender its dominant place for the first time since the 1920s. The collapse of the US economy is a "sign of autumn," as the historian Ferdinand Braudel put it; our autumn is China's springtime. Linked to this 2016 date is yet another: 2034. The US governmental data shows that by

2034 the United States will have a rate of inequality that matches Mexico. The United States *today* is *more unequal* than Pakistan and Iran. The rate of inequality has risen steadily since 1967; it is going to become catastrophic by 2034.

By 2042, the country will be majority minority. By 2034, it will be as unequal as Mexico, with the economy shrinking and formal unemployment steadily rising.

By 2042, people of color will inherit a broken country, one that is ready to be turned around for good, not ill.

part 3: conservatism

IN *SUICIDE OF a Superpower*, Pat Buchanan bemoans the decline of the United States and of white, Christian culture. What is left to conserve, asks the old warrior for the Right? Not much. He calls for a decline in the nation's debt and an end to its imperial postures (including an end to its bases and its wars). These are important gestures. Then he falls to his knees, begging for a return of the United States to Christianity and Whiteness. Buchanan knows this is ridiculous. He makes no attempt to say how this return must take place. His is an exhortation.

But Buchanan is not so far from the general tenor of the entire political class, whether putatively liberal or conservative. It is not capable of dealing with the transformation. It is deluded into the belief that the United States can enjoy another "American Century," and that if only the Chinese revalue their currency, everything would be back to the Golden Age. It is also deluded into the belief that the toxic rhetoric about "taking back the country" is going to silence the darker bodies, who have tasted freedom since 1965 and want more of it.

The idea of "taking back the country" produces what Aijaz Ahmad calls "cultures of cruelty." By "cultures of cruelty," Aijaz means the "wider web of social sanctions in which one kind of violence can be tolerated all the more because many other kinds of violence are tolerated anyway." Police brutality and domestic violence, ICE raids against undocumented workers and comical mimicry of the foreign accent, aerial bombardment in the borderlands of Afghanistan and sanctified misogyny in our cinema—these forms of routine violence set the stage for the "more generalized ethical numbness toward cruelty." It is on this prepared terrain of cruelty that the forces of the Far Right, the Tea Party for instance, can make their hallowed appearance—ready to dance on the misfortunes and struggles of the Migrants, the Workers, and the Dispossessed. The pre-existing cultures of cruelty sustain the Far Right, and allow it to appear increasingly normal, taking back the country from you know who.

The Right's menagerie sniffs at all the opportunities. It is prepared, exerting itself, feeding off a culture that has delivered a disarmed population into its fangs. *They* are ready for 2034 and 2042, but only in the most harmful way.

part 4:
multiculturalism

OBVIOUSLY MULTICULTURALISM IS the antithesis of Buchananism. But multiculturalism too is inadequate, if not anachronistic. Convulsed by the fierce struggles from below for recognition and redistribution, the powers that be settled on a far more palatable social theory than full equality: bourgeois multiculturalism. Rather than annul the social basis of discrimination, the powers that be cracked open the doors to privilege, like Noah on the ark, letting specimens of each of the colors enter into the inner sanctum—the rest were to be damned in the flood. Color came into the upper reaches of the Military and the Corporate Boardroom, to the College Campus and to the Supreme Court, and eventually to the Oval Office. Order recognized that old apartheid was anachronistic. It was now going to be necessary to incorporate the most talented amongst the populations of color into the hallways of money and power. Those who would be anointed might then stand in for their fellows, left out in the cold night of despair.

The same politicians, such as Bill Clinton, who favored multicultural advancement for the few strengthened the social policies to throttle the multitudinous lives of color: the end of welfare,

The few luxuriate, the many vegetate: this is the social effect of high rates of inequality, the trick of jobless growth.

the increase in police and prisons, and the free pass given to Wall Street shackled large sections of our cities to the chains of starvation, incarceration, and indebtedness. Meanwhile, in ones and twos, people of color attained the mantle of success. Their success was both a false beacon for populations that could not hope for such attainment, and a standing rebuke for not having made it. There is a cruelty in the posture of multiculturalism.

When Barack Obama ascended the podium at Grant Park in Chicago on November 4, 2010 to declare himself the victor in the presidential election, multiculturalism's promise was fulfilled. For decades, people of color had moved to the highest reaches of corporate and military life, of the State, and of society. The only post unoccupied till November 4 was the presidency. No wonder that even Jesse Jackson, Sr., wept when Obama accepted victory. That night, multiculturalism ended. It has now exhausted itself as a progressive force.

Obama has completed his historical mission, to slay the bugbear of social distinction: in the higher offices, all colors can come. Obama's minor mission, also completed, was to provide the hard-core racists with a daily dose of acid reflux when he appears on television.

What did not end, of course, was racism. That remains. When the economy tanked in 2007–08, the victims of the harshest asset-stripping were African Americans and Latinos. They lost more than half their assets, which amounts to the loss of a generation's savings. As of 2009, the typical white household had wealth (assets minus debts) worth $113,149, while Black households only had $5,677 and Hispanic households $6,325. Black and Latino households, in other words, hold only about 5% of the wealth in the hands of white households. Latinos have the highest unemployment rate in the US (11%), the greatest decline in household wealth from 2005 to 2009, the greatest food insecurity with a third of households in this condition, and 6.1 million children in poverty, the largest number for any ethnic group. These are the social consequences of living in a recession, governed by politicians in the pockets of banks. The myth of the post-racial society should be buried under this data.

Even Obama knew that it was silly to speak of post-racism. Before he won the presidential election Obama told journalist Gwen Ifill for her 2009 book, *The Breakthrough*, "Race is a factor in this society. The legacy of Jim Crow and slavery has not gone away. It is not an accident that African Americans experience high crime rates, are poor, and have less wealth. It is a direct result of our racial history. We have never fully come to grips with that history." The jubilation of Obama's victory meant that we were in a post-multicultural era. Racism is alive and well.

Multiculturalism is no longer a pertinent ideology against the old granite block.

part 5: occupy

IN 1968, JUST before he was killed, Martin Luther King, Jr., said, "Only when it is dark enough, can you see the stars."

It is now dark enough.

Out of the social woodwork emerged the many fragments of the American people and the impetus to occupy space that is often no longer public. It began in New York, and then spread outward. The framework of the Occupy Wall Street movement is simple: society has been sundered into two halves, the 1% and the 99%, with the voice of the latter utterly smothered, and the needs of the former tended to by bipartisan courtesy. Why is there no list of concrete demands is equal to the broad strategy of the movement? (1) It has paused to produce concrete demands because it is first to welcome the immense amount of grievances that circle around the American Town Square; and (2) it has refused to allow the political class to engage with it, largely because it does not believe that this political class will be capable of understanding the predicament of the 99%.

From September to November 2011, I travelled to several encampments between Boston and Chicago, talking to the people who had come to sleep in tents or who had come in during the day to participate in solidarity actions and discussions. It was an exhilarating period: conversations that rarely take place were now at the forefront, and a new kind of energy took hold of people who had begun to slump into despondency.

Jeffrey Harris had recently lost his job in Hartford, and then his wife died. Heading home from his wife's deathbed

In 1968, just before he was killed, Martin Luther King, Jr., said, "Only when it is dark enough, can you see the stars."

It is now dark enough.

in the hospital on a public bus, Jeffrey saw the tent city at the intersection of Broad and Farmington. He got off at the nearest bus stop, walked over and remained at the encampment. The epidemic of joblessness and foreclosures in the city angered and saddened Jeffrey, a pleasant man who wore his life's tragedies with grace. "It's crazy," he said of the inequality in the city. "It's a bunch of bullshit. These guys, the corporate elite, have to back down and give us something. It's crazy man. When the system's not working, then it has to be fixed."

Jess and Ken sat outside their tent on New Haven Green. Jess lost her family when she was very young, and went from foster home to foster home, faced physical and sexual abuse as a routine part of her life, and learned about power through her fraught exchanges with social workers. "I had to learn how the system works to survive," she tells me. "If you are poor, you need to educate yourself to have power. You can't let them take away your free will. No change comes from silence." Ken lost his job, his apartment, and his girlfriend, got on his bike in New Hampshire and began a journey to Florida. He stopped in New Haven four years ago, and now lives by his wits, with his corncob pipe, his bicycle, and his friends. "When I lost my job, I lost my life," he told me wistfully.

I met Loren Taylor and Brittney Gault in the Rainbow-Push offices in Chicago. They are with Occupy the Hood-Chicago, where Brittney is lead organizer. She tells me, "The system isn't going to change. We are preparing for five years from now when the problems will be greater." Trying to reposition the resources available to the disposable class, Brittany is leading a survey of what people are already doing to survive in dire times and is producing a network to link movements and individuals to each other. One of the lessons of the Occupy dynamic was that although we have a million grievances and are trying out our million experiments for change, our work has been lonely. Occupy tried to invalidate the loneliness of suffering and struggle. A direct line runs from Brittney and Loren to anti-eviction organizers like J. R. Fleming (Chicago Anti-Eviction Campaign), to youth organizers like Shamar Hemphill (Inner-City Muslim Action Network), to community organizers like Amisha Patel (Grassroots Collaborative), to healthcare fighters like Matt Ginsberg-Jaeckle (Southside Together Organizing for Power), and to the young people of Fearless Leading by the Youth (FLY). "A movement has been created," Loren told me. "Anything you think you want to do or what you've already been doing: now is the time to step up your game."

When I asked the rapper Jasiri X about Occupy, he echoed Loren Taylor. "This is the time to get off the couch," he told me. Occupy is not the encampments alone. It is the new political momentum toward a new horizon. Hip Hop's ubiquitous presence within Occupy belies the claim that

Occupy was not diverse. It is of course true that some silly people at the heart of OWS made the claim that racism is now over (we are "one race, the human race, formerly divided by race, class," said the draft declaration). Hena Ashraf, Sonny Singh, Manissa McCleave Maharawal and others contested this assertion, arguing that the divides have not been superseded. They remain, have to be recognized, and have to be fought. They cannot be wished away. Along the grain of the People of Color Working Group came Hip Hop Occupies, pushed by DJ Kuttin Kandi, Rebel Diaz, Emcee Julie C, and a host of others. "Rise and Decolonize: Let's get free," they said. "Our presence at Occupy," DJ Kuttin Kandi told me, "is to claim our space, to represent our concerns and struggles, and ourselves as people of color."

When I asked Toni Blackman, a rapper with the Freestyle Union, what she thought of the Occupy dynamic, she said that it brought her "a sense of relief. I exhaled and thought, 'finally.' I believe the energy will be contagious. Hip Hop is inching closer and closer to the Occupy movement. Soon singing about your riches and your bitches will be less and less acceptable. The Occupy movement has agitated the stagnant air just enough for artists who felt powerless to being acknowledging their power again."

Occupy is not a panacea, but an opening. It will help us clear the way to a more mature political landscape. It has begun to breathe in the many currents of dissatisfaction and breathe out a new radical imagination. In *Dreams of My Father*, Obama relates how he was motivated by the culture of the civil rights

The new radical imagination vitalized by Occupy forces us to break with the liberal desires for reform of a structure that can no longer be plastered over, as termites have already eaten into its foundation.... We require something much deeper, something more radical. The answers to our questions and to the condition of bare life are not to be found in being cautious. We need to cultivate the imagination, for those who lack an imagination cannot know what is lacking.

movement. From it he learnt that "communities had to be created, fought for, tended like gardens." Social life does not automatically emerge. It has to be worked for. The social condition of "commute-work-commute-sleep" or of utter disposibility does not help forge social bonds. Communities, Obama writes, "expanded or contracted with the dreams of men—and in the civil rights movement those dreams had been large." Out of the many struggles over the past several decades—from anti-prison to anti-sexual violence, from anti-starvation to anti-police brutality—has emerged the Occupy dynamic. It has broken the chain of despondency and allowed us to imagine new communities. It has broken the idea of American exceptionalism and linked US social distress and protest to the pink tide in Latin America, the Arab Spring, and the pre-revolutionary struggles of the *indignados* of southern Europe.

The new radical imagination vitalized by Occupy forces us to break with the liberal desires for reform of a structure that can no longer be plastered over, as termites have already eaten into its foundation. It forces us to break with multicultural upward mobility that has both succeeded in breaking the glass ceiling, and at the same time demonstrated its inability to operate on behalf of the multitudes. Neither liberal reform nor multiculturalism. We require something much deeper, something more radical. The answers to our questions and to the condition of bare life are not to be found in being cautious. We need to cultivate the imagination, for those who lack an imagination cannot know what is lacking.

part 6. the impatience of the elite

FROM OAKLAND TO New York City, the police received authorization to use maximum force and eject the manifestations. Harsh techniques of counterinsurgency were softened by the choir of the corporate media, which bemoaned the inconvenience of the encampments. Occupy had to make the police repressions the fundamental issue, given that it is the security state that works hand-in-glove with corporate interests to manage the social costs of making so many millions disposable. It was not a distraction to focus on the police. They are one part of the two-headed monster: Money is one head, and the other is Power. As in an old William Blake etching, the Zombie's heads, Money and Power, sway side by side, seeking to devour the vast mass. The patience of the elite has been tested, and found wanting. They want their country back.

The counter-attack is not new to American history. In 1786, the farmers of western Massachusetts were angered by the denial of the right to vote in their new republic and by the shoddy treatment of the veterans of the revolutionary wars. One farmer, Daniel Shays, led his band of veterans and farmers in Springfield, where they marched around with fife and drum to prevent the court from hearing cases against rioting farmers. Shays' movement then marched toward Boston, where the Senate's President Sam Adams signed a Riot Act and sent General Benjamin Lincoln to crack some heads. Northampton, where I live, was the home of the trails of the trials of the captured rebels, many of whom were put to death.

From Paris, France, Thomas Jefferson wrote to James Madison about Shays' rebellion, "I hold it that a little rebellion now and then is a good thing, & as necessary in the political world as storms in the physical." Few listened to these sage words.

Midway between 1786 and now, in May 1932, seventeen thousand veterans came to Washington, DC on a Bonus March. They were fed up. Their friends and relations had been thrown by the wayside, and promises made to them had been betrayed. Across the Potomac River from Washington's offices, the Bonus Army created an encampment. It would soon be given the name, Hooverville, in honor of President Herbert Hoover, and imitated across the country. Hoover sent General Douglas MacArthur (later of the Asian wars) to quell the peaceful Bonus Army. MacArthur unleashed tanks and tear gas. But the Hoovervilles continued.

The sedimentary nature of Power fears the chaos of protest. What the 1% knows as Stability, the Middle Class knows as Convenience. Protest is unstable and inconvenient. It pushes here and there, seeking ruptures in the fabric of the present. Success is not guaranteed. What is clear, however, is that the time of the present, of the possible has become irrelevant to thousands, if not millions of people. They are seeking the time of the future, of the impossible: Occupy is a stepping-stone to that time of the future. The encampments are no longer, but the spirit lingers, pushing here and there.

Molly Crabapple

Last fall Occupy Wall Street happened outside my window.

At first, I was a typical cynic. "White guys in dreadlocks. Drum circles. Mumia. Cliches. Fuck that." Then, one day after brunch with some equally cynical friends, I saw OWS had taken over Broadway.

"Join us" a beautiful young woman cried, and while I didn't (and probably for the best, as that was the day Officer Tony Bologna maced three girls while they were herded like cattle behind police nets), the next day I brought tarps down to Zuccotti.

Occupy was a participatory uprising. You didn't have to speak leftist theory. You just had to cook food, or wash dishes, or donate books, or just be there—occupy. Suddenly a mini-city based on mutual aid sprung up in one of NYC's most unlovely concrete squares. There was a Spanish language newspaper and a tree hung with union helmets, a poetry journal, a medic tent, a place for kids to play. All friendly, all free.

It was an unseasonably warm night. I sat in the park, listening to a kid play viola and another kid recite poetry, reading a book from the People's Library, eating free ice cream scooped by Jerry himself. It had all the hope, all the loveliness, of a new world.

I started drawing portraits of the protesters, because the media said they were dirty crazies. They weren't.

Later I did signs for the People's Library, for general strikes, for unions. I hate consensus. I'd rather stab out my eyes than sit through a General Assembly. But something rare and important and fragile was happening, and I wanted to help however I could. Or capture it at least.

I turned my apartment into a pressroom, inviting journalists from all over the world in to get warm, file reports over my wifi, and drink my scotch.

I was in London when they smashed Zuccotti's mini-city. The cops threw all the books into garbage trucks, cut up the sturdy military tents. A few dozen brave guys and girls linked arms around the makeshift kitchen.

The cops arrested them and held them in jail for days. The police banned reporters from watching what was going down in Zuccotti, so my friend Laurie Penny, a British journalist, scampered down my rickety fire escape at 3AM to get behind police lines. She was nearly arrested.

In an icy rage, I drew a poster of the Wall Street bull eating books. It was a sign on the streets within two hours.

That fall, it was the fall of living urgently, and caring passionately, and talking to everyone. I don't know what will happen with OWS, if it will come back or succumb to infighting. I know, however briefly, we took care of each other. I know we made them afraid.

Josh MacPhee

A QUALITATIVE QUILT BORN OF PIZZATOPIA

The following essay could not have been written without my
partner in occupation Dara Greenwald, whose insights color
everything below. In addition, and in the spirit of Occupy, this
piece is truly a collaboration, coming out of conversations and
work done with Lindsay Caplan, Jesse Goldstein, and Cindy
Milstein.

*All photographs taken by Josh MacPhee at Zuccotti Park between
September 19 and October 3, 2011.*

DURING THE EARLY DAYS OF THE OCCUPATION OF ZUCCOTTI PARK MANY
renamed it "Liberty Square," but more often than not we jokingly referred
to it as "Pizzatopia." A magical place where all we had to do was think of
pepperoni and a pizza would arrive, someone volunteering to distribute
slices to all. This seemingly infinite volume of saucy pie pointed to the possibility of other surpluses, many of which would be quickly realized. Other
kinds of healthier and heartier food were served multiple times a day, an
infinite collection of books were available to read, basic medical services
were set up, even vast little pyramids of cigarettes were hand rolled for those
convinced that lung cancer is both rebellious and a quintessential part of
the revolution.

The pizzas arrived with a purpose and a message; they were sent as gestures of solidarity from people not only in New York City, but also from
Egypt, Tunisia, and around the world. This was a tactic borrowed directly
from Wisconsin and the labor uprising in Madison that had occurred the
previous February. Feeding people while raising spirits was the goal, but
one unintended side effect was hundreds of cast-off cardboard boxes. Being both a creative and environmentally-conscious crew, park denizens con-
verted this refuse into artists' canvas, just one of the many alchemical tricks
I witnessed at Zuccotti Park.

First one hand-painted sign, then another, and another, emerged from the pile of empty boxes. Within days the entire northwest quadrant of the park became a corrugated tapestry of slogans, exhortations, and grievances. Not only that, but enterprising occupiers quickly democratized the tools of production, setting up self-expression ateliers with piles of cardboard, paint, and markers. A couple of the people sleeping in the park even became impromptu curators of the signs, laying them out each morning in new patterns, and quickly sheltering them under tarps when it threatened to rain.

Being a graphic designer and artist, it was clear to me that few of these signs would pass muster as successful, or compelling, political graphics. But it was also apparent that that was never the point. Whether it was Wisconsin activists paying back the generosity they received for fighting to save the right to collective bargaining, veterans of the Egyptian Revolution sending over a slice of solidarity, or sympathetic neighbors looking down on cold and hungry kids huddled in sleeping bags, the desire—no, the *need*—to eat was plain to all those who sent pizzas. What might not have been so evident was the similarly deep need in people to express themselves freely and publicly. And the occupation did far more than provide a venue for self-expression; it furnished an equally important yet much less obvious part of the equation: an audience to not only hear that expression but take it seriously and be mobilized by it as well.

This cardboard phenomenon was no minor sideline—no art project

This cardboard phenomenon was no minor sideline—no art project outgrowth of the "real" political activity—but instead a central aspect of both the culture of Zuccotti Park and the larger Occupy movement. As much as anything else, the common space to speak and be heard was the characteristic that most distinguished Occupy from the status quo of corporate representative democracy.

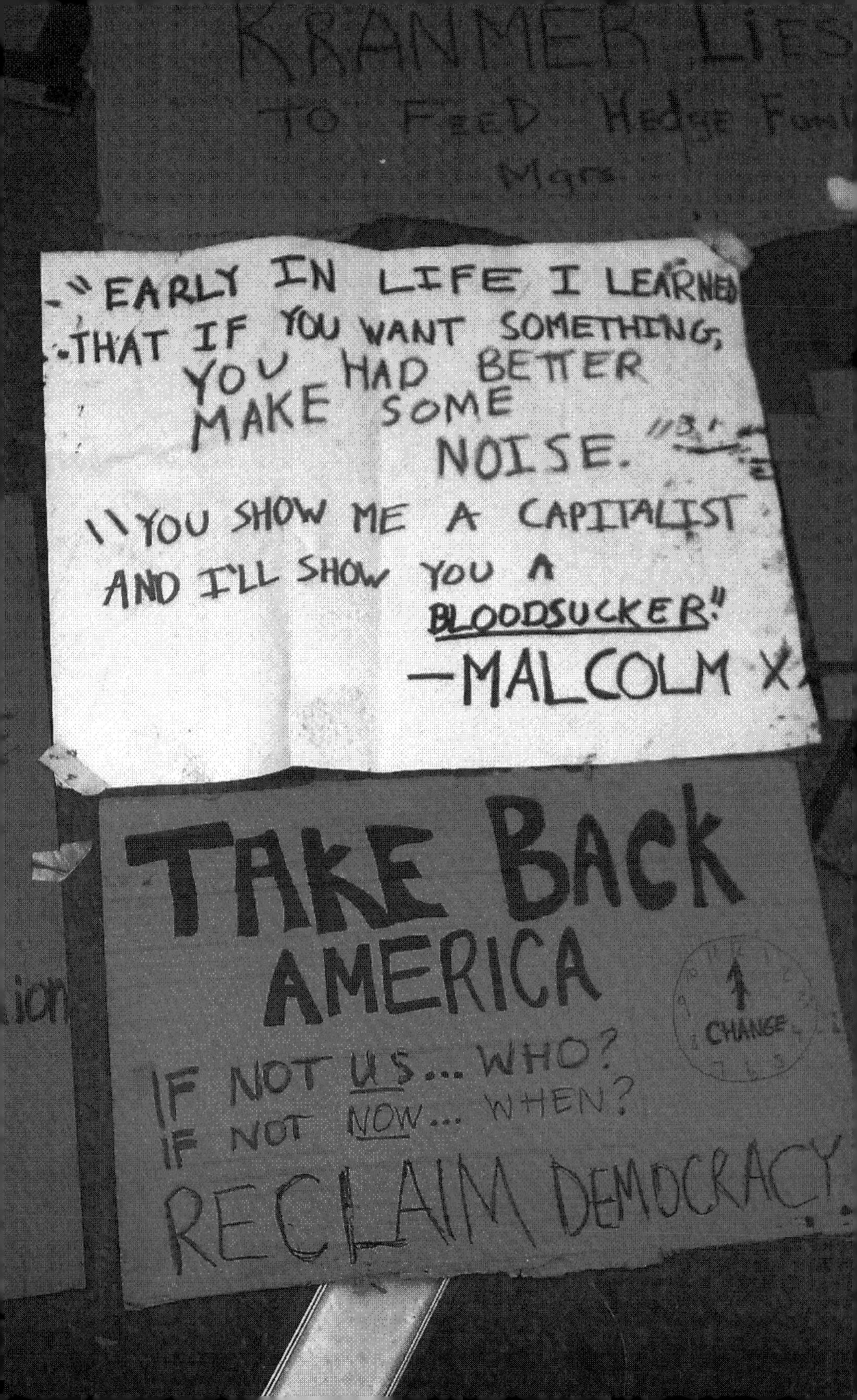
KRANMER LIES
TO FEED Hedge Fund
Mgrs
"EARLY IN LIFE I LEARNED THAT IF YOU WANT SOMETHING, YOU HAD BETTER MAKE SOME NOISE."
"YOU SHOW ME A CAPITALIST AND I'LL SHOW YOU A BLOODSUCKER!"
—MALCOLM X
TAKE BACK AMERICA
CHANGE
IF NOT US... WHO?
IF NOT NOW... WHEN?
RECLAIM DEMOCRACY

outgrowth of the "real" political activity—but instead a central aspect of both the culture of Zuccotti Park and the larger Occupy movement. As much as anything else, the common space to speak and be heard was the characteristic that most distinguished Occupy from the status quo of corporate representative democracy. Prior to September 2011, most political organizations were intently focused on quantitative goals: recruiting members, influencing policy, garnering press coverage, or mobilizing increasing numbers of people for demonstrations. Few, if any, existing political organizations would have proffered this form of expression, deeply qualitative in nature, as either a central pillar of its work or a meaningful need of its constituents, so it is not that surprising that no preexisting formal political organization played a serious role in the early development of Occupy.

The art supplies, the cardboard, and the social fabric of the park allowed anyone to express themselves on a sign, or a dozen. Teenagers painted big circle As, student activists scribbled out slogans about *Citizens United*, and down-and-out former professionals carefully painted out aspects of their life stories, laying the blame for their misfortunes at the feet of the banks in broad, unwavering strokes. There were a thousand signs for a thousand experiences. While no one sign could clearly speak to the reasons people were in the park—and if we're to be honest, many of the signs actually made little sense unto themselves—the web they wove was a compelling statement about where we found ourselves in late 2011. Many spoke to being

While no one sign could clearly speak to the reasons people were in the park—and if we're to be honest, many of the signs actually made little sense unto themselves—the web they wove was a compelling statement about where we found ourselves in late 2011.

DAUGHTER AND
E IN POVERTY
S TO WALL ST
Y MAKERS
ND

E GREED

BACON

WAR

EAT
JAIL THE
RICH!

JUSTICE

DISSENT
IS
PATRIOTIC!

NO STOCKS

College
taught Me

Nothing
(but they got my money)

bulldozed by a massive recession, the paucity of employment opportunities, avenues of foreclosed homes, and a student debt tickling a trillion dollars. Others confronted a government infected by corporate glad-handing and a financialized economic system unregulated, untethered from responsibility, and unhinged from any ethical or moral compass.

Intentional or not, the signs became real-world "status updates" to a population increasingly familiar with the form and function of social media and networking. And like on Facebook, where I can and am encouraged to repost the updates of others, in the park I could make my own sign or pick up someone else's. Day traders on their lunch breaks carried signs around the park exhorting love over money, whimsically painted by youthful hippies. Communist union organizers stood at the edges of the park holding up signs about God's hatred of greed scrawled by middle-aged black churchgoers. The ideas expressed were both broad and pointed, both complicated and naively simple. Many were internally contradictory or politically incoherent, boldly utopian or issue specific with exacting language.

The creation of signs fostered an aspect of a new identity, a new definition of citizen. In the world in which I would want to live, to express oneself in public would not merely be a right but also a social good, something of value in and of itself. I caught a glimpse of this world in Zuccotti Park. It was messy and raw, but blissfully unmediated by the prerequisites that exist for participation in public dialogue in our present society. No education or specific skills were required, no access to complicated distribution mechanisms or expensive technological delivery systems. All we needed to do was eat a lot of pizza, and share lifetimes of frustration and anger, excitement and joy.

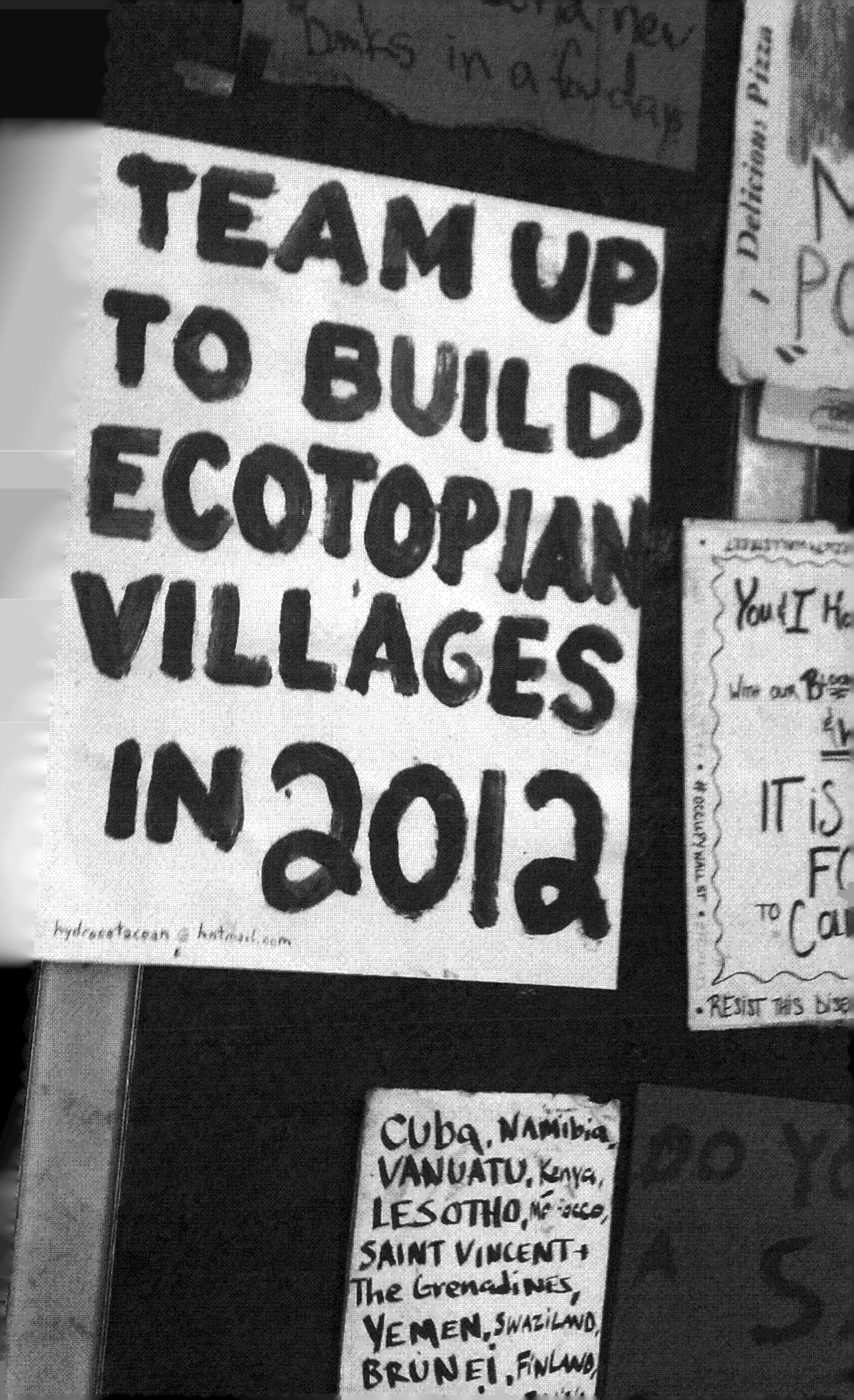
TEAM UP
TO BUILD
ECOTOPIAN
VILLAGES
IN 2012
Delicious Pizza
Cuba, NAMIBIA,
VANUATU, Kenya,
LESOTHO,
SAINT VINCENT +
The Grenadines,
YEMEN, SWAZILAND,
BRUNEI, FINLAND,

CORPORATIONS
ARE
NOT
They want to execute Troy Davis on Sept. 21
Don't let Georgia Kill an Innocent Man!
Join the struggle to save his life!
Call 212.633.6646 or iacenter.org

Annie Cockrell

It was early in the morning of the first of January; the early hours of the first day of a new year, and I found myself carrying a black flag down the streets of Seventh Avenue in New York City. In between shouting alternating cries of "Close the gap!" and "Slow down!," I was also dodging the New York Police Department's scooters, which seemed hell-bent on keeping me and my colleagues off the streets, and it was in that moment, of evading New York's finest and leading the crowd protesting against economic and moral injustice, that I finally felt my first true sense of power.

Being at Occupy Wall Street for New Year's was nothing new for me—I've been an active member of the movement since its second month, a Brooklyn Bridge veteran who never looked back—but this sense of true power in numbers was something that I'd been missing. In my non-Occupy life, I'm a second-year economics student at an overly-privileged liberal arts school; until Occupy, and specifically that moment, I'd felt as though I was a part of a giant hamster wheel, a cog in a machine, destined to follow a certain path until expiration.

What Occupy Wall Street has done for me—and my peers, those with whom I feel comfortable enough discussing politics, religion, and taxes—is that it has reinstated a hope for a better tomorrow. A world of equality of opportunity, a world without complex hierarchy, a world of our own making—it all seems possible, plausible, a reality well within the grasp of not only the 99%, but the one hundred percent of the world. Working together now is something to strive for, not laugh at; a option, no longer to be dismissed within the cynicism of self-interest.

No longer must we be shackled down by idealism; by the ideas that we are improper, flawed, disorganized masses needing rules and laws to keep our unruly natures in check. Social movements in the vein of Occupy have inspired me to realize that humanity needs neither gods nor masters to rule, to govern, to impose force. We have the power and determination within ourselves to take over a bridge, to take over Times Square, to take over the world and carve into it our own Utopia.

But then, of course, there is the question—what would this Utopia look like? What is this world we imagine? But to me, at least, this is no problem at all; the problem with Utopias arises when you only have one.

And so I look forward to the rest of the movement, to the future of Occupy, and the inspiration from which I learned the power to create my own Utopia.

Crystal Grover,
2010

George Ciccariello-Maher[1]

FROM OSCAR GRANT TO OCCUPY
THE LONG ARC OF REBELLION IN OAKLAND

IN *THE BLACK JACOBINS*, C.L.R. JAMES, THE GREAT REVOLUTIONARY AND historian of the Haitian Revolution, rejected any suggestion that human history moves inevitably forward toward a *telos*,[2] emphasizing instead not only the minute strategic considerations and switchbacks, and the victories and defeats, but also the stark reality that what little progress we have achieved comes not from the best intentions, but often from the worst. "Sad though it may be," he insisted, "that is the way that humanity progresses. The anniversary orators and the historians supply the prose-poetry and the flowers."[3] This is a warning that we must take with the utmost seriousness when discussing the trajectory of the Occupy Movement.

We must disrupt the sorts of self-congratulatory historical narratives which, through a sort of voluntary myopia, constrain and limit the bounds of our imaginations in ways that crucially reinforce the pretenses of the very system that the Occupy phenomenon could be seen to oppose: the idea that we live in a democracy, that we must only raise our voices to be heard, and only be heard to be listened to, the dogmatic belief that only nonviolence gets the goods, and that by collectively coming together we have already won. The "prose-poetry and the flowers" here serve not so much to commemorate the past as to contain future possibilities, and our task must be precisely the opposite. We revise and indeed decimate this sort of historical understanding by evoking memories of Occupy's antecedents, antecedents which—I will argue, at least, in the case of Oakland— give presence to very different dynamics and provide powerful lessons for both Occupy and its aftermath.

---

1   Originally presented at the Pre-Occupy Symposium at University of Wisconsin-Milwaukee on April 13 2012. Thanks to Annie McClanahan for organizing this event.

2   "An ultimate object or aim." —Ed.

3   C.L.R. James, *The Black Jacobins* (New York: Vintage, 1963), 63.

ON JANUARY 1, 2009, in the dawning hours of the Age of Obama, Oscar
Grant was shot in the back on a train platform by a transit cop, Johannes
Mehserle, while handcuffed and lying face down. The bullet ricocheted off
the platform and re-entered his body, and after being denied emergency
care by the police present, Grant died almost immediately. The shooting
was captured by dozens of passengers on cellphone videos, and while they
should have been treating Grant, officers were instead attempting to con-
fiscate people's phones. The defiance of the crowd was threefold: heckling
the police for their racial profiling and subsequent murder, the very act of
filming itself, and finally the attempts by many to hide cellphones in an effort to smuggle the footage out to the public.[4] This effort proved successful,
and the gut-wrenching footage of Oscar Grant's murder went viral, viewed
hundreds of thousands of times in a short week. In the meantime, Mehserle
had been questioned, refused to talk, and eventually resigned his post to
avoid speaking. He was not arrested, and the anger that percolated during
that week resulted as much from this failure by the state to act as from the
murder itself.

One week later, a hastily-formed coalition, largely comprised of radical
nonprofit workers close to the city administration, called a rally at the station where Grant was shot. It soon became apparent that whatever their
intentions for the day, those gathered were justifiably angry and would not
be contained, and thus we had the first of the Oscar Grant rebellions, as several hundred took off on an unpermitted march toward and then through
downtown Oakland, hemmed in briefly at the by-now familiar flashpoint
that is 14th and Broadway, before being pushed down 14th Street amid
the smashing of windows and the burning of cars. National headlines were
garnered; attention had been gotten.

In the acrimonious debates, the opportunistic maneuvers, and counterinsurgency strategies that circulated in Oakland the following week,
something fundamental happened. As the date of the promised January
14 follow-up march approached, and as the threat of another riot-rebellion
became tangible, the wheels of political power in the state, county, and city,
groaned reluctantly into motion. Under pressure from the state Attorney
General and the Mayor, Johannes Mehserle was arrested, and he was arrested *to prevent a second riot*. But popular power is not so easily tamed: the
second rebellion did in fact occur, as a sort of promise that the people would
not be so easily placated, and it was followed by a third on January 30,
when Mehserle—already a demonstrated flight risk—was granted bail. It is

---

4   For the best account of this and subsequent events, see Raider Nation Collective, *From the January Rebellions to Lovelle Mixon and Beyond* (Oakland, 2010).

these three rebellions and the high tide of radical organizing that emerged from their example, demands, and lessons, that represent the fundamental precursor to what would become Occupy Oakland.

from oscar grant to occupy

WHEN ATTEMPTING TO map the national dynamics of the Occupy Movement, it becomes necessary to grapple with the peculiarity of Occupy Oakland. How was it that a movement emerging from the bowels of the great eastern financial metropolis saw its center of gravity shift dramatically to a small city in the west (so small, in fact, that it is popularly know as "The Town")? Amid the swirling tear gas of its first eviction, Occupy Oakland leapt somewhat unexpectedly to the head of the Occupy Movement nationwide, or rather not to the head so much as to the heart: Occupy Oakland was soon serving as the simultaneous inspiration and benchmark for mobilizations nationwide, as though by striking one, the "whip of the counterrevolution" had educated one hundred.[5] But it was not merely the repression that had cemented its leadership. Vague suggestions regarding Oakland's "radical legacy" are also on the right track, but too imprecise to explain much. Some cite the California student occupations of 2009 and 2010, but here we are hard pressed to see how these were fundamentally distinct from those in New York, or why they would have drawn energy toward Oakland instead of Berkeley or San Francisco.

I'm going to insist as stubbornly as possible, that if there was a fundamental source, not for the *presence* of Occupy Oakland, but for its peculiar *radicalism* and the mantle of national leadership it assumed, this source was to be found in the Oscar Grant rebellions and the political lessons these rebellions contained. But to be clear, I'm less interested in claiming the superiority of one movement over another, and more interested in the lessons contained *within* these movements. I will make this argument not merely historically or quantitatively: the Oscar Grant rebellions indeed preceded the student occupations, and many participants in the former played key roles in Occupy, but more fundamental were the lessons imparted by this struggle, lessons in mass strength gleaned in the streets. In classically dialectical fashion, however, even quantitative participation was more importantly qualitative: relationships built, debates undertaken, intersubjective lessons internalized.

The more crucial lessons, however, lay beyond the intersubjective challenges of crafting a multiracial revolutionary movement, and here the qualitative aspects I speak of stray into the realm of the immeasurable, the

---

5 This famous if enigmatic phrase is often attributed to Marx, and refers to the dialectical impact of reactionaries in spurring revolutionary processes forward.

difficult to pinpoint, the sensed rather than seen. These can be summarized in the generalized sentiment that, after the seismic shift of the Oscar Grant rebellions, *Oakland was a different place*. In what follows, I will nevertheless attempt to pinpoint three elements of this transformation, which swirl around the great triad of revolutionary thought comprising C.L.R. James, Frantz Fanon, and W.E.B. Du Bois.

1. c.l.r. james

ESPECIALLY ON THE day of the first Oscar Grant rebellion, the masses of people in the streets exceeded, leapt beyond, and quite literally *ran past* the organizations attempting to represent, mediate, and moderate their will. This ability and determination is a central element of Jamesian politics, and has powerfully dialectical implications: the practice of autonomy provides a lesson in one's own power. This lesson was not limited to the organizations attempting to calm passions on the street, but this unmediated expression of popular rage holds yet another, more powerful lesson. After all, this mass power had provided a rare example of a moment in which popular demands are quite literally *forced* upon the state. This was a lesson not soon forgotten in Oakland.

"The rich are only defeated when running for their lives," James reminds us, in many ways updating Marx's dictum that "material force must be overthrown by material force."[6] This is a powerful lesson that the Occupy Movement ought to have taken to heart, but did so only very partially, with many Occupations instead naively believing that the police and the city government were on their side (this lesson was egregiously overlooked in Philadelphia, where I now live). In Oakland, by contrast, the fruit of this history was clear, carried forward by many who had cut their political teeth in the Oscar Grant struggles only to then throw their weight into Occupy: permits were rejected, politicians banned *a priori*, and autonomy against the police fiercely and jealously defended. For those unaware, it was in Oakland that police were first banned from the encampment and a security force instituted to defend it.

2. frantz fanon

FANON WAS PECULIARLY attentive to the pernicious role of intermediary sectors in the struggle, and this lesson played out above all on the second night of the Oscar Grant rebellions. Confronted with the impatient violence of the masses, Fanon writes, the official "leaders" of the struggle, "cloaked in their

---

6 James, *The Black Jacobins*, 78; Karl Marx, "Introduction" to *A Contribution to the Critique of Hegel's Philosophy of Right* (1843).

experience ruthlessly reject 'these upstarts, these anarchists.'"[7] In the case of Oakland, these mediating and moderating sectors were largely comprised of ostensibly radical nonprofits, many tied directly to ostensibly progressive city leaders, in 2009 Mayor Ron Dellums and today Mayor Jean Quan.

Throughout the Oscar Grant struggle, such nonprofits protected the state and the administration by both turning anger away from political leaders and channeling it down the tried-and-true failure that is the non-profit industrial complex, which views every angry youth as a bargaining chip for more funding. This function was laid bare during the second rebellion, when organizers provided their own orange-vested security force in an effort to prevent anger from spilling beyond the bounds of the acceptable. But once again popular rage spoke as clearly as it did eloquently, tossing off this yoke and taking to the streets once again.

Here active intervention was crucial, with many organizers exposing this function with words and theory as participants had exposed it with feet and in practice. By fiercely attacking this "buffer" role, the movement was successful in discrediting the nonprofits, many of which then withdrew to leave the field of battle more open and well-defined.[8] By July 8, 2010, when Mehserle's conviction on the insultingly paltry charge of involuntary manslaughter was delivered, the position of many nonprofits could not have been clearer: they released a series of public service announcements aimed not at justice but at preventing yet another riot, and comparing the death of Oscar Grant to the windows that were broken in a desperate but ultimately effective gamble.

Fanon's lesson here—which is again more qualitative than quantitative—has very similar implications to that of James.

> **Enlightened by violence, the people's consciousness rebels against any pacification. The demagogues, the opportunists and the magicians now have a difficult task. The praxis which pitched them into a desperate man-to-man struggle has given the masses a ravenous taste for the tangible. Any attempt at mystification in the long term becomes virtually impossible.[9]**

The point is this: the practice of rebellion transforms its participants, revealing their own power as the machinations of their opponents become more transparent. To put it in clichéd terms: the Oscar Grant struggle

---

7   Frantz Fanon, *The Wretched of the Earth* (New York: Grove Press, 2004), 77.

8   See Advance the Struggle, "Justice for Oscar Grant: A Lost Opportunity?"

9   Fanon, *Wretched*, 52.

allowed us to both know our enemies and to know ourselves. Or better still: having learned of their own power by forcing the enemy to act, and having removed from the field those who would weaken and mislead that power by delivering it up on the altar of those same enemies, the people had gained a qualitatively advanced position.

To turn again to Occupy Oakland, I want to insist that this discrediting of the ostensibly radical nonprofit sector was massively important. The justified suspicion of nonprofits carried over into Occupy, effectively preventing any serious attempt to corral or channel Occupy toward more moderate ends. This did not prevent less-serious and utterly clumsy attempts, however, as when Mayor Quan's own nonprofit attempted to move the encampment, or when some nonprofiteers attempted to broker a meeting to shore up support for the Mayor in the aftermath of the brutal first eviction.

3. w.e.b. du bois

I TURN TO Du Bois as both a culmination and a concretization of the first two historical lessons of the Oscar Grant Struggle. This was not just any shooting, not just any victim, not just any police force, and not just any state. It was instead, a young Black man, shot by a white cop working for the glorified slave catchers that are American police who was protected and ultimately sacrificed by a white supremacist state. The police in the United States have always functioned to uphold the color line, from day one, when policing as an occupation emerged as the material side of what Du Bois called the "wages" of whiteness, with smug superiority serving as its psychological counterpart.[10] Today, amidst the mass incarceration and lynching that Michelle Alexander has deemed the "New Jim Crow," this function is not *less important*, but *more so*.

Moreover, Du Bois is among those who have shown that struggles against white supremacy in the United States have a peculiar resonance and impact, often qualitatively exceeding their quantitative importance. In this view, white supremacy serves as a linchpin holding together a system of domination, in part through a racial division of the working classes, and attacking that linchpin has the potential to unleash broader waves of rebellion. Thus the Radical Reconstruction of the 1870s preceded first-wave feminism and socialism, and the Civil Rights Movement of the 1950s and 60s very clearly inspired and drove forward the rebelliousness of students, women, queers, and other oppressed groupings. By struggling toward what Du Bois called "abolition democracy," we broaden the horizon of radical democracy and social equality more generally, not only in the United States, but globally as well.

---

10 W.E.B. Du Bois, *Black Reconstruction in America* (New York: Free Press, 1998), 701.

In a sense, all that I have said above stands as yet another testament to this truth: the Oscar Grant rebellions constituted a seismic shift in Oakland's political terrain, opening a radical space for subsequent struggles by students and occupiers alike. We must build upon the strategic implications of this understanding: seeking out struggles against white supremacy that bear within them the potential to unleash a chain reaction of broader rebelliousness. Here there is faith, of course, because faith is to be found everywhere that we tie the past to the future via action in the present. But this is a faith backed with strategic insight, drawing for sustenance upon the concrete historical function of the police and the state to attack strategically where the system is weakest.

postscript: trayvon martin

THE LESSON OF Du Bois regarding the centrality of struggles against the police and white supremacy is, unfortunately, the one that has been least learned by any Occupy, Oakland included. At the same time that radical nonprofits attempted to use questions of race as a leverage point to once again infiltrate struggles in Oakland, others have responded with an unnecessarily hyperbolic attack on what is being called "privilege politics" that threatens to abandon the importance of race entirely. This critique of privilege politics has emerged again in the case of Trayvon Martin: another Black man killed, another legal system forced into motion by popular pressure from below. This time, however, the ethnicity and authority of the assailant are in question: a multi-ethnic fake cop, George Zimmerman, attempted to buy into whiteness by voluntarily policing Blackness.[11]

If there is a lesson from the Oscar Grant struggle for the present, it is to throw our most radical energies and hope into the struggle unleashed by Trayvon Martin's murder, but also to do so without losing sight of *why it is* that this case is important. Identifying white privilege *within* movements is fundamental, but it is useless if we don't then turn toward the revolutionary practice of attacking white supremacy as a system. As with the arrest of Johannes Mehserle, officials in Florida are currently attempting to save a system by sacrificing an individual, simultaneously responding to the dictates of and attempting to undermine popular force. If there is a national struggle today with strategic importance, it is that of Trayvon Martin and all those who come after him. As our recently departed teacher, mentor, and comrade Joel Olson put it in his essay included in this volume: "When the pillars of the white democracy tremble, everything is possible." *Let's shake those pillars!*

---

11 For a more sustained analysis of this, see George Ciccariello-Maher, "The Dialectics of Standing One's Ground," *Theory & Event* 15.3 (September 2012).

Joel Olson

WHITENESS AND THE 99%

OCCUPY WALL STREET AND THE HUNDREDS OF OCCUPATIONS IT SPARKED nationwide are among the most inspiring events to take place in the United States in the twenty-first century. The occupations have brought people together to talk, to occupy, and to organize in new and exciting ways. The convergence of so many people with so many concerns has naturally created tensions within the Occupy movement. One of the most significant tensions has been over race. This is not unusual, given the racial history of the United States. But this tension is particularly dangerous, for unless it is confronted, we cannot build the 99%. *The key obstacle to building the 99% is left colorblindness, and the key to overcoming it is to put the struggles of communities of color at the center of this movement.* It is the difference between a free world and the continued dominance of the 1%.

left colorblindness is the enemy

LEFT COLORBLINDNESS IS the belief that race is a "divisive" issue among the 99%, so we should instead focus on problems that "everyone" shares. According to this argument, the movement is for everyone, and people of color should join it rather than attack it.

Left colorblindness claims to be inclusive, but it is actually just another way to keep whites' interests at the forefront. It tells people of color to join "our" struggle (who makes up this "our," anyway?) but warns them not to bring their "special" concerns into it. It enables white people to decide which issues are for the 99% and which ones are "too narrow." It's another way for whites to expect and insist on favored treatment, even in a democratic movement.

As long as left colorblindness dominates our movement, there will be no 99%. There will instead be a handful of whites claiming to speak for everyone. When people of color have to enter a movement on white people's terms rather than their own, that's not the 99%. That's white democracy.

BIOLOGICALLY SPEAKING, THERE'S no such thing as race. As hard as they've tried, scientists have never been able to define it. That's because race is a human creation, not a fact of nature. Like money, it only exists because people accept it as "real." Races exist because humans invented them.

Why would people invent race? Race was created in America in the late 1600s in order to preserve the land and power of the wealthy. Rich planters in Virginia feared what might happen if indigenous tribes, slaves, and indentured servants united and overthrew them, so, they cut a deal with the poor English colonists. The planters gave the English certain rights and privileges denied to all persons of African and Native American descent: the right to never be enslaved, to free speech and assembly, to move about without a pass, to marry without upper-class permission, to change jobs, to acquire property, and to bear arms. In exchange, the English poor agreed to respect the property of the rich, help them seize indigenous lands, and enforce slavery.

This cross-class alliance between the rich and the English poor came to be known as the "white race." By accepting preferential treatment in an economic system that exploited their labor, too, the white working class tied their wagon to the elite rather than the rest of humanity. This devil's bargain has undermined freedom and democracy in the US ever since.

As this white race expanded to include other European ethnicities, the result was a very curious political system: the *white democracy*. The white democracy has two contradictory aspects to it. On the one hand, all whites are considered equal (even as the poor are subordinated to the rich and women are subordinated to men). On the other, every white person is considered superior to every person of color. It's democracy for white folks, but tyranny for everyone else.

In this system, whites praise freedom, equal opportunity, and hard work, while at the same time insisting on higher wages, on access to the best jobs, on the right to be the first hired and the last fired at the workplace, on the

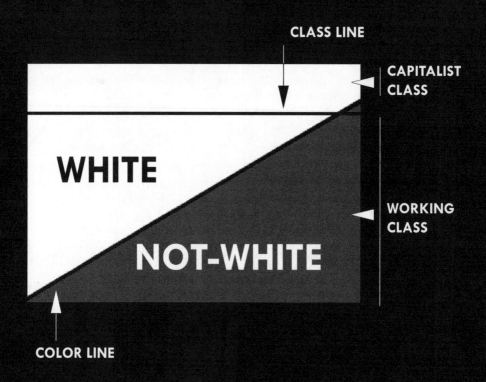

The cross-class alliance that makes up the white race.

full enjoyment of civil rights, and on the right to send their kids to the best schools, to live in the nicest neighborhoods, and to enjoy decent treatment by the police. In exchange for these "public and psychological wages," as W.E.B. Du Bois called them, whites agreed to enforce slavery, segregation, reservation, genocide, and other forms of discrimination. The tragedy of the white democracy is that it oppressed working class whites as well as people of color, because with the working class bitterly divided, the elites could rule easily.

The white democracy exists today. Take any social indicator—rates for college graduation, homeownership, median family wealth, incarceration, life expectancy, infant mortality, cancer, unemployment, median family debt, etc.—and you'll find the same thing: whites as a group are significantly better off than any other racial group. Of course there are individual exceptions, but as a group whites enjoy more wealth, less debt, more education, less imprisonment, more healthcare, less illness, more safety, less crime, better treatment by the police, and less police brutality than any other group. Some whisper that this is because whites have a better work ethic. But history tells us that the white democracy, born in the 1600s, lives on.

the distorted white mindset

NO ONE IS opposed to good schools, safe neighborhoods, healthy communities, and economic security for whites. The problem is that in the white democracy, whites often enjoy these *at the expense of communities of color.* This creates a distorted mindset among many whites: they praise freedom, yet support a system that clearly favors the rich, even at the expense of poor whites. (Tea Party, I'm talking to *you.*)

The roots of left colorblindness lie in the white democracy and the distorted mindset it creates. It encourages whites to think that their issues are "universal" while those of people of color are "specific." But that is exactly backwards. The struggles of people of color are the problems that everyone shares. Anyone in the Occupy movement who has been treated brutally by the police has to know that Black communities are terrorized by cops every day. Anyone who is unemployed has to know that Black unemployment rates are always at least double that of whites, and Native American unemployment rates are far higher than that. Anyone who is sick and lacks healthcare has to know that people of color are the least likely to be insured (regardless of their income), have the highest infant mortality and cancer rates, and the lowest life expectancy rates. Anyone who is drowning in debt should know that the median net wealth of Black households is twenty times less than that of white households. Only left colorblindness can lead us to ignore these facts.

This is the sinister impact of white democracy on our movements. It encourages a mindset that insists that racial issues are "divisive" *when they are at the absolute center of everything we are fighting for*.

To defeat left colorblindness and the distorted white mindset, we must come to see any form of favoritism toward whites (whether explicit or implicit) as an evil attempt to perpetuate the cross-class alliance rather to than build the 99%.

the only thing that can stop us is us

THROUGHOUT AMERICAN HISTORY, attacking the white democracy has always opened up radical possibilities for *all* people. The abolitionist movement not only overthrew slavery, it kicked off the women's rights and labor movements. The civil rights struggle not only overthrew legal segregation, it kicked off the women's rights, free speech, student, queer, Chicano, Puerto Rican, and American Indian movements. When the pillars of the white democracy tremble, everything is possible.

The only thing that can stop us is us. What prevents the 99% from organizing the world as we see fit is not the 1%. The 1% cannot hold on to power if we decide they shouldn't. What keeps us from building the new world in our hearts are the divisions among us.

Our diversity is our strength. But left colorblindness is a *rejection* of diversity. It is an effort to keep white interests at the center of the movement even as the movement claims to be open to all. Urging us to "get over" so-called "divisive" issues like race sound inclusive, but they are really efforts to maintain the white democracy. It's like Wall Street executives telling us to "get beyond" "divisive" issues like their unfair profits because if you work hard enough, you too can get a job on Wall Street someday!

Creating a 99% requires putting the struggles of people of color at the center of our conversations and demands rather than relegating them to the margins. To fight against school segregation, colonization, redlining, and anti-immigrant attacks is to fight against everything Wall Street stands for, everything the Tea Party stands for, everything this government stands for. It is to fight against the white democracy, which stands at the path to a free society like a troll at the bridge.

occupy everything, attack the white democracy

WHILE NO SINGLE essay or book can capture everything a nationwide movement can or should do to undermine the white democracy and left colorblindness, below is a short list of questions people might consider asking in movement debates. These questions were developed from actual debates in occupations throughout the US:

- Do speakers urge us to "get beyond" race? Are they defensive and dismissive of demands for racial justice?
- If speakers urge developing "close working relationships with the police," do they consider how police terrorize Black, Latino, Native, and undocumented communities? Do they consider how police have attacked occupation encampments?
- If speakers urge us to hold banks accountable, do they encourage us to focus on redlining, predatory lending, and subprime mortgages, which have decimated Black and Latino neighborhoods?
- If speakers urge the cancellation of debts, do they mean for things like electric and heating bills as well as home mortgages and college loans?
- If speakers urge the halting of foreclosures, do they acknowledge that they take place primarily in segregated neighborhoods, and do they propose to start there?
- If speakers urge the creation of more jobs, do they acknowledge that many communities of color have already been in chronic "recessions" for decades, and do they propose to start from there?

Attack capitalist power—attack the white democracy.
Build the 99%!
People of color at the center!
No more left colorblindness!

STATE
TROOPER

SCHOOL

SAVE
OUR
YOUTH

Casey McKeel
January 16, 2012
Schools Not Jails, Baltimore

Lester Spence and Mike McGuire

OCCUPY AND THE 99%

When I saw Occupy Rochester form, I saw a bunch of white folks. I was like, okay, we'll start from here. But then I started seeing where the ideas were coming from. I started to see where the exclusions were coming from. They were occupying a park that had been used by homeless people, now the homeless people came to the park and were told "Look, we don't want you around here." These homeless guys were people of color, they were black people. I was automatically like, where are you going with this? You're kicking out people you need to be your allies. He said, "Well, they're stealing food, they're doing this..." I said, okay, when people donate food to you, you eat it, you just do it. But if they eat it, it's stealing. So automatically there were divisions. So I'm saying whoa, it's the reality of an occupation where people are trying to change the world, but haven't started changing themselves. This is just a popular thing they're doing to be a part of it. But they're not looking at the people, the ones that are directly affected by the society they live in. Then I started looking at other things. Where do these guys come from? They come from suburbia, not from the inner city, so they didn't identify with people that are having direct problems in the inner city which they were occupying. So they already had a relationship issue. Then you look at the educational base of the occupation. People think "Well, I'm educated. I've got a PhD. I'm well spoken..." Then I started to see exclusions. Decision making: all white folks. You start seeing these things and you start saying "I know there's not many of us here, but we should be included in the decision making part regardless of education or status.

—Hubert Wilkerson, Take Back the Land, Rochester

ADBUSTERS[1] CALLED FOR A SEPTEMBER 2011 OCCUPATION OF WALL STREET to rail against the economic crisis.[2] No one expected the outcome. For the

---

1   *Adbusters* is an organization of self-proclaimed "culture-jammers" founded in Canada.

2   According to *Adbusters* they were partially influenced by the political uprisings

first time in a generation, hundreds of thousands of men, women, and children forced a debate on economic inequality by taking to the streets and plazas of American cities. From Wall Street, the protests swiftly spread through hundreds of cities worldwide. But as Hubert Wilkerson notes above in reference to Occupy Rochester, these protests have not always reconciled the desire for economic justice with the desire for racial justice. Joel Olson, recognizing this, wrote "Whiteness and the 99%" as a strategic intervention. In this essay, we expand on his work. In constructing the 99%, we do have to recognize the role race plays in agenda setting. However agenda setting is not the only site of "left colorblindness."

In April 1966, *Monthly Review* published James and Grace Boggs' "The City Is the Black Man's Land," one of the first attempts to define and argue for black power. The city was the black man's land, they argued, because of the principle of majority rule (blacks were swiftly becoming the majority in dozens of American cities) and because African Americans were in the best geographic and social position to create more humane ways of life.

> … the stark truth of the matter is that today, after centuries of systematic segregation and discrimination and only enough education to fit them for the most menial tasks abandoned or considered beneath their dignity by whites, the great majority of black Americans now concentrated in the cities cannot be integrated into the advanced industrial sector of America except on the most minimal token basis. Instead, what expanding employment there has been for Afro-Americans has been in the fields of education and social and public service (teaching, hospitals, sanitation, transportation, public health, recreation, social welfare). It is precisely these areas of activity that are socially most necessary in the cybercultural era. But because the American racist tradition demands the emasculation of blacks not only on the economic and sexual but also on the political level, the perspective of black self-government in the cities cannot be posed openly and frankly as a profession and perspective toward which black youth should aspire and for which they should begin preparing themselves from childhood. Instead, at every juncture, even when concessions are being made, white America makes clear that the power to make concessions remains in white hands.

in Egypt and Tunisia.

> The result is increasing hopelessness and desperation on
> the part of black youth, evidenced in the rising rate of
> school dropouts, dope addiction, and indiscriminate vio-
> lence. Born into the age of abundance and technological
> miracles, these youths have little respect for their par-
> ents who continue to slave for 'the man' and none for
> the social workers, teachers, and officials who harangue
> them about educating themselves for antediluvian jobs.
> (P. 164)

Their gendered language was problematic. Their assessment of the potential of black political power was unrealistic. And, writing their piece after
American immigration laws were changed, they mistook a demographic
shift that would make American cities increasingly non-white for a more
particular demographic shift that would make American cities increasingly
black. However, their general ideas about the city and the role of race seem
remarkably prescient.

As a result of the neoliberal turn, manufacturers and whites left cities
like Detroit and Baltimore first for the suburbs and then, in the case of
manufacturers, for third world nations. Urban public school systems increasingly under-educated citizens, churning out graduates for jobs that no
longer existed. By the mid-eighties, cities were bifurcated between haves
and predominantly non-white have-nots. As a partial consequence of urban disinvestment, political officials increasingly turned to casinos, sports
stadiums, prisons, and downtown development, turning away from social
service provision and working class neighborhoods. They also increasingly
treated have-nots with the heavy hand of the state, articulating and supporting policies that increased incarceration rates (particularly of black men) as
well as punitive workfare policies that penalized working class single mothers (particularly black women). Although the end result of the neoliberal
turn is increased anxiety and inequality and decreased political control, the
American public generally accepted it because urban have-nots in particular
were represented as non-white. But when the have-nots were no longer concentrated among people of color, whites became much less likely to accept
the turn. And, when *Adbusters* proposed an occupation of Wall Street, the
idea spread like wildfire.

Joel Olson was an antiracist political scientist and activist (not to mention committed father, husband, and punk rock musician) who spent the
better part of the past decade organizing in Arizona against Juan Crow laws
until his sudden passing in 2012. One of the first political scientists to recognize the possibilities of the Occupy movement, he was also cognizant of
its potential for reproducing colorblind racism. His pamphlet "Whiteness

and the 99%" (which he offered as an essay for this volume, just before his death) represented an early attempt to get activists to think critically about racial justice. For Olson, the central question Occupy faced was not necessarily whether it should become involved in traditional politics or not. Rather, the central question was whether it would embrace racial justice, or fall victim to "left colorblindness." For him it was "the difference between a free world and the continued dominance of the 99%."

The bulk of the pamphlet details the elite construction of race, racial hierarchy, and racial democracy. The end result of this construction is a system that produces stark inter-racial inequities between populations defined as "white" and populations defined as "nonwhite." Under this system it is no coincidence that the 1% is not only incredibly wealthy, but incredibly white, while the 99% is not only comparatively poorer but racially diverse. Any attempt to deal with economic inequality that ignores the racial diversity of the 99% in effect casts non-white interests and needs aside in favor of white ones. Privilege allows people the luxury of being blind to the realities that surround them. Olson calls this *left colorblindness*—though, technically, he should be more specific. In as much as racism doesn't allow many non-white leftists to stay colorblind, it's more accurate to call this dynamic *white* left colorblindness.

For Olson, white left colorblindness largely plays itself out in agenda setting, in activists determining what issues are important, what issues are worth mobilizing against/for, and what issues are unimportant. He concludes the essay by asking a set of questions designed to assess the extent to which racial issues are either ignored or put aside in movement debates, effectively bringing the racial politics of inequality and the potential racial politics of Occupy to the fore.

The pamphlet represents an important intervention in the nascent movement. And it's important to note that white left colorblindness has a long history in America. However, we suggest that the racial politics of Occupy require a bit more unpacking and that the dynamics of occupation and displacement, agenda-setting, and funding networks require examination. We explore these areas below.

occupation and displacement

WHEN *ADBUSTERS* CALLED for an occupation of Wall Street they imagined themselves taking back space (both physical and virtual) taken over by financial capital. For *Adbusters*, the term "occupation" was a progressive term connoting reclamation, and to the extent the fight against financial capital actually *is* a war, the term also emphasized the fundamental nature of the struggle. It emphasized solidarity with the struggles of other progressive forces around the world—the Arab Spring looms large here. In North America, though, the term "occupy" also has a deeply regressive meaning—it denotes the white settler colonialism that led to the brutal suppression of indigenous peoples, and to the creation of the Atlantic Slave Trade. Furthermore, in the American context, the term also refers to the contemporary urban policy of gentrification—a policy that often ends up displacing poorer populations of color in favor of middle and upper income white populations.[3] The nomenclature of Occupy and the decision to "occupy" spaces that were (in many cases) already occupied led to the symbolic and physical displacement of people of color. While understandably chosen, the use of the term "occupy" largely ignores the role of historical occupations in subjugating people of color.

Occupy Wall Street took over Zuccotti Park because it appeared easy to occupy and maintain, and because it was located near Wall Street. The park had no semi-permanent human population before Occupy Wall Street convened there.[4] However, other formations took

Occupy Wall Street took over Zuccotti Park because it appeared easy to occupy and maintain, and because it was located near Wall Street. The park had no semi-permanent human population before Occupy Wall Street convened there. However, other formations took spaces that were already occupied. In some instances they took over places used by homeless populations, in some instances Occupies took over places frequented by drug-using populations.

3 A number of organizations called for new nomenclature as a result (*Liberate* Baltimore and (Un)Occupy Albuquerque, for example).

4 The park is itself a geographic manifestation of the neoliberal turn, as it is one of dozens of New York City parks owned and managed by private developers for public use in exchange for lowering density regulations. Originally named "Liberty Plaza," it was renamed in 2006 after John Zuccotti, the chairman of Brookfield Office Properties (the park's

spaces that were already occupied. In some instances they took over places used by homeless populations, in some instances Occupies took over places frequented by drug-using populations. In most of these instances, they took over places used by people of color. In some instances these populations were able to coexist. Some argue that the homeless population was actually safer in Occupy encampments than in other spaces. However, occupiers socially displaced and marginalized poor populations of color, creating formal and informal rules that precluded these populations from using the spaces in the ways they saw fit, and from fully participating in the various discussions and political actions taken by the activists. Many Occupies created anti-drug and anti-liquor regulations that prevented poor populations from using the spaces to self-medicate. Even though these rules were hard to enforce, they still worked to literally displace a predominantly non-white population from spaces they had, in many instances, already claimed. Although the politics and the processes were very different, many of the various formations acted as a progressive form of gentrification of public spaces.

agenda setting and structural dynamics

OLSON'S ESSAY FOCUSES on the way race is ignored or shunted aside by speakers and in various occupation debates. Colorblind supporters of economic justice may ignore the specific ways that economic inequity harms communities of color in discussions and in debates. Similarly when people of color bring up issues that are important to them, *they* may be ignored in discussions and debates. Even worse they may be derided. This has the effect of centering organizing efforts on issues most important to whites.

When people think of open source movements like Occupy, they tend to think of movements that require little more than a social network of some sort that can be deployed in the service of progressive politics. To the extent that resources and networks are needed or are developed, they are presumed to come about more or less "naturally," and these resources are deployed horizontally rather than vertically between people who have relatively equal levels of resources themselves. The reality is a bit more complicated. These open source movements are both created and sustained by pre-existing networks that are themselves connected to other pre-existing networks. These networks consist of individuals and institutions who have

---

current owners). Policies designed to prevent poor populations from using the park are the likely results of private management.

some combination of experience and capital,[5] and are deployed whenever an action is called for and whenever resources are required that cannot be garnered by the individuals directly. These networks make the open source movements possible in the first place—one of the reasons Occupy Wall Street formed was because pre-existing networks used the opportunity provided by the *Adbusters* call to organize. These pre-existing networks then created the infrastructural backbone that provided heft to Occupy.

In part because of the decimation of the non-white left through COINTELPRO,[6] in part because of the reduced capital non-white groups have (as a result of white supremacy), the networks tend to be white and tend to be connected to other predominantly white networks. Even though the movement itself has open elements, the networks that lend resources to the movement are often closed.

These networks helped to shape, though not determine, the trajectory of Occupy, and continue to do so, by shaping structures of leadership and by the selective use of funding. In the case of funding in particular, there are, broadly speaking, two different ways this can be (and to a certain extent *has been*) played out.

One way is "inside-out." When competing ideas are proposed that themselves require independent funding streams, individuals who are already connected to funding streams have a two-fold advantage over other individuals: they know the resource providers that exist while other individuals do not; and furthermore, they are *known* by the resource providers while other individuals may not be. The racial dynamic embedded in the 1% dynamic is critical here—white communities possess much greater wealth than black or Latino communities. Thus, it is no surprise that these networks tend to exist more in white communities than others, making it more likely that projects by (and for) whites will be funded. A number of Occupy formations have taken steps to deal with the agenda setting dynamics laid out by Olson. However in as much as they may also be interested in pursuing "broader goals," the knowledge advantage can alter the degree to which racial justice is actually pursued. Furthermore, as pursuing racial justice

---

5   We include some movement groups that would likely call themselves horizontal but that we call vertical because participation can be dependent on years of working together and are thus exclusive.

6   It is quite important to remember the FBI's Counter Intelligence Program (COINTELPRO) in this context. The sixties and seventies were host to the types of urban struggles that the Boggs' foresaw. However, the FBI very intentionally killed and jailed the leadership of the black, Puerto Rican, Hawaiian, and Native American movements. Unlike most of the white movements of the era, these were not allowed to grow, mature, and pass on practices to future generations. This loss is still deeply felt more than thirty years later.

entails building the institutional capacity of people of color to organize and develop their own work, leaving this knowledge advantage uninterrogated further reduces that institutional capacity by locking people of color out of these networks.

The other way we can think of as "outside-in." As soon as Occupy was recognized as legitimate, a number of individuals and institutions offered activists grants. These grants represent implicit attempts to shift the agenda of the movement and its constituent groups. We would not go as far as to say that these represent cooptation attempts. In many cases the grants connected with pre-existing goals and desires of Occupy members. However, in as much as the universe of grants tend to reflect pre-existing power relationships on the left, it is fair to say that these attempts tend to move Occupy away from the causes of racial justice and tend to reproduce colorblindness.

There is a third way that we can also think of as "outside-in," but rather than being colorblind it is almost color *conscious*. People of color have been organizing on their own in communities across the country, largely because people of color have been dealing with economic crisis for the past several decades.[7] Some of these groups have been able to get funding from vertical networks, but it is largely zero-sum. For every dollar people of color receive some other group does *not* receive it. When Occupy began, a number of vertical networks shifted their resource allocation towards it and away from pre-existing organizations led by and for people of color.

the interesting cases of take back the land and occupy our homes

THE OCCUPY MOVEMENT was far from the first initiative in the US that used encampment as a way to challenge an economic system that leaves most of us on the margins. One recent example is Take Back the Land (TBtL), which was founded by Black activists in 2006 in order to combat the class and racial gentrification of predominantly black Liberty City. TBtL activists took over a park in Miami, building a community they named the Umoja Village. The community was composed of poor people, mostly people of color, and they managed their own space for six months, until a fire and police occupation ended the project. But TBtL swiftly morphed as Florida became ground zero of the foreclosure crisis, expanding its mission to include foreclosure defense and home liberation, and eventually expanding to include work in other cities such as Madison, Wisconsin and Rochester, New York.

---

7 Even during the supposedly plush Clinton years, black unemployment has dwarfed white unemployment.

Take Back the Land, and its most recognizable representative Max Rameau,
have been a major influence on the Occupy Movement's focus on foreclosure
and eviction defense. In spite of this,
TBtL chapters did not proliferate after
Occupy Wall Street. However, Occupy
Our Homes (OOH) did. In the case of
Madison, Wisconsin, the founders of
OOH approached M. Adams of TBtL
for help. The OOH folks developed a
program very similar to TBtL, but still,
the mostly white OOH decided that
they needed their own organization,
thus dividing the two groups and leaving
one with a mostly black leadership and
the other with a mostly white leadership.
This division was reproduced at the national level as well, in one case leading
a foundation to choose between funding
TBtL and OOH. For those that are curious, OOH got the money.

steps in the other direction

UNTIL NOW WE have mostly discussed
structures and networks that form
through uncritical expressions of privilege. However, there are options beyond
the unconscious reproduction of inequi-
table race relations. Neither we nor Joel
Olson are the first to notice that white
supremacy is reproduced in social movements unless it is directly challenged and
undermined. How do we do this? First,
our task is to explicitly identify the reproduction of white supremacy within
our movements as a problem. This
means overcoming white left colorblindness as a precondition for building inter-
racial alliances. Second, we must very

First, our task is to explicitly identify the reproduction of white supremacy within our movements as a problem. This means overcoming white left colorblindness as a precondition for building inter-racial alliances. Second, we must very intentionally build beyond existing racial networks and share human and financial resources.

intentionally build beyond existing racial networks and share human and financial resources. This must be done without patronization or tokenization—two dynamics that generate greater mistrust. And finally, those with privilege must learn to use their privilege strategically. If you float in a network that is resource-rich, share that access. Use it to open doors to other communities. Similarly, if your life has allowed you a great breadth of experience, share that experience with others. If the criminal justice system treats you with greater favor, you might consider taking greater risk. Here are a couple of examples of recent actions that take these suggestions to heart.

may 12 coalition, nyc, 2011

IN RESPONSE TO NYC Mayor Michael Bloomberg's draconian budget that proposed slashing thousands of teacher jobs (among other things), New York City unions and community groups prepared for a week of actions demanding that Bloomberg cancel the cuts and balance the budget by making major banks and financial firms pay local taxes. The week of actions was coordinated by a veteran white organizer, who planned the week with a diverse set of actors including (but not limited to) the United Federation of Teachers, VOCAL New York, and New York Communities United. The coalition set the agenda through meetings of coalition partners, and through surveying individual members. The goals of the week of actions were to stop Bloomberg's budget cuts, make banks pay their fair share, and train a new generation of New Yorkers in direct action. The leadership of the unions and community groups tended to be whiter than the membership, but it was the members that participated in the training and the week of action, which is to say, the actions were meant to empower a group that was majority people of color. The trainers themselves were white women and men.

The week of action was packed full of experience and reflection. Groups flew from one action to another, day in, day out, leaving time only for meals and debriefs. In the course of three days, a street team of a hundred took over bank, hotel, and hedge fund lobbies, did street theater outside of Goldman Sachs, blocked intersections, interrupted a conference, protested outside of the Bank of America building, distributed thousands of fliers, and called a flash mob into the World Financial Center building. The twice-daily debriefs were fundamental spaces to reflect on the actions and what worked or didn't work, and to plan roles for the next series of actions. The week culminated in a march on Wall Street of more than 20,000.

The members took on a lot of leadership in the meetings and on the streets, where they were paired up with more experienced activists on some of the more difficult tasks of the actions. Participants in that week went on to plan more actions themselves, and to participate strongly in the Direct Action Working Group of Occupy Wall Street.

schools not jails, baltimore, january 2012

SEVERAL YEARS PRIOR to the start of Occupy, the State of Maryland announced plans to build a new $112 million youth detention facility in Baltimore, a majority Black, working class, postindustrial city. This in a context where the city is closing schools, firehouses, and swimming pools, and refusing to fund or privatizing Recreation Centers due to budget shortfalls. A broad coalition of largely Black organizations working on youth, education, and incarceration issues had been pushing hard against this jail. When Occupy Baltimore was evicted from McKeldin Square, a proposal was floated to occupy the youth jail site. This set up an interesting dynamic: Occupy Baltimore was a racially-mixed group, but was identified by many as a white group in a Black city. Poor black youths were the primary target of the youth jail. Further, black youth-led organizations such as the Baltimore Algebra Project (BAP) were holding down the struggle against the youth jail.

Before launching the effort to occupy the youth jail site, Occupy Baltimore participants approached the BAP to get their approval and invite collaboration. In the end, the action was a close collaboration between Occupy Baltimore and the BAP, with members from both organizations taking leadership, making decisions, risking arrest, and gaining experience.

The actions unfolded over the course of a week. On the first day there was a rally at the youth jail site while some activists entered the fenced in lot and built a schoolhouse on the proposed youth jail site. Six people were arrested that night. Other actions continued throughout the week.

The legal fallout was somewhat predictable. Of those arrested, it was a young Black male that was targeted for harshest treatment. However, all of the codefendants stood together and minimized the negative impact on that individual. Occupy Baltimore and the BAP will be co-litigants in a lawsuit against the city for its seizure of a Recreation Center facade during one of the week's protests. The collaboration between the two organizations has continued and deepened.

conclusion

NOTE THAT IN these cases we still see race doing work. In large part due to the systematic decapitation of a radical black activist leadership, many (if not most) of the activists with the deep knowledge and deep repertoires of direct action are white. With both the May 12 Action and the Baltimore Schools not Jails project, we see whites in significant leadership roles.

However, instead of taking the 99% and the issues of the 99% for granted, note here that in both cases white activists intentionally chose to cooperate and work through racial difference as opposed to glossing it over. In the May 12 action, activists created space for two types of engagement—for engagement between formal representatives on what the issues and the direct actions were to be, and for engagement between (predominantly white) activists and people of color. The first type of engagement deals directly with the issues Olson reflects on. Who gets a chance to say what the issues are? How is race to be treated? Activists not only took this on by surveying a wide body of representatives, they also took this on by way of several phone conferences intentionally designed to ensure that the issues the action dealt with were issues that reflected broad and deep consensus. The second type of engagement deals with another issue that Olson doesn't wrestle with, but which is important nonetheless—training. As noted above, the institutional memory that would be present in black and other non-white communities is largely absent because of the systematic decapitation of radical black leadership, and also because of the degree to which the election of black representatives itself shunts off radical action. The activists in the May 12 instance took the time to train people of color in direct action techniques, reducing the skills gap that exists between them.

The Baltimore Schools not Jails action was a creative response to two actions by state officials. The first was the forced removal of Occupy Baltimore from McKeldin Square by police. Occupy Baltimore, like other Occupies, began to expend more and more mental and fiscal resources on maintaining their physical occupation—resources that to an extent precluded them from thinking about other activities. When police forced occupiers out of the square, members began to think about other sites more carefully. The second action was the Baltimore Algebra Project's decision to contest the youth jail site. Instead of taking the action without involving the Baltimore Algebra Project, Occupy Baltimore engaged in discussions with the BAP to ensure that the ongoing campaign of a young, Black organization would not be unintentionally "occupied." As with the May 12 Coalition, the intention was to open the door for a sharing of skills and other resources.

These two examples point the way toward positive forms of inter-racial collaboration. It is not bad for organizing to occur separately in white communities and Black communities (we need everyone fighting in whatever way they can…). However, the scale of change we need will not happen without people making connections between issues and organizations, developing a systemic analysis of the problems, and working together towards a common solution. It is especially urgent that formations like the Occupy Movement, majority white movements in majority non-white cities, realize that meaningful, transformative change is not going to happen if they don't look beyond their networks and issues and learn from, work with, and share with the majority populations.

James and Grace Boggs' "The City Is the Black Man's Land" remains incredibly prescient. The Boggs predicted the economic crisis, they predicted the demise of the industrial age, they predicted the fall of labor, they predicted the growing obsolescence of urban youth. And they were correct in noting the importance of racial dynamics and the importance of the city as a site of political action. As Joel Olson notes, the fight for the 99% should center on the fight for racial justice as people of color and the communities they reside in serve as ground zero. These communities were hit hardest by the economic crisis we currently wrestle with, and they have struggled the longest. It is our suggestion here that the battle against white left colorblindness must occur along multiple fronts. Along the linguistic front, future iterations should take care to use symbols that reflect the realities of settler colonialism and refrain from using language that denotes "occupation." Along the geographic front, if Occupies continue to use the tactic of physical occupation they should do so in a way that highlights rather than reproduces oppression. Along the agenda-setting front, activists should work to ensure that issues particular to communities of color be made central. A number of Occupies already have committees dedicated to not only dealing with issues of racial justice but also with making sure that the Occupies themselves are sensitive to the ways left colorblindness can disrupt organizational processes. Along the structural network front, people should work to make sure that funding streams are transparent and made available to everyone. And finally, along the relationship front, activists need to push beyond current fragmented and segregated relationships and start working through the challenges and joys of organizing beyond their current networks. Without that, we're unlikely to move very far beyond our current situation no matter how hard we try.

Brendan Maslauskas Dunn
Occupy Utica
Occupying a Small Rustbelt City

I lived and worked in NYC when OWS started. After Zuccotti Park was cleared, the call to action that resonated most with me was to spread the occupation in your community. I answered the call and moved back to my hometown—Utica, New York.

Utica shares a common fate with many smaller cities in the Rust Belt. It was once an economic center for knitting mills and General Electric, but most of the major manufacturing left the city over the past fifty years. Its current population is half what it was during its industrial heyday. Some of the larger employers currently in the area are prisons and a Walmart distribution center. The city is a shadow its former self. Capitalism has not been kind to Utica, but Occupy was a recent injection of hope.

Utica does not have a reputation for protests of any sort, but when Occupy erupted overnight, 400 people showed up to the first Occupy Utica demonstration and a public space was occupied. The camp eventually folded, forcing us to shift the struggle into the community. A nightly radio show called Occupied Radio was set up at occupiedradio.net and acts as a resource to Occupy nationally. It still airs every night at 10PM EST. It was through the radio show we found John McDevitt, an Afghan War veteran who had over $25,000 stolen from his Bank of America account while he was overseas. After a march and picket of BofA, and national media coverage, Occupy Utica was able to do what BofA, government agencies, and lawyers were either unwilling or unable to: force corporate headquarters to give every cent back to McDevitt. He's now one of the most active members of Occupy Utica.

Another battle we picked up was one over austerity measures in the city schools. Over 200 teachers, sports teams, and numerous programs were threatened with termination.

Trinh Truong, a fellow Occupier and 14-year-old high school student, helped organize over 50 students to picket outside the Board of Education. It was through that action we found another student whose father was facing deportation to Jamaica and was locked up in an ICE detention center. Occupy helped his family and fought to prevent the deportation. We organized the first May Day rally in Utica in recent memory, and are active in the struggle to prevent the closure of the only psychiatric center in town, which could mean life or death for some patients and would terminate 150 union jobs. The April announcement of one of the last major manufacturers in the area, Orion Bus, which employs over 500 workers, prompted us to start organizing workers there to fight the closure of the unionized plant. We also picked up a campaign to help fifteen workers and contractors who were fired from their jobs and had $30,000 stolen from them by their boss. An official city newspaper, *The Utica Phoenix*, helps spread our message by devoting a section of their paper to Occupy stories.

As the summer heats up, so too does Occupy Utica. There is no shortage of plans and we're grassroots organizing to get into the community to: start a Copwatch against a brutal police force, organize tenants to fight evictions, organize homeowners to fight foreclosures, and organize workers to fight for better working conditions. Utica has had a rough and tumble past but Occupy helped create a small but growing culture of resistance. It is in small cities like Utica where the real power of a social movement is measured and where parallel grassroots power can thrive.

Occupy Research and DataCenter
Christine Schweidler, Pablo Rey Mazón, Saba Waheed,
and Sasha Costanza-Chock

RESEARCH BY AND FOR THE MOVEMENT
KEY FINDINGS FROM THE OCCUPY RESEARCH GENERAL DEMOGRAPHIC & PARTICIPATION SURVEY (ORGS)

occupy research

OCCUPY RESEARCH WAS CREATED AS AN OPEN, DISTRIBUTED RESEARCH NET-work. As movement researchers, we are committed to advancing the theory and practice of research justice for movement building.[1] The Occupy Research General Demographic & Participation Survey (ORGS) was designed to: 1) create a better understanding of who participates in Occupy, who does *not* participate, and why; 2) identify, document, and challenge race, class, gender, sexuality, age, disability, and other inequalities reproduced within movement spaces; 3) support movement actors to share ideas, strategies, and tactics; 4) spread research skills, tools, and methods more broadly throughout the 99%; 5) challenge dominant narratives about the movement by creating and sharing data that highlights the views of Occupiers in their own words.

methods

OCCUPY RESEARCH DESIGNED ORGS through an open, collaborative process that included Occupy participants and researchers from across the globe. Although it was initially designed as a face to face survey, after most Occupy camps were displaced by police we focused on gathering responses

---

1   For more about research justice, see http://www.datacenter.org/research-justice/.

online. ORGS was open from December 7, 2011, to January 7, 2012. We gathered 5,074 completed surveys.

limitations

OUR SAMPLE OF respondents was non-random: therefore, our findings cannot be assumed to reflect all participants in the Occupy movement. ORGS was primarily accessed online, so our results are biased towards those with greater levels of Internet access. The survey was conducted in English only, so it fails to reflect non-English speakers. That said, ORGS contains data from several thousand self-identified Occupiers, and the findings are relevant to movement-building analysis and strategy.

The following pages highlight a small subset of our key findings. For the full ORGS report, including methodology, survey instrument, training guides, complete data sets, and extended analysis, please see http://www.occupyresearch.net/category/survey.

demographics

ORGS RESPONDENTS ARE of diverse age, educational and class backgrounds, and are almost equally divided amongst men (44%) and women (53%), with 1% reporting as transgender. In terms of sexual identity, the majority (76%) identify as heterosexual/straight, while 16% identify as Lesbian, Gay, Bisexual, and/or Queer. The average age of survey respondents is 42.

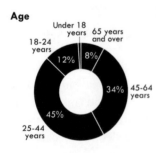

Age

Occupy faced difficulty connecting to communities of color: eight out of ten respondents (81%) are white. People of color participated extensively in many Occupy locations, but overall ORGS respondents were just 5% Latino/a, 5% Asian/Pacific Islander, 4% Native American, and 3% African American.

Almost half of respondents identify as working or lower middle class. Despite right-wing rhetoric about "jobless" Occupiers, about one third are employed full time, 8% are underemployed, and 18% are students, while just 9% report being unemployed. In terms of housing, almost half are renters, and 41% are homeowners. The annual household income breaks down as follows:

Annual Household Income

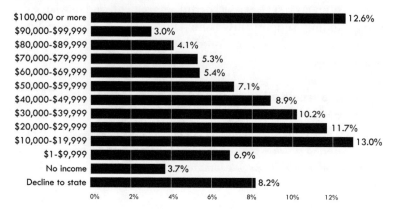

$100,000 or more	12.6%
$90,000-$99,999	3.0%
$80,000-$89,999	4.1%
$70,000-$79,999	5.3%
$60,000-$69,999	5.4%
$50,000-$59,999	7.1%
$40,000-$49,999	8.9%
$30,000-$39,999	10.2%
$20,000-$29,999	11.7%
$10,000-$19,999	13.0%
$1-$9,999	6.9%
No income	3.7%
Decline to state	8.2%

media use

MANY ARGUE THAT social media play a key role in the current global cycle of struggles. We sought to better understand how Occupiers used various kinds of media to seek and circulate movement information:

Word of mouth was the most crucial form of communication, followed by Occupy movement websites. Social media was quite important, although our results are biased by the high proportion of respondents who arrived at the survey via Facebook. Email remains popular; Twitter, blogs, and Tumblr, as well as print newspapers, were used by less than a quarter of Occupiers during the past day. Nearly a fifth (19%) reported using a livestreaming video site during the past 24 hours: more than TV or radio (17%).

Usage of different types of sources for news and information about the Occupy movement.

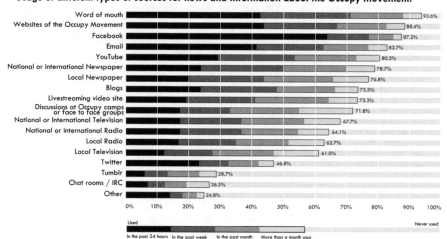

Word of mouth	93.6%
Websites of the Occupy Movement	88.4%
Facebook	87.2%
Email	82.7%
YouTube	80.3%
National or international Newspaper	78.7%
Local Newspaper	76.8%
Blogs	73.5%
Livestreaming video site	73.3%
Discussions at Occupy camps or face to face groups	71.8%
National or International Television	67.7%
National or international Radio	64.1%
Local Radio	62.7%
Local Television	61.0%
Twitter	46.8%
Tumblr	28.7%
Chat rooms / IRC	26.5%
Other	24.8%

Used — Never used

In the past 24 hours   In the past week   In the past month   More than a month ago

participation

OCCUPY DESCRIBED ITSELF as a "leaderful" movement, and to a large degree the survey findings support this claim: 41% said they volunteered to help with food, 40% participated in workshops or events, and 38% took part in a working group:

Type of participation in the camp . . . . %

Attended a General Assembly 69

Marched in a protest. 69

Volunteered to provide food or services to people at the camp . 41

Participated in workshops or events hosted at the camp 40

Taken part in a working group 38

Slept in an Occupy camp 17

Got arrested 4

Other. 26

civic engagement

OCCUPIERS ARE ALSO highly engaged in diverse forms of civic activity. While many said that Occupy was their first social movement, more than half (59%) said they had previously been involved in other movements. Beyond Occupy, they take part in civic life: the majority belong to nonprofit organizations (57%) and political parties (52%); during the past year, most (91%) signed petitions, boycotted, or buycotted (89.9%); more than two thirds (77%) contacted a civil servant to express their views, and 67.7% donated money or raised funds for a social or political activity. Most are actively involved in electoral politics: 87.3 % voted in the 2008 presidential elections. More than a third (38.4%) were independent or did not identify with any political party; almost an equal number were Democrats (37.9%).

why i occupy

WE ASKED PEOPLE to name their top three reasons for participating in the Occupy Movement:

In this visualization of responses, the most commonly occurring terms (like *inequality, corporate,* or *corruption*) appear larger; word proximity is based on co-occurence within a single response. As this book goes to print we are coding the results from these and other open-ended questions, for our full analysis see the complete report.

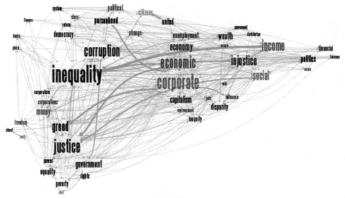

conclusions

Occupy has successfully mobilized large numbers of people to protest, take direct action, and engage in prefigurative politics. Occupy struggles to build the world we want, now, and Occupiers from a range of backgrounds work together under stressful conditions of surveillance and police repression. Of course, the movement reflects the broader social context, and white supremacist capitalist patriarchy, developed over centuries, is not a system that can be simply dismantled in a few months. We hope that these findings will be used by Occupiers to strategize about how to grow stronger social movements, center the participation, experiences, knowledge, and leadership of women, people of color, immigrants, and queer folks, and meaningfully challenge privilege and internalized oppression.

future work

The Occupy Research network and DataCenter (http://www.datacenter. org) are currently analyzing the ORGS dataset to inform insights that can help our movements grow stronger. The complete report, including the datasets, along with more information about the ORGS survey and the Occupy Research network, are available at http://occupyresearch.net.

("Reasons Why We Occupy" graphic above by Don Blair.)

OCCUPY

Grégoire Vion
HTTP://WWW.GRGWR.COM

Yvonne Yen Liu

WHERE IS THE COLOR IN OCCUPY?

WHEN THE GREAT RECESSION SANK ITS FANGS INTO THE VEINS OF THIS country in December 2007, for the first time, millions of white people woke that morning to a different world. Unemployment and poverty are not unfamiliar bedfellows to people of color: Black unemployment has been at least double that of the rate for whites from 1973 to 2009; Latinos were 1.5 times more likely to be unemployed than whites for 28 out of the 37 years.[1] The white middle class wasn't able to get a job, pay their mortgage or healthcare bills, were in danger of losing their home to foreclosure, or applied for food stamps for the first time.[2] In short, the white middle class joined the ranks of people of color who have faced unemployment, low wages or poverty, and lack of wealth and assets throughout the history of this country.[3]

It should not be surprising that two years later, after the recession technically ended (June 2009, according to the National Bureau of Economic Research)[4] yet unemployment stayed steady at 9.1%,[5] thousands of members of the white middle class, many young and college-educated, but with

1 Applied Research Center. May 2009. "Race and Recession: How Inequity Rigged the Economy and How to Change the Rules." http://arc.org/recession (accessed 5/13/12).

2 Appelbaum, Binyamin and Robert Gebeloff. 2/11/12. "Even Critics of Safety Net Increasingly Depend on It." *New York Times.* http://www.nytimes.com/2012/02/12/us/even-critics-of-safety-net-increasingly-depend-on-it.html (accessed 2/13/12).

3 Sullivan, Tim et al. 1/12/12. "State of the Dream 2012: The Emerging Majority. United for a Fair Economy." http://www.faireconomy.org/dream (accessed 4/15/12).

4 "US Business Cycle Expansions and Contractions." 9/20/10. National Bureau of Economic Research. http://www.nber.org/cycles/cyclesmain.html (accessed 4/15/12).

5 "Employment Situation News Release." 10/7/11. Bureau of Labor Statistics. http://bls.gov/news.release/archives/empsit_10072011.htm (accessed 4/15/12).

no hopes of breaking into a job market, answered the call to Occupy Wall Street.[6] Many flocked to Zuccotti Park, eerily close to the negative space of Ground Zero, to roll out sleeping bags onto hard concrete, claiming to be the 99%. Surveys, such as those conducted by Occupy Research, confirmed what many of us already knew: over 80% of Occupy participants identified as white.[7]

Occupy Research is a global network of academics and independent researchers, dedicated to both understanding the movement as well as aiding it.[8] The informal network was started by Sasha Constanza-Schock, a media studies professor at MIT, and Chris Schweidler of DataCenter, a movement-based research think tank. A number of research projects were incubated under the Occupy Research umbrella, for example, Oakland carried out campaign research into the city's interest rate swap payments to Goldman Sachs. The Occupy Race, Class, and Gender working group was interested in two specific questions:[9]

1. What were the dynamics of race, class, and gender in the Occupy movement?
2. What are the ebbs and flows of Occupy, in its progression from a moment into a movement?

To answer these questions, researchers devised several methods, including cultural text analysis and focus groups. Focus group conversations with youth organizers involved in Occupy in three cities—Oakland, New York, and Atlanta[10]—yielded insights into how race is conceived within the movement.[11] In both Oakland and Atlanta, cities with strong traditions of racial justice movements, focus group participants identified their actions as

---

6   Unemployment rates for young adults between 20 and 24 in age are higher than that of the general population. But, youth of color face higher rates consistently over time. From 1977–2009, the highest rate of unemployment for white youth, 13.9% in 2009, does not reach even the lowest rate for Black youth, 14.3% in 2001 (ARC, 2009, Race and Recession).

7   Occupy Research. Preliminary Findings: Occupy Research Demographic and Political Participation Survey. 3/23/12. http://www.occupyresearch. net/2012/03/23/preliminary-findings-occupy-research-demographic-and-political-participation-survey/ (accessed 4/15/12).

8   Occupy Research, http://occupyresearch.net (accessed 7/24/12).

9   Occupy Race, http://occupyresearch.wikispaces.com/occupyrace (accessed 7/24/12).

10 Youth defined as anyone between the ages of 18 and 30.

11 Focus groups sponsored by the Applied Research Center (publisher of Colorlines.com). Each group had 10–12 participants; the gatherings were publicized through Occupy social networks.

distinct from entrenched nonprofit institutions (often referred to in conversation as the "nonprofit industrial complex"). "Nonprofits led by people of color are pissed that they weren't asked to join Occupy Oakland," explained Oliver, a white man in his early twenties, who favored long hair topped by theatrical flourishes, such as a top hat.[12]

In Atlanta, Anna is a single mother in her late twenties, originally from Eastern Europe, who named Camus and Sartre as authors that influenced her politics. She and her son lived with a Black family in a rapidly gentrifying working class neighborhood, helping the family to defend their home from foreclosure. Anna explained the city's politics: "The ossified Black civil rights leadership has been bought off; they don't allow grassroots movements to flourish. Nonprofits kill movements, they replace [movements] with themselves."

Emily is a 19-year-old white woman, who moved to Atlanta from the surrounding suburbs a year ago. She wore t-shirt advertising a punk band, with an anarchy-A in the logo, and sat for most of the conversation with her knees hugged to her chest. Emily remarked "Troy Davis was a huge thing here. The Black leaders urged us all to vote and pray, yet [Davis] was still murdered. It was a turning point, where we started to reject the vote and pray stuff."

Aisha is an 18-year-old Black woman who smiled to reveal a mouthful of braces. She lived in another home being defended from foreclosure, located

Aisha is an 18-year-old Black woman who smiled to reveal a mouthful of braces. She lived in another home being defended from foreclosure, located in a neighboring suburb, owned by a former Black Panther. Aisha added, "Blacks are always affected by things like police brutality or the recession, but our leaders just tell us to be good, 'pray and vote.'"

---

12 Names have been changed to maintain anonymity.

in a neighboring suburb, owned by a former Black Panther. Aisha added, "Blacks are always affected by things like police brutality or the recession, but our leaders just tell us to be good, 'pray and vote.'"

Almost everyone I talked to concurred that racial disparities were important for Occupy to address. Nathan, a 22-year-old white male in New York, suggested that "you can't talk about the financial crisis without talking about race. The movement fails if it doesn't address race as a pillar, along with sexism and patriarchy. You need an intersectional analysis." However, white participants were more likely to be "colorblind" in their view of economic inequalities and movement processes. "Capital doesn't discriminate," stated Oliver. "Asians make more than whites." Tom, a 30-year-old white male in Oakland, who arrived with a giant rucksack stuffed with a sleeping bag and his clothing covered in travel dust, complained, "I am lumped unfairly as a white middle-class male; bigotry cuts both ways."

Liberal commentators such as Chris Hedges have attempted to divide the movement into good, nonviolent activists versus bad, violent troublemakers.[13] This debate has plagued other movements before, the alter-globalization movement for example, conflating violent tactics with those who adhere to an anarchist orientation. Although several voices within Occupy have criticized this conflation,[14] youth in the focus groups uphold the correlations, perhaps unconsciously. Emily, for instance, described Occupy as a "white organizing culture," where "the consensus model pushed people of color away." She thought that when "Representative John Lewis wasn't allowed to speak out of process, people defended the process… But, defending that process was defending white organizing culture."

Oliver in Oakland cited a Black Panther party leader, who praised anarchists for their willingness to take direct action.[15] But, he referred to anarchists as "white kids," thereby assigning a racial identity to a philosophical tradition, ignoring any heterogeneous identification within the community. "Brother Freeman says people of color run nonprofits, but white kids get stuff done." Again, there is the equation of the politics of representation with an entrenched leadership, protecting the status quo.

While these binaries of nonprofits/insurgence, people of color/white anarchists, nonviolence/violence from past movements persist in Occupy, I take hope in the Occupy generation, those newly politicized, who are

---

13 Hedges, Chris. 2/6/12. "The Cancer in Occupy." *TruthDig*. http://www.truth-dig.com/report/item/the_cancer_of_occupy_20120206/ (accessed 4/15/12).

14 Graeber, David. 2/9/12. "Concerning the Violent Peace-Police." *N+1*. http://nplusonemag.com/concerning-the-violent-peace-police (accessed 4/15/12).

15 Soynoise. 7/14/08. What does Black Panther Party think about Anarchists? http://www.youtube.com/watch?v=tHCrueoYYuA (accessed 4/15/12).

encountering the vagaries of race, class, gender, and sexuality in daily life, yet struggle to reconcile an intersectional analysis with their thirst for a better world. Nick, a white male in his late twenties in New York, said that his vision of a better world was a temporary autonomous zone, without state or capital. He remembered being in the Occupy Wall Street kitchen one day, where a young woman of color asked a white man to clean the dishes he left in the sink. "The young white man said to her, 'You do it, I'm doing important work.' But, who's going to do the important work of washing dishes?"

Langley, a 20-year-old white male, who wore an oversized green army jacket that engulfed his thin frame, contemplated Nick's question for a minute. He and a friend were the only white residents of a home in east New York, which was liberated by the movement in early December.[16] "Doing the dishes is revolutionary."

---

16 Harkinson, Josh. 12/6/11. "Occupy Movement Targets Foreclosed Properties." *Mother Jones.* http://motherjones.com/politics/2011/12/occupy-our-homes-wall-street-squatters-foreclosures (accessed 4/15/12).

Anonymous
Excerpt from a 26-page rioter's manual
produced during the 2011 Egyptian uprising

HOLD YOUR GROUND, EGYPTIAN!
Block the truncheon with your shield as
you're spraying them in the face.

Croatoan

WHO IS OAKLAND?
ANTI-OPPRESSION ACTIVISM, THE POLITICS OF SAFETY, AND STATE COOPTATION

synopsis[1]

THIS ARTICLE, ORIGINALLY PUBLISHED IN UNABRIDGED FORM AS A PAMPHLET, was written collaboratively by a group of people of color, women, and queers—and is offered in deep solidarity with anyone committed to ending identity-based oppression and exploitation materially. The fact that we must specify our identities in advance before making an argument is an index of how powerful, widespread, and largely unquestioned is the premise that arguments always reduce to identity positions.

While twenty-first century anti-oppression politics in the US is an evolving, ad hoc patchwork of theories and practices, we argue for the necessity of identity-based organizing while criticizing how anti-oppression activism

---

1   We feel that many of the observations and arguments in the "Who Is Oakland" pamphlet are regionally specific to the Bay Area and to what we witnessed as participants in Occupy Oakland. In Occupy Los Angeles, the informal "leadership" of many of the committees and the General Assembly have discussions about the role of the police and how the "unity" of the 99% is complicated by racism, sexism, and patriarchy. In Los Angeles, this culminated in an incident where a "participant in Occupy LA distributed fliers at the October 4, 2011 General Assembly with the names and photos of 25 individuals associated with the Committee to End Police Brutality and accusing these participants ... of trying to highjack and destroy the movement and provoking the police." Obviously such dynamics were present in Occupy Oakland, but our pamphlet also explores how Occupy Oakland's relatively greater racial and ethnic diversity, and the city's peculiar radical history, impacted its immediate, nationally unpopular stance on the police, city government, and Democratic Party pressure groups like MoveOn. For more context on Occupy LA, please see the two statements at this site—the first from Decolonize LA and the second from Paracaidistas Collective at http://unpermittedla.wordpress.com.

has been dominated by an unquestioned rhetoric of checking individual privilege, by a therapeutic idealization of cultural identities and origins, and finally by the assumption that identity categories describe homogeneous "communities" of shared political beliefs. We argue that a politics of individual privilege, cultural idealization, and cultural homogenization minimizes and misrepresents the severity and structural character of identity-based oppression and exploitation in the US.

According to the dominant discourse of "white privilege" for example, white supremacy is primarily a psychological attitude which individuals can simply choose to renounce instead of an entrenched material infrastructure which reproduces race at key sites across society—from racially segmented labor markets to the militarization of the border. Whiteness simply becomes one more "culture," and white supremacy a psychological attitude, instead of a structural position of dominance reinforced through institutions, civilian and police violence, access to resources, and the economy. At the same time a critique of "white privilege" has become a kind of blanket, reflexive condemnation of any variety of confrontational, disruptive protest while bringing the focus back to reforming the behavior and beliefs of individuals.

Anti-oppression, civil rights, and decolonization struggles clearly reveal that if resistance is even slightly effective, *the people who struggle are in danger*. We maintain that the choice is not between danger and safety, but between the uncertain dangers of revolt and the certainty of continued violence, deprivation, and death.

identity-based organizing is non-negotiable

WE ARE NOT spokespersons for Occupy Oakland. As a group of people of color, women, queers, and poor people coming together to attack a complex matrix of oppression and exploitation, we believe in the absolute necessity of autonomous organizing. By "autonomous" we mean the formation of independent groups of people who face specific forms of exploitation and oppression and who organize *as* people of color, women, queers, trans* people, gender nonconforming people, or queer people of color. We also recognize the political value of forming networks which try to cross racial, gender, and sexual divisions.

No demographic category of people could possibly share an identical set of political beliefs or personal values. The violent domination and subordination we face on the basis of our race, gender, and sexuality do not immediately create a shared political vision even though it may describe a shared experience of discrimination and violence. Identity categories do not indicate political unity or agreement. But the uneven impact of identity-based oppression across society creates the conditions for the diffuse emergence of autonomous groups organizing on the basis of common experiences and a common political understanding of those experiences. There is a difference between a politics which places an idealized cultural identity or heritage at the center of its analysis of oppression, and autonomous organizing against forms of oppression which impact members of marginalized groups differently.

occupy oakland, "outside agitators," and "white occupy"

WHEN OAKLAND MAYOR Jean Quan and Alameda District Attorney Nancy O'Malley claim that Occupy Oakland is not part of the national Occupy movement, they're onto something. From the start, Occupy Oakland immediately rejected cooperation with city government officials, wildly flexible state and media definitions of "violence," and by now largely discredited arguments that the police are part of "the 99%."

The press releases of the city government, Oakland Police Department, and business associations like the Oakland Chamber of Commerce continually repeat that the Occupy Oakland encampment, feeding nearly a thousand mostly desperately poor people a day, was composed primarily of non-Oakland resident "white outsiders" intent on destroying the city. For anyone who spent any length of time at the encampment, Occupy Oakland was clearly one of the most racially and ethnically diverse Occupy encampments in the country—composed of people of color from all walks of life, from local business owners to fired Oakland school teachers, from college students to the homeless and seriously mentally ill.

From the beginning the Occupy Oakland camp existed in a tightening vise between two faces of the state: nonprofits and the police. An array of community organizations immediately began negotiating with the Mayor's office and pushing for the encampment to adopt nonviolence pledges and move to Snow Park (itself later cleared by OPD despite the total compliance of the individuals who settled there). At the same time, police departments across the Bay Area were readying one of the largest and most expensive paramilitary operations in recent history.

The city's reaction to Occupy Oakland is a case study in how much anti-racist politics has changed since Bobby Seale and Elaine Brown attempted to run for Oakland mayor and city council respectively in 1973 against a sea of white incumbents. Oakland's current city government—including the mayor's office, city council, and Oakland Police Department—is now staffed and led predominantly by people of color.

By borrowing a charge used against civil rights movement participants and 60s-era militants of color like Stokely Carmichael and H. Rap Brown, and even Martin Luther King Jr., as "outside agitators," City Hall has tried to claim that the interests of all "authentic Oaklanders" are the same. The month-long Occupy Oakland encampment was blamed by the Oakland Chamber of Commerce and its city government partners for everything from deepening city poverty to the failure of business-led development, from the rats which have always infested the city plaza to the mounting cost of police brutality. An encampment which fed about a thousand people every day of its month-long existence, and which witnessed a 19% decrease in area crime in the last week of October, was scapegoated for the very poverty, corruption, and police violence it came into existence to combat.

If you believe the city press releases, "authentic Oaklanders" are truly represented by a police force which murders and imprisons its poor black and brown residents daily (about 7% of OPD officers actually live in the city) and a city government which funnels their taxes into business-friendly redevelopment deals like the $91 million dollar renovation of the Fox Theater—$58 million over budget—which line the pockets of well-connected real estate developers like Phil Tagami. In a complete reversal of 60s-era militant antiracist political movements, we are told by these politicians and pundits that militant, disruptive, and confrontational political actions which target this city bureaucracy and its police forces can only be the work of white, middle class, and privileged youths.

People of color who were not only active but central to Occupy Oakland and its various committees are routinely erased from accounts of the encampment. In subsequent months the camp has been denounced by social justice activists, many of whom work directly with the mayor's office, who have criticized it as a space irreparably compromised by racial and gender privilege. Racism, patriarchy, homophobia, and transphobia were all clearly on display at Occupy Oakland—as they are in every sector of social life in Oakland.

There is clearly a need to reflect upon how the dynamics of the encampments quickly overwhelmed the capacity of participants to provide services and spaces free from sexual harassment and violence. But to describe the participants of Occupy Oakland as primarily white men is not only factually incorrect, it ultimately prevents participants from being able to look honestly at the social interactions which occurred under its auspices.

the new politics of privilege, culture, and "community"

WE BELIEVE THAT privilege politics and cultural essentialism—that is the belief that cultures are the bounded, timeless, inherently liberatory property of racial and ethnic groups—has incapacitated antiracist, feminist, and queer organizing in this country. Representing significant political differences as differences in privilege or culture places politics beyond discussion and reinforces stereotypes about the political homogeneity and helplessness of people of color. It's important to keep in mind that the interracial designation "people of color" is itself a recently invented identity category which implies communal experience while at the same time concealing emerging forms of nonwhite interracial conflict and obscuring the central role that antiblack racism plays in maintaining America's racial order.

In the Bay Area, the state has appropriated a peculiarly repressive, depoliticized ideal of "community" which invokes mythologies of shared cultural origins and of communal experience as an authentic, non-hierarchical space of political belonging. In the wake of Oakland's regular police murders of unarmed black and brown youths, politicians, clergy, and nonprofit leadership spring into action and relentlessly promote a rhetoric of "healing the community," which expressly forbids the "community" from ever attacking or disrupting the oppressive systems which terrorize them in the first place.

It is a well-worn activist formula to point out that "representatives" of different identity categories must be placed "front and center" in struggles against racism, sexism, and homophobia. But this tokenistic gesture is meaningless if the political beliefs of these individuals are simply ignored. The US Army is simultaneously one of the most racially integrated and oppressive institutions in American society. Racial, gender, and sexual "diversity" alone is an empty political ideal which reifies culture, defines agency as inclusion within oppressive systems, and equates identity categories with political beliefs.

For too long there has been no alternative to this politics of diversity and representation, and so rejecting this liberal political framework has become synonymous with a refusal to seriously address racism, sexism, and homophobia in general. Even and especially when people of color, women, and queers organize and act independently of this increasingly rigid politics, they are persistently attacked as white, male, and privileged by the cohort that maintains and perpetuates the dominant praxis.

protecting vulnerable communities of color and "our" women and children

WE ARE CONSTANTLY compared to children in the paternalistic idiom of contemporary privilege discourse. Even children can have a more savvy and sophisticated analysis than privilege theorists often assume! "Communities of color" have become, in this discourse, akin to endangered species in need of management by sympathetic whites or "community representatives" assigned to prevent political conflict at all costs. For this brand of politics, identity-based oppression is legitimate and recognizable only when each gender is in its proper place, and only if it speaks a language of productivity, patriotism, and moral prostration. We must remain peaceful, unthreatening, morally deserving "others."

Yet the vast majority of us are not "safe" simply going through our daily lives in Oakland, or elsewhere. When activists claim that poor black and brown communities must not defend themselves against racist attacks or confront the state, including using illegal or "violent" means, they instead reproduce stereotypes about the passivity and powerlessness of these populations. In fact it is precisely people from these groups—poor women of color defending their right to land and housing, trans* street workers fighting back against murder and violence, black, brown, and Asian American militant struggles against white supremacist attacks—who have waged the most powerful and successful uprisings in American history.

We are told that the victims of oppression must lead political struggles against structures of domination by those who oppose every means by which we could actually overthrow these systems. We are told that resistance lies in "speaking truth to power" rather than attacking power materially. We are told by an array of highly-trained "white allies" that the very things we need to do in order to free ourselves from domination cannot be done by us because we're simply too vulnerable to state repression. At mass rallies, we're replayed endless empty calls for revolution and militancy from a bygone era while in practice being forced to fetishize our spiritual powerlessness.

In a country where the last eruption of widespread political unrest was nearly forty years ago, when the police go to war it is called "force." Militant protests in Egypt are characterized as heroic, "nonviolent" struggles for freedom, while in Oakland movement peace marshals who claim to represent vulnerable communities of color assist the police in enforcing amplified sound permits.

In an October 24, 2011 letter, Egyptian activists, keenly aware of the distorted media accounts of their revolution in the US, offered a bit of timely advice for the Occupy movement:

> In our own occupations of Tahrir, we encountered people entering the square every day in tears because it was the first time they had walked through those streets and spaces without being harassed by police; it is not just the ideas that are important, these spaces are fundamental to the possibility of a new world. These are public spaces. Spaces for gathering, leisure, meeting and

interacting—these spaces should be the reason we live in cities. Where the state and the interests of owners have made them inaccessible, exclusive or dangerous, it is up to us to make sure that they are safe, inclusive and just. We have and must continue to open them to anyone that wants to build a better world, particularly for the marginalised, the excluded and those groups who have suffered the worst.

[...]Those who said that the Egyptian revolution was peaceful did not see the horrors that police visited upon us, nor did they see the resistance and even force that revolutionaries used against the police to defend their tentative occupations and spaces: by the government's own admission, 99 police stations were put to the torch, thousands of police cars were destroyed and all of the ruling party's offices around Egypt were burned down. Barricades were erected, officers were beaten back and pelted with rocks even as they fired tear gas and live ammunition on us. But at the end of the day on 28 January they retreated, and we had won our cities.

It is not our desire to participate in violence, but it is even less our desire to lose. If we do not resist, actively, when they come to take what we have won back, then we will surely lose. Do not confuse the tactics that we used when we shouted 'peaceful' with fetishizing nonviolence; if the state had given up immediately we would have been overjoyed, but as they sought to abuse us, beat us, kill us, we knew that there was no other option than to fight back. Had we laid down and allowed ourselves to be arrested, tortured and martyred to 'make a point,' we would be no less bloodied, beaten and dead. Be prepared to defend these things you have occupied, that you are building, because, after everything else has been taken from us, these reclaimed spaces are so very precious.[2]

2   Comrades from Cairo. "To the Occupy Movement: the Occupiers of Tahrir Square Are with You." *The Guardian*. Guardian News and Media, 25 Oct. 2011. Web. 06 Aug. 2012. http://www.guardian.co.uk/commentisfree/2011/oct/25/ occupy-movement-tahrir-square-cairo.

PLAZA—RIOT—COMMUNE

RELEASED ON BAYOFRAGE.ORG ON OCTOBER 10, 2011

WE ARE THE GENERATION OF THE ABANDONED, THE BETRAYED. Tossed up on the shores of the present by 150 years of failed insurrection, by the shipwreck of the workers' movement, the failure of a hundred political projects. But it is not only our once-upon-a-time friends who have departed. Today, even our enemies flee from us, even capital abandons us: no more its minimum promises, the right to be exploited, the right to sell one's labor power. Abandoned, we greet the world with utter abandon. There is no longer any possible adequacy of means and ends, no way of subordinating our actions to the rational or the practical. The present age of austerity means that even the most meager of demands require the social democrats to pick up bricks. Betrayed by democracy, betrayed by the technocrats of socialism, betrayed by the dumb idealism of anarchy, betrayed by the stolid fatalism of the communist ultraleft. We are not the 99%. We are not a fucking percentage at all. We do not count. If we have any power, it is because we are the enemies of all majority, enemies of "the people." As the old song goes, *we are nothing and must become everything.*

Though it is a key characteristic of capitalism that each generation of its victims has, in its way, considered its persistence beyond a few decades unlikely if not preposterous, the difference between us and them is that in our case it just happens to be true. Now, not even capital's footservants can paint a convincing portrait of a future based upon markets and wages—all the sci-fi dystopias of flying cars and robot servants seem truly ridiculous. No, the future only presents as ruin, apocalypse, burning metal in the desert. It is easier to imagine the end of life on earth than our own old age.

This is why anxieties over the implicit statism of anti-austerity struggles are baseless. With the exception of a few benighted activists and media ideologues, everyone understands quite well that the Keynesian card was played long ago, blown on wars and bailouts, the victim of its own monstrous success. There will be no rebirth of the welfare state, no "reindustrialization" of society. This much is obvious: if there is an expansion of the state, it will be a proto-fascist austerity state. Nor is there any longer a "Left" in any meaningful sense, as a force that desires to manage the existing world on different terms, in the name of the workers or the people. Those radicals who, tired of the weakness of the loyal opposition, imagine themselves called upon to "destroy the left" find that their very existence is predicated upon this old, vanished enemy. There is no Left left: only the great dispirited mass of the center, some wild and misdirected antagonism at the fringes.

The hopelessness of deflecting the state from its current course; the realization that even a slight reform of the system would require collective violence of a near revolutionary intensity; the attendant awareness that we would be idiots to go that distance and yet stop short of revolution—all of this gives many anti-austerity struggles a strange desperation and intensity. Our hope is to be found in this very hopelessness, in the fact that, in the current cycle of struggles, means have entirely dissociated from ends. Tactics no longer match with their stated objectives. In France, in response to a proposed change in the *retirement age*, high school students barricade their schools; roving blockades confuse the police; rioting fills city center after city center. In Britain and Italy, university struggles recruit tens of thousands of youth who have no hope of attending the university, nor any interest in doing so for that matter. There is no longer any possibility of a political calculus that matches ideas with tactics, thinking with doing. Do we suppose that French children are really concerned about what will happen to them once they are ready to retire? Does any young person expect the current social order to last that long? No, they are here to hasten things forward, hasten things toward collapse. Because it is easier to imagine the end of the world than retirement. Because anything is better than this.

For the neo-Leninist *philosophes* who build their cults in the shells of the dying universities, such an impossibility of lining up means with ends is nothing but a barrier or block. Where is the revolutionary program in the Egyptian revolution, they ask, where is the program in the streets of Britain or Greece? Who will discipline these bodies for their final assault on the palaces and citadels? For such thinkers, only an idea can guarantee the efficacy of these bodies. Only an idea—the idea of communism, as some say—can make of these bodies a proper linkage between means and ends out communism is not an idea nor an idealism. It means freeing bodies from their subordination to abstractions. Thankfully, we are skittish, faithless and flighty people. We have trouble listening. For us, communism will be material or it will be nothing. It will be a set of immediate practices, immediate satisfactions, or nothing. If we find discipline and organization, it will come from what we do, not what we think.

By "idea" the *philosophes* mean something like "the Party." They intend to make themselves and their ideas mean, as structure and social form. They intend to cement the old pact between the intelligentsia and the workers' movement. But there is no intelligentsia anymore and there certainly is no workers' movement to speak of. The entire structure of duty and obligation—Christian in origin—upon which the classical programmatic parties were built no longer exists, because capital no longer needs morality for helpmeet. There is acting *for ourselves*; there is acting *with others*; but there is no sustained acting *for another*, out of obligation.

OUR INDISCIPLINE MEANS that among political ideas only the one idea which is, by its very nature, determined to remain an idea, an ideal, can gain any purchase here: *democracy*. From Tunisia to Egypt, from Spain to Greece, from Madison to Wall Street, again and again, the "movement of the squares" buckles under the dead weight of this shibboleth. *Democracy*, the name for the enchantment of the people by its own image, by its potential for endless deferral. *Democracy*, a decision-making process becomes political ontology, such that the form itself, the form of the decision, becomes its own content. *We democratically decide to be democratic! The people chooses itself!*

In the present era—the era of the austerity state and the unemployment economy—radical democracy finds its ideal locus in the metropolitan plaza or square. The plaza is the material embodiment of its ideals—an blank place for a blank form. Through the plaza, radical democracy hearkens back to its origin myth, the *agora*, the assembly-places of ancient Greece which also served as marketplaces (such that the phrase "I shop" and "I speak in public" were nearly identical). These plazas are not, however, the buzzing markets filled with economic and social transaction, but clean-swept spaces, vast pours of concrete and nothingness, perhaps with a few fountains here or there. These are spaces set aside by the separation of the "political" from the economy, the market. Nowhere is this more clear than in the most recent episode of the "movement of squares"—Occupy Wall Street—which attempted, meekly and rather insincerely, to occupy the real agora, the real space of exchange, but ended up pushed into a small, decorative park on the outskirts of Wall Street, penned by police. This is what building the new world in the shell of the old means today—an assembly ringed by cops

If there is hope in these manifestations, it lies in the forms of mutual aid that exist there, the experimentation people undertake in providing for their own needs. Already, we see how the occupations are forced against their self-imposed limits, brought into conflict with the police, despite the avowed pacifism of the participants. The plaza occupations—with all their contradictions—are one face of the present dissociation of means from ends. Or rather, they present a situation in which means are not so much expelled as sublimated, present as the object of a vague symbolization, such that the gatherings come to pre-enact or symbolize or prefigure some future moment of insurrection. At their worst, they are vast machines of deferral. At their best, they force their participants toward actually seizing what they believe they are entitled to merely want.

How far we are from Egypt, the putative start of the sequence. There, the initial assembly was an act of symbolic violence, decidedly so, which everyone knew would open onto an encounter with the state and its force. And yet, even there, the separation from the economy—from the ways in which our needs are satisfied—remained inscribed into the revolution from the start. In other words, the Egyptian insurrection was not *deflected* to the sphere of the political but started there to begin with. And all of the other episodes in the so-called "movement of squares" repeat this primary dislocation, whether they remain hamstrung by pacifism and democratism, as in Spain, or press their demands in material form, as in Greece.

This brings the plaza occupations into relation not only with the entire development of orthodox Marxism, from Lenin through Mao, which places the conquest of state power front and center, but also its apparent opposite in this historical moment: the riots of Athens and London and Oakland, which, bearing the names of Oscar Grant, Alexis Grigoropoulos, or Mark Duggan, treat the police and state power as both cause and effect, provocation and object of rage. Though the looting which always accompanies such eruptions points the way to a more thorough expropriation, these riots, even though they seem the most immediate of antagonistic actions, are also bound by a kind of symbolization, the symbolization of the negative, which says what it wants through a long litany, in letters of fire and broken glass, of what it does not want: *not this, not that.* We've seen their limits already, in Greece—even burning all of the banks and police stations was not enough. Even then, they came into a clearing, a plaza, swept clean by their own relentless negations, where negation itself was a limit. *What then? What will we do then? How do we continue?*

Between the plaza and the riot, between the most saccharine affirmation and the blackest negation—this is where we find ourselves. Two paths open for us: each one, in its way, a deflection from the burning heart of matter. On the one hand, the endless process of deliberation that must finally, in its narrowing down to a common denominator, arrive at the only single demand possible: a demand for what already is, a demand for the status quo. On the other hand, the desire that has no object, that finds nothing in the world which answers its cry of annihilation.

One fire dies out because it extinguishes its own fuel source. The other because it can find no fuel, no oxygen. In both cases, what is missing is a concrete movement toward the satisfaction of needs outside of wage and market, money and compulsion. The assembly becomes real, loses its merely theatrical character, once its discourse turns to the satisfaction of needs, once it moves to taking over homes and buildings, expropriating goods and equipment. In the same way, the riot finds that truly destroying the commodity and the state means creating a ground entirely inhospitable to such things, entirely inhospitable to work and domination. We do this by facilitating a situation in which there is, quite simply, *enough of what we need*, in which there is no call for "rationing" or "measure," no requirement to commensurate what one person takes and what another contributes. This is the only way that an insurrection can survive, and ward off the reimposition of market, capital and state (or some other economic mode based upon class society and domination). The moment we prove ourselves incapable of meeting the needs of everyone—the young and the old, the healthy and infirm, the committed and the uncommitted—we create a situation where it is only a matter of time before people will accept the return of the old dominations. The task is quite simple, and it is monstrously difficult: in a moment of crisis and breakdown, we must institute ways of meeting our needs and desires that depend neither on wages nor money, neither compulsory labor nor administrative decision, and we must do this while defending ourselves against all who stand in our way.

Research & Destroy, 2011

Andrew Stern
November 20, 2009
UC Berkeley Occupation

Joshua Clover

THE COMING OCCUPATION

OCCUPY EVERYTHING DEMAND NOTHING. This would turn out to be the baseline formulation of tactics and strategy for "the Occupy movement" (an awkward yet inescapable designation).

It was a stance at first implicit and then increasingly evident at Wall Street (#OWS); it was explicit from the outset at the more militant Occupy Oakland (#OO). What is almost unrecognized is that there were actually three distinct political positions, or theoretical analyses, concealed within this slogan. These three logics in turn imply different directions of struggle. My goal is here is, accordingly, to set forth the three logics—perhaps focusing on the one which has been the least remarked, the logic which escapes the ongoing public opposition of 'liberals' and 'anarchists' (an opposition often conducted by people with little sense of what these terms actually mean, hence the scare quotes).

The question of tactics and strategy is a forward-looking one. Nonetheless, to grasp the three logics behind the slogan "OCCUPY EVERY-THING DEMAND NOTHING," I want to travel backward to one of the immediate and domestic roots of the Occupy movement—specifically the US student occupation movement that began in New York in late 2008 and peaked in California in 2009.

One reason for such a return is that communities of struggle which formed in those situations would contribute significantly to #OWS and especially #OO; that the two epicenters of the Occupy movement would appear precisely in the places of the two student occupation waves is manifestly significant. But another reason to return is that the mythical moment of inception for the Occupy movement—*Adbusters'* call—itself drew heavily from the experiences of 2009 at the University of California, and from a single document circulating in that moment.

I do not want to exaggerate the significance of this history, nor promise it any primacy among origins. There are many available. There are the events in the Maghreb and Mashreq known as the Arab Spring; there is the movement of the squares, largely in Europe; there are anti-austerity insurrections in Greece, the UK, Chile, and more than a handful of other hot spots. In the Bay Area itself there was the committed militancy following the police murder of Oscar Grant earlier in 2009. Herein, I mean only to track down the arrival onto a broad political stage of the slogan OCCUPY EVERYTHING DEMAND NOTHING, so that it can be thought in full.

Despite *Adbusters'* initial reference to a "Tahrir moment," the forensics are decisive in leading us to the Bay Area. *Adbusters'* braintrust, founder Kalle Lasn and his aide-de-camp Micah White, formulated their scheme in June of 2011. Lasn chose the name on June 9, but was unable to pass it along immediately, as White, a Berkeley resident, "had already left for the University of California's Doe Library, where he spends his afternoons looking for snippets of radical thought." So wrote *The New Yorker*, adding that it was "the point in his day when he leaves behind his electronic devices to seek what he calls a 'burst of clarity.'"

As it happens, Doe had been occupied by 600 antiprivatization protesters the October before. We don't know if White was present for that burst; we do know he was present on November 20, 2009, when 40-odd people occupied Berkeley's Wheeler Hall and engaged in a protracted, rainy standoff with hundreds of riot cops looking for blood and sometimes getting it. We know because he wrote about it.

"An Open Letter to Students" offers a clear sense of what White and *Adbusters* did and did not grasp from that struggle. Clearly White got the occupation part: "Students, I write this letter in celebration of your passion. The campus occupation movement is now a global phenomenon: from the recent actions in California to last year's events in New York and the occupations in the UK to the almost 70 universities currently locked down in protest in Austria and Germany."

The letter continues, "In protesting against your 'absent future,' the student movement has the potential to spark a cultural insurrection against consumer capitalism." Note the adjectives here: "cultural insurrection," "consumer capitalism." These register not the commitments of the campus occupation movement but *Adbusters'* house politics, opening onto White's final passage. "It is time to acknowledge that there is no going back—neither to the days before climate change nor to the times when state governments were flush with money." This is a clear material account, which ascends suddenly into the purest idealism: "I call on you, students of the 'first world,' to shift your struggle and link arms with us as we build a mental environment movement capable of smashing corporations, downsizing consumer spending, and building egalitarian communities." It cannot be surprising, given a program of building mental environments, that the horizon of revolution will turn out to be "downsizing consumer spending." ¡Hasta la Victoria Siempre!

The letter ends with a rhetorical flourish: "Together, the future is ours." Such optimism is a far cry indeed from the "absent future" previously mentioned. Nonetheless, it is evident enough that some significant portion of the *Adbusters* program and its account of the situation, and the tactic of occupation as a response to economic and political crisis, is drawn from this moment.

Many readers will recognize the document that White would use without quite citing, would borrow without quite grasping, and which would articulate the reason and rhetoric of the OCCUPY EVERYTHING DEMAND NOTHING platform. "Communiqué from an Absent Future: On the Terminus of Student Life" had been circulating widely that fall (hosted digitally by AK Press among others). Among its topics is the matter of demands: "Our task in the current struggle will be to make clear the contradiction between form and content and to create the conditions for the transcendence of reformist demands and the implementation of a truly communist content.... We must constantly expose the incoherence of demands for democratization and transparency. What good is it to have the right to see how intolerable things are, or to elect those who will screw us over? We must leave behind the culture of student activism, with its moralistic mantras of nonviolence and its fixation on single-issue causes. The only success with which we can be content is the abolition of the capitalist mode of production and the certain immiseration and death which it promises for the twenty-first century."

"We must constantly expose the incoherence of demands for democratization and transparency. What good is it to have the right to see how intolerable things are, or to elect those who will screw us over? We must leave behind the culture of student activism, with its moralistic mantras of nonviolence and its fixation on single-issue causes. The only success with which we can be content is the abolition of the capitalist mode of production and the certain immiseration and death which it promises for the twenty-first century."

It then defines the tactic of occupation as itself contrary to demands, and thus logically intertwined with the refusal of demands (I take this to be in fact an early formulation of what would become #OWS's answer to the question asked over and over: "The occupation is its own demand").

> Occupation will be a critical tactic in our struggle, but we must resist the tendency to use it in a reformist way. The different strategic uses of occupation became clear this past January when students occupied a building at the New School in New York.... While the student reformers were focused on leaving the building with a tangible concession from the administration, others shunned demands entirely. They saw the point of occupation as the creation of a momentary opening in capitalist time and space, a rearrangement that sketched the contours of a new society. We side with this anti-reformist position. While we know these free zones will be partial and transitory, the tensions they expose between the real and the possible can push the struggle in a more radical direction.
>
> We intend to employ this tactic until it becomes generalized.

This would be the fall of 2009's antiprogram. It was not clear what it would look like but swiftly it came into focus. In the end, it would be far larger than anyone expected, the largest wave of campus activism since the Sixties. There would be a massive student, staff, and faculty walkout across the UC system, several union strikes, teach-ins and teach-outs and hue and cry. And occupations. One at Berkeley failed. Another, at Santa Cruz, was an odd but brilliant success. Its slogan, circulated via handbill and banner drop, was OCCUPY EVERYTHING DEMAND NOTHING.

But this is not to say that the spirit of the communiqué held sway, or simply transmigrated intact to Zuccotti Park. Obviously it did not. In some sense the series of transfigurations between the antagonistic call of 2009 and the variegated response of 2011 is entirely understandable via a clear-headed account of what populism is, and how it must always turn away from any hint of nihilism, much less political-economic eschatology.

But I think these concepts around "the future," or more accurately about the possibilities that retain actuality within the present situation, are significant. They are also inseparable from the question of demands itself, a question which is for me a decisive characteristic of the Occupy movement, alongside the lived practice of mutual aid and care. Let me then set forth the three logics as I understand them.

The first is a negative one. In this regime, the fomenting of a new political hegemony allows an endless array of individual grievances, but precludes any single demand to which everybody must submit, as its particulars might exclude some portion of the everybody hailed by the formula of "the 99%." Michael Levitin, managing editor of *The Occupied Wall Street Journal*, wrote in October, 2011, "Let's get something straight: this movement has issued no demands…. As we wrote in the editorial that appeared in the second edition of *The Occupied Wall Street Journal* on Saturday: 'We are speaking to each other, and listening. This occupation is first about participation.'"

The second logic affirms that there is no one who could meet our demands. Judith Butler has articulated this logic eloquently, drawing in turn on Gayatri Spivak. It is this rejection of demands that has generally been adduced to the "theoretical wing" of Occupy:

> But anyone who argues that demands must be capable of being satisfied assumes that there is someone or some existing institutional power to whom one could appeal to have one's demands satisfied. Union negotiations backed by the threat of strikes usually do have a list of demands which, if satisfied, will avert the strike, and if not, will commence or prolong a strike. But when a company, corporation, or state is not considered a legitimate partner for negotiation, then it makes no sense to appeal to that authority for a negotiated settlement. In fact, to appeal to that authority to satisfy the demand would be one way of attributing legitimacy to that authority.

The third logic insists that the meeting of any demand worth making is an impossibility within the present social arrangement. This may initially seem to blur together with the previous logic—no one can meet our demands, they can't be met—but is finally quite distinct. It does not concern itself with power and political legitimacy, but with the conditions of possibility for the meeting of needs. It rests on the basic contradiction: the lacks that are worth making demands about were produced by the current political-economic order. It exists by producing these lacks, this immiseration. It cannot stop doing this and continue to exist. Demanding an end to immiseration would be tantamount to asking capital to abolish itself.

These three logics can be schematized in a couple of different ways. There are some terminological difficulties here, and the schemas will remain figural; they are meant to show resonances and relations more than rigid structures.

The first schema notes that these three logics come from three different philosophical traditions: liberalism, post-structuralism, and Marxism. One might continue by associating these analytic frames with political forms, albeit imperfectly: democracy, anarchism, communism (though here we must allow a strong distinction between Soviet or PRC communism and the idea of communization embraced in the "Communiqué"). I believe in particular that this schema usefully limns the affinity between anarchist politics and poststructuralist thought which has increasingly manifested among the remarkable autodidacts and theorypunks of the west coast anarchist milieu (and perhaps others, though I am not positioned to know either way). It is an affinity for the identity-problematizing thought of Butler and Hocquenghem, but also for the Tiqqunist embrace of Foucault and Agamben, for the rhetoric of the biopolitical and "forms of life."

In a cavalier way, we could also add that the disciplinary markers here would be those of political science (the apologetics of liberal democracy), ethics (which undergirds the "legitimacy" in Butler's reasoning), and economics (said to be the "last determining instance" of Marxism). This schema doesn't stand up to real scrutiny, as we would want the distinction of political economy for the lattermost, and we would want in general to take seriously the ambitious and sometimes tendentious debates of the last two decades or so regarding the status of the political as such. I am happy to leave this debate to Badiou, Rancière, Žižek, Esposito, Moreiras, and the like. That is to say, the political as a purified zone is now the province of philosophers, just as economics is now the province of mathematicians and financiers. Political economy barely registers, much less critiques thereof. This has turned out to be true in the Occupy movement as well; the third logic, though demonstrably central to the Occupy movement's conceptual core—the very one which *Adbusters* appropriated—now goes unremarked and unrecognized in assessments of the political situation. This remains true even as "anticapitalism" remains on everybody's lips.

Anticapitalism is by now only common sense; one scarcely need be a Marxist to arrive at such a position. Perhaps the time has come to ask: toward what end does one engage in such schematizing, such parsing of various logics, when all parties have come to congruent if not identical conclusions?

As I suggested before, it concerns the future of the movement, if it has any at all. But even if something else, like and unlike Occupy, is constituted next in this global cascade of misery, militancy, and experiments in social antagonism, the question of strategy and tactics will remain for us. Logistics too, but that is another discussion.

Occupation is the tactic. Demandlessness is a strategy. There is some general agreement on both. It is clear, in the "Communiqué"—just as in the

Argentine factories in 2001, to choose perhaps the most relevant corollary— why this tactic and this strategy are mutually constitutive rather than merely yoked together. This, we might say, is the distinctive feature of the analysis on offer: the conjunction itself, the insistence that objective conditions implied OCCUPY EVERYTHING DEMAND NOTHING as indivisible tactic and strategy. This generalized itself more than anybody foresaw, but the analysis which bound the two halves of the slogan into a unity did not survive this generalization in any meaningful way.

As a result of this dissolution, the tactic and the strategy became divisible, and each lost some fraction of its material force. Thus we have seen some slippage, some mutations, which we cannot elide. Occupation has traversed the threshold from inside to outside to nowhere—from the buildings to the squares to "Occupy Love" and "Occupy Elections"—scarcely tactics at all. In defense of this slippage we must concede that such traversals have to do with quite serious matters—most evidently, the struggle to outmaneuver or at least avoid violent physical and legal repression. The truncheon is one sort of materialism. But its imperatives cannot finally do away with that other materialist analysis, with the questions of production, circulation, and reproduction. And these matters will occasion what it is we occupy next.

And so I must apply one final schema, this time with my thumb on the scale. I would suggest that the first logic, the *Adbusters* analysis that passes easily through OWS, concerns little or nothing of materiality—hence the language

The lacks that are worth making demands about were produced by the current political-economic order. It exists by producing these lacks, this immiseration. It cannot stop doing this and continue to exist. Demanding an end to immiseration would be tantamount to asking capital to abolish itself.

of "cultural insurrection" or modulations in the intensity of "consumer capitalism." This logic functions in the realm of the idea, the informed choice. The shadow of this is cast most distressingly in the dual fascination with reciting passages from the Bill of Rights, and with such matters as *Citizens United* or Glass-Steagall: concerns which accede to the regime of legislation, of almost absolute indifference to the question of immiseration locally, much less globally.

In turn, the second logic finally avails itself of distributive solutions; it returns again and again to the promise that maldistribution of everything from food to time is a consequence of power itself, with its disciplinary regimes and differentiations—power which must therefore not be recognized or legitimated. Once power is broken, goes the proposition, its artificial scarcities and imposed separations might be overcome.

And the third logic of demandlessness, predictably by now, seeks its truth in production. This is the meaning of our "absent future." Some authors of the "Communiqué" would eventually argue that the span from 1973 onward was in fact a single variegated and extended crisis of value production, periodically masked and deferred by various kinds of what Robert Brenner calls "Asset Price Keynesianism"—and that 2007–2008 was the end of the line for such strategies, and thus a "terminal crisis" in the terms of Giovanni Arrighi.

"Absent future" did not mean apocalypse, exactly. But it did mean, to retain the theological tonality, that the debts imposed on or elected by all beings in this era (human, corporate, and state beings) would not be redeemed in that airless vault of the future—that the current regime of value production could promise no such redemption. And with the amount of value being produced relative to population waning decisively, no redistributive approach could succeed—it would simply be an increasingly brutal struggle over diminishing resources, not even zero-sum but negative-sum. This is part of what is meant by a crisis of reproduction—the productive forces no longer have need, nor ability, to reproduce a nonetheless increasing population.

This brings me, via the future and the past, to the present. I do not think there is any way out of this crisis for the global working and sub-waged population that is not a fundamental reorganization of production. But this opens onto the problem of the present structure of capitalism, and the limits of the "Communiqué." It is with these that I should end.

As some of us have begun to understand, the failure of production cannot be understood simply as a failure to produce value adequate for capitalism to continue along its course, in the classical Marxian account. What we have seen in the last four decades is a decisive shift of production into the sphere of circulation itself. Indeed, unbeknownst to Hardt and Negri and many others, the much-ballyhooed rise of immaterial labor is not so much a dematerialization as a departure from the factory floor of production via a leap into circulation, toward the reduction of what David Harvey calls Socially Necessary Turnover Time—be it Walmart supply chains, massive development of communications networks, containerization, or vast deployments of financial liquidity.

This cannot reverse the directionality of the value catastrophe; on that we are agreed. But it does shift the terrain of antagonism, of direct and immediate intervention which occupation both signaled and was. And in this regard the slippage away from the indoor occupation—for which the locus classicus is always the clangorous industrial factory, with its greasy brick and huffing smokestack—toward some other space of flows, is not a mistake, but an intuition. The occupation is elsewhere: in the spaces where capital conveys itself ever more swiftly through the circuits, drawing production and circulation ever closer even as they press against the limits of space and time. In that sense some of the mistakes of Occupy have in fact been incomplete inventions, unfinished thoughts—and I believe we are still thinking.

OCCUPY EVERYTHING DEMAND NOTHING: THREE LOGICS

MARXISM	POSTSTRUCTURALISM	LIBERALISM
		1
communism	*anarchism*	*democracy*
	2	
political economy	ethics	political science
3		
PRODUCTION	CIRCULATION	LEGISLATION

LA BEAUTÉ

EST DANS LA RUE

Atelier Populaire
Poster from Paris '68

Immanuel Wallerstein

UPSURGE IN MOVEMENTS AROUND THE GLOBE[1]

1) The World Class Struggle: The Geography of Protest

WHEN TIMES ARE GOOD, AND THE WORLD-ECONOMY IS EXPANDING IN TERMS of new surplus-value produced, the class struggle is muted. It never goes away, but as long as there is a low level of unemployment and the real incomes of the lower strata are going up, even if only in small amounts, social compromise is the order of the day.

But when the world-economy stagnates and real unemployment expands considerably, it means that the overall pie is shrinking. The question then becomes who shall bear the burden of the shrinkage—within countries and between countries. The class struggle becomes acute and sooner or later leads to open conflict in the streets. This is what has been happening in the world-system since the 1970s, and most dramatically since 2007. Thus far, the very upper strata (the 1%) have been holding on to their share, indeed increasing it. This means necessarily that the share of the 99% has been going down.

The struggle over allocations revolves primarily around two items in the global budget: taxes (how much, and who) and the safety net of the bulk of the population (expenditures on education, health, and lifetime income guarantees). There is no country in which this struggle has not been taking place. But it breaks out more violently in some countries than in others—because of their location in the world-economy, because of their internal demographics, because of their political history.

An acute class struggle raises the question for everyone of how to handle it politically. The groups in power can repress popular unrest harshly, and many do. Or, if the unrest is too strong for their repressive mechanisms, they

---

1   Part 1 originally published as Commentary No. 330, June 1, 2012, Fernand Braudel Center. Part 2 adapted from a talk delivered at the 2640 Space in Baltimore MD, November 3, 2011.

can try to co-opt the protesters by seeming to join them and limiting real change. Or they do both, trying repression first and co-option if that fails.

The protesters also face a dilemma. The protesters always start as a relatively small courageous group. They need to persuade a much larger (and politically far more timid group) to join them, if they are to impress the groups in power. This is not easy but it can happen. It happened in Egypt at Tahrir Square in 2011. It happened in the Occupy movement in the United States and Canada. It happened in Greece in the last elections. It happened in Chile and the now long-lasting student strikes. And at the moment, it seems to be happening spectacularly in Québec.

But when it happens, then what? There are some protesters who wish to expand initial narrow demands into more far-reaching and fundamental demands to reconstruct the social order. And there are others, there are always others, who are ready to sit down with the groups in power and negotiate some compromise.

When the groups in power repress, they quite often fan the flames of protest. But repression often works. When it doesn't and groups in power compromise and co-opt, they often are able to pull the plug on the protesters. This is what seems to have happened in Egypt. The recent elections are leading to a second-round runoff between two candidates, neither of whom supported the revolution in Tahrir Square—one the last prime minister of the ousted president Hosni Mubarak, the other a leader of the Muslim Brotherhood whose primary objective is instituting the sharia in Egyptian law and not implementing the demands of the those who were in Tahrir Square. The result is a cruel choice for the about 50% who did not vote in the first round for either of the two with the largest plurality of votes. This unhappy situation resulted from the fact that the pro-Tahrir Square voters split their votes between two candidates of somewhat different backgrounds.

How are we to think of all of this? There seems to be a rapidly and constantly shifting geography of protest. It pops up here and then is either repressed, co-opted, or exhausted. And as soon as that happens, it pops up somewhere else, where it may in turn be either repressed, co-opted, or exhausted. And then it pops up in a third place, as though worldwide it was irrepressible.

It is indeed irrepressible for one simple reason. The world income squeeze is real, and not about to disappear. The structural crisis of the capitalist world-economy is making the standard solutions to economic downturns unworkable, no matter how much our pundits and politicians assure us that a new period of prosperity is on the horizon.

We are living in a chaotic world situation. The fluctuations in everything are large and rapid. This applies as well to social protest. This is what we are seeing as the geography of protest constantly shifts. Tahrir Square in Cairo yesterday, unauthorized massive marches with pots and pans in Montréal today, somewhere else (probably somewhere surprising) tomorrow.

2) 1968 Redux

WE'RE ALL LIVING A VERY SPECIAL moment. A couple of years from now you'll think of this as the Occupy moment, and it's been a remarkable experience because it's a world experience. It has spread incredibly, and you have to link it in with an awful lot of other things that have been going on the last year, two, three years, across the world. Relatively a lot in North America, Latin America, and Europe, a little in the Arab world, a little but thinner in Asia, pretty much in Africa too. This is obviously the heir of the world-revolution of 1968. Of course, this is forty-odd years later and the world has moved on and the present upsurge is different in some significant ways. So I would like to start by talking a little about what I think 1968 was, and then talk a little bit about what has happened in the world since 1968, and then get us to where we are today and where we may be heading.

First of all, 1968 is a symbolic year. What I am actually talking about went on from about 1966 to about 1970 and it went on everywhere. It was a world-revolution. In those days we talked about three worlds: the First World, which was the pan-European world (western Europe, the United States, Australia and so forth); the Second World, which was the Communist or socialist world, or

The Old Left was composed of, in our language of today, vertical movements. That is to say, they argued that only one movement was allowed to exist per country and it had to control everything else. If you weren't part of that, you were counter-revolutionary.

whatever you want to call it; and the Third World, which was Asia, Africa, and Latin America. We talked in those terms and we thought in those terms.

One of the remarkable things about 1968 and the world-revolution is that it occurred in all three of these worlds, which is something that almost no one at the time expected or really understood. Of course, to say that it occurred in all three worlds depends on what you include in the world-revolution of 1968. I think of what went on in western Europe (France, Germany, Great Britain, Italy, and so forth) and of course in the United States. I was personally in the middle of the Columbia uprising in April of 1968. I keep reminding my French friends that this was one month before they started things in Nanterre. So some of us think of the French as having copied the US, and not the other way around. I also think of the cultural revolution in China as part of the world-revolution of 1968. And there was a long list of countries in the Third World which had uprisings at that time. Nearest to home were the very dramatic and tragic events in Mexico.

What was remarkable about the world-revolution of 1968 was that it was a double revolution. It included a double set of demands, almost every-where. The first was the denunciation of US hegemony in the world-system, with special reference to the fact that we were in the middle of the Vietnam War. It was a denunciation, however, not only of US hegemony but, for virtually everyone who was involved in the world-revolution of 1968, what was considered to be the collusion of the Soviet Union with US hegemony. So, when the Chinese talked about the split in world politics, they pictured it as the US and the Soviet Union on one side, and everybody else on the other side. It is hard to get your mind around that these days.

The second central theme derived from something we have forgotten, which is how strong the antisystemic movements were in the period of 1945 to 1968. They suddenly came to power everywhere, albeit in different forms. What does that mean? A third of the world was the so-called social-ist world, in which there were Communist parties in power. These parties had been part of the historic antisystemic movements. If you look at North America, western Europe, and Australasia, what you see is that the Social-Democrats were in power, alternating power to be sure, but dominating the scene. I include New Deal Democrats as Social-Democrats. They didn't use the same name for themselves, but they pursued parallel policies. In the Third World, you had the national liberation movements, who for the most part also came to power in Asia and Africa, and comparable populist move-ments in Latin America.

It was a remarkable situation in which, out of nowhere, all these move-ments suddenly achieved this objective of coming to power. What the revo-lutionaries in 1968 said to all these movements who came to power—the Communist movements, the Social-Democratic movements, the national liberation movements is: "You promised us that when you came to power, you would transform the world. And you've come to power, but you haven't transformed the world." So there's something wrong there.

In sum, there was a double revolt on one side against US hegemony and Soviet collusion, and on the other side against the Old Left. The Old Left was composed of, in our language of today, vertical movements. That is to say, they argued that only one movement was allowed to exist per country and it had to control everything else. If you weren't part of that, you were counter-revolutionary. The movement was structured from the top down. Whether you were dealing with Social-Democratic, Communist, or national liberation movements, they were vertical movements. The 1968 revolutionaries came and said: The women have been forgotten. The ethnic groups have been forgotten—Black Power, etc. The people with other sexualities, they've been forgotten. The Old Left movements had always said, "You have grievances, but just wait until the revolution comes and we'll solve that problem later." The 1968 revolutionaries said "There is no later it's now. We have legitimate demands, as legitimate as the claims of the so-called central actors or subjects of history. We're subjects of history too."

These were the themes of 1968. And 1968 blew up very powerfully everywhere. Then it died out or got repressed, and by about the mid-1970s it was to be seen almost nowhere. Nowhere but everywhere, because it transformed the situation in the world. And that's what's important to see.

History is on nobody's side. There's nothing in this situation that is inevitable. We may end up, by 2050, in a much better world, or we may end up in a worse world. No one can say now which of the two will win out. It's up to us. We've got to work hard, unceasingly, and with no illusions.

So, what happened? The revolution undid some very important things. One, it undid the singular legitimacy of centrist liberalism. Centrist liberalism had emerged in the nineteenth century as a dominant theme asserting that yes, everything has to change, but slowly, in controlled ways, rationally. The changes had to be led by sophisticated people who knew how to do it correctly. They marginalized both the conservatives and the radicals, making them accept the legitimacy of this centrist path. 1968 exploded that, and it liberated the conservatives, who went back to being real conservatives.

The people you see today as conservatives weren't around in the 1950s. Just take a simple thing: Milton Friedman was an academic joke in the 1950s. No one took him seriously. By the 1980s, he's the legitimating figure of the economics profession. Now that's a real transformation. That's the re-legitimation of genuine conservative thought. And there was as well the re-legitimation of genuine radical thought, which we're experiencing strongly today.

The second was the widespread rejection by those active in the movements of verticalism. It was widely replaced by what we now call horizontalism. Horizontalism is the view that there are multiple kinds of justice movements and these movements should speak to each other, deal with each other, without any one movement on top. They should be legitimating each other, rather than denouncing each other. Such horizontalism is what you see very much now in the Occupy movements.

The movements of 1968 thus transformed not merely the world-system, but the social movements as well. The heirs of the Old Left movements have changed their language, adapting themselves to the new language of the movements of the forgotten peoples. Read any newspaper put out by an Old Left movement in the 1950s, and compare it with that same newspaper in the 1980s or in the 2010s. You will notice a transformation in the language. They discuss the issues insisted upon by these other movements such as gender or race or environment, issues they used to deprecate as secondary, and suddenly they acknowledge that they are indeed legitimate issues of the present.

The next thing that we have to put into this picture is how a world-system works. All systems fluctuate. So does the modern world-system. There are two very important kinds of fluctuations. One has to do with the expansion and contraction/stagnation of the world-economy. Some people call them Kondratieff cycles (I do), and others give it other names. It doesn't matter. The second one is hegemonic cycles in which one state manages to set the rules by which the interstate system functions. Kondratieff cycles have tended to last 50–60 years. Hegemonic cycles are much longer, perhaps 100–150 years.

The expansionary phase of each is made possible by a quasi-monopoly—in one case of leading products, in the other of geopolitical strength. But quasi-monopolies are necessarily self-liquidating. Those who are not the beneficiaries of these quasi-monopolies work very hard to break them, and eventually succeed, leading to the downturn or stagnation. Resuming the upward path is always possible at first, but it always requires some concession to the transformations. The moving equilibriums take the form of a ratchet (two steps up, one step back). Therefore, over time, there are structural trends moving towards asymptotes.

We've learned a lot from the people in complexity sciences. All systems—from the universe as a whole, to supersmall subatomic systems, to medium-size historical social systems—have lives. They are not eternal. They come into existence at some point. They have rules which govern their normal lives, and then they begin to move further and further from equilibrium. At a certain point, the system moves too far from equilibrium and it bifurcates, and when it bifurcates the system is in structural crisis, which is a chaotic situation. When a system is in structural crisis the only thing that is certain is that the system can't survive as a system. Bifurcation means that there are two quite different possible ways of ending the chaos and stabilizing a new system. It is intrinsically impossible to predict which alternative will prevail. Our present world-system of capitalism is in precisely such structural crisis since at least the early 1970s.

What happens when you're in structural crisis? First of all, structural crises are not crises of a day, or a year, or even a decade. They last fifty, seventy-five years. There is a struggle between groups pushing alternative visions of the future world-system or systems. At some point, the collective "choice" tilts definitively, and one or the other of the two kinds of new system wins out.

The language I use to describe the politics of the struggle between the two visions of the future system is this: I say one of the alternatives is "the spirit of Davos" and the other is "the spirit of Porto Alegre." I talk of "spirit" since the particular organizations that are emblematic of the two spirits may or may not survive much longer.

What do I mean by that? What is capitalism as a system? It's really a system that is hierarchical, exploitative, and polarizing. Over the 500 years of its existence, the difference between people on top and people on the bottom has grown bigger and bigger in every way. Now, finally, we're really talking about that. That's the language of the Occupy movement, when they spoke of the 1% versus the 99%.

Capitalism is not the only way you can construct a system that's hierarchical, exploitative, and polarizing. There are many other ways, and what "the spirit of Davos" is looking for is precisely this other way, since they know that capitalism can't survive any more. They're looking for an alternative, and this alternative isn't necessarily better than capitalism as a system. It might be much worse than what we have now.

What then is "the spirit of Porto Alegre?" It is the search for a world-system that is relatively democratic, and relatively egalitarian. Don't ask me "What does that exactly look like?" I don't know what that exactly looks like, and you don't know what that exactly looks like.

I always say to people, "Look, suppose in the year 1500, or 1450, or thereabouts, you were sitting around in a small group, and you were saying, 'The feudal system in Europe is in structural crisis, and we're in the middle of a bifurcation.'" And one possible outcome is a capitalist system. It's not the only possible outcome, although it's the one that actually won out. It's a long story of why it won out, but it doesn't matter in this analysis. Who, in that small group, in 1450 or 1500, would have been able to describe the institutional structures that have developed over 500 years in a capitalist system? Nobody today can work out the institutional parameters of a future system. All one can do is outline the main thrust that you hope will underlie the future system.

Now the question is, "What do we do?" That is our problem, and that is our issue. I have no simple answers to that. It is a matter of keeping a balance between being too narrow, in terms of who we pull into the movement, and too broad. And that's a very, very tricky question. Not easy at all. It's constant work on everybody's part. And will things happen in the next two years, four years, six years? No, you've got another twenty, thirty, forty years of struggle ahead of you before it clicks, before enough momentum shifts in this direction rather than in that direction. You don't know who's going to win. But you do know that you affect who's going to win by your actions, by your reality. But you've got to think in the long haul, think thirty or forty years ahead, because that's what it's going to take for us to come to "the spirit of Porto Alegre"—the relatively democratic, relatively egalitarian world-system that we've never seen before. It will be a new thing in the history of the world.

There's no model for it. There's no previous model to learn from. We don't know what's going to go right, and how we do it, but we've got constantly to do three things: analyze the options, choose our preferences, and develop a winning political strategy. So it's a triple demand: an intellectual-analytic, a moral judgment, and a political-tactical set of decisions. It's not easy, but it's doable, provided that you don't assume that history is on your side.

The last thing I want to say is this: history is on nobody's side. There's nothing in this situation that is inevitable. We may end up, by 2050, in a much better world, or we may end up in a worse world. No one can say now which of the two will win out. It's up to us. We've got to work hard, unceasingly, and with no illusions.

Atelier Populaire
Poster from Paris '68

Grassroots International
October 6, 2009
Paranatinga, Mato Grosso, Brazil

Janaina Stronzake

PEOPLE MAKE THE OCCUPATION AND THE OCCUPATION MAKES THE PEOPLE
THE OCCUPATION OF LAND AS PART OF CLASS STRUGGLE

introduction

IN THE HISTORY OF CLASS STRUGGLE, THE STORY OF OCCUPATIONS OR TAKing of spaces is not unusual. Native Americans occupied Spanish cities, women occupied food ships during the British famine of the seventeenth century, rural workers occupied plantations all over Latin America and other continents.

Occupation is the material taking of a space and is heavily symbolic. For the Movement of Landless Rural Workers of Brazil (MST), occupying land is the first step in the construction of a new society.

Founded in 1984 by female and male rural workers expelled from their land, the MST made their first slogan "Land for those who work it," denouncing the concentration and hoarding of unproductive land throughout the country. The chosen form of struggle was the occupation of plantations, reclaimed as part of land reform. In addition to the objectives of "land" and "agrarian reform," the MST also decided to struggle for a new society, and for social transformation.

Agrarian reform became part of Brazilian law in 1964. The nation's Land Statute prescribes the "social function of property," and that function includes three main aspects: It should be environmentally sustainable and respectful and cannot degrade the environment; it should be socially responsible, working conditions must never be degrading; and, there must be specific regionally-established production minimums.

These production minimums are in the Productivity Index, a norm established by the federal government, which is supposed to be updated every

ten years. The indexes in place today were established in 1975. The plantation owners put great pressure on the government to keep them from being
updated, as these reviews would reveal many unproductive areas subject to
appropriation.

The GINI index of land distribution in Brazil in 1985 was 0.815. The
closer this number is to zero, the greater the equality of distribution. The
closer it is to 1, the greater the concentration. According to the level of
concentration noted by Caparroz (1997), Brazilian land is at a "high or very
high" level of concentration (between 0.700 and 0.900). In 2006, the GINI
index was 0.872, according to the agricultural census.

Considering such a concentration of land, and the agrarian reform law,
the women and men of the MST chose occupation as one method of denouncing current conditions, recuperating land, and democratizing access.

We defend the rural way of life in the struggle between the small farmers
and agribusiness. There is an effort on the part of the established powers
(economic, media, state, and military) to maintain an absolute separation
between countryside and city and to eliminate small farmers. The rural way
of life at times joins and mixes with urban life, and both relate to each other
with solidarity, responsibility, autonomy, sovereignty.

The cry of the MST, "Occupy, Resist, and Produce," is being renewed in
occupied urban plazas and is acquiring new dimensions in accordance with
the new social, political, economic and cultural moment.

In this brief text, we seek to reflect on this act of occupation from the
perspective of the MST and show how occupation can be a tool in class
struggle.

occupation: when people say "enough!"

OCCUPATION IS ONE of the trademarks of the MST. It is a symbol of identity. It is a form of struggle.

The act of occupation carries risks. One is death or physical harm carried
out by the "guardians" of the property. Another is moral harm, promoted
by the spokespeople of conservatism, who accuse anyone who threatens the
sanctity of private property as "thieves." There is also the threat of exhausting the struggle, which we will address below.

An occupation can be a strategy in class struggle. It is a step among many
others and contains a series of processes and elements which fall into a sequence of planned struggle, with objectives that go beyond the occupation.

If occupation is the only objective, it will lose its meaning once the
occupation is won. If the occupation is immediately evicted, perhaps the
movement will last until the next opportunity to occupy, or perhaps the
movement to occupy ends.

This characteristic of occupation as an act in and of itself is not uncommon. Quite to the contrary, it is very common. When a person decides to occupy, they confront the risks already noted as well as others such as hunger, cold, separation from their partner, family abandonment, etc. When people reach that point, it is generally motivated by a profound despair with a concrete situation and they say "Enough!" in response to their own impotence.

Occupation is an act, an attitude, and a demonstration of power on the part of an individual and a collective.

During their first occupation it is often the case that the women and men of the MST direct themselves exclusively to the struggle for the land that is being occupied. If the land is won, the struggle is over, each one organizes their life, and personal dignity is restored through the exercise of collective power.

But this would be a fragile victory, as it does not change the structure of social relations of exploitation. In time, the family that has won land and ended their struggle can become a petite bourgeois exploiter, an exploited rural worker, or both.

If the struggle ends in the immediate conquest of land, class consciousness also tends to end in this stage. The *campesina* or *campesino* now becomes an owner of the means of production and might, in a capitalist world, ascend economically by exploiting the work of other *campesinas* or *campesinos* who still have no land, the paid rural workers.

Simultaneously the land could also be exploited by large capitalists through the existing models of production and technology such as the seed market, chemical fertilizers, machines, and medicines. Unless the *campesinas/campesinos* organize other commercial conditions, they may have to sell their product to very few buyers, like the large food conglomerates Bunge, Monsanto, or Nestle.

After saying "enough!" to the conditions predating the land occupation, the *campesina/campesino* has to organize into communities and study, reflect, and establish goals that go beyond immediate need. The land itself runs the risk of being an agent of capital, an agent that promotes the same structure against which they rebelled when they decided to occupy the plantation.

the place for praxis: transformative action-reflection

THE FIRST THING learned is sentient: concrete contact with the real world. After coming in contact with this reality there can be theorizing and reflection. New action and new contact with the real world provide the opportunity for further action and reflection.

In this process of concrete appropriation, reflection and new action, the human agent is transformed. The act of changing the world also transforms the human who is working for change.

As Vinicius de Moraes, a Brazilian poet, writes in his poem "Construction Worker:" "the worker makes the thing, and the thing makes the worker." The same happens in an occupation: the person occupies the land, and the process of rebellion, the shift in perspective, slowly occupies the person.

An occupation is not enough to revolutionize the world. Before and after the occupation there is a revolution in each person, if they allow it. How does that revolution happen?

The occupation is the first step in the learning process, the first contact with the real, concrete world. If people get stuck in that, they do not advance towards a more transformative contact with the world, a *praxeological* contact. Study and reflection is needed, coupled with action.

One has to reflect on every action: Why are we doing this? What do we want in the future? Who is on our side? Where do we want to go and how do we want get there? Is there anyone else in history who wanted the same, or something similar? What did they do, and what happened?

These and other reflections help us broaden our view to become more historic and identify which actions are tactically intelligent and which ones are strategic, as well as who our allies and adversaries are. It also helps form an analysis of our conjuncture, which helps us make the best decisions possible.

In the MST, these decisions are made collectively, after a lot of study in all our spaces. An occupation is a result of meetings, lectures, and educational sessions in which we try to understand the environment, how capitalist society works, Brazilian law, the agrarian situation, etc. We also discuss the best moment to occupy land and what land should be occupied.

In these preparatory moments, the movement takes on its organic nature. The families organize themselves in Base Cells, which contain ten to fifteen families. They then divide the tasks among them, forming sectors of activity: education, communication, health, gender, culture, youth, security, and human rights, and others that may be necessary. In each Base Cell there is at least one person from every sector.

The Base Cell is the place for study, debate, and decisions. The activity sectors are the place for study, debate and execution. The sectors can send a decision back to the Base Cell, together with an argument about the decision. Each space should be one of thought and action.

Upon occupying, people already know which tasks are their direct responsibility. People participate through the Base Cells. It is also through these Cells that they influence and suggest guidelines for the activity sectors. Through participation in the activity sectors, everyone in the encampment is responsible for the life of an occupation.

In this day to day activity, this assumption of responsibility for the collective and for each person, everyone progressively constructs a common identity, and ways of seeing the world and acting to shape it. They also construct norms of conviviality, and ways in which collective and personal well-being are assured.

It is in this arrangement of living together with shared responsibilities that we try to change capitalist culture: machismo, racism, power relations in general. An example of this in the MST is the kindergarten.

Mothers have responsibilities in the collective; they may be in education, production, or another sector. The girls and boys need a group that takes care of them while their mothers are working. What responsibility the fathers ought to have for the little ones was an initial discussion. But it was immediately noted that the care of children and the elderly is a social issue, not just a familial issue.

We are the working class, and we will end class, gender, and ethnic exploitation.

In a society like the one we want to build, we are all responsible for every one of its members. With this thinking, we started building the kindergartens as a type of day care with a different philosophical base.

The kindergartens should be spaces for socialization, care, affection, education, and attention for girls and boys from zero to six. The intention is raising new women and men capable of acting in solidarity and of being responsible, autonomous, and critical.

Today the MST wants the kindergartens to extend to all our spaces and involve men and women in the tasks of educating, caring for and respecting the little ones. This would enable the little ones to have a space for transformative education, and beyond that, for new relations among themselves and with the adults. The entire collective becomes involved in child education, perceiving it as a collective problem whereas it had previously been seen as the work of women.

When one has a vision of an occupation that is broader than the conquest of physical space, but keeps in mind the concrete needs of people, you can advance a process of education and change within a *praxeological* framework that moves the collective beyond its immediate needs.

When one has an historic and dialectic perspective on struggle, and maintains a vision of class struggle, occupation is the first tactical step within a series of other processes that together compose a desire for a new society. That desire is objectified in the occupation and in other steps and processes beyond it.

conclusion

> When arriving on land, remember those that want to come;
> When arriving on land, remember there are other steps to take
> —MST song, "When Arriving on Land"

AN OCCUPATION CAN exhaust itself without ever representing structural change, or it can be an effective and efficient part of class struggle and positively impact the achievements of the working class.

To have that range, perhaps one of the first conditions is recognizing that you belong to the working class. When one feels part of that class, one develops an interpretation of reality, and a plan of action, with goals for the victory of the working class, within class struggle.

Class identity is a condition and result of class struggle. That is, we carry out struggles, sometimes starting with occupations, because the person feels that they are part of the working class. Upon struggling, upon participating in the occupation, upon the material and symbolic taking of one of the bases of power of the bourgeoisie, one starts to have working-class consciousness.

Material conditions of concrete struggle, the "social being" in struggle, make the "social consciousness" of the working class, as Marx and Engels said in *The German Ideology*.

If this materialist, historic, dialectic perspective of struggle is not achieved and situated in class struggle, an occupation closes in on itself. It never projects a subject capable of realizing structural changes in society.

Without broadening the struggle of an occupation and making it part of class struggle, the historic value is lost due to a lack of the maturity that leads to an international struggle and class solidarity. An occupation that is reduced to nothing more than an occupation tends to end without changes to social reality or to the people that were involved.

As a result of much collective study and reflection, the MST has defined from its founding that it has three objectives: land, agrarian reform, and social transformation.

The occupation of land is a step toward the first goal. In many cases the land that we've conquered, with education, health, leisure time, sports, etc., are steps towards agrarian reform, which is nothing more than the fulfillment of Brazilian law.

However, a new society is not inscribed in laws. It must be built in practice and theory every day. New gender relations are not decreed, they come to be when we build consciousness that women are capable and have the same rights as men. How do we build that consciousness? In a daily reality in which we search for these new relations through our practices.

How do we build autonomy, sovereignty, responsibility, the freedom of a people, in the countryside and the city? Perhaps by starting with the occupation of land, plazas, schools, universities, or factories. And continuing beyond that, studying, weaving networks, practicing solidarity, organizing other and new concrete actions, without ever losing this perspective: We are the working class, and we will end class, gender, and ethnic exploitation.

sources:

Caparroz, João Miguel (1997). *Concentraçao de terras no Brasil—1940 a 1985*, Pontificia Universidade Catolica, São Paulo

Censo Agropecuario Brasileiro (2006). Instituto Brasileiro de Geografia e Estatística (IBGE), Governo Federal, Brasilia

Marx, Karl, and Friedrich Engels (s/d). *A ideología alemã*. Versão obtida em http://www.dominiopublico.gov.br/pesquisa/DetalheObraForm.do?select_action=&co_obra=2233

Santos, Leandro de Lima, Cleuler Barbosa das Neves, and Carlos Leão (2009). *Uma década de politica de reforma agraria no Brasil: Índice de Gini e estrutura fundiaria—1985 a 1995*, 47º Congresso SOBER, Porto Alegre

Andrea Clambra
June 19, 2011, Barcelona

Ryan Harvey

OCCUPY BEFORE AND BEYOND

The only way out is to organize with everyone; all who struggle and suffer from these policies of starvation that leave us marginalized from everything. And yes, to organize in order to build something else, something different… It's a process that won't happen from one day to the next or even one year to the next, but our starting point is organizing differently.
—Neka, Argentina, interviewed in Marina Sitrin's
Horizontalism

For it is undeniable that most participatory democratic groups have struggles to survive past their founding, let alone realize politically transformative aims. The challenges that they have faced in coordinating large numbers of people with little preparation time and scarce resources have been daunting, and the economic and legal pressures on them to mimic conventional organizations equally so.
—Francesca Polletta, *Freedom Is an Endless Meeting: Democracy
in American Social Movements*

WE LIVE IN AN INTERESTING TIME. THE WORLD SOCIAL MOVEMENT THAT erupted at the end of 2010 in Greece has led us to, or helped to inform and inspire, the Arab Spring, the uprisings of the *indignados*, the mass student strikes in Chile and Québec, the Occupy movement, the protest movement around the elections in Mexico, and more. It also spurred significant protests in Nigeria, Portugal, Iraq, and Ireland, among others.

Perhaps more significant that the physical protests is the effect this wave of movements has had in the social sphere. Sitting in Dublin, Ireland finishing this essay, I reflect on the year that has passed since I was last in Europe, when the Occupy movement broke out. Here in Ireland, and elsewhere, friends seem to agree: Occupy's greatest achievement might be that it declared, in a popular language and with great public support, that the financial system of unregulated capitalism and corporate control over life is the key political and economic problem we face today. It renders democracy useless, it attacks life, the environment, and the rights of people, and it serves the interests of what the majority of Americans now refer to as "the 1%." That simple framing of the issue, that analysis, existed before either in private or public only in what would be considered fringe circles. Now it's out in pop culture, and it's controversial to not recognize the problem.

As the movement portion of this wave wanes in the US, there is a great discussion about what is happening and what has happened. This conversation is talking taking place in Egypt, in Spain, in Ireland, and beyond, in regards to their respective mass movements.

In the US, many suggest that "Occupy" is a conversation and an idea, a term used to describe the states of mind of a large group of people in the post-Arab Spring United States, as well as a way to describe a new (to the US, at least) way of doing protest and decision-making. Others argue that it is a defined movement rooted in Zuccotti Park, Oscar Grant Plaza, McPherson Square in DC, and in countless other public assembly points throughout the country (and the world).

As an idea, Occupy remains relevant as a major juncture point in an emerging climate of political and social upheaval, as well as a reference point for an entire generation of young activists. It shattered the silence around the economic crisis and ushered in a new era of mass, grassroots democracy. Within political movements in the US, it is hard to imagine hierarchical organizing becoming popular among a generation that was brought into politics through Occupy.

As a defined movement, Occupy is clearly a diminished force that is struggling to keep itself relevant. The reality is that Occupy will never be what it was again, it will only be different. And that's not a bad thing, it's a reality that movements often struggle with and a reality that opens space for an endless list of possibilities.

Occupy grew out of a specific social, economic, political, and cultural context. Mass ruptures in the future will grow out of their own contexts as well. Perhaps Occupy will become a reference point that helps define and inspire movements that we cannot even imagine today, just as we could not have imagined what began in Tunisia in December of 2010.

a rupture in conventional politics

SINCE THE 1970S, mainstream political discourse in the United States has been in a continual shift towards the right, a trend kicked off with the introduction of domestic neoliberalism under the Reagan administration and an almost religious emphasis on pro-business policies that would "trickle-down" to the rest of us. In the last few years, the cultural component of this current has manifested most publicly as the Tea Party, which rode a wave of anti-Obama sentiment stemming from a mixture of racism and genuine disillusionment with American liberalism.

Many activists from the grassroots of the Tea Party saw the party's emergence as something was counter to the more properly organized and funded right wing, and those activists considered the entry of people like Sarah Palin into the Tea Party ranks as a cooptation by the Republican Party. Interestingly, but perhaps not so surprisingly, some of the same folks have found themselves moving further toward socially-liberal, economically-conservative libertarian politics. Some of have found themselves at Occupy gatherings around the country.

Meanwhile, the funded, organized Republican side of the Tea Party has been successful at winning some popular support, and a small group of billionaires managed to buy several key elections, which were followed by a coordinated legislative attack on immigrants, unions, students, women, the elderly, and the poor.

We can't divorce Occupy from the domestic political context from which it emerged, stemming from a decade-long anti-war movement, an eruption of immigrants' rights marches in 2006 and again in Arizona a few years later, and a growing frustration with the refusal of the Obama administration to make any significant changes from the Bush years.

Arizona, Georgia, and Alabama have all passed bills in the last few years that require police officers to check the immigration status of people they think could be undocumented—essentially, the legal sanctioning of racial profiling

Within political movements in the US, it is hard to imagine hierarchical organizing becoming popular among a generation that was brought into politics through Occupy.

of brown-skinned people. These bills also take state funding away from un-documented people and require public schools to check immigration status before allowing children to enroll. In Arizona, the introduction of SB1070 catalyzed a massive wave of street protests. Protests also erupted in Georgia when a similar bill was introduced. In Wisconsin, Indiana, and Ohio, a bill authored by the same think-tank that wrote SB1070 in Arizona, the Ameri-can Legislative Exchange Council (ALEC), was pushed through (a Ohio referendum, however, blocked its passage there).

Equally important in the history of Occupy as a homegrown Ameri-can mass movement is the international context of the Arab Spring, which quickly stretched far beyond the Arab World. Alongside and immeasurably inspired by the Arab Spring was the mass social movement that rose up in Wisconsin to challenge the imposition of Tea Party policies. This, in the immediate sense, marks the beginning stage of the recent wave.

In Wisconsin, the "budget repair bill," which sought to break public unions, privatize university control, increase student tuition, and cut funding for Wisconsin's public healthcare program, was introduced in early February 2011. Hundreds of people occupied the Capitol building in Madison for a month and coordinated marches of over 100,000 people, the largest demon-strations in the state's history, to try to stop the bill from taking effect.

On top of this new wave of right-wing activism and popular reaction, the wars in Iraq and Afghanistan, and recent interventions in Somalia, Lib-ya, Yemen, and Pakistan, have increasingly given rise to a public perception that is wary of what might be seen as an imperial agenda in United States foreign policy. Afghanistan, now the longest and most expensive war in US history, is still raging, and attempts by Obama to market the withdrawal from Iraq as a "profound" success have been met with an almost universal cynicism.

"I think the Arab Spring and Occupy Wall Street kind of mark the end of the 9/11 era," an Iraq War veteran turned anti-war activist told me re-cently. Indeed, since the 2008 economic crash, many people across class lines who have been pushed out of their houses by the same banks that ben-efited from a $1 trillion federal bailout package have gained a new aware-ness that remained largely suppressed during "the 9/11 years." And while the foreclosure crisis that precipitated the recession had a wide impact on both the poor and middle class, serving to bring together those forces in a unified anger against the big banks and financial institutions, it hadn't yet manifested on the streets.

The Wisconsin protests may mark the first successful move toward such a manifestation, though Arizona and the immigrant marches of 2006 may mark the first real attempt at sparking something larger. (And, they did spark a large movement, one focused on immigration, but did not manifest as a general movement against the economic system.) Though viewed as somewhat unsuccessful in a political vein, the Wisconsin protests were themselves a major social and cultural breaking point that ended a silence, especially among lower and middle-income white workers in the US, surrounding neoliberal policies. The protests also sent a message that effective protest must transcend traditional methods and doctrine if they are to be successful in the current US climate.

One of the main things that this Wisconsin-to-Wall Street wave has achieved is that it has catalyzed a large number of people to give voice to their extreme disenchantment and anger with the financial institutions, as well as at the specifics of American corporate capitalism. This is not to say that these protests were all "anti-capitalist;" rather, they were a strange combination of anarchists, socialists, communists, progressive liberals, conservative-identified libertarians, and even some who identify as Republicans but see the hyper-rich as exploiters of the Republican values they identify with. That said, the issues raised at Wall Street and the discussions surrounding them are quite critical of what we on "the left" call *capitalism* or what some on "the right" call *corporatism*. Perhaps such common ground simply hadn't been recognized before Occupy Wall Street emerged.

the global roots and practices of occupy

IN MY OPINION, Occupy really started in Wisconsin, just not by name. When I arrived there as both an independent journalist and as a general participant in the protests against the Tea Party Governor Scott Walker, I saw signs referencing Egypt on the walls of the occupied Capitol building. It was mid-February and the occupation was just over a week old. Though word of its events had only begun spreading to the rest of the country and the world, the power of a broad and spontaneous social movement had clearly established itself.

As word spread, giant stacks of pizzas would be delivered to the "Peoples' House," as some had dubbed the occupied Capitol, purchased through the Internet by people in dozens of countries and from all fifty states in the US Inside the shop, Ian's Pizza, a list was posted showing the countries of origin of the purchases; it included Iraq, Egypt, and Tunisia.

While Wisconsinites hung posters referencing the then-emerging revolution in Egypt (like one that read "Cairo on the Yaharo"), a young Egyptian posted a photo of himself in Tahrir Square with a sign reading "Egypt Supports Wisconsin Workers: One World, One Pain." Another Egyptian sent a message to a Wisconsin organization's Facebook account that folks inside the occupied Capitol would turn into a poster reading: "I want Scott Walker to know that he is not just dealing with the people of Wisconsin, he's dealing with the people of the world."

Just as the Egyptians referenced Tunisia in Tahrir Square and the Wisconsinites referenced Egypt in the Capitol, the *indignados* of Spain would take to their plaças in May of 2011 and reference the social movement in Iceland that ousted the government in 2008, going on to become the only country in Europe to successfully reject IMF austerity measures. And though my *indignado* friends in Barcelona knew little of the protests in Wisconsin (very little info on it was available in Spanish), their movement bore so much resemblance that it is hard to believe they were not directly influenced. In Chile, too, *indignados* rose up in the largest protests in decades, led by massive student organizations.

It is hard to map the way that influence and solidarity spreads. In fact, I don't know of any tools—intellectual, physical, or otherwise—that one could use to do such a thing, and I probably wouldn't trust them if I saw them used. At the same time, as someone who lived the experience of Wisconsin, visited with participants of some of the European and North African movements of that following year in Tunisia, Scotland, England, Spain, Portugal, and Ireland, and experienced both Occupy Wall Street and many of the "Occupies" that popped up around the country afterwards, I can say with confidence that a definite, and at times mysterious, lineage existed and continues to exist between these world events.

The characteristics that have defined these movements are numerous, but there are a few that stand out as overwhelmingly clear and (almost) universally-accepted behaviors or procedural similarities. Among those are the coordination of spontaneous mass movements through social-networking technology; the emergence of movements not born from established political parties or activist networks and organizations; the reclamation of public space as a commentary on the "right to the city" or the right to houses of government; the reclamation of public space as a source of movement power and internal development; mass consensus and "lower-case d democracy" as a central way of doing but also as a prefigurative model; a general rejection of established economic systems (from both the right and left); and the putting forth of imaginative and "unrealistic" goals (one could also read this as *revolutionary*, though the media labels it as *goal-less*).

In some ways, these movements are similar because they are all tied to and are fighting against similar economic and governmental systems. Iceland, Spain, Portugal, Iraq, Chile, and Ireland, for instance, are all the products of recent or, in Chile's case, long-seated neoliberal policy and IMF control.

In Europe, young and old alike are facing the dissolution of what have long been considered staples of western European social democracies: England's health care system is on the privatization block; the right to squat abandoned houses is being stripped in England and The Netherlands; the International Monetary Fund has tightened its grip on Greece, Ireland, and

Portugal with increasing austerity measures; and tuition rates for students across the continent are rising dramatically.

In Egypt, the downward pressure of wages from neoliberal policies has resulted in an increasing number of strikes across various industries in the last decade. Egypt's rupture, however, was tied to the other uprisings that would precede and follow it throughout the Middle East, which, unlike the movements of southern Europe, hold characteristics specific to the legacy of western imperialist policy in the region.

In Tunisia, for example, a generation of young people educated in universities found themselves with few job options. In 2008, they watched the government of Ben Ali kill protesting miners in the southern city of Gafsa; student organizations and bloggers began publicly agitating for major changes. This, according to an anonymous friend from Tunis, marks the start of the movement that eventually toppled Ben Ali.

Iraq, too, had an Arab Spring that saw mass demonstrations and police repression. Rising from the wreckage caused by both the US war and the IMF-designed economic policies that accompanied US troops into the country, the movement sought not only to fight for economic and political justice, but also in many ways to establish a new civil society in the face of a slow US withdrawal.

It must be said that these recent uprisings and revolutions were not the first of their kind in this era of global economic depression and austerity, and not the first to launch high-profile, game-changing tactics and strategies in the public sphere. Iran's Green Movement, however, was one of the first world "ruptures" to be largely initiated and coordinated through social media technology, the other being perhaps the 2008 uprising in Greece, which spread quickly through similar channels.

The Green Movement preceded the uprising in Tunisia by a few years and offered some examples of new ways of fighting. It was a largely secular uprising against a religious regime that was trying to assert itself as heroic and anti-American while simultaneously repressing large segments of the population and domestic social movements.

Yet there are other factors that have led to such moments. Though tied closely and often directed by the major political parties, the airport occupation in Bangkok, Thailand in late 2008, while not initiating a wave of immediate protests globally, certainly inspired people (including me) around the United States towards thinking about new ways of doing public politics.

Even more forgotten, perhaps, are the massive protests that erupted in Burma in 2007 against the IMF-imposed economic policies and military rule after Burma's military government caused massive increases in fuel and food throughout the country when they cut subsidies on the advice of the IMF. These protests, in many ways, preceded the coming crisis-responses in southern Europe.

Shortly before the protests in Burma, a rebellion broke out in Oaxaca, Mexico. Starting as a strike initiated by a small group of teachers, it soon grew into a citywide movement. In Oaxaca City, the *Zócalo* became one of the central areas of revolt and grew into an encampment that resembled, in many ways, Tahrir Square.

public spaces as movement centers

THE CENTRALITY OF public space as a platform for both the coordination of protest and, I would say more so, the spontaneous and organic development of new forms of politics, is perhaps the most important dynamic of this wave of movements. Though the concept itself is nothing new, what feels wholly unique at this particular moment is the newfound and conscious understanding of the power of such locations, coupled with the application of those understandings in central public spaces across the world.

Such centers of power also are a physical manifestation of consensus-driven models of organizing; they are public, open, and they exist for all. In this sense, the adaptation of both mass democratic processes and the organization of social movements through open, public centers combined to form a perfect and essential formula for the current movements.

"It was never something we had anticipated, that a community was going to form and live in this space and be sort of the focal point of the resistance to the budget repair bill and the beginnings of a social movement," my friend Erika Wolf, who played a key role inside the occupation of the Capitol in Wisconsin, told me. "As far as I know nobody had set out to say 'we are going to occupy our state Capitol,'" Charity Shmidt, a University of Wisconsin grad student who was there the first night of the occupation, said in a separate interview. "I don't think the decision ever actually happened," said another UW grad student, Mario Bruzzone.

It was in this way that the occupation in Wisconsin began, not exactly as an accident, but far from a coordinated political mobilization. That's partly why the occupation was so widely felt, because it did not come from a specific group with a specific goal but from a general mass of people with a shared general understanding of why they had gathered together, and with an understanding of their different motivations.

Whereas many movements struggle constantly to find collective space, usually through the hosting of regular marches or demonstrations, the establishment of such spaces as the encampments and the creation of such public social spaces has allowed these movements to experience fast-paced social change and collective transformation, which has often led to a more horizontal arrangement of power within them—as well as to a lot of frustration born from a uneasiness around working with folks across various differences in opinion, experience, and political goals. But within that frustration, these spaces have hosted real debate and dialogue around issues of power, privilege, and movement direction(s).

Thus "taking the square" became a central way of participating globally after Tahrir's example. Soon, Pearl Roundabout in central Bahrain, Syntagma Square in Athens, the Capitol Building in Madison, the Plaça Catalunya in Barcelona, Zuccotti Park in Manhattan, and Oscar Grant Plaza in Oakland became both the focal points of movement activity and the reference points for the movements that brought them to global awareness.

The importance of these spaces to their participants on a solely emotional level is also key. In both Madison and Barcelona I saw fresh tattoos on participants of the protests commemorating their time in the shared public spaces of those movements. In Oakland, the establishment of Oscar Grant Plaza, referencing the young man murdered by transit police on New Year's Day 2010, sent a strong emotional message to the people of the city and made it clear that the protests were as much about Oakland as they were about a vague solidarity with Occupy Wall Street.

Politically, these spaces became the central locations of power. In Cairo, many were murdered by the police as they attempted to re-enter the areas around Tahrir Square. In one famous YouTube video, a military convoy mutinies and leads a massive crowd across one of the bridges leading to Tahrir, facing off with a line of soldiers and police at the other end. In Oakland, Iraq veteran Scott Olsen had his skull broken by a police tear gas canister hurled into the middle of a crowd of demonstrators attempting to re-take Oscar Grant plaza after a violent eviction. In New York, the arrest of over 700 activists in a march over the Brooklyn Bridge to Zuccotti Park turned the relatively small protests there into a national movement almost overnight.

on the importance of "isms" and the irrelevance of "ists"

SOMETHING THAT SEEMED so obvious to me both in Wisconsin and in my conversations with *indignados* in Spain was that while both anarchists and non-party socialists played extremely important roles in the movements in these places, they didn't play those roles as members of or ambassadors of their respective "isms." Rather, they came into movements that were bursting with a *new politics* and those that wanted to remain relevant within those movements participated as such.

In the US, the lineage of these new politics can be found in many places, including anarchism, socialism, and libertarianism. It is no secret that many within the Occupy movement came into activism initially through the grassroots electoral campaign of Ron Paul and the Liberty Movement that grew around it. Similarly, in Spain, many identifying generally with right-wing policies joined those from both the organized and non-aligned left currents in the *plaças*. In Cairo's Tahrir Square and in central Tunis, people from varying political shades united in the context of the Days of Rage that gave birth, at least for a number of participants, to something new—at least temporarily.

It is clear that Occupy has been extremely powerful and rather broad in part because of the diverse and vague nature of its politics. Many participants have said that relatives and other people in their lives who have never been politically active before have been moved by Occupy.

To me, as a practical anarchist, I see these political developments as one of the more exciting things to happen in the recent past. I have long believed that if a radical movement for economic and social justice of any sort was to emerge in this country, it had to somehow find a balance, or a recognized alliance of cooperative differences, with folks from a large segment of the population. What this means in reality is precisely the sorts of strange alliances that formed at almost all Occupy sites between anarchists, socialists, communists, liberals, libertarians, and non-aligned people. It also means groups like anarchists, which often carry a strong rejection of organized religion, have to work alongside folks from communities of faith, and both parties need to at least respect that they are fighting for *most* of the same things.

Talk of such alliances may alarm radicals in the US, which perhaps is a good thing. I would ask if they are also alarmed by what happened in squares across the Middle East, specifically in Egypt and Tunisia, when secular peoples, Christians, leftists, anarchists, and Muslim Brotherhood members, among many others, united in mass movements. There, as well as across Spain, participants were discouraged from holding political party banners and slogans at the squares, to avoid infighting and to hold focus on the common enemies. "They were opposed to all political parties and to the established unions," a Greek friend tells me of the protests in Syntagma Square in mid-2011. "They were very broad, involving both the poor and the middle classes."

On one side, these alliances allowed for the power to take root that eventually ousted the autocratic rulers of both Tunisia and Egypt. On the other hand, in Egypt for example, political Islamicists from the Salafi (the right-wing of the Islamic movement) attacked anarchists after the revolution and accused them of causing the violence in Tahrir Square. Coptic Christians also became the victims of brutal attacks by Islamicists, resulting in marches across Egypt against the violence by folks from across the spectrum, including Muslim parties.

In the US, this alliance has not only involved grassroots participants from various political spheres spanning the right and the left, it has also involved cross-organizing between major unions and countless community organizing projects. In Wisconsin, the role of unions was simultaneously extremely important to the swelling of the protests and politically problematic when paired with the mass democratic, grassroots spontaneity of the occupation. In some ways, the overlap worked, in other ways, it caused tension and, perhaps, kept some from taking the occupation to another level.

Still, such alliances brought tens of thousands of people together from various backgrounds to participate in spontaneous and organic assemblies that seriously challenged established forms of power, from Wisconsin to Tahrir Square. It may be that this is simply an initial step of a longer process that will continue to challenge established ways of doing grassroots politics in the US.

the movement after occupy

SOMETHING THAT SEEMS very clear to me at this juncture in the Occupy movement (the early spring of 2012) is that Occupy was the initiator of a new era of political development and social movement emergence in the US. It will not likely continue to be, however, *the* movement, as many perhaps expected it to be in the winter. While it has manifested in smaller, localized campaigns like the defense of houses facing eviction, it has also morphed in concept.

Alongside groups with direct lineage to Occupy that have moved beyond the public centers (Occupy Our Homes, Occupy the Hood), there have been moments like the murder of Trayvon Martin in Florida that gave birth to massive demonstrations throughout the country that, when looking at the whole, seem to be at least referentially inspired by Occupy. They also share with Occupy a significant characteristic: they were organized through social media networks, not through the conventional networks of top-down organizations of personalities like Jesse Jackson and Al Sharpton that have so often held sway in similar outpourings in the past.

But something present in these movements, in relation to Occupy, is an inability, or worse a refusal, of Occupy activists to see that their role within the larger social movement that they may well have inspired is not what it was in October. It has shifted due to many factors, perhaps in part because it failed to defend itself from consistent evictions, perhaps because many of its participants took from it what they could and have moved on to other projects and campaigns.

That temporary space that Occupy, and the *indignados* in Spain, were able to hold in 2011 and early 2012 may be gone, but the breaking point they oversaw has lasting effects. It is not our job nor in our interest to try to map those effects out; that is a slippery slope between admitting our impact and attaching ourselves to situations and movements that carry with them their own contexts and trajectories.

Gabriella

Our General Assembly meets on the courthouse steps, facing busy Water St. and the jail. This is the "face" of Occupy Santa Cruz, complete with a heated geodesic dome and an easy-up pavilion sheltering literature and a donation box. The camp, the "heart," is located in a valley behind the courthouse, hidden from public view. The camp floods as it rains, reflecting the movement's social hierarchy.

Today's discussion is whether to move three of our seven General Assemblies to the other courthouse steps *facing the camp*. Proponents of the proposal argue that it will promote camp-GA unity and campers may be more likely to participate if they can hear and see us. Opponents argue this location diminishes our visibility to the public on Water Street, rejecting the very real audience of the camp while prioritizing engagement with another class of people.

More homogenous than the camp, the GA is mostly white and housed. Politicians and bureaucrats threaten to shut us down if we can't address the "problems" of the camp and speakers on the steps re-iterate their orders. The plight and desires of "homeless people" are asserted and behaviors such as drug use, theft, and violence are salient. In actuality, the camp is very diverse, made of people of different identities and class status. There are traveling kids, experiencers of long-term poverty, people who use drugs, and those recently removed from the middle class. However, over-simplifications are made; the "hard-core occupiers" camp nearest to the courthouse steps while it's claimed that the "opportunists" in the back of camp will "scatter like cockroaches when the cops come."

I am in the in-reach working group focused on the relationship between GA and camp. At the "All Camp Meetings," we stand or sit in a circle instead of using the GA model. Speakers stand in the middle with two minutes to speak. Some folks are talking rebellion and I am moved. One person said, "We all are the 99%, but we are the bottom 1%." This is the revolution I dream of. I channel a patronizing savior mentality without asking, "What do you want?" I assume I have the knowledge and tools this marginalized population needs in order to activate, although many have been resisting capitalism longer than me. Several "all camp" meetings later, my partner introduces the hand signals. I make assumptions about their intellectual capacity and think "This is too complicated for them." My own classism wraps itself around my shoulders.

I do not remember his name, the houseless fellow who took a liking to me, but I shut him down at one of the GAs. He was talking; it wasn't relevant, but he had waited his turn. I could tell the people who sit still on cold concrete steps, stick to the topic, and follow the meeting rules, were frustrated. Gently I approached him, whispered "that's enough" and led him away from the steps. Once we were alone, he said I insulted him and he had only walked away out of respect for me. I realized I had silenced and removed him from the process because he was not participating in the efficient way we understood and valued. Later, I was congratulated and thanked for my handling of him. However, I was disgusted that my actions were recreating the power dynamics I seek to eradicate.

How can we start a revolution without doing internal work on ourselves? The in-reach group provided the opening stages for this, but there remained a perceived fragility of the movement. We feared extensive conversations about race, gender, and class would stall us and everything would fall apart. It fell apart anyway.

IT'S GETTING DARKER AND COLDER

Margaret Killjoy
December 7, 2011
Occupy Santa Cruz evicted

Morrigan Phillips

ROOM FOR THE POOR

THE OCCUPY PHENOMENON IS CONFUSING. DUE IN PART TO THE INCRED-ible fluidity of process structures and in part to the wide variety of participants, Occupy confounds many established patterns of organizing and action building. Composed largely of a confluence of people increasingly dispossessed by current economic trends, fueled by outrage over economic gluttony and seeming impunity on Wall Street, the Occupy Movement took hold of a kernel of anger lying deep in the hearts of thousands of people: the economic pinch was being felt by too many. Pop! A would-be movement sprang forth representing those to whom the promise of prosperity in exchange for hard work had been made and broken.

A common refrain birthed by the Occupy Movement and now a part of popular discourse is the chant of "We Are the 99%." This important slogan has galvanized a mass of disassociated people into feeling some level of connection ... but who, really, makes up this so-called "99%"? In Boston, this broad classification includes both Harvard graduates making $400,000 per year, and those who make far less. And while many of the people in the 99% are likely buried in debt, many also enjoy more social privilege and access then masses of people falling through the growing holes in the safety net and living without homes, health care, and education. The Occupy Movement, interestingly, does include people from both of these extremes of "the 99%," but more common are occupiers aged between 20 and 40, who have some social privilege.

Given this, it's not hard to make the argument that the mobilization of the Occupy movement will be strongest if it includes, at its core, a realistic understanding and analysis of poverty and poor people's movements, and an understanding of the disparities of wealth and resources that exist within the so-called 99%. This is not to say that Occupy is, or should be, a poor people's movement, but it does need to own what it is. Plenty of people active in Occupies throughout the country are hurting and letting that hurt fuel their rage and conviction. But it will not serve anyone for Occupy to continue without an analysis of poverty. This is about the top 10% versus the bottom 20%. Occupy can choose to align itself with either. But an Occupy movement that joins its interests with the interests of a poor people's movement in a shared vision of economic justice would be remarkable and bold.

a brief primer on poverty, poor people's movements, and the importance of a safety net

POVERTY IS, AS the most basic definition states, the lack of resources sufficient for someone to live comfortably in society. For many, credit cards and loans have kept them in enough comfort that they have been able to put off acknowledging the grim realities of our economic system, but the myth of comfort and stability has fallen apart in recent years as the economic crisis has pushed more people into the uncomfortable position of realizing how close they are to a financial crisis of their own. Meanwhile, according to new poverty measures and census data, rates of poverty, particularly in rural communities and urban communities of color have risen to a 52-year high.

The scattered analysis that has emerged from Occupy has focused on issues of corporate personhood, bank bailouts, executive bonuses, and general Wall Street excesses at the expense of real democracy. Personal stories have defined the Occupy narrative: stories about multiple years of unemployment, of home foreclosures, of bankruptcy due to medical expenses, of untenable student loan debts, and more. These are the stories of people for whom the promise of security was broken. These, too, are those who are broke, but for whom that sense of being able to live comfortably in society is somewhat attainable. But for thousands, a promise of security was never made. No part of the system has ever worked in their favor, and for decades the economy has failed them in boom or bust.

Amidst a seeming abundance of stuff and general prosperity, the poor pull together a patchwork living that is a mere shadow of what many others are able to attain. In our overly commercialized and consumption-driven society, being poor can mean being left out and left behind. Left to create and build as best one can with limited resources but never looking like everyone else. Never seeing your life reflected back to you on TV, in the news, in advertisements. Not even close. This alone makes it less likely that the poor will take up in protest with Occupy. The society that Occupiers are working to defend never included the poor in the same way.

This, of course, does not mean the poor will not organize and rise up. Poor peoples' movements have played and continue to play an important role in social and community movement work. Statistically speaking, however, the poor hold the space at the bottom of the 99%, earning less then $22,314 for a family of four. For an individual, the poverty threshold comes in at $10,890 a year in earnings, or around $900 a month. For most federal and state programs, individuals are eligible for assistance within 200% to 300% of the federal poverty line. More than a reflection of earnings, the poor are a class unto themselves. They not only have precarious livelihoods, experiencing frequent economic disruption; they also live in communities where there is generally less stability. Poor communities are often isolated either by location (i.e. rural isolation) or through systematic disenfranchisement. We need only look at examples like poor public transportation options, the closing of public hospitals in poor communities, and a lack of supermarkets, parks, walkable streets, and sound infrastructure in many cities to see that this is unquestionably true.

In our overly commercialized and consumption-driven society, being poor can mean being left out and left behind. Left to create and build as best one can with limited resources but never looking like everyone else. Never seeing your life reflected back to you on TV, in the news, in advertisements. Not even close. This alone makes it less likely that the poor will take up in protest with Occupy. The society that Occupiers are working to defend never included the poor in the same way.

making room for the poor

ALMOST A YEAR from its inception, Occupy looks very different. The camps are gone and with them much of the daily labor that kept people tied together in work. The media spotlight has dimmed somewhat and while many of the conversations Occupy helped to start or reframe continue in the media and elsewhere, there is less emphasis on the protests.

A small list of examples of poor people's movements:

- Coalition of Immokalee Workers

- The National Welfare Rights Movement

- Domestic Workers Bill of Rights

- Take Back the Land

- City Life/Vida Urbana anti-foreclosure organizing in Boston

- United Farm Workers

- The unemployed workers movement during the great depression

- Poor People's Campaign organized by Martin Luther King, Jr. and the Southern Christian Leadership Conference

- Poor People's Economic Human Rights Campaign

- All of Us or None: An organization of prisoners, former prisoners and felons, to combat discrimination.

- Formerly Incarcerated and Convicted People's Movement

- Western Regional Advocacy Project

Some people have dispersed and returned to their pre-Occupy lives to ruminate and move on. Others have hunkered down and continue to be a part of working groups, attend general assemblies, and plan events. Others have taken the messaging, energy, and heart from Occupy as they have dived back into the organizing that was in the works before Occupy. Occupations of mental health clinics in Chicago and eviction blockades in Minneapolis, and the transformation of Occupy Oakland into Oakland Commune, all signal that Occupies are shifting and absorbing or being absorbed, to varying degrees, by existing community work.

Parallel to all of this has been the ever-escalating conservative fiscal fervor in Washington DC and on the presidential campaign trail. From Obama to Romney to Paul Ryan and Fox News this escalation has meant an escalation of the war on the poor.

In today's political discourse, it is the loss of the middle-class dream that is most lamented. Every political candidate, pundit, and journalist seems to be looking to champion the middle class. But few want to champion the poor, or even acknowledge their existence. This goes, too, for much of the discourse emerging from the Occupy movement.

Just as so much of society excludes the collective experience of the poor, so too has Occupy. At Occupy Boston, at least, from the very beginning there was a striking lack of an analysis of poverty present in the discussions and messaging of actions. Demands and grievances focused on personal gains rather than collective objectives:

a middle-class desire for debt relief; the focus on individual corporations or banks rather than on the system of capitalism; a practice of policing individuals without a larger reflection on provocateurs; and a collective reflection on the societal disrespect toward the mentally ill, homeless, or substance-addicted.

It should be made clear that Occupy Wall Street and the multitude of Occupies that have come alive around the US are not orchestrated, nor primarily constituted, by financially-comfortable, gainfully-employed, resource-rich individuals. Plenty of unemployed, underemployed, and broke-ass people are taking on roles of organizers within Occupies. There are also those who rely on various forms of public assistance, both safety net programs like subsidized public housing and social security programs like unemployment. Occupy camps also drew many from those forgotten and neglected corners of our communities: the houseless, those with mental health issues and substance use problems. So long as camps remained, so to did these communities' members.

The aforementioned eviction blockade work in Minneapolis, as well as in other cities throughout the US, has brought Occupy activists into the dynamic and growing eviction defense movement that has been building since the beginning of the housing crisis. This work, as well as the defense of mental health clinics in Chicago, Occupy the Farm in California, and other regional efforts, shows that in some areas Occupy groups have connected in deep ways to local social and economic justice work. But given the shifting and transient nature of this new movement, building an analysis of poverty that is shared by the collective Occupy identity is a challenging task. More than a national vision, if it is really to be accomplished, this framework would have to be one that individuals could with them into meeting spaces and working groups.

what would an analysis of poverty within the occupy framework look like?

Historical reference points: Messaging and demands would be rooted in a historical analysis of the years of cuts to social welfare spending and the toll those cuts have taken on communities of color in the United States. Economic recovery, when it does come, often leaves scars in poor communities that look like cuts to social services and public welfare spending, including funding for economic development, housing, food assistance, aid to the elderly, education, and job training. Additionally, since the Reagan era, poor communities have been blamed, bullied, marginalized, and subjected to slander in the media.

Engage the process … and then mess it up: In his 2011 State of the Union address, President Barack Obama mentioned poverty only once, and that was only in passing. Shortly after, presidential hopeful Mitt Romney said he was "not concerned about the very poor." This was followed by the release of a new budget proposal by Republican Representative Paul Ryan of Wisconsin, entitled "A Road Map to America's Future"—an entire budget based on the false premise that aid to the poor and those in need is what is causing our national deficit and bankrupting our economy. Ryan's budget is not likely to be the budget that becomes law, but it sets the stage and the terms for the fight ahead.

The conversion of programs like Medicaid and SNAP (food stamps) into block grants is a central feature of Ryan's budget—a move that would gut both programs over the next 10 years. Understanding the implications of converting funding for social safety net programs to block grants is one example of how Occupies can begin to align their work and messaging with the fight ahead that will be necessary to stop the cuts. Engaging the budget rhetoric through protest, through savvy media messaging, and through solidarity work with community organizations, as well as bird-dogging candidates, could bring the energy and anger that fuels Occupy to the front lines of the fight to stop the continued attacks on the poor.

Let's talk about Austerity: Movements in the Global South and in Europe have been talking about (and protesting against) austerity for decades. This is the time for that conversation to come to the US. Austerity is at the heart of fiscal policies rooted in corporate capitalism and free trade. Escalating the fight on multiple fronts—from attacks on higher education and funding cuts to programs that aid the poor to unemployment and infrastructure—could mark the beginning of an anti-austerity movement in the US. But for this to work, the language of Occupy needs to shift away from the focus on big banks and Wall Street, and instead transition to a discourse that highlights the connection between public policy and capitalism.

This is neither the first, nor the last moment: This is not the last time in which people will face economic hardships; things have been getting worse on the ground for decades: Both the political and popular discourse around poverty in the United States has always boiled down to the "deserving" and "undeserving" poor. The US welfare state was birthed out of a legacy of Elizabethan Poor Laws which placed the onus of one's poverty squarely on the shoulders of the poor. The only ones deserving of assistance were widows with children and anyone who could not work. The influence of this philosophy is felt throughout the history of the creation of the very limited US welfare state. There is no culture of poverty. But there is a culture of reluctance and outright disdain for aid to the poor in American political discourse.

Occupy is not the first time that people have risen together against the dominant structures of oppression and greed. But perhaps it can become something more nuanced and lasting, if it manages to shift focus.

A more nuanced and developed meme: The idea that the 99% meme is useful and popular should not overshadow the importance of examining power and privilege within the 99%. For example, the foreclosure crisis is amounting to the largest loss of land in the black community since the African slave trade tore people from their land. Unemployment among black men is at Depression-era levels. Again, economic hardship hits some communities harder due to historical disenfranchisement, oppression, and economic exclusion. Economic inequality is better represented in the US by looking at the 10% at the top versus the bottom 20%.

Beyond individual interests: We must move to a collective understanding of shared interests for economic justice. Improving the social safety net and protecting entitlement programs such as unemployment insurance, food stamps, foreclosure protection, and so on needs to be the context in which other demands such as financial industry regulation and an end to corporate personhood are placed. Messaging and tactics using the distinctive Occupy analysis that are deployed against direct attacks to the social safety net that hit poor communities the hardest, illuminating the relationship between economic hardship and big finance, could be powerful. A move in this direction would also create an opening for solutions to the immediate needs of people now, as well as in the long-term. Solidarity means that even if you win, you stand with everyone until everyone wins.

Thinking global and local: The analysis that Occupy formulates should invoke economic justice and economic rights and be born from the messages that have been raised up by poor people's movements in the US and Global South for decades. We also must acknowledge that the relative prosperity here in the US relies on the exploitation and subjugation of the Global South.

A shift in praxis: The way in which the economic crisis is conceived of and organized against needs to be informed by a systemic analysis of power, culture, history, and economics that moves deeper into a social change model, one that re-envisions how our society meets the needs of everyone. Ending corporate personhood, for example, will not restore funding to much-needed programs and services. It will not restore dignity and comfort to those left in the cold each night by homelessness. Only a cultural and societal change that internalizes an analysis of poverty and the poor will do that.

A diversity of organizing structures: We must be inclusive of people of homeless and other economically-stigmatized communities. While my own experience of the Occupy Boston camp provides a good example of the issues at stake here, the situation in Boston was far from unique. The Dewey Square Occupation in Boston was, like so many Occupy camps around the country, consumed in conflict that revolved around the role homeless people played in the camp. Sometimes called "junkies," other times called "trouble," from the get-go there was little capacity within the camp to deal with these challenges. The now-infamous structures of Occupy—General Assemblies, consensus process, and working groups, among others—showed their limits when confronted with the necessity of being inclusive of people who live in those dim and frequently forgotten parts of society. The promise of meals every day, protection in numbers, and community drew the homeless to Occupy camps. Those struggling with mental health issues, living on the streets or in the shelter system, and those whose struggle is compounded by substance use and addiction live frustrating lives every day. Occupy camps offered the promise of a space that could address some of their needs.

But the organizing structures built at Occupy Boston mostly showed the divide between the priorities of the middle of the 99% and the needs of the bottom 10%. Violent and admittedly-unstable personalities were present at Occupy Boston, but it was those personalities among the houseless (the preferred term of those members of the community active in Occupy Boston) population that drew the most scorn. Plenty of young, white, housed, and comfortable men showed outright oppressive tendencies. But it was not these participants in Occupy Boston to whom the Good Neighbor Agreement was directed. Solutions sought within the established process almost exclusively targeted problematic personalities within the houseless community. What is more, the use of the police and criminal justice system was at times viewed as an acceptable option, without any larger discussion of the role these forces play in the oppression and criminalization of homelessness.

There are many organizing models and many examples of empowering organizing work that don't rely on forcing marginalized and unheard communities with varying capacities to fit into our preferred process. Occupy needs to examine how its processes can and often do recreate the societal norm of excluding the voices of people living on the fringes. These dynamics are not as apparent now that there are so few occupations, but an understanding of poverty and the inclusion of a poor people's agenda will only help a movement of "the 99%"

The Prison Industrial Complex (PIC): The PIC, the criminal justice system, and the police serve as methods of oppression and destruction in poor communities. The 99% analysis needs to acknowledge that for the bottom 10% to 20%, the police, prison guards, and other agents of the criminal justice system are not allies and are certainly not "in it together" with poor communities of color. This is not about income but about the role these agents play in the criminalization of poverty. The approach to addressing inequality and societal disparities must not only look at income but also the roles people play in the systems of inequality. Occupy for Prisoners is an excellent example of solidarity between Occupy Oakland and prison abolition activists, a pointed recognition of the fact that there are many thousands locked up on the inside that can not join us in our meetings or in the streets as we fight for justice.

As anti-poverty activists, as organizers, and as community members, we need to dig deep and assess how the many voices, campaigns, organizations, groups, and networks that exist today can join together in a national, anti-poverty, poor people's movement for economic justice. We all deserve better, but what is better for some should not come without, or at the expense of, the poor.

Yotam Marom
Bloombergville to Occupy
Liberating the Impossible

In June of 2011, as the fight against austerity spread from Athens to Wisconsin and everywhere in between, New York City activists set up Bloombergville, a two-and-a-half-week occupation of a street corner outside of the City Council building near City Hall. The occupation stood alongside a broad resistance to a New York City budget that would cut funding from schools, hospitals, daycare centers, elderly homes, fire-houses, AIDS clinics, homeless shelters, transportation, and other vital services, while the big banks and millionaires made record profits from an economic crisis they had caused. On June 14, we occupied, intending to take a last stand against the budget. We slept on the street, held assemblies, engaged in direct action, hosted teach-ins, made art, and built relationships with groups across the city.

Late in the evening of June 24, after weeks of negotiations and grassroots struggle, the city council called a an emergency meeting to make a deal that would save some of the social programs and jobs under threat, but leave most of the cuts intact. Members of the council, select press, and the mayor's office made their way to the Tweed Courthouse—just around the corner from Bloombergville—for their victory press conference. It was late, 10PM—maybe because it had been a long day of haggling or maybe because they didn't want many protesters or cameras—but that didn't stop people at Bloombergville from calling on partners from around the city to converge at the press conference.

I showed up at Tweed, a bit late and out of breath, to see my friends—working people, union members, activists, homeless people, and parents—chanting, banging drums, and picketing at the bottom of the stairs. The press conference was inside, the doors between the regal pillars of the building were locked, and about five policemen stood on the stairs leading up, announcing that we had to stay on the sidewalk. Sometimes, I guess, it's hard to realize how much power you have, but the contrast between the large, defiant crowd at the bottom of the stairs and the handful of cops protecting the politicians at the top was too stark to miss. One of us shouted, "Why are we down here if they are up there?" and then marched up the steps, chanting "This is what Democracy looks like!" Everyone joined the procession, with barely any hesitation—the first of us slipped through the police lines like drops of water, and as they chased us and broke their formation, the rest charged up in a tidal wave. The cops were overwhelmed, taken by surprise and outnumbered, and within moments we were at the top of the stairs against the doors, drumming and chanting. We could see the proceedings, and they could sure as hell hear us. Someone tweeted from inside that it felt like Tweed was under siege. It was.

A few days later, we delayed the final vote by staging a sit-in in the lobby of the City Council building, while a thousand people surrounded the building and went marching in the streets for hours. But, as we were hauled off to New York's Central Booking in handcuffs, the budget passed, with some gains but most of the vicious and unnecessary cuts still to take effect. Bloombergville packed up a few days later, taking many of us back to the drawing board. It had not been as big as Occupy would be, nor as glamorous; there were lots of lessons we hadn't learned yet, and it didn't catch like many of the events that would unfold shortly after. Nonetheless, many Occupiers look back at Bloombergville fondly as a sort of predecessor, and we have learned a lot from its successes and failures.

That moment on the stairs of Tweed has stuck with me more than any other. It was one of those rare moments in which a group recognizes its potential and understands its strength, when something just clicks to allow people to see just how much stronger they are than they thought they were. We only climbed 20 steps or so, no big deal, but the leap was enormous—from one stage of struggle to another. You could see that shift in consciousness on people's faces, that sense of empowerment in people's eyes: it was a flicker of possibility in a world where we are told there is none.

In a bigger sense, this is what Occupy Wall Street has done too. It has shown us our collective strength, helped us recognize our power in the face of crumbling systems, punctured a small hole in the narrative of impossibility, and opened pathways to another world that might be if we fight for it. We are sprinting up the stairs and opening doors; one breathless step at a time, we are liberating the impossible.

DECLARATION OF THE OCCUPATION OF NEW YORK CITY

This document was accepted by the NYC General Assembly on September 29, 2011

As we gather together in solidarity to express a feeling of mass injustice, we must not lose sight of what brought us together. We write so that all people who feel wronged by the corporate forces of the world can know that we are your allies.

As one people, united, we acknowledge the reality: that the future of the human race requires the cooperation of its members; that our system must protect our rights, and upon corruption of that system, it is up to the individuals to protect their own rights, and those of their neighbors; that a democratic government derives its just power from the people, but corporations do not seek consent to extract wealth from the people and the Earth; and that no true democracy is attainable when the process is determined by economic power. We come to you at a time when corporations, which place profit over people, self-interest over justice, and oppression over equality, run our governments. We have peaceably assembled here, as is our right, to let these facts be known.

- They have taken our houses through an illegal foreclosure process, despite not having the original mortgage.
- They have taken bailouts from taxpayers with impunity, and continue to give Executives exorbitant bonuses.
- They have perpetuated inequality and discrimination in the workplace based on age, the color of one's skin, sex, gender identity and sexual orientation.
- They have poisoned the food supply through negligence, and undermined the farming system through monopolization.
- They have profited off of the torture, confinement, and cruel treatment of countless animals, and actively hide these practices.
- They have continuously sought to strip employees of the right to negotiate for better pay and safer working conditions.
- They have held students hostage with tens of thousands of dollars of debt on education, which is itself a human right.
- They have consistently outsourced labor and used that outsourcing as leverage to cut workers' healthcare and pay.
- They have influenced the courts to achieve the same rights as people, with none of the culpability or responsibility.

- They have spent millions of dollars on legal teams that look for ways to get them out of contracts in regards to health insurance.
- They have sold our privacy as a commodity.
- They have used the military and police force to prevent freedom of the press.
- They have deliberately declined to recall faulty products endangering lives in pursuit of profit.
- They determine economic policy, despite the catastrophic failures their policies have produced and continue to produce.
- They have donated large sums of money to politicians, who are responsible for regulating them.
- They continue to block alternate forms of energy to keep us dependent on oil.
- They continue to block generic forms of medicine that could save people's lives or provide relief in order to protect investments that have already turned a substantial profit.
- They have purposely covered up oil spills, accidents, faulty bookkeeping, and inactive ingredients in pursuit of profit.
- They purposefully keep people misinformed and fearful through their control of the media.
- They have accepted private contracts to murder prisoners even when presented with serious doubts about their guilt.
- They have perpetuated colonialism at home and abroad.
- They have participated in the torture and murder of innocent civilians overseas.
- They continue to create weapons of mass destruction in order to receive government contracts.[1]

To the people of the world,

We, the New York City General Assembly occupying Wall Street in Liberty Square, urge you to assert your power.

Exercise your right to peaceably assemble; occupy public space; create a process to address the problems we face, and generate solutions accessible to everyone.

To all communities that take action and form groups in the spirit of direct democracy, we offer support, documentation, and all of the resources at our disposal.

Join us and make your voices heard!

---

1   These grievances are not all-inclusive.

Joe Lustri
October 15, 2011
OWS General Assembly at Washington Square Park

Marisa Holmes

THE CENTER CANNOT HOLD
A REVOLUTION IN PROCESS

the assembly

IT BEGAN WITH A BREAK IN PROCESS. GEORGIA SAGRI STOOD UP IN THE middle of the crowd and shouted, "This is not an assembly!" With that statement a breakout group formed the first real NYC General Assembly.

New Yorkers Against Budget Cuts had initially called for the meeting. Earlier in the summer the group organized an occupation called Bloombergville. The three-week encampment was intended as a protest against the city budget cuts. I had participated in Bloombergville out of curiosity but never made a formal commitment. While I supported their declaration I knew the coalition to be run by the institutional left, mainly the ISO (International Socialist Organization), Workers World (a Marxist Leninist group), and Organization for a Free Society (dominated by followers of Parecon).

In late July of 2011, I received their Facebook invitation entitled *The People's General Assembly*. It was to convene on Tuesday, August 2 at 4:30PM in front of the charging bull. While the idea of an assembly intrigued me I was skeptical of both *Adbusters* and New Yorkers Against Budget Cuts. I wanted nothing to do with the institutional left, and thus I did not attend the meeting.

Later that week I was invited to a dinner party, where I was entertained by the anecdotes of anarchists and autonomous Marxists from the 16 Beaver Group. Everyone was a bit astonished that they were able to break away and reveled in the possibilities ahead. I realized there was an opportunity to have a General Assembly that was horizontally organized. After a bit of coaxing I made a commitment to building the assembly.

My first General Assembly was in front of the Irish Potato Famine Memorial on August 9, 2011. Sixty or so assembled under a great stone arch, which protected us from the oppressive August heat. Amin Hussein facilitated in an even and deliberate voice, but there was confusion over process. The process group (i.e. the break-out group from the first meeting) gave a reportback. They had decided to use modified consensus, but not everyone was clear about what this meant. We spent an hour or so discussing the consensus process before deciding to use a modified consensus, which would drop to ¾ majority in case of a block. We would use hand signals when needed, progressive stack, and keep notes of meetings. This seemed to appease everyone in the group. We then discussed future meeting times and decided to meet for the foreseeable future at Tompkins Square Park under the Hare Krishna tree every Saturday evening.

On Saturday, August 13, I co-facilitated the first Tompkins Square meeting with David Graeber. I remember both of us being a bit reticent to facilitate, but no one else stepped up to the task. Thus, we began by opening the space for agenda items. This consisted of reportbacks from working groups, announcements, and a discussion around messaging. The Outreach Working Group was eager to begin publicizing for the 17th. We heard from the other various groups. At that time there were the Student contingent, Arts and Culture, Media, Internet, Tactical, and a loosely defined "process group," which later became the Trainings Group. We then began a discussion of demands. *Adbusters* had told us we needed demands, and some people actually wanted them. The democratic socialists in attendance were adamant about having clear messaging and one demand, but these arguments fell on deaf ears. The agenda item was tabled.

Every Saturday, with the exception of August 20 (due to Hurricane Irene), we met under the Hare Krishna tree. On September 3, 2011 the NYC General Assembly consented to the following definition:

> **NYC General Assemblies are an open participatory and horizontally organized process through which we are building the capacity to constitute ourselves in public as autonomous collective forces within and against representative politics, cultural death, and the constant crisis of our times.**

We imagined many assemblies in New York City and beyond.

We decided not to have demands, not to have police liaisons, and not to work within a legal framework. The Tactical Group presented several sites of convergence. We would begin at noon in Bowling Green Park, and then move to the next location at 3PM. The action on the 17th would be an assembly. We would not ask permission. It would be an experiment in direct democracy.

day one

WHEN OCCUPIERS AT Occupy Wall Street refer to "day one" they mean September 17.

It was a strange convergence. About a hundred or so people circled around the bull chanting something about corporate bullshit, the Arts and Culture group held a rally in Bowling Green Park by the American Indian Museum, a performance artist walked down the street in a giant inflatable bubble, and LaRouche members in hooded white robes began singing.

Throughout the afternoon our numbers grew and by 3PM there were close to a thousand people in attendance. We began marching up Broadway to Zuccotti Park chanting, "Whose streets? Our Streets."

The plans were in flux. We had arrived at our second choice destination and needed to determine next steps. David Graeber, Lisa Fithian, Marina Sitrin, Amin Hussein, Mike Andrews, Matt Presto, and I met in the southwest corner of the park as the Trainings Group. We were worried about the size of the crowd and our makeshift megaphone rig wasn't working properly. We decided to use the people's microphone and stepped up to address the crowd. "Mic Check!" We screamed. The crowd responded, "Mic Check!"

The assembly had begun. Everyone sat down and broke out into groups to discuss the world they saw around them and the world they wanted to live in. One by one people shared their stories. Some people had lost their homes. Others were facing mounting credit or student debt. Still others were experiencing police brutality and deportations. Regardless of their backgrounds everyone agreed that Wall Street was the enemy.

We ate together. It was a wonderful meal of peanut butter sandwiches and bananas. Then, at 7PM we convened for a massive assembly. By then the crowd was large enough that one mic check would not suffice. We needed rounds of mic checks, so that everyone could hear. We asked whether or not people wanted to occupy and discussed this for hours before, at around 10PM, reaching consensus to occupy Zuccotti Park. We renamed it Liberty Plaza.

the occupation

MOST OF US did not come to Liberty Plaza prepared for an occupation. We thought the police would come in early on—maybe even the first night. At most we anticipated staying for three or four nights. Armed only with a three-day supply of peanut butter, cardboard, and markers, we began to occupy.

Suddenly, there was a need to make decisions, lots of them. In the first few weeks of the occupation we held two assemblies a day—one at 1PM and another at 7pm. When we chanted, "All day. All week. Occupy Wall Street," we meant it. As the resident facilitator I was called on to help with the assemblies. There were many days in which one assembly bled into the other and I was facilitating for eight hours straight.

At the beginning it was clear that most people had no conception of the consensus process. Thus, on day three of the occupation David Graeber and myself convened the first facilitation working group meeting. There were about a dozen or so in attendance including Andy Smith and "Ketchup," who would both go on to play major roles in the group. We went thru the hand signals first. This seemed like the best place to start for Consensus 101.

Twinkles: Waving your fingers up if you feel good and down if you don't feel good. This allows the facilitator(s) to get a sense of the group. It is not binding.

Point of Process: Making a triangle with both hands to signify a concern about the structure of the conversation.

Point of Information: Relevant and factual information regarding the topic at hand.

We explained that we used progressive stack. This meant that everyone wanting to say something was put on a list and encouraged to wait their turn. Traditionally oppressed groups and those who spoke less often were given more weight and bumped up the stack. We then went thru a formal consensus process including questions, concerns, objections, and blocks. We did not use stand-asides early on. Objections were in place of stand-asides.

We had a bullhorn, but whenever we used it the police would give us trouble, so we decided it was better to just use the people's microphone. Jason Ahmadi had given a training prior to the 17th introducing the practice for use in crowd communication. The people's microphone had been used for this purpose over the course of decades. It was not until occupy, however, that it became a symbol of free expression.

One night, when Matt Presto and I were co-facilitating, Russell Simmons came to the General Assembly. He wanted to be bumped up on stack to give a speech. I told him, "You can get on stack like everyone else."

When I am asked about my experience in the occupation this is a defining moment. For me the assembly was about leveling the playing field. It didn't matter where you came from, how well known you were, or how much money you had. Everyone was equal in the assembly.

the spokescouncil

By October occupy was a global movement. Hundreds of Occupies around the world were holding their own assemblies and using some form of consensus. However, all was not well in Liberty Plaza.

The General Assembly was becoming a form of entertainment. All sorts of people, who weren't involved with working groups and weren't sleeping in the park, started coming to visit. They wanted to see the authentic, original General Assembly in action.

Meanwhile, the original General Assembly, which had been intentionally built, could not withstand the pressures of a constant public and permeable space. Individuals misinterpreted the process to mean that they could say whatever they wanted whenever they wanted. Everyone had a voice to the extent that they didn't prevent others from speaking, but this was difficult to convey. In a body of strangers there was no respect for one another. It became a body ruled by the mob or "ochlocracy."

There was also, of course, the money. By October donations were flowing into OWS coffers. The finance committee estimates that there was on average $10,000 a day in cash donations not to mention online donations. We had over half a million in the bank.

The facilitation group was bombarded by proposals. We didn't ask for them at first, but they were given to us. 2/3 of them were financial proposals. In order to deal with the influx a proposal point committee was established to post proposals on the website and give adequate notice (24 hours in advance).

In short the General Assembly was becoming a bureaucratic, money-allocating machine of the mob. This was completely counter to its original intention.

I began to think about stakeholders. It did not make sense for all those most committed to the movement, who were doing most of the work, to be absent from the decision-making process. It seemed they should be central to it since they were most invested and effected by the outcomes.

Working groups had no need for the assembly anymore. They realized it was far more efficient to work on their own. They wanted to be autonomous and not burdened by the GA. Most working groups were even scheduling regular meetings that conflicted with the General Assemblies.

There was a need for a coordinating and decision-making body for working groups. This would take into account stakeholders and provide accountability and transparency of the work being done. A spokescouncil seemed to be the best model for this particular need.

Enter Brooke Lehman. Before David Graeber left for Austin he introduced me to Brooke Lehman, who had been involved with DAN (Direct Action Network) during the alter-globalization movement. She knew a great deal about process, but was often textbook in her approach. Instead of posing questions she brought answers. Instead of listening to the group as a whole she developed consensus organically in a small group. In a movement founded on inclusivity and transparency, this approach failed miserably.

Brooke and I had many conversations during this period resulting in an open approach toward consensus building. We ushered in the Structure Working Group and decided to pass a proposal in the General Assembly. Thus, the Great Spokescouncil campaign of 2011 began.

The Structure Working Group recruited others to help draft the spokescouncil proposal. Nicole Carty, Sully Ross, Stefan Fink, Ethan Buckner, Annie Desmond Miller, and Tim Ambrose Desmond contributed a great deal as did Suresh Naidu and Adash Daniel. We took the first draft of the proposal to GA in mid October, but it was tabled for further discussion. The following concerns were raised: that the council was a representative system, that it would hold too much power especially the power to make financial decisions, that it would silence those who were most disenfranchised in the movement, and that the difference between operations groups and movement groups was not made clear.

At the time my heart sank. The Structure Working Group met to review the feedback, made amendments, and came back to GA only to be tabled again. We went a third time and were tabled. At this point there seemed to be a need for educational public forums, so that everyone would better understand Spokescouncil and connect it to their immediate needs.

Adash, Suresh, and I sat at 60 Wall Street for a solid week all day every day with a sign that said Structure. One by one people came to us, berated us, and then began to understand what we were doing. We explained that spokescouncils came from indigenous traditions, that they were horizontal, accountable, and empowered caucuses. We explained that the inclusivity of working groups and rotation of spokes ensured that it would not become an elite representative body.

On October 28, the Spokescouncil proposal went to the General Assembly. Adash and I presented the proposal. We gave a compelling argument, answered questions, and it passed by modified consensus. Hundreds of people were in attendance and they began singing, "Get up. Get Down. There's revolution in this town!" This was the high point of Spokescouncil.

the dark days

Two weeks after the Spokescouncil proposal passed we were raided. The NYPD came in with a vengeance—tearing thru tents, beating people with batons, pepperspraying, and clearing every last vestige of the occupation. Hundreds were displaced, scattered throughout the city. Many were housed in churches, but this was a temporary fix, and we had very little in the way of infrastructure. Spokescouncil became a place to work out conflicts after the raid. While this context is important it does not explain the entirety of why spokes failed miserably.

There were fundamental flaws in the execution of spokes. First, there was the membership question. We outlined categories for membership in the Operations Spokescouncil. A group could be an Operations Group or a Caucus, and we gave definitions for both. All other groups were considered "Movement Groups," and, not wanting to hold too much power, the Structure Group left the application process up to the Spokescouncil itself. This created confusion and resentment as groups turned on each other and questioned their commitment to OWS.

Second, there was the relationship of Spokes to GA. In our first draft for spokes we outlined that all financial decisions would be made by spokes and not by the GA. This didn't play well in the GA. People saw it as a power grab. Thus, we watered down the proposal to allow both bodies to make decisions. We thought people would come to spokes because it would be easier than GA and the process would organically unfold. Instead, we created dueling bodies with the same powers.

Third, we did not set Community Agreements or implement an Accountability process early enough in establishing spokes. This should have been first on the agenda. Instead, we became embroiled in a war over membership, which left many casualties.

I attended every meeting of Spokescouncil for the first two months of its short life. I facilitated at least four or five of them. It was an abusive space. Individuals would come with the stated purpose of disrupting meetings and dissolving Spokescouncil. They held the room hostage by couching their criticisms in anti-oppressive language. This was a disservice to the caucuses, which were effectively silenced as a result.

At the same time the General Assembly sank further into chaos. After the eviction assemblies continued to be held in Liberty Plaza, but the space was contested. Often police tried to contain or move the assemblies making it difficult to meet. While the winter was relatively mild for New York, the cold was still a lot to take hours on end. Finally, the GA was moved to 60 Wall on colder nights, but there were private security officers there, which created a new set of tensions. There were so few working group members in attendance that reportbacks were dropped from the agenda. The only people left in the assembly were con artists, informants, and the mentally unstable.

In both Spokescouncil and GA, facilitation teams were verbally and at times physically assaulted. We tried desperately to de-escalate and move forward. Many different individuals and groups tried to reform the structures, but were having little if any success.

open spaces and ows community dialogues

THE FIRST SIGN of resistance came from Open Spaces. A break-off group from Facilitation including Leo Eisenstein, Daniel Thorson, Ambrose Desmond, Annie Desmond Miller, and Kelly McGowan began discussing less structured and fluid approaches to group meetings. They recognized a need for this at the end of November. Kelly McGowan created a Facebook event for December 3 entitled *OWS is Moving Forward Together: An Open Space for Conversation*. The description read the following:

> Since OWS lost its encampment, the Occupiers haven't had a space for deeper discussion and creative reflection together and the 99% haven't been able to witness the full breadth of the movement. This Saturday, OWS activists will be piloting an Open Space gathering to look at what we value, what we've accomplished, and where we are going. This is an open invitation to the 99% to participate. Please invite friends, family or any others who you want in this conversation.

Every other Friday, Open Spaces convened. Kelly, Leo, and others initiated a scheduling grid and people came to post their topics for discussion. Whoever brought the discussion would bottom line, and they would harvest the results thru text or images.

While the GA and Spokes were faltering the Open Spaces meetings were flourishing. In Open Spaces there were no decisions made. Discussions only happened if people wanted them to happen. The container created was flexible.

The downside to open spaces was the lack of continuity. Every meeting was its own space. New topics could arise but they were self-contained. It was difficult to carry a conversation from one meeting to the next. This isn't to say Open Spaces as a philosophy and/or model isn't capable of continuity. In these particular Open Spaces this was not the case.

Lisa Fithian came to town at the end of January. I knew Lisa to be a great pinch hitter and this time was no exception. She flew in, executed a series of trainings, and helped initiate the OWS Community Planning Meeting. Lisa, myself, and other facilitators, drafted a call, which included the following language:

> Dear OWS Family,
>   This is an invitation to caucuses, working groups, affinity groups, and any other member of the OWS community to be a part of a planning brunch for a larger

community-wide discussion on core issues we are all
grappling with. These issues include but are not limited
to:
- Accountability
- Transparency
- Structural and interpersonal dynamics of privilege
- Hierarchies within OWS

The meeting was held on Sunday February 5. Brunch was served, people mingled, and slowly we came together for reflection.

Open Spaces wasn't a decision-making body, and the existing bodies were not functioning. In response to this, many working groups had broken off into affinity groups. Some of these were actually affinity groups in the historical sense and others used the term to veil vanguardist activities including those of political parties, nonprofits, and other interests. In short the movement was becoming less accountable and transparent and collapsing under its own weight. It was time for an intervention.

The planning meeting was part anti-oppression training and part open spaces. We began with a circle. People stepped in if they had power or privilege. This allowed us all to get a sense of who was in the room. From there we identified stakeholders in the various topics, existing projects, and planned to meet again.

There were seven follow-up meetings in what came to be known as the OWS Community Dialogues. Nicole Carty, Tashy Endres, and myself carried them through, stewarding the process. We began with more of a training structure and then broke out into discussions in Spokes, GA, and Open Space format. Our goal in these conversations was to sow the seeds of an intentional horizontal movement. We started first with identifying power, privilege, and access to resources. Then we went on to define resources, which created openings around money in the movement. Hundreds of people participated in these discussions. When asked about resources no one said money. More often than not they said people were our greatest resource.

We rooted the principles of horizontality, inclusion, openness, anti-oppression, and participation in personal experience and grew stronger as a result. Finally, at the end of March we came together for next steps, which included reforming GA and Spokes, a Grievance and Accountability Process, Trainings and Skill Shares, The NYC Movement Assembly (not an assembly but a clearing house model), Project List and Permabank, and the Fun Committee. OWS was starting to feel like a community again.

the coming of spring

THE REFORMING GA and Spokes next step group came away from the Community Dialogues with a clear sense of purpose. We determined that the General Assembly should be an outward facing, discussion-based body, and that it was ill equipped for decision-making. We determined that a Spokescouncil for working groups did not make sense if people were moving away from working groups and into a more inter-disciplinary and project-based practice. We recognized a need to make some collective decisions, but we wanted to be very clear about what these decisions were in order to avoid unnecessary bureaucracy. We were adamant about not making decisions about political statements or declarations (i.e. endorsements). If there were decisions about resource allocation to be made, then we wanted a separate body for this purpose. We also, on the whole, wanted less meetings.

I took on the responsibility of carrying forward the project of reforming GA and Spokes. On March 27, I sent an e-mail to the Facilitation Working Group entitled *What's Next?* It included a brief reportback from the Community Dialogues and then the following:

> Let's shake things up!
> Come to a GA and Spokes meeting!
> Thursday, March 29th
> Union Square
> @5PM
> (meet at the Gandhi statue)
> See you there!
> In solidarity,
> Marisa

Ten days earlier was the six-month anniversary of OWS. An attempted re-occupation of Liberty Plaza had ended in a bloody battle with police. However, a small crew of occupiers made their way to Union Square. They raised an Occupy Wall Street banner in defiance and staged an occupation.

The OWS community had not decided to buy into another occupation. Many, myself included, were against it, but there was potential in Union Square for an open forum. Working groups, affinity groups, and projects were all relocating to Union Square as a soft occupation. Thus, the Facilitation Working Group met at the Gandhi statue.

It was a bit cold to sit outside, so we sought refuge in Barnes & Noble. There, occupying the humor section, we plotted next steps. The existing structures were illegitimate. Reforming GA and Spokes would only reify them.

We needed a revolution.

The difficulty, as in any revolution, was the transition. What would we do with the existing structures? How would we build new ones? When would we destroy and when would we create? We decided to boycott the existing institutions thereby removing our consent while creating new structures. We sought to create flexible containers that would adapt to changing needs.

Jose Martin (also known as Chepe), who contributed to the meeting, drafted a call, which included the following language:

> When we Occupy Wall Street, we build new, temporary structures to fulfill our needs. We construct them as needed, and let them whither away as their purposes end. We don't seek to create new corruptible or abusive institutions that become ritualistic or static, that exist simply for the sake of existing. When there are new needs, there must be new experiments to create space for direct democracy. Where experiments become stale, we prepare to experiment once again.

It is in this spirit that we gathered on April 4, 2012 to assemble anew in Union Square. On the anniversary of the death of Rev. Martin Luther King Jr. we came together to dream. We asked, "What world do we live in?" and "What world do we want to see?" It was a beautiful scene, echoing all the visionary potential of the early days of the assembly. We affirmed our roots and looked toward the future.

revolution

THE STRUCTURES WE created in OWS were far from ideal or permanent. They were susceptible to the same social and political pressures of the society we live in. They replicated patterns of power, privilege, and control over resources. They oppressed us.

In bringing forward new processes and structures I am cautious. I do not pretend to know the answers or impose models, but rather I enter processes humbly in the spirit of questioning. Revolution will never be finished. It is a constant process.

AGREE

UNSURE

DISAGREE

BLOCK

POINT OF PROCESS

POINT OF INFORMATION

I HAVE A QUESTION

WRAP IT UP

Adam Koford
"Untitled"

Andrew Cornell

CONSENSUS
WHAT IT IS, WHAT IT ISN'T, WHERE IT COMES FROM, AND WHERE IT MUST GO

THE WORD "CONSENSUS" MEANS, GENERALLY SPEAKING, THAT ALL PARTIES involved in discussing a topic or making a decision have reached agreement or have come to share the same opinion. Since the 1970s, progressive and radical social movements in the United States (and elsewhere in the world) have developed a range of procedures intended to help participants in movement organizations, campaigns, and counter-institutions arrive at agreement about the direction these initiatives should take. Consensus has been especially useful for smaller groups, efforts dependent only on self-selecting participants, and political projects in which participants share fairly similar key values, visions, and/or levels of experience. Groups of activists who staff infoshops, edit alternative newspapers, and participate in campus-based organizations, to cite a few examples, have honed consensus process to their particular needs, often finding that it serves as an orderly method of interacting and running meetings, which promotes the active engagement of everyone involved in the work. Consensus has also historically served as a useful tool for coordinating large-scale direct actions such as occupations and blockades that depend on the collaboration of committed activists from different parts of the country who may have never before worked with one another.

In the early days of OWS, experienced organizers taught participants many of the procedural elements of consensus, honed through trial and error in earlier campaigns. Elements such as the order in which conversation should flow, the role of a facilitator, and, especially, the use of hand signals to efficiently indicate the opinions and concerns of participants became part and parcel of the nascent movement. Indeed, consensus process seems to have affected OWS in a variety of ways, both positive and negative. Manissa Maharawal, active in the occupation of Zuccotti Park, told *Al-Jazeera*, "If you're going to join Occupy, you have to get on board with horizontal decision-making. In my mind it's the reason why this thing has grown so much. Its structure is what allows it to be something that is fairly inclusive." The fact that everyone who showed up could help set the direction of the movement provided a sense of excitement missing from the highly scripted, pre-planned protest events typical of many unions and progressive organizations. The use of a General Assembly (GA) linked the action to events in Egypt and Spain, while the procedural aspects of consensus (taking stack, terminology like "process point," straw polls, etc.) brought some order to the chaos of thousands of strangers suddenly trying to communicate their political desires with one another. The Zuccotti Park GA, like many others, quickly adopted a 90% threshold of agreement as their standard rather than absolute consensus, leading participants to speak of modified consensus or horizontal decision making.

In statements by participants in occupations throughout the country, consensus operates as one term in a whole chain, or cloud, of associated concepts. This chain includes: participation, empowerment, horizontalism, direct democracy, participatory democracy, community, prefigurative politics, anarchism, and perhaps other terms as well. Because relatively little has been written about consensus and because many learn the term and how to practice it in the excitement and chaos of moments of rapid social movement expansion, the meaning of these concepts are often conflated or their relationship to one another is blurred.

One result of this imprecision is that, today, the left in the United States is once again debating if consensus is a tool (a technique helpful when applied in certain times and places), a primary goal of the left (a central aspect of a better way of organizing social life promoted by the movement), or both. Some thoughtful commentators like David Graeber and Cindy Milstein have made some version of the claim "Consensus is both our ends and our means of struggle." Here consensus functions as a synecdoche—a part rhetorically standing in for a greater whole. In this case, the whole that consensus stands in for is a participatory, egalitarian, self-determining movement, on the one hand, and, on the other, a society with the same characteristics.

But the term consensus has also grown to serve as an antonym to a whole range of social institutions and ways of behaving. Social movement organizations devoted to using consensus are often seen as alternatives to social movement organizations run using "democratic centralist" principles, parliamentary procedure, or those directed in non-transparent ways by anointed or self-appointed individuals. Most commonly, these turn out be traditional Marxist parties, mainstream labor unions, and liberal nonprofit organizations, respectively. The commonality in these widely divergent types of organizations is that a subset of participants make decisions (by whatever method) that a remainder are strongly encouraged or required to follow. Pro-consensus activists have often convincingly connected these organizational features to the difficulties these organizations have had achieving broad transformations in social life, though the drawbacks to consensus and "flat" organizational schemes are less scrutinized.

Consensus process is also seen by many as an alternative to parliamentary procedure and majority-rule voting. Parliamentary procedure (also known as Robert's Rules of Order) is accused of limiting open discussion by allowing procedural manipulation, while majority rule overrides the opinions of sizeable minorities and fosters a competitive mode of political debate. Finally, consensus is sometimes seen as an alternative to bourgeois representative democracy itself. In this case, the fact that everyone involved is encouraged to help make decisions is the quality that ties consensus to "direct democracy"—the process of making collective decisions without delegating power to representatives. Ideals of direct democracy have been especially compelling over the past year, since a central charge of OWS is that, across the board, elected political representatives have been corrupted by the wealthy.

The use of consensus has become a hot-button issue because it goes directly to the questions of "What is the left aiming to achieve?" and "What is the most realistic strategy for achieving this vision?" What looks to some like a minor procedural matter appears to others as a question determining the entire fate of the struggle for social justice. To put it a different way, the consensus process has come to perform deep signifying work (meaning-making) above and beyond the facilitating work that it accomplishes.

For this reason, I believe OWS and future radical movements in the US will be stunted until they better understand and find more common ground regarding consensus.

In order to see how these associations developed, it is useful to review the means by which consensus historically rose to its current place of prominence in US social movements.

where consensus comes from

IT CAN OFTEN seem that consensus doesn't have a history. To some it appears to have emerged whole cloth out of the mind of some brilliant organizer. Those who view consensus as a brand-new solution to age-old problems of democracy often insist that testing it in real life be adopted as a top priority of the movement. To others, consensus can appear as received wisdom, an article of faith—the way the movement has always functioned, and therefore the way it always should. But consensus does have a history, and a relatively finite one at that.

It is not true that anarchists invented consensus. There are no accounts of Errico Malatesta twinkling his fingers to signal agreement with an idea suggested by Peter Kropotkin. However, anarchists have long been concerned with what their political vision implies about how they should structure their movements. And it is equally true that anarchists have been important in the development and popularization of consensus as political tool for more than sixty years.

Perhaps counter-intuitively, the use of consensus in radical political organizations has roots in the religious beliefs and practices of the Society of Friends, better known as Quakers. Quakers believe that God speaks to all believers directly, or exists as an inner light within them, removing the need for clergy to interpret God's will. Traditionally, Quakers worship by sitting together silently until members of the congregation feel moved, ostensibly by God, to share a message with the community. Quakers model their meetings to handle church business and social or political initiatives on this pattern. Participants take turn expressing ideas, and refrain from responding directly to one another or voting to set policy. Instead, discussion continues until there is a sense that all participants share a general agreement about what is to be done, or can at least accept the position of their compatriots. Though this process can be time consuming, Quakers are invested in it because they believe the process of reaching consensus to, in fact, be the practice of divining God's will.

Pacifism and stewardship towards others are fundamental tenets of Quakerism. As such, Society of Friends members pushed for conscientious objector legislation following World War I and were prominently involved in other liberal causes during the interwar years. Impressed by the collaborative and deliberative character of this approach, WWII-era liberal organizations such as the American Friends Service Committee and an early association of intentional communities adopted versions of their consensus-seeking practices (usually stripped of their religious underpinnings). It appears that the first *radical* political organization to adopt consensus as its internal decision making process was Peacemakers, formed in 1948. Peacemakers was an organization dedicated to revolutionary nonviolence that grew out of connections made between religiously motivated pacifists and anarchists imprisoned together for resisting the draft during the WWII, including notable figures such as David Dellinger, Bayard Rustin, George Houser, and David Thoreau Wieck.

Members sought to combat white supremacy, halt nuclear proliferation, and resist US warmongering as the Cold War revved into high gear. Many chose to live in intentional communities based on shared political values as a ballast against the McCarthyist political climate, and as a means of practicing their politics in daily life to the greatest extent that they could. This focus on "being the change one wants to see" and living in communities of like-minded revolutionaries derived in larger measure from Gandhi's influence, but also from a variety of anarchist and utopian socialist traditions.

Rustin and other founding members had been raised in the Quaker faith, and it is likely that they suggested adapting the consensus method to suit their needs. Peacemakers was specifically seeking to develop a new form of political organization that could serve as an alternative to the top-down centralism of the Communist Party and to liberal "membership organizations" that asked members only to pay dues and left day-to-day work to an executive committee or a small paid staff. The group structured itself as a network of small cells that elected a steering committee, but operated autonomously from one another in pursuit of the organization's defined goals. As historian Scott Bennett writes, Peacemakers hoped this experimental form of organization "could challenge and eventually replace centralized, hierarchical institutions." While Peacemakers never grew beyond a few hundred members, those involved helped to relay the ethics of nonviolence and consensus to individuals and organizations at the center of the mid-century movement for African American civil rights, including the Student Nonviolent Coordinating Committee (SNCC).

SNCC developed out of a wave of sit-ins organized by African American college students at segregated lunch counters and other facilities in the US south beginning in 1960. The historian Clayborne Carson explains that early SNCC activists "strongly opposed any hierarchy of authority such as existed in other civil rights organizations." Ella Baker, an experienced organizer who helped found the organization, believed

The use of consensus in radical political organizations has roots in the religious beliefs and practices of the Society of Friends, better known as Quakers.

that the mark of a good leader was his or her ability to share responsibility and develop leadership capacities in others; accordingly she advocated "group-centered leadership." Instead of carrying out a program designed by a few leaders, SNCC members engaged in long discussions in which those not used to speaking up were supported and gently urged to participate alongside the more loquacious. The organization attempted to reach consensus on major programme and strategy decisions—a technique introduced by participants such as James Lawson, who were affiliated with Congress of Racial Equality and influenced by Peacemakers. Talking issues through until they reached a general agreement about methods and expectations helped build the sense of trust and commitment among the group needed to engage in the potentially deadly work of trying to break the back of Jim Crow in the Deep South.

The sociologist Francesca Polletta claims this way of operating also accrued to SNCC a "developmental benefit." That is, people who previously had little experience speaking publicly or developing strategy gained skills and confidence through their active engagement in the group's inner workings. As SNCC shifted its energies from direct action against segregation to organizing poor black men and women to register to vote, staff members such as Bob Moses sought ways to extend the process of perpetual leadership development beyond the organization itself to all the people who SNCC staff members worked with in their voter registration efforts. In this way, SNCC developed in its day-to-day organizing work an ideal of local, grassroots democracy that demanded ordinary people be able to make the decisions that affect their lives. By 1964, leadership in SNCC shifted toward organizers who, influenced by national liberation movements in Africa and other formerly colonized areas, claimed the need for a more centralized form of organization.

In its early years, SNCC served as an important model for many of the white, middle-class northern college students who formed Students for a Democracy Society (SDS) in the early 1960s. In its famous founding document, *The Port Huron Statement*, SDS enunciated the concept of "participatory democracy" as the goal it sought to achieve, loosely defining the concept as "people having a say in the decisions that affect their lives." (Some added later, "in proportion to the degree that those decisions impact them.")

Beginning in the late 1960s, radical feminists launched a critique of male domination and male leadership styles in the civil rights and anti-war movements. Women involved in consciousness-raising groups, especially, suggested the possibility of non-hierarchical and "leaderless" organizations, which could make use of consensus. Though some participants famously noted that unofficial, and therefore less accountable leaders, typically emerged in such situations, the concept of leaderless movements (rather than SNCC's "group-centered leadership") found traction especially in movements where counter-cultural/prefigurative lifestyle and community was deemed an important aspect of movement strategy.

Another important conduit of consensus in the 1970s was Movement for a New Society (MNS). MNS grew out of a radical Quaker organization and took inspiration from the nonviolent revolutionaries of the 1940s. Many members had been active in the civil rights movement and New Left, and they again sought new organizational forms, which could balance movement-building activities with personal development initiatives. MNS attempted to combine organizing campaigns that made use of nonviolent direct action with the development of counter-institutions and intentional communities in which members could "live the revolution now."

MNS helped make consensus a defining feature of the radical anti-nuclear campaign of the 1970s and 1980s. In 1976, more than 1400 people were arrested for occupying the site of a proposed nuclear power plant near the town of Seabrook, New Hampshire. MNS trained participants in the consensus method and in what they called the "small-to-large group decision making method"—what later became known as the "spokescouncil" model of coordinating affinity groups and working groups. Jailed for more than a week in a set of open armories, the arrestees were able to convene daily and make decisions as a group using consensus. Their successful collaboration built an intense sense of community among the participants in a manner similar to that experienced by many of those camping together during OWS. This experience of joyful cohabitation in medium-sized groups successfully coordinated through consensus has created a sense among some participants that pursuing such forms of community can, in itself, have a transformative impact on the wider world—as a model of a better way of living. This was, and remains a claim that has not been demonstrated historically. MNS trained activists throughout the world on how to use the consensus method in short workshops and through publications such as *The Resource Guide for a Living Revolution*, affectionately known as the "Monster Manual."

Food Not Bombs grew out of the anti-nuclear movement in 1980 and became a vital conduit of consensus within anti-authoritarian circles over the next three decades. It adopted a decentralized network structure and the use of consensus, growing to hundreds of local chapters throughout the world. Food Not Bombs cofounder C.T. Butler helped systematize the process in publications such as *Conflict and Consensus*. Food Not Bombs' popularity with anarchists strengthened associations between consensus and anarchism during the same years that anarchist theorist Murray Bookchin was conceptualizing the possibility of more direct forms of democracy at the city-wide level. Earth First! and other radical environmental organizations likewise began to rely on consensus in the 1980s and 1990s.

Earth First! treesitters and veterans of the anti-nuke movement worked together in 1999 to organize the infamous demonstrations and direct actions that shut down the World Trade Organization meeting in Seattle and fired up the alter-globalization movement of the early 2000s. The Seattle demonstrations uneasily united activists based in the US nonviolent direct action tradition with those taking cues from European autonomous movements that tactically valued property destruction and confronting police forces. One result was that after Seattle, anarchists and sympathizers placed heavy emphasis on the use of consensus in organizing protests while also insisting that other activists endorse the use of a "diversity of tactics," which often included political rioting. It could be argued that this represents a corruption of the ideal of consensus, in that the goal of reaching and sticking to agreement on which tactics will best benefit the movement is abandoned.

In the series of mass actions and local organizing campaigns that came to be known as the Global Justice movement of the early 2000s, a common intra-movement criticism was that the new wave of protest felt inhospitable to many activists of color or unintentionally excluded them in a variety of ways. Some authors noted that white and non-white radicals and progressives frequently participated in (and built an identity from) social movement cultures based on different norms, including the significance placed on the consensus process. As that movement began to wane, a variety of participants debated ways in which a process meant to be inclusive might have served to distance potential allies from each other, and what discussions or compromises might instead cement those alliances. Though these issues were never fully resolved, the criticism seems to have become muted as horizontal forms of organizing (sometimes including the use of consensus) began to spread to additional sectors and institutions of the left, such as the committee organizing the US Social Forum, likely influenced by the "horizontalism" exhibited by movements of the Global South and incorporated into the structure of the World Social Forums.

Reviewing this admittedly partial, and only partially-digested history, we can begin to see how the use of consensus grew throughout the second half of the twentieth century, and how the significance attributed to it changed as it was taken up by different groups. For Quakers, consensus was a technique used amongst a bounded community of belief as a means for discerning revealed truth. Peacemakers linked the practice to the search for new organizational forms that could bolster radical efforts in a conservative period and to Gandhi's insistence on social justice movements setting a high moral standard and living in line with their beliefs. SNCC used consensus to critique forms of leadership that in some ways reproduced dynamics the movement was struggling against. They found using consensus could increase group solidarity and help members develop political skills. SDS announced participatory democracy as a political ideal and long-term movement goal, while expressing support for SNCC's style of organizing, perhaps implying a causal link between participatory movement structures and social order they sought to achieve. In MNS and sections of the women's liberation and anti-nuke movements, consensus again became associated with building counter-cultural communities and lifestyles. Participants hotly debated whether incubating progressive values in such communities was transformative or retreatist. Food Not Bombs linked consensus with the contemporary anarchist movement and presented it as a norm for a generation of antiauthoritarian radicals at a time when other sectors of the left were weak. The Seattle demonstrations, and the global justice movement that arose in their wake, served to unfasten consensus from its nonviolent moorings. In OWS, consensus has melded with the process of mass general assemblies of citizens and has become intimately associated with a faith in the new terminology of prefigurative politics. It is important to recognize that over the course of these seventy years, in some quarters, the belief that means and ends be in accordance has been transformed from a moral responsibility, to an empirical argument about what tactics generate the best results, to a mystical faith that following the proper means guarantees the desired ends.

Understanding this history gives us access to the lessons previous generations

To avoid some of the muddled strategic thinking that often accompanies an introduction to consensus, organizers must stop teaching consensus in a way that entrances activists into thinking that the quality of their inter-movement conversations are alluring enough to revolutionize society by weight of example.

of activists have derived from their experiments with consensus. To conclude, I will enumerate a few such lessons—primarily those derived from MNS, the consensus-based organization I am most familiar with.

what consensus must become

IF WE ARE to win more victories for humanity, we need to articulate a clear and compelling vision of a better way of organizing our lives together. We also need to unite the disparate fragments of the left as it exists today and learn how to attract and maintain the involvement of millions of people not currently involved in our movements. To do this we need to develop more complex and realistic views of what consensus can and can't do. We need to de-fetishize it, so that we stop attributing powers and significance to it that have never been demonstrated in the actual practice of social movements.

It is noteworthy that the term "consensus" has come to refer both to the ideal or value of reaching near agreement or acceptance amongst movement or organization participants, a set of practices for structuring discussions and fielding proposals amongst diverse bodies of people, and an assumption that groups should seek to accommodate the beliefs or satisfy the desires of each member. We might distinguish these as an ethic of agreement, an ethic of participation, and an ethic of non-conflictual decision-making. Differentiating between them allows us to judge the efficacy and importance of each ethic on its own merits and try to test how functional each is in establishing democratic procedures that tend to result in more egalitarian outcomes. In doing so, we should note that democratic procedures for social movements and for societies-at-large will be different from one another, since more political agreement is bound to exist between comrades on the same side in a social struggle than is likely to exist amongst an entire, diverse polity. Being more realistic about consensus and about the much larger concept of direct democracy also means developing a multi-faceted idea of freedom that includes the ability to participate in decisions that affect one's own life as well as the freedom to spend one's limited amount of time doing things besides laboring to arrive at collective decisions.

To avoid some of the muddled strategic thinking that often accompanies an introduction to consensus, organizers must stop teaching consensus in a way that entrances activists into thinking that the quality of their inter-movement conversations are alluring enough to revolutionize society by weight of example. Concretely, this means that they need to use and teach additional methods for making decisions in political work and help less-experienced activists determine when each are most useful. Proponents of "direct democracy" need to define what this means in much more concrete terms, acknowledging the complexity of determining popular will in contemporary societies. Some good starting points for this exist in the work of proponents of "deliberative democracy," communitarian political philosophers, and the ideas about radical democracy propounded by Cornelius Castoriadis, Chantal Mouffe, Enrique Dussell, and others.

OWS has directly and publicly raised the question as to whether our elite-dominated system of representative politics can make good on the political and social promises embedded in the concept of democracy. Participants and their philosophically-minded allies now have to clarify their ideas about what a more deeply democratic society will look like, but they also have to build a strategic, tactically and organizationally-flexible movement that can improve the lives of millions of people, proving in concrete terms—not just in theory—what it means to satisfy everyone's needs.

Manissa McCleave Maharawal
So Real It Hurts

On a Thursday night in late September 2011, I went to the General Assembly of Occupy Wall Street with some South Asian friends. That night the General Assembly was discussing and passing the "Declaration of Occupy Wall Street," which we were handed a working draft of when we got there. The night before, I'd heard the Declaration read aloud at the General Assembly and turned to my friend, Sonny, after noting a line that had hit me in the stomach: "As one people, formerly divided by the color of our skin, gender, sexual orientation, religion, or lack thereof, political party and cultural background…" Initially we'd shrugged it off as a rhetorical flourish. But now we realized this was about to become *the* declaration of the movement, a document sent out to the world as defining the purpose of the occupation. The proposed text ignored people from countries that have been colonized, communities right here in New York where democratic participation is anything but a given, as well as countless histories of oppression and inequality. This was not something I could get behind. But I couldn't walk away from the document, or from this movement, either.

So our radical South Asian contingent stood up. My friend Hena addressed the crowd of hundreds with our concern, and we were told to send an email that could deal with it later. Hena persisted, and again the facilitators at the General Assembly tried to bypass our grievance and push it off until later. They warned us that to "block" the Declaration was a serious act. We knew it was a serious act. And that is why we did it.

It is intense to speak in front of hundreds of people, but it is even more intense to speak in front of hundreds of people with whom you feel aligned—and to say something to them that they don't necessarily want to hear. We told the General Assembly that we wanted a small change made to the language, but that this change represented a larger ethical concern. To erase a history of oppression in this founding document, we said, was not something that we could let happen. We proposed that they cut out the offending line, and after a few minutes of debate, the Assembly accepted our proposal. Task accomplished, we withdrew our block. My friend Sonny looked me in the eye and said, "You did good," words I truly needed to hear at that moment.

After the assembly concluded, we spoke with some of the people who had written the document to re-write the line and to explain why we thought it needed to be re-written. Let me tell you what it feels like as a woman of color to stand in front of a white man and explain privilege to him: It *hurts*. It makes you tired. Sometimes it makes you want to cry. Sometimes it is exhilarating. Every single time it is hard. Every single time, I get angry that I have to do this; that this is my job, that it shouldn't be my job. Every single time, I am proud of myself that I've been able to say these things because it took hard work to be able to and because some days I just don't want to.

In that small circle following the assembly we offered a crash course on white privilege, structural racism, and oppression. We did a course on history and the declaration of independence and colonialism and slavery. It was real. It was hard. It hurt. But people listened. Sitting there on a street corner in the Financial District at 11:30 at night, talking with twenty people, mostly white men, it all felt worth it. Explaining the way that women of color like me experience the world—and the power relations, inequalities and oppressions that govern that world—felt for me like a victory ... and like a victory not only for myself and others who feel the way I do, but a victory for the movement. As I biked home that night over the Brooklyn Bridge, the world seemed somehow, just a little bit more, in that moment, to be mine. It seemed somehow like a world that could be all of ours.

Clayton Conn
October 4, 2011
Occupy Baltimore Day of Encampment

Manissa McCleave Maharawal

REFLECTIONS FROM THE PEOPLE OF COLOR CAUCUS AT OCCUPY WALL STREET

During the past nine months, the months since Occupy entered my life, time has operated differently. It has sped up and then slowed down again, stretching and changing its rhythm. The movement has changed too, sometimes at a seemingly frenetic pace. I am often asked where the movement is now in terms of issues of inclusiveness, and dynamics of race and gender, but the truth is that I'm never sure how to answer this question because "the movement" is not a single thing and because the answer to this question, of course, looks different depending on who you ask and who they have been working with. And, of course, these dynamics have shifted and continue to shift as the movement shifts. What I *can* say is that as the movement has changed, I have changed too. Through my experiences organizing and working with Occupy, and in particular the People of Color caucus at Occupy Wall Street, I have experienced some of the steepest learning curves in my life. In what follows, I will try to distill some of the content of these learning curves by reflecting on the People of Color caucus.

The very first time I visited Occupy Wall Street, before I was intimately involved, one of the things I did when I entered the park was observe how many other visibly non-white people there were (more than I thought), and then start asking around about whether or not there was any sort of POC space/working group/meeting, or just some sort of informal gathering or group of people. This wasn't because I don't work with white people or because I don't like them or because I like to be divisive and exclusionary, but simply because I was looking for a way to plug into the movement and potentially find people who think similar things as I do about racial justice, oppression, and the need for safe spaces to discuss these dynamics.

I was looking for something like this because I have found these spaces to be extremely important at various times in my life, whether they have been formal spaces or groups, or just informal gatherings. In fact as I write this piece, I sit in the Women of Color office at my university; here my friend K sits across from me and works on her proposal, and I am surrounded by colorful posters from various social movements (including Occupy), pictures of Frida Khalo, flowered tapestries, and books by Zora Neale Hurston, Grace Lee Boggs, Ruth Wilson Gilmore, and Frantz Fanon, to name a handful. Academia is still overwhelmingly dominated by white men and this office is often a refuge from that reality, a reality in which I, and other women of color in the academy, are too often confronted with the ways we have to work harder to legitimate ourselves, our writing, our work, and our experiences. In some ways, this was the sort of space I was looking for at Occupy, a space where, in the midst of the hustle and bustle of that park when it was "occupied," in the midst of the inspiring work that was going on there, I could come together with other people who identify as people of color and talk about our experiences in the movement, talk about the ways being a person of color impacts our organizing and political consciousness, and talk about how to organize around these issues together. Very simply, a place where we could come together and work together.

After the night my friends and I blocked the Declaration [see "So Real it Hurts," above], creating this space seemed all the more urgent because it had suddenly become painfully clear to me that Occupy had yet to build an analysis around race and its impact *within* the movement. And as many people have said before me: movements that pretend racism doesn't exist, that ignore oppression, that deny homophobia, sexism, and ableism, these movements not only alienate people, but ultimately do not succeed, as they fail to articulate a vision of social justice. Occupy Wall Street needed to take these issues on not only in order to succeed, but also to achieve its goal of serving as a model or a pre-figuration of the world it wanted—through caring for each other, through horizontal organization, through creating a space for everyone's voice to be equally heard and respected. OWS absolutely *needed* to prefigure a world in which oppression within the movement, as well as racial justice as connected to economic justice outside of the movement, was an integral part of the analysis.

It was with all of this swirling around in my mind—the need for such a space along with the need for a larger analysis around race, power, and privilege—that I and others started the People of Color working group. We didn't know what the space would be like, we didn't know what it would exactly look like, we didn't know who would come, if anyone would come, or if people would be interested. We knew that some people within Occupy were nervous about starting a POC group, that at the General Assembly where we became a working group, people had questions around the inclusivity of such a group, that the working groups at Occupy were all open and that this didn't fit into that ethos. But many others understood the necessity of having a POC group and supported us in starting it.

On a Sunday afternoon in mid-October, the second meeting of the POC working group was held underneath the red sculpture on the southeast corner of the park. I was late that day, and when I got there I was surprised to see over a hundred people. I could barely see the facilitators through the crowd, but I heard my friend Thanu in the center of the circle taking stack. I can't even really remember what was discussed at that meeting. Perhaps it was at this meeting that we started the different working groups of the larger POC space, working groups that mirrored the working groups of Occupy, or perhaps we discussed whether or not the group should be exclusively for people of color, or perhaps we discussed structure and meeting times. Yet while I don't remember what was exactly discussed, I do vividly remember what it felt like to be standing in a meeting with over a hundred other people of color inspired by Occupy who were also interested in carving out a space in which to work seriously on issues of race within the movement. I remember feeling that this was an important step: that a POC space was vital for people of color who were unsure about Occupy and where they fit in, or how they could engage in a movement that was, for the most part, white.

After that second meeting, much of my time organizing within Occupy became about organizing through the POC working group and caucus as part of its Structure and Process sub-group.

Movements that pretend racism doesn't exist, that ignore oppression, that deny homophobia, sexism, and ableism, these movements not only alienate people, but ultimately do not succeed, as they fail to articulate a vision of social justice.

This meant that I sent emails about the meetings, typed up minutes, or facilitated meetings, along with the other members of Structure and Process. Doing this work meant that I often felt really inwardly focused—that is focused on the inner workings of one working group within Occupy rather than focused on the larger social justice goals of Occupy.

In looking back on this experience, I have begun to distill some important lessons which I will take forward with me into future organizing spaces. The first lesson is that the inwardly-focused work on the structure and logistical coordination of the group needs to be shared and distributed as evenly as possible. I believe that it is only through such sharing that a sustainable collectivity can be created. Not only does sharing responsibilities like facilitating, emailing, building agendas for meetings, etc. make for a more equitable division of labor, it also can serve as an antidote to the tendency for those who do this labor to be seen as the *de facto* "leaders" of the group. A more equitable sharing of such work also allows all members of the group to contribute to a movement in multiple ways, instead of creating a structure where some participants spend almost all of their time on the nitty-gritty of keeping the group going. And a more equitable sharing of this work is particularly important in POC spaces because of the identity politics inherent within them. Because we exist in a world in which racialized and gendered divisions of labor are integral to maintaining capitalism and its oppressions, any group that is attempting to challenge capitalism must also challenge these hierarchies and ensure that they are not re-creating them. As people of color working together, we need to make sure that we don't also recreate these divisions and oppressions amongst ourselves.

A second set of lessons and experiences that I have been grappling with are, broadly, the issues of identity and difference as they played out within the caucus. POC spaces are, of course, spaces that are about identity politics, which is to say, the politics of who you are (and how you define yourself) and the way that affects your social politics. In the POC caucus at Occupy, there were many of us from a variety of different racial, ethnic, and immigrant backgrounds: we were black, brown, mixed, some of us passed as white, we were straight and queer and trans, and we were of different religions from Christian to Muslim to Sikh to Jewish. We were of different economic backgrounds, of different educational levels, of different immigration statuses, of different genders. In this respect, all that we had in common was one very general aspect of our identity—that of not identifying as white—and one very general manifestation of oppression—how not identifying as white (or more often being identified as white) meant that we experienced racism in one of its ugly manifestations. This was, in many ways, what brought us together—this was also, in other ways, what caused some of the largest problems within the caucus and arguably what precipitated its eventual collapse.

And, our meetings reflected this. Often they became spaces for us to share our experiences of racism within the movement as well as outside of it. We shared the ways that this racism affected our organizing, our politics, and our lives. But just because we all identified and came together as people of color in that space, it never meant that we agreed on or shared the same political positions. Often it was precisely our differences of race and class and gender and sexual orientation that became the fault lines along which our politics frayed, and sadly we didn't always know how to take these issues on. Sometimes these differences led to misunderstandings, resentments, and disagreements that we didn't always have the skills to deal with. And because the POC caucus was so inwardly focused, these differences were increasingly highlighted.

This was a steep learning curve for me. I had worked and organized within many POC spaces before, but never one as challenging as at Occupy. The caucus really did reflect something of the complexity of what Occupy Wall Street was and is: a movement that attracted many different people with many different sets of politics and sets of issues that they believed in fighting for. This was part of the beauty of Occupy: it was not just a movement against corporate greed, but one that connected a myriad of issues, and in so doing, gave so many people a way to plug in. This was also what led to a variety of tensions within Occupy: in connecting so many people there were bound to be massive differences of opinion between us.

My experiences of racism as a mixed-Indian woman who has a white mother and an Indian father is related to the racism that a black man experiences in New York City, but they are not the same.... This does not mean that we can not build together; on the contrary, it is necessary that we do, and I truly believe that we are stronger when we can. But it is critical that these differences be respected, acknowledged, and overtly taken up within the self-understanding of the group.

These tensions were also at the heart of Occupy's rallying cry, chanted over and over again on the streets: "We are the 99%!" It was a cry that empowered people, but also potentially and perilously erased important differences. The POC caucus was an attempt to take on this erasure and make some of our differences visible. In this way, I stand by its importance and necessity, despite the fact that in actual practice, I don't think we were prepared or knew how to take on our own differences of race and class and gender within the caucus.

As I've tried to think through this in the past months, I have thought about how we could have been better organized and how we could have better addressed these differences. I don't have a perfect answer to these questions, but I have a few ideas. The first of these is fairly self-evident: we must be constantly aware that oppression is not experienced the same way by everyone. My experiences of racism as a mixed-Indian woman who has a white mother and an Indian father is related to the racism that a black man experiences in New York City, but they are not the same. I have not been stopped and frisked, and while my brother and father have, while they have been detained while trying to board planes, and while they have been called terrorists, these sets of oppressions are different than the systematic disenfranchisement and racism that black men in New York City face daily. This does not mean that we cannot build together; on the contrary, it is necessary that we do, and I truly believe that we are stronger when we can. But it is critical that these differences be respected, acknowledged, and overtly taken up within the self-understanding of the group. I also strongly believe that people of color spaces, groups, and communities need to be aware that racism and oppression can still occur within these spaces—that unless we work very hard and explicitly to not re-create racism or sexism or homophobia or ableism, we run the risk of falling into the same societal traps we seek to overcome. I also believe that our organizing always needs to be intersectional: we need to be aware of and own our differences of class and gender and race along with our similarities. This is the important and intensive *internal* work that such spaces require.

Another lesson I learned was that this internal work cannot be all of what we do. The work of making sure that we don't re-create racism and other sets of oppressions is paramount, and the creation of a POC space where we can talk about and organize around these experiences is also necessary and fundamentally important. But in order to truly build power together, we must also always be connecting our internal work to larger external projects. At Occupy Wall Street, this meant connecting the movement's analysis of Wall Street and economic injustice to questions of racial injustice. Our job was to put forward an analysis that made it clear that economic justice is not possible without racial justice, and to push for a racial justice framework to become a core part of the movement's organizing tools. This is the important and intensive *external* work that the POC caucus pursued with varying degrees of success and failure.

In this way, the POC caucus was fighting on three levels: (1) we were taking on various sets of oppressions and racisms within Occupy Wall Street (e.g. through organizing a variety of anti-oppression and structural racism workshops and teach-ins); (2) we were taking on the ways that these oppressions were also manifested within the caucus itself; and (3) we were trying to connect the economic crisis and Occupy Wall Street's response to the crisis to an analysis of structural racism and an understanding that it has been communities of color that have been disproportionately affected by the economic crisis.

This work was exhausting but also some of the most valuable work I have ever done. It was valuable both on a personal level, and, I believe, on a movement level. Building the POC caucus, even if it was at times a difficult and politically-challenging space, was absolutely necessary. The issues that the POC caucus raised are fundamental ones: they are questions of difference and how, as Audre Lorde challenges us, these differences can be more than merely tolerated, but also productive. For a movement like Occupy to survive, for any large-scale popular movement to grow, we can't be scared of taking on these differences. Instead we need to exist together in, as Angela Davis said in her October 15 address to Occupy in Washington Square, a "complex unity" in which there is space for us to learn and build together.

Luther Blissett
November 20, 2011
NYC

Max Rameau

OCCUPY TO LIBERATE
OCCUPATION, LAND LIBERATION, AND EVICTION DEFENSE

THE LAST FEW YEARS HAVE BEEN HARD FOR US: RECORD FORECLOSURES, high unemployment, drastic cuts in social services, and government actively doing the bidding of big business at the expense of regular people.

With a combination of bewilderment and frustration, concerned global citizens had asked one question over and again: when and where are people in the US going to rise up and take to the streets?

Turns out, the answer was September 17, 2011 on Wall Street.

Of course, for all its simplicity and elegance, that answer is not entirely accurate. Communities of color, albeit in smaller numbers and with less media, have taken to the streets for years around issues of police brutality and the impacts of the economic crisis, particularly gentrification, foreclosures, and evictions.

Since 2007, the Take Back the Land movement has identified vacant government-owned and foreclosed homes and "liberated" them by breaking in and transforming vacant houses into homes for families. Our objective is to transform land relationships to secure community control over land and elevate housing to the level of a human right. With the crisis deepening, many more organizations are liberating land or waging eviction defenses with increased success.

This one grand crisis, then, has elicited two very different responses, each strong and each relevant to its core constituency. With the combination of low-income communities of color and working- and middle-class whites taking to the streets, this society is on the cusp of a major social movement, the likes of which have not been experienced in the US in more than a generation.

Far from homogeneous, this budding movement is evolving towards parallel, but interrelated campaign tracks: #Occupy and Liberate. The two look similar in many regards, but are distinguished by three important characteristics: composition, primary frame, and target/base.

1. Composition: #Occupy has mobilized mainly, though not exclusively, disaffected young and impacted working- and middle-class whites. Liberate is mainly low- and middle-income people of color.

2. Primary Frame: #Occupy's primary frame is the economic system and the injustice it produces. Liberate frames issues in terms of land control and use (such as housing, farming, and public space).

3. Target/Base: #Occupy targets those symbols, institutions and persons responsible for perpetrating the economic crisis—the 1%—through the "occupation" of public and private spaces, most notably New York's financial district, the Oakland seaport, and individual bank branches. Liberate's base are the victims of the crisis, who are protected via land liberation and eviction defense.

Social movements are not single celled creatures on a linear path, but dynamic complex organisms with multiple moving parts, each responsible for a different series of tasks. Such a division of labor must be understood, appreciated, and fully embraced. This movement is a complex organism with two tracks, and each track performs unique and critical functions.

Two intractable images of the housing crisis include the banks responsible for this financial mess and the homes from which families are evicted. This movement must take the fight to the banks, protesting and occupying them on their turf. Those same banks are occupying our communities, neighborhoods, and homes. We must end that occupation through Liberation and eviction defense. The crisis simply cannot be resolved by choosing to fight on either one front or the other.

Not only must we both #Occupy and Liberate, but the chances of success for one track increases exponentially with the actual success of the other. Therefore, the Occupy/Liberate dichotomy is not an antagonistic one; it is complementary.

We must occupy the 1% and liberate the 99%.

That is not the job of one organization, but the mission of everyone's movement.

There is growing awareness of the two tracks, their characteristics, strengths, and limitations. As we struggle to properly understand and define this relationship, we must resist the tendency towards two competing orientations:

The first tendency is to examine both tracks, note their size, frames, and composition and conclude that each track actually represents its own separate and unique movement essentially unrelated to the other. The second, and polar opposite, tendency is to remark the similarities in approach and tactics and conclude the tracks are effectively identical and must be merged into a singular monolithic track. Both tendencies are wrong.

We must take care not to expect large numbers of Blacks, Latinos, indigenous, and other oppressed nationalities or immigrants, each with particular historic relationships to the police, to "occupy" banks and financial institutions. In fact, it is not clear that #Occupy could have succeeded if first executed by people of color. We must also resist the temptation to allow 1,000 young white kids to "occupy" historically people of color communities that are still reeling from the more onerous occupation of gentrification. At the same time, we must find creative, effective, and empowering ways to work together through parallel, supportive, and even joint actions and campaigns.

While engaging the dual tracks in parallel actions is a prerequisite to building a holistic and powerful movement, it is not sufficient to guarantee trust and success. Two sets of actions, even during the same time frame and in the same city, will not result in an instant movement.

Forging these dual tracks into a cohesive movement with mutually supportive actions requires at least three basic understandings:

1. Basis of unity: Why are we fighting and what are we fighting for? Do we want the same things or are we just doing the same thing in order to get to different places? What is the basis of our unity?

2. Framework of unity: How are we working together? How are decisions made? What do we do when one track disagrees with the other?

3. Next steps: What are we doing next? How can we move this movement forward?

We must Occupy to Liberate!

SOLIDARITY IN PRACTICE
FOR THE STREET
DEMONSTRATIONS

WE ARE VERY DIFFERENT GROUPS. WE ARE NOT NECESSARILY immediate allies nor are we each other's greatest enemy. There are many things on which we do not agree. But, we will be in the streets together to protest this war. We know that the police and media are trying to divide us in order to crush our movements. Solidarity is the way in which our diversity becomes our strength, we build our movements and we protect each others' bodies, lives and rights.

We believe we have some things in common. We believe in basic human rights and the need to live with respect and dignity. We believe we must protect this planet—our air, water, earth and food or we will all die. We believe these global corporate and political institutions are serving only the interests of the rich. We all agree it's time for fundamental and radical change.

As we take to the streets together, let us work to be in solidarity with one another. The following suggestions offer ways in which we can make our solidarity real.

personal

- Challenge and critique other groups and individuals in constructive ways and in a spirit of respect.
- Listen without getting defensive. Be open in thinking, not rigid in positions.
- Don't make assumptions no matter what a person looks like or what groups they belong to.
- Don't assume tactics are the only way to measure militancy or radicalness.
- Refrain from personal attacks, even with people whom strongly disagree. (Focus on how you feel, not what they did.)
- Understand that even though we may disagree we have come to our politics, strategies and choice of tactics through thoughtful and intelligent consideration of issues, circumstances and experiences.

street

- Do not intentionally put people at risk who have not chosen it.
- Do not turn people over to the police.
- Do not let people within our own groups interfere with other groups.
- Respect the work of all medics, legal observers, independent media people.
- Share food, water, medical and other supplies.
- Support everyone who is hurt, gassed, shot or beaten.
- Respect other groups' rights to do a certain type of protest at certain times and places. If you choose to participate, do so within the tone and tactics they set. If you do not agree, do not participate in that protest or bring another protest into that time and space.
- Understand that our actions and tactics have repercussions that go beyond ourselves and our immediate groups. And that some tactics overrun the space of others.
- If you choose to negotiate with the police, never do so for other groups to which you are not a part

media

- Do not denounce other demonstrators.
- Talk about your strategy, not others.
- Acknowledge other groups' existence and role they play in creating change.
- Acknowledge that we sometimes disagree about strategy and tactics.
- Avoid using the word violence.
- Condemn police repression and brutality.
- Share media contacts and do not monopolize the media's attention.

jail solidarity:

- No one is free until everybody is free.

—the RANT Collective

Paul Dalton

Occupy is facing something of an identity crisis. Fractious debates over tactics and goals have laid bare fundamental differences between the three components of Occupy—radicals, progressives, and the "discontented 99%."

Occupy's success comes from joining these groups together, each bringing something of its own to the table: Progressives bring political and economic resources. Radicals add the emphasis on direct action and direct democratic process. The discontented 99% bring numbers to the street and, most importantly, social relevance.

As the heady early days have faded into the reality of police oppression, participant burnout, and internecine conflict, a fractured and unsure movement faces the question of how to go forward. This is where fissures between the three camps show most clearly.

This is quite apparent around confrontational tactics and violence. Doctrinaire nonviolence folks contend loudly that any aggressive tactics, including property destruction and confrontation with the police, reduce Occupy's relevance. This is rooted in the faulty assumption that violence and confrontation inherently alienate people. Hogwash. People do not universally reject violence, although progressives and liberals generally do. Violence in Egypt, Libya, and Syria has not reduced support for those struggles. The Black Panthers entering the California legislature armed certainly drew more new supporters than it lost older ones. When people claim violence will alienate people from Occupy, they are right, but only partly so.

The question is: who are we alienating, and who are we attracting? Tactics like prayer vigils, street theater, pickets, flyering, boycotts, and marches—all can and do alienate some people. They also attract others.

Part of the problem is that so many radicals were once liberals and/or progressives. Moreover, we tend to work together as part of the same larger movements, and often share social and cultural attitudes and interests.

But sharing political and social milieus leads to the almost reflexive belief that winning liberals and progressives over to radicalism is the key to growing a relevant and powerful movement. As much sense as this seems to make, it is both fundamentally flawed and hugely problematic. Radicals should be oriented toward the discontented 99%—those with a shared outrage over economic inequality, but who don't readily associate with political activism. The radical left should care less about what Whole Foods shoppers think and more about what Walmart shoppers do.

"Diversity of Tactics" is not a cover for violence—it is a necessary framework for attracting and building a movement capable of challenging power. I am not asserting black blocs, Molotovs, and rock throwing will draw the masses to Occupy. It will draw some and repel others. I, for one, am more interested in attracting people willing to directly, aggressively challenge the cops and the State than those who think enlightenment, ecstatic dancing, and clever signs will save the world.

Occupy is already a success. If it is to sustain itself, it will need to grow deeper roots with poor, working class, and people of color communities—the discontented 99%. Progressives and liberals will come around eventually. Even if they don't, it isn't much of a loss. As a rule they make poor allies—they undermine, split, and control whenever possible.

I believe we have much more potential goodwill in the world than we think. We should aim to build from this deep reservoir of discontent. A strong, effective, street based direct action movement—one that strategically embraces aggressive and even violent tactics—has as much potential to capture the imagination and support of the Discontented 99% as does a movement that lionizes Gandhi and vilifies glass breakers.

THIS IS CLASS WAR

just wi baby

Margaret Killjoy
November 2, 2011
Oakland General Strike

Emily Brissette and Mike King

OVERCOMING INTERNAL PACIFICATION
THE UNCOMPROMISING FAITH OF FANATICISM

This chapter is dedicated to the late Joel Olson. A true inspiration and missed comrade, who not only theorized fanaticism, but embodied it in everything he did.

STRUGGLES FOR SOCIAL CHANGE ARE STRUGGLES NOT JUST AGAINST CONtemporary configurations of power or modes of distribution and exploitation, but also against their internalization: against the internalized and debilitating belief in the naturalness and permanence of the existing order and the way that it shapes the categories through which we apprehend the world and understand ourselves as subjects. It is in confronting and shaking loose these internalizations that we emerge personally and collectively transformed. This is not an easy process.

The Occupy movement today is challenging the political and economic inequalities engendered by late capitalism/neoliberalism and its spawn: financial speculation, home foreclosures as dispossession, and austerity measures fraying the remnants of the meager social rights of generations past. But this challenge has been uneven, varying significantly in the degree to which it seeks a radical transformation of the status quo or hopes only to check some of its more egregious excesses. Although accused for months of lacking demands, Occupy Wall Street and the broader movement have never lacked for proposals, put forth by people who earnestly see themselves as part of the movement. Some of these proposals have been for modest changes: new financial regulations, greater oversight, progressive taxation. And many who see themselves as part of the movement put their faith in electoral politics, ballot initiatives, and petitions to effect these changes. But the movement has also had a strong and vibrant radical dimension that has privileged direct action and mutual aid—blockades, strikes, and home reclamations alongside the communalization of care and nourishment—in its struggle for a more profound transformation of the conditions shaping our lives.

We need to be wary of drawing too stark a line here between radicals and liberals. Radicals may be less invested in the status quo, but *all* of us have work to do to confront the way our thinking is shaped by the dictates of power, using its categories, its preoccupations, its terms to define the terrain of struggle, assess the value of various strategies, or determine how we relate to one another. At our best, we are all still in a dialogue with the terms of the existing order; we are not wholly autonomous, selecting our slogans, our analyses, our dreams in an unconstrained way. Everything we do is conditioned and informed by the situation we find ourselves in. Which is in part to say: social control is not simply something imposed on us but something that becomes so naturalized that we impose it on ourselves. We all come to the movement from different places, with different lived experiences and different personal and political identities. What we share is the internalized baggage of having been raised in a culture marked by hierarchy, exploitation and domination, oppressions and privileges, individualism, competitiveness, and so on. This shapes us and our movement in varying ways and to varying degrees, often unconsciously, affecting our desires, imagination, and sense of possibility. We call the various conscious and unconscious ways we internalize systems of power that seek to dominate us—and so become desiring agents of our own subjugation—internal pacification. Internal pacification constrains and limits our ability to be radical and to imagine radical social change. It frustrates our relationships and muffles our desires, and even though we may say that another world is possible, we often have a hard time believing that to be true.

To understand internal pacification requires a sense of the forms in which it is expressed. We offer three examples of different forms that internal pacification can take. These do not exhaust the possible ways internal pacification can manifest itself, but they are forms that we have seen and experienced in Occupy Oakland. We offer these, and our accompanying analysis, as an opportunity for reflection in the hopes that by being aware of the problem we can all individually and collectively subject these tendencies to critique. Being open and willing to confront our assumptions and affective responses, to stop and question why we feel as we do, why we experience fear, discomfort, and anxiety, enables us to critically engage the way we apprehend the world, cognitively, morally, and emotionally—and to begin to sharpen our responses, to wield them more effectively as tools—and weapons—of social transformation.

becoming an agent of the state

IN THE FILM *The Matrix*, the people who remain plugged into the dream world cannot think beyond the terms imposed by the existing order and are invested in its preservation despite their exploitation and dehumanization. If the existing order is threatened, if anything out of the ordinary should occur to disturb or disrupt expectations, any one of them can morph into an agent, an enforcer of the status quo. This is not simply science fiction, but a metaphor for our own lives. We see a similar dynamic play out within and around struggles for social change, with the agents often appearing first as elected officials, journalists, and others with substantial privilege within the existing order. But just as in the film, sometimes "ordinary" people with only marginal privileges can become impassioned defenders of the status quo as well.

One of the ways in which this has occurred within the Occupy movement can be seen in responses to acts or stances deemed to be "violent." The state has a clear interest in defining a wide range of behaviors—anything that is disruptive or potentially threatening of entrenched power and exploitation—as violence. This includes blockades (Mayor Quan called the shutdown of the Port of Oakland "economic violence" and others in City Council called it "domestic terrorism"); essentially defensive—but visually provocative—measures such as carrying shields and wearing helmets; and, of course, property destruction. As we have written elsewhere, and as many within Occupy Oakland or larger radical circles would argue, equating property destruction with violence partakes in the state and capital's definition of the situation, privileging property over human life, the latter of which is routinely subject to various forms of harm by the current capitalist order. In a just and humanist view of the world, the definition of violence would be restricted to that which causes harm to people and other living things. It would include home foreclosures and evictions that create insecurity/precariousness around the basic human need for shelter; it would include food deserts, polluted neighborhoods, closed schools, shuttered libraries, reduced bus service and escalating bus fares, profit-driven health care; and it would include the more overt forms of violence in war, incarceration, and police brutality.

That many continue to see (corporate) property destruction as a form of violence is understandable, given the extent to which the capitalist sanctification of property and its concomitant dehumanization of people suffuses our common sense. This common sense found expression in proposal after proposal brought before Occupy Oakland's General Assembly advocating the adoption of principles of nonviolence and the repudiation of property destruction and other "violent" tactics, and in less formal discussions about the putative need to create an internal police force or to actively collaborate with the police in identifying and prosecuting the "violent" elements thought to be marring the movement. All of these proposals were soundly rejected at Occupy Oakland, but have been more common elsewhere around the country.

But this common sense did not just present itself to a democratic process of deliberation, where it could be rejected after often heated debate; it also found expression in acts of vigilantism. For example, on November 2, 2011, during the General Strike called and organized by Occupy Oakland, an anti-capitalist march targeted bank windows and greeted a Whole Foods store with ten-foot high lettering spelling out the word "strike" on the side of the building. In the midst of this, some within the march morphed into agents, seeking to vigorously defend the sanctity of corporate property (they would say they were protecting the movement) by tackling, brandishing chairs and sticks at, or unmasking and photographing those thought to be involved in the graffiti and property destruction.

In other cases, rejecting the divisiveness inherent in isolating and targeting those deemed "violent," and therefore other, was enough to provoke a vigilante reaction. One such case occurred on the night of October 25. Hundreds of people gathered in downtown Oakland that night in an attempt to reclaim Oscar Grant Plaza, the site of the encampment which had been raided in the wee-hours that morning. They were met by several hundred police in riot gear—OPD plus reinforcements from seventeen other police agencies—and volley after volley of tear gas, CS gas, flash bang grenades, and rubber bullets. It was during one of these rounds that Marine veteran Scott Olsen was hit in the head with a tear gas canister at close range, resulting in a significant brain injury. For hours the people faced off against the police, dispersing in the face of a barrage of weaponry, only to reassemble minutes later.

In the midst of all the smoke and gas, some in the crowd tried to appeal to the police. One older white man with a megaphone, standing next to members of the media and in front of the police line, just feet from where Scott Olsen had been critically wounded earlier, talked to the police about how we are all on the same side and that they are part of the 99% too. When a group of youth started to throw plastic bottles at the police, who were clad in full riot gear, megaphone man shifted to protest cop, declaring, "This is a peaceful movement. Violent people are not part of this movement," and pointing in the direction from which the plastic bottles had come. At this point, one of authors (Mike) intervened, shouting the man down and telling him that he was doing the cops' work and dividing the movement. A group of people moved in to encircle Mike while he was told by a young white man: "We are making a citizen's arrest." The group attempted to grab his wrists and arms, but he managed to pull free and walk away. In this moment, shouting down megaphone man—obstructing one of the peace police in carrying out his self-appointed duty—was construed as an act of violence, so threatening that it elicited a perverse reaction. This is internal pacification on a power-trip, the morphing of self-avowed "peaceful protesters" into agents of order, a peoples' militia for the police State.

protection racketeering

SOCIOLOGIST CHARLES TILLY once likened the state to organized crime, arguing that the state runs a protection racket by offering to protect people from a threat that it creates.[1] This offer of protection from real or imagined threats becomes a key justification for the state's prerogative power, its "legitimate" arbitrary rule, its monopoly on violence. In some origin stories, the state emerges from the threat of roving warrior bands and its mirrored response, the promise of patriarchal protection. As Wendy Brown and other feminists have argued, this promise of protection is fundamentally masculinist, entrenching patriarchal power in the name of securing those deemed weak and vulnerable, incapable of defending themselves or acting on their own behalf.[2] This offer of protection is simultaneously an imposition, seeking to elicit compliance while denying the protected the subjectivity and capacity to deliberate, consent, or act in any meaningful way. As with the Mafia, it also contains an implicit threat: accept this protection and its associated costs—or else. Those seen to be outside the protection of some constituted authority become vulnerable to attack, not primarily because the threat from which they ostensibly need protection is credible, but because they might delegitimate the protector through the example of their refusal.

We reproduce this logic of state power within our movements and our relations with one another whenever we seek to protect others—whether from police violence and state repression or from perceived threats from "infiltrators," "agents provocateurs," and other "violent" elements. A paternalistic claim of protection has been a recurrent presence within Occupy Oakland, and while it has been challenged and checked at (nearly) every turn, it remains an issue and a tendency to be confronted. The logic of protection has been invoked during the debates on each of the nonviolence proposals ("we have to create a safe space for women and children and the elderly to come participate"), in some of the labor solidarity work #OO has been involved in ("we have to march on the sidewalk because there are

---

1   Tilly, Charles. 1985. "War Making and State Making as Organized Crime." Pp. 169–186 in *Bringing the State Back In*, edited by Peter Evans, Dietrich Rueschemeyer, and Theda Skocpol. Cambridge: Cambridge University Press.

2   Brown, Wendy. 1992. "Finding the Man in the State," *Feminist Studies* 18(1):7–34; Young, Iris Marion. 2003. "The Logic of Masculinist Protection: Reflections on the Current Security State," *Signs* 29(1): 1–25.

undocumented workers here and this is what our permit says"), and most egregiously and explosively in the efforts of a small group from the media committee to smear an Arab-American member of #OO (simultaneously) as a terrorist and police infiltrator. Whatever motivations may have been behind this move, the justification they gave to the GA was that they did it to protect the movement.

At the heart of each of the incidents is a denial of others' subjectivity and agency, dressed up as benevolence and heartfelt concern. It may well be that in each case, those claiming to protect others truly believed they were acting with the best of intentions, in good faith. At the same time, they reproduced the fundamental logic of state power in their relations with others in the movement, constituting themselves as an authority (or seeking to constitute that authority in the GA) to protect others thought to be incapable of speaking or acting on their own behalf. They reproduced the logic of naturalized racial and gender hierarchies and a long history of benevolent paternalism, of knowing what's best for others and erasing their standing as active subjects in the process. In these moments, as in the examples of megaphone man and the militia kids above, there is an odd mix of entitlement and subservience embedded in the same actions. There is a sense of entitlement in the claim to know what's right and best for others. Indeed, some were so sure of the justice of their position that they willingly became vigilantes: seeking to detain, arrest, or expose the perceived threat, in some cases with physical force and in others behind the veneer of objective journalism, all ostensibly in order to protect the young movement from itself.

But in effect these efforts serve only to protect the existing order from a potentially disruptive and ungovernable challenge. And in this sense they exemplify a subservience, born of the internalization of an often unacknowledged belief in the naturalness of the existing order. None of the liberal militia-kids ever thought to place the police under "citizen's arrest," if only rhetorically. The police and their social role are naturalized like water or air—or in this case chemical gas-filled air; there is a internalized belief among many in the legitimate function of the police ("to *protect* and serve") that engenders a sense of deference and obedience and an erasure of one's own capacities for action. The other examples also display an internalization of norms and discourses associated with the existing order we seek to transform, internalizations which mitigate or contain agency. We see traces of the idea of the white man's burden to act on behalf of poor people of color exemplified in claims to protect undocumented immigrants; of masculinist protection dressed in pseudo-feminist clothing in calls to repudiate militancy so as to make actions safe for women and children to participate; and of statist discourses of threat, and statist forms of profiling, in the invocation and appellation of terrorism. When we invoke any of these ideas we reproduce claims to hierarchical forms of power among one another, we reproduce elements of the existing order that will frustrate and contain our efforts at transformation. All of this needs to be made plain and subject to sustained reflection and critique. Recognizing the ways our thought and actions continue to be informed by pernicious and unacknowledged forces is a necessary first, and continual, step in freeing our imaginations to envision a transformed world and in freeing our energies to act.

fencing the imagination

> If a society is identical with its structures—an amusing hypothesis—then yes, desire threatens its very being. It is therefore of vital importance for a society to repress desire, and even find something more efficient than repression, so that repression, hierarchy, exploitation and servitude are themselves desired.
> —Gilles Deleuze & Félix Guattari, *Anti-Oedipus*

WHAT WE HAVE been calling internal pacification throughout this piece involves both an acquiescence to and identification with power, as well as a disciplining of our desires and imaginations so that we come to want our exploitation, dehumanization, and repression. We learn to behave and to find gratification and satisfaction in doing so. We grow to be properly disciplined subjects, our common sense and affective responses determined by power. We learn to see the world through the lens of capital's prerequisites and the state's claim to secure order, and we move through the world accordingly, displaying the appropriate forms of behavior. We conform to expectations, comply with official requests and demands, and thus constrain and contain our own capacities for action. Hannah Arendt defines action as the setting into motion something new, as the momentary and spontaneous instantiation of freedom, always and only in community with others. Radically at odds with behaving, acting disrupts the inertia of existing processes, breaks the still surface of social reproduction and ripples out and through social relations, unleashing transformative potential. Action is inherently unpredictable, its ultimate reach unforeseeable and for that reason uncontainable. In the process of struggling for social change, our disciplined selves can begin to break down, we can begin to awaken, to question, to take risks—to act. But our disciplining runs deep, and precisely because acting invites the unknown, it can elicit fear, uncertainty, or hesitation among people long accustomed to behaving.

We saw this in the wake of the first raid on the encampment, when the city erected a simple, 6-foot-high chain link fence around the grassy part of Oscar Grant Plaza to deter us from re-occupying it. The night after OPD's tear-gassing of downtown, people returned for a General Assembly and found that the only open space at the plaza was the concrete amphitheater directly in front of City Hall, a space too small to accommodate the crowd of two thousand. In order for a democratic mass meeting to occur, one where everyone could assemble, listen, and participate, the fence would have to be confronted—and not just the physical fence preventing the congregation from assembling as one, but the fence in the minds of many there. The physical fence represented a claim by city authorities to the space, and although there were no police in sight to enforce the claim, and no posted order on the fence itself, the presence of the fence was enough to evoke a disciplined, and disciplining, response.

As a small group of us opened a hole in the fence, a larger group of people grabbed the fence away from us and closed it back up, fencing us in, as an even larger crowd of people looked on. Some in the crowd yelled at us, labeling our actions "violent" and "typical male behavior," calling us "vanguardist" and "agents provocateurs" for attempting to re-occupy a public park with a group of people who were there, ostensibly, to do one thing—occupy that same park. The General Assembly met for a full hour, with well over a thousand people cut off, unable to hear announcements and proposals, unable to participate in discussion, because at that moment there was more respect for a metal fence than for democratic assembly. One of the handful of us fenced in started to chant "Off the Pig ... in your head! Tear down the fence." Eventually several small groups tore down the fence from different vantage points and those previously cut off from the General Assembly poured in to fill the entire park.

Before the fence was successfully torn down, the vast majority of people assembling that night understood the message fences convey—"keep out," "no trespassing"—and *behaved* accordingly. Whether they unthinkingly accepted the fence's presence or actively feared police reprisal or hesitated before the unknown that might be unleashed with its removal, many were willing to accede to the city's (ultimately weak and unenforced) claim to manage and corral dissent and struggle. That people assembled that night as Occupy Oakland were willing to grant legitimacy, however tacitly, to the forces that oppose us, and to their real and metaphorical fences, is indicative of how deeply disciplined we are. But we can take heart from this example as well: the fences eventually came down that night and something powerful was set in motion, as nearly two thousand people deliberated and voted on a call for a General Strike. Over the course of the next week many put in countless hours of work and were joined on November 2 by more than 30,000 others to celebrate the Oakland Commune and to shut down the Port of Oakland.

embracing revolutionary zealotry

> The living, vital truth of social and economic well-being will become a reality only through the zeal, courage, the non-compromising determination of intelligent minorities, and not through the mass.
>
> —Emma Goldman

WE INTERPRET THE quote above not as a slight against "the mass," but as an honest and realistic evaluation of how revolutions are made. There are two possible readings here, one loosely defined as vanguardist, the other radically democratic. One could read this to suggest that the mass is inherently reactionary and that the revolution will be made by a small group of militant insurrectionists; this was the stance taken by the Weathermen. While we have a great deal of admiration for the Weather Underground and see many positive lessons to be learned from them, we find this premise ultimately short-sighted and nihilistic. We think Emma meant something different: that revolutions are made by revolutionaries, people who are uncompromising and clear on what needs to be done, eschewing what we might call pragmatism in the zealous pursuit of their vision. This is not to say that the broader public is unimportant or incidental to the struggle; for a radical democratic movement it is central. Social revolutions are made by significant portions of a population, but the groundwork and framework for struggle is laid by revolutionaries. The distinction between the vanguardist and radical democratic approaches hinges largely on the question of building a constituency. Revolutionaries need their vision to resonate with and to mobilize millions of people; they need to reach beyond their own groupings and translate their radical politics in a way that people can respond to. The obvious question is: how?

In order to address how we in the movement should relate to the broader public, we must distinguish between that nebulous and ever-manipulable creature called "public opinion" and the public as a collection of human beings, largely disciplined and constrained, but full of hopes and dreams—and a potential capacity for action. We should not let public opinion, largely constructed by the structures we seek to abolish, determine the limits of our vision or the tactics and strategies through which we seek to realize that vision. Public opinion, real or imagined, serves as another form of internal pacification when we defer to it, when we seek to be as broadly appealing as possible so as to secure a favorable public image. Seeking to avoid offense is an inherently conservative position. But its opposite, writing off the public as reactionary and thereby absolving oneself of having to engage a broader audience, is an equally untenable position. What both of these very different orientations share is a fundamental lack of faith that the average person can be won over to radical politics. The liberal believes such a process impossible, the insurrectionist leaves it up to unlikely chance.

A third option lies in the history of radicals who deliberately set out to annihilate the existing order by building or transforming mass movements into mass revolutionary movements. The radicals we have in mind here combined an unwavering and ruthless critique of the existing society with a particular way of engaging the broader public that transformed their radical critique into an immanent revolutionary threat. John Brown and many other Abolitionists, Mother Jones and the early Wobblies, Malcolm X and the later Black Power movement all share this unique combination of qualities. Joel Olson, in an interview with AK Press, describes their revolutionary relentlessness as fanaticism, zealotry, extremism.[3] The negative connotation these words typically have in our language is indicative of the broader social order in which our language is situated and a political culture where pragmatism, moderation, centrism, compromise, and (dare we say) consensus have been cardinal virtues. Truly effective radical zealots not only held to their principles unwaveringly, often losing their lives in the struggle, but did so in a way that redefined the terms of the debate. They created a revolutionary pole in opposition to the status quo and embraced a polarizing approach, seeking to hollow out the middle by drawing clear lines and forcing people to choose sides. According to Olson, the fanatic: 1) refuses to compromise on basic principles; 2) divides the world into friends and enemies; 3) puts pressure on the moderate middle; 4) tries to build a constituency; 5) engages in legal and illegal direct action; and 6) seeks to build a new cultural hegemony or common sense.

Fanaticism is thus a conscious political praxis that seeks popular support but does not waver or compromise in trying to achieve it. Exemplary fanatics from our radical past used plain and direct language to make explicit the various hypocrisies of the existing order in a way that made any "middle ground" completely unintelligible or fraudulent. Simple, radical demands can redefine the goals of a movement while exposing the hypocrisy of the enemy, forcing those on the fence to choose sides and clarifying the terrain of struggle, what is to be done, and why. The Wobblies' direct action around free speech, filling jails with soapboxers, exposed the hypocrisy of the liberal State in crowded public places, radicalizing cities and towns as they went. Malcolm X's use of plain, blunt language, his relentless critique of the hypocrisy of American "freedom," and his lack of fear helped to transform the nature of the Civil Rights movement—centering decolonization and self-determination in the movement—upon which the Black Panthers and

---

3 http://www.revolutionbythebook.akpress.org/radically-democratic-extremism-an-interview-with-joel-olson/. See also: 2007. "The Freshness of Fanaticism: The Abolitionist Defense of Zealotry." *Perspectives on Politics* 5(4): 685–701.

others would build after his death. The Panthers' 10-Point Program was both a reasonable set of demands that fit squarely within America's promise of "life, liberty, and the pursuit of happiness" and an inherently revolutionary statement, laying bare the duplicity of that promise which was never intended by the founders to apply to people of African descent. The lesson to be drawn from these examples is to think, speak, and organize in such a way that makes internal pacification visible, subjects it to radical critique, and develops revolutionary consciousness in its place, not just for a minority of militants, but for the movement as a whole and beyond.

Radicals in Oakland envision a new world, a complete transformation of the existing order. We are deliberately not just tinkering around on the margins of the existing system, suggesting new regulations or working on behalf of a candidate. We are working towards something not-yet-seen, an unknown that can be frightening or just unimaginable for people. Part of the struggle is to make that radical vision imaginable, so that people can come to see themselves in the picture and to join the struggle for its realization. This requires that we engage the public in a meaningful way, seeking to draw people out and into the movement, into a deeper commitment to radical transformation. But we shouldn't try to appeal to the public as a mass or seek to curry favor with public opinion; we need to engage people as individuals and in human terms. The existing order makes its own enemies on a million fronts each day. Revolutionaries need to reflect peoples' capacity to act politically, outside of the bounds of what has been deemed acceptable. Our goal is to harness that reality, painting a portrait of the existing order in terms that make its destruction not only desirable, but necessary, justified, imperative—not just for the already-initiated but for millions and millions of people. Reflexively confronting internal pacification is a fundamental step in this process. As radicals, we must confront our lack of faith both in "the mass," in its various manifestations, and in ourselves and our capacities, for this lack of faith thwarts our ability to become the fanatics we must be in order to win.

Coco Curranski
November 17, 2011
New York City

Kristian Williams

COPS AND THE 99%

THE FIRST WEEKS OF THE OCCUPY MOVEMENT WERE PUNCTUATED BY TWO incidents of police violence which, thanks to video, received widespread public attention.

On September 24, 2011, in New York City, Deputy Inspector Anthony Bologna gratuitously peppersprayed nonviolent Occupy Wall Street protesters whom police had trapped in a "kettle"—plastic net barriers used to contain crowds.[1] A month later and a continent away, on October 25 in Oakland, California, cops fired tear gas at Occupy protesters, hitting Iraq war veteran Scott Olsen in the face and severely injuring him. They then attacked the medics who rushed to Olsen's aid.[2]

These are only the most famous in a long series of similar incidents. In November, *Alternet* ran a perverse sort of "top ten" list, collecting images of unprovoked police attacks against Occupy, not only in New York and Oakland (the most visible centers of Occupy activity), but also Portland, Seattle, Davis, and Denver. They show cops using fists, clubs, tear gas, pepperspray, and concussion grenades against people who are peacefully seated, people who have gone limp, people who are simply walking away, and, as mentioned above, against people who have been trapped in police "kettles" and medics trying to treat the injured. They show police indiscriminately attacking crowds, using violence against very young people and against very old people—including 84-year-old retired school teacher (and self-described "all-around troublemaker") Dorli Rainey.[3] Keep in mind that the list only

---

1 Jim Dwyer, "A Spray Like a Punch in the Face," *New York Times*, September 28, 2011.

2 Adam Gabbatt, "Scott Olsen Injuries Prompt Review as Occupy Oakland Protests Continue," *Guardian.co.uk*, October 26, 2011.

3 Joshua Holland, "Caught on Camera: 10 Shockingly Violent Police Assaults on Occupy Protesters," *Alternet.org*, November 18, 2011. "Troublemaker" quote from [Dorli Rainey], "About the Old Lady," *Old Lady in Combat Boots*, 2009. http://www.oldladyincombatboots.com/?page_id=2.

represents the most circulated images, and that it was compiled in mid-November of that year, just two months into the movement.

The police attacks are interesting, in part because the Occupy movement has been overwhelmingly peaceful, and in part because elements within it have pushed a slogan that "Police are part of the 99%."[4] Yet, in city after city, the cops responded to the peaceful encampments with violence.

And that is, of course, exactly what we should have expected.

To understand why, we need to look beyond slogans about the 99% and examine the role of the police in our society, which requires in turn some understanding of the way our society is organized.

percentages and classes

THE 99% TROPE makes for clever propaganda, but analytically it is nearly useless.

For one thing, 99% is merely a kind of metaphor to identify the aims of the Occupy movement—whatever they are—with the interests of the vast majority. It is just another way of saying "the people" or "the masses."

In fact, the 1% we've been hearing about so much lately only controls 34.6% of the country's wealth. I say "only" because the top 10% control 73.1%. The top 20% control 85%.[5]

But the numbers are largely beside the point. To understand social and economic inequality we need to think not only in terms of *percentages*, but in terms of *classes*.

One percent or ten percent, the point is that at the top of our economic pyramid there is a group of people whose only function is to accumulate vast quantities of wealth—that's called *profit*. They then use that profit to determine how resources will be allocated. As one might expect, some of that money goes toward making more money. That productive wealth is called *capital*; the people who control it are called *capitalists*; and this system, taken as a whole, is called *capitalism*.

---

4   See, for example: Jeremy Kessler, "The Police and the 99%," *N+1* (npluso-nemag.com), October 10, 2011. For images of protest signs on the theme, see: "Sometimes We Need a Reminder," *OccupyPolice.org*, January 20, 2012, http://www.occupypolice.org/2012/01/20/sometimes-we-need-a-reminder-ows-oc-cupypolice-ocpo-solidarity-occupy-policearethe99too-vision/.

Early in 2012, I was amused to see a "We are the 99%" lawn sign by the employee entrance (and smoking area) of an office that the Portland Community College Department of Public Safety shares with the Portland Police Bureau.

5   Dave Gilson and Carolyn Perot, "It's the Inequality, Stupid!" *Mother Jones*, March/April 2011. http://motherjones.com/politics/2011/02/income-inequal-ity-in-america-chart-graph; and E.D. Kain, "We Are the 80%, Not the 99%," *Forbes.com*, October 11, 2012.

Now the capitalists, as we've seen, are the minority. The rest of us—the overwhelming majority, whether or not it is exactly 99%—have to rent ourselves out to the capitalists. This rent—our wages—is usually at a set rate and, since the aim of the capitalists is to make money, it is almost always far less than the wealth that we actually produce.

If the capitalists are good at what they do, then we workers make a little, and they take the rest. If they're bad at it, then they start to lose money, and since the whole idea is to make money, they close up shop and we lose our jobs. Or—as has been happening lately—the government just gives the capitalists money and maybe (but only maybe) we keep our jobs.[6]

Now, if this all sounds like an enormous scam—well, you've got the right idea.

cops and capitalism

So WHAT DOES that have to do with the cops?

The role of the police, at its most basic, is to keep this system of extortion in place, and in particular, to keep it in place by using surveillance and violence to control those portions of the population most likely to cause it trouble. In other words, to control workers and poor people and—since the US is stratified by race as well as class—people of color in particular.

This goes back to the very origin of policing. The modern institution of the police force, as I argue in *Our Enemies in Blue*, evolved from an earlier type of organization called the slave patrols. These slave patrols were militia-based groups charged with keeping slaves on the plantations and, just as importantly, preventing revolts. Over the course of decades, the slave patrols gradually became professionalized and acquired additional responsibilities, transitioning just after the American Revolution into a body easily recognizable as a modern police force.[7]

---

6   PNC Financial, for example, received $7.58 billion as part of the Troubled Asset Relief Program, and then laid off 5,800 workers. PNC's CEO, James Rohr, was paid $14.8 million that year. Likewise, American Express received a more modest $3.39 billion, and laid off 4,000 employees while CEO Kenneth Chenault earned $16.8 million. Sarah Anderson, *et al. CEO Pay and the Great Recession: 17th Annual Executive Compensation Survey* (Washington, DC: Institute for Policy Studies, September 1, 2010) 8.

7   This essay's argument about the history and function of policing summarizes the more detailed account from my book: Kristian Williams, *Our Enemies in Blue: Police and Power in America* (Cambridge, Massachusetts: South End Press, 2007). The discussion concerning the origins of American policing can be found on pages 36–50.

This dual social function—preserving racial and class inequality—is a much better indicator of what the police are going to do than are either the law or concerns about public safety. That function has remained remarkably stable over the two centuries since the institution emerged, even as laws have changed. For example, in terms of day to day policing, police enforced pass laws to prevent slaves from traveling, enforced legal segregation in the days of Jim Crow, and now—in an era of legal equality—they still engage in racial profiling, which has the effect of limiting the mobility of people of color and restricting their access to resources.[8] Similarly in the nineteenth century, the cops enforced vagrancy laws, and today—without having to change their behavior in the least—they enforce laws against sleeping on the sidewalk, trespassing under bridges, and panhandling.

It is no surprise, then, that collective action intended to address these social inequalities is met with police repression. The cops, historically, have been the enemies of both the labor movement and the civil rights movement. They've attacked picket lines, broken up demonstrations, raided offices, tapped phones, opened mail, sent informants and agents provocateurs into organizations, jailed organizers, and assassinated leaders.

That's the job. That's what they do. Why should we expect any different?

police work and police unions

WELL, THE TRUTH is that some people did expect different—or at least they hoped for something better. That was the impulse behind the slogan about police being "part of the 99%."

An uncharitable person might note that this mistake points to the vacuity of the "99%" idea. However, one does also have to admit that, by some measures, the police may qualify as working class: they tend to come from working-class families, they work for wages, have low social status, and are organized in unions. All of that—plus, perhaps, the short-lived support some cops showed for labor demonstrations in Wisconsin early in 2011[9]— may have led some in Occupy to expect that the cops would be on our side.

What these rather optimistic observers failed to recognize, apparently, is the fact that the cops' job, in large part, is to monitor and control the working population. As I argued in *Our Enemies in Blue*, that leaves them

---

The authoritative source on the slave patrols is: Sally E. Hadden, *Slave Patrols: Law and Violence in Virginia and the Carolinas* (Cambridge, Massachusetts: Harvard University Press, 2001).

8   David A. Harris, *Profiles in Injustice: Why Racial Profiling Cannot Work* (New York: The New Press, 2002) 98–9 and 102–5.

9   Kristian Williams, "Cops for Labor?" *Dollars and Sense*, Sept/Oct 2011.

in something of an ambivalent class position.[10] Patrol officers may stand at the bottom of their institutional hierarchy, but their profession, taken as a whole, has to be considered part of the managerial apparatus of capitalism. Wherever their personal sympathies may lie, their institutional role makes them the representatives and guardians of the interests of the capitalists. And curiously, the police union is one of the mechanisms that has developed to ensure they remain reliable in that role.

Just as police work is not like other work, police unions are not like other unions. Following World War II, as cops began to show an interest in collective bargaining and other municipal employees gained the right to organize, police commanders very cannily opened an avenue that would simultaneously allow for negotiation and avoid the dangers of police joining a broader labor alliance. Police administrators started allowing, encouraging, or in some cases creating police-only unions.

From the perspective of the local authorities, these police unions had several advantages: they institutionalized negotiations, which allowed conflict within the police department to be resolved through legalistic, routinized means. Further, separate unions meant that the police could be always treated as a special case during budget planning and contract talks, granting them pay, benefits, and pensions far better than those of other government workers. Police unions organized the cops *as cops* rather than as workers, encouraging an identification with the police institution as a whole and cementing a kind of vertical solidarity. And for all these reasons, police unions allowed local governments to keep the police in reserve, away from the main body of the labor movement, and ready to act against striking workers.

The implication is that, while some cops may offer signs of support—from a word of encouragement to a refusal to fire their tear gas—these actions should be appreciated for what they are: individual expressions of sympathy, or small acts of resistance. Their source will likely be the conscience of the officer, and the police union will usually not be the vehicle through which it finds expression. We should encourage this sort of dissent within the ranks, and, should the need arise, support whistle-blowers or cops who refuse to perform riot duty.[11] But we should not kid ourselves about the ultimate significance of such acts, or their potential to blossom into mutiny. Most of these gestures are exactly that—*gestures*. They may mean something, but they don't necessarily do very much to change the situation. On the other hand, an abundance of sympathy for the

---

10 Williams, *Our Enemies in Blue*, 137–8. The analysis of police unions follows, on pages 138–143.

11 For a chronology of cops—mostly, former cops—speaking out in favor of the Occupy protests and criticizing the police attacks against them, visit: http://OccupyPolice.org.

police may have real consequences, not only in terms of discouraging militant resistance, but also in alienating people of color and anyone else who has good reason to mistrust people who try to align with the cops.

My rather cynical take on the issue is this: to the degree that the cops identify with the workers, *good*. To the degree that the workers identify with the cops, *bad*.

crowd control: escalated force and negotiated management

I SAID EARLIER that we should have expected the police assault, but that's not to say that I *did* expect it. What I expected instead was that the first, mostly symbolic, fairly non-confrontational Occupations would be ignored—or face, at worst, pre-negotiated, symbolic arrests—and therefore fade away owing to a combination of winter weather, strategic directionlessness, general boredom, and a growing sense of futility.[12]

Instead the cops decided to pour gasoline on what was initially a very small flame. Detective Bologna single-handedly pushed Occupy Wall Street into the headlines,[13] and suddenly Occupy was transformed from an ignorable constellation of tent cities into a political force that politicians had to grapple with.[14] Police violence, in other words, made Occupy a political problem.

That surprised me. Partly it surprised me because it seemed shortsighted, but mostly it surprised me because I thought the police had learned this lesson.

During the Civil Rights and Vietnam War period, police generally responded to demonstrations with extremes of violence—not just arrests and

12 It seems I wasn't alone in this assumption. See, for example: E.D. Kain, "How Not to Respond to a Peaceful Protest," *Forbes.com*, October 26, 2011.

13 Nate Silver used a database of 4,000 news outlets to track reporting on Occupy Wall Street in the period from September 17 to October 7, 2011. He found that "coverage was all but nonexistent" until the pepperspray incident of September 24. "The next day, the volume of news coverage increased to … about six times its previous rate." And it continued to increase with each subsequent confrontation. "[The] volume of news coverage has tended to grow in a punctuated way rather than a smooth and linear fashion … [and] coverage has remained at something of a new equilibrium after each of the incidents, rather than falling back to its previous levels…". Nate Silver, "Police Clashes Spur Coverage of Wall Street Protests," *Five Thirty Eight*, October 7, 2011. http://fivethirtyeight.blogs. nytimes.com/2011/10/07/police-clashes-spur-coverage-of-wall-street-protests/.

14 Dylan Scott, "Mayors Opt for Balanced Response to Occupy Protests," *Governing.com*, October 28, 2011. The protests also shifted the national debate: Esmé E. Deprez and Catherine Dodge, "Occupy Wall Street Protests Inject Income Inequality into Political Debate," *Bloomberg.com*, November 9, 2011.

billy clubs, but fire hoses, police dogs, and sometimes live ammunition. The violence did not surprise civil rights activists; it was, in fact, part of the plan. Their strategy relied on revealing the brutality of the Jim Crow South, shocking the conscience of the nation—meaning, really, white northern-ers—and embarrassing the US internationally. The more the cops respond-ed with violence, the more people sympathized with the demonstrators and the more influence the movement won.[15]

In the decades that followed, the cops largely gave up their "Escalated Force" model for handling unrest and developed, instead, a strategy of "Nego-tiated Management." That orientation, which predominated throughout the eighties and nineties, took a more flexible approach to political demonstra-tions. Rather than prohibit them, the cops sought to regulate them through permit requirements and agreements with responsible protest leaders. The cops would allow demonstrations, and even accommodate certain forms of civil disobedience; but in exchange, protesters were limited—or, more often, they limited themselves—to types of action that were minimally disruptive.[16]

The peaceful protest/peaceful police ideal of the contemporary liberal fantasy points back to this tradition of symbolic actions, symbolic arrests. The point to remember, however, is that the cops didn't adopt this approach out of concern for civil liberties. Their strategy changed, but their aims remained the same. They moved from hard tactics to soft ones because the soft tactics seemed like a better way of controlling, and therefore neutral-izing, social movements.

In some places, the cops seem to have adroitly adopted this approach to handling Occupy.[17] Not long ago, I found myself at lunch with a man who described himself as a "fixer" for the mayor of a mid-sized western city. He told me that, so long as the Occupy movement's actions remain symbolic, as in his city they had, they aren't really that much of an issue. The protesters may symbolically break laws, and the cops may symbolically arrest them. No one gets hurt, nothing gets broken, and no one loses any money. The cops—with their polite, peaceful, symbolic arrests—are important to this strategy, but they are much less important than the protest organizers, with their polite, peaceful, symbolic tactics. As the Fixer confided in me, he was, as "liaison to the Occupy

---

15 Doug McAdam, "Tactical Innovation and the Pace of Insurgency," *American Sociological Review* (December 1983).

16 Clark McPhail, *et al.*, "Policing Protest in the United States: 1960–1995," in *Policing Protest: The Control of Mass Demonstrations in Western Democracies*, ed. Donatella della Porta and Herbert Reiter (Minneapolis: University of Minne-sota Press, 1998).

17 See, for example: George Corsetti, "Detroit Police and the Occupy Movement: A Lesson in Restraint," *CounterPunch*, November 25–27, 2011.

movement," in direct contact with "some of the older people—guys in their fifties and sixties," and felt that they could be relied on to control the younger and more militant types.[18] It was interesting for me to see how well the authorities understood the situation—much better than the protesters: the Fixer, the mayor, and probably the police recognized that, without a confrontation, the protests were largely meaningless, while protest leaders naively believed that by avoiding a confrontation they were actually winning. In fact, the protesters made police repression unnecessary by making themselves irrelevant. The protest could be tolerated precisely because it presented no challenge.

toward strategic incapacitation

HISTORICALLY, NEGOTIATED MANAGEMENT worked because both sides developed a shared set of expectations that nothing *too* serious would happen at demonstrations—and for the most part, nothing did.

But as the civil rights movement had out-smarted Escalated Force, it fell to the anti-globalization movement to outsmart Negotiated Management. On November 30, 1999, tens of thousands of protesters converged in Seattle and, using direct action tactics largely developed over years of struggle in the environmental movement, blockaded the streets of downtown Seattle and disrupted the ministerial meeting of the World Trade Organization. The police, unprepared for the "new paradigm of disruptive protest,"[19] reverted to simple force.

Over the next several years, police around the country embarked on a period of clumsy experimentation. From the outside, their actions often seemed strangely contradictory. For instance: at the 2000 Democratic National Convention in Los Angeles, police launched an unprovoked attack against a crowd listening to music in one of the permitted demonstration areas; a few days later, when dozens of protesters enacted a sit-in at the Ramparts station, an LAPD commander accepted a list of their demands, and shook their hands while politely placing them under arrest.[20]

Slowly, the police fumbled their way toward a new strategy, which John Noakes and Patrick Gillham describe as "Strategic Incapacitation."[21] This

---

18 Our meeting was an accident, a matter of us having a mutual friend. And as it was a private conversation, I will do the Fixer the courtesy of naming neither him nor the city where he works.

19 Seattle Police Department, *The Seattle Police Department After Action Report: World Trade Organization Ministerial Conference: Seattle, Washington, November 29–December 3, 1999* (Seattle: April 4, 2000) 4.

20 The result, as one observer astutely noted, "was a PR/media opportunity to showcase the [cops'] civility." Quoted in Williams, *Our Enemies in Blue*, 194.

21 John Noakes and Patrick F. Gillham, "Aspects of the 'New Penology' in the

new approach incorporates some of the features of Negotiated Management, selectively applied to cooperative protesters—but, instead of being established through negotiation, the conditions for demonstrations are unilaterally dictated by the police. At the same time, the cops also employ many of the coercive tactics associated with Escalated Force. These, too, are applied selectively, targeting groups the cops consider potentially disruptive—by definition, anyone who doesn't cooperate with their process or abide by their rules. But Strategic Incapacitation is not just a blend of the two older forms. It also includes: extensive surveillance; the management of space to restrict movement and contain public assemblies; the sharing of information between police departments (and other agencies); and, focused campaigns to shape public perception of the protests through the news media.[22]

Within this framework, the attacks on the Occupy encampments make some sense. Though the camps were, by any sober assessment, purely symbolic and no real threat to anyone, they had positioned themselves outside the police-regulated framework of managed protest. In a sense, they represented a rejection of the cops' right to dictate the conditions under which

The police recognized that, without a confrontation, the protests were largely meaningless, while protest leaders naively believed that by avoiding a confrontation they were actually winning. In fact, the protesters made police repression unnecessary by making themselves irrelevant. The protest could be tolerated precisely because it presented no challenge.

Police Response to Major Political Protests in the United States, 1999–2000," in *The Policing of Transnational Protest*, eds. Donatella della Porta, *et al.* (Hampshire: Ashgate, 2006).

22 Patrick F. Gillham, "Securitizing America: Strategic Incapacitation and the Policing of Protest Since the 11 September 2001 Terrorist Attacks," *Sociology Compass*, July 2011.

free speech occurs, and at the same time, they embodied the public's right to control urban space. In other words, the police had switched the game, and the Occupy movement switched it again. Therefore the Occupiers were, in the eyes of the cops, disruptive "bad" protesters. Notice that this assessment has nothing whatsoever to do with the question of violence or nonviolence, or even really with basic legality (since the Constitutional guarantees of the right to peacefully assemble ought, in theory, to trump local ordinances against sleeping in parks).

What happened next should have been perfectly predictable: the cops attacked. They attacked violently, in coordinated raids. The used tear gas, billy clubs, pepperspray, horses. They confiscated tents and made arrests. They attacked in the press, with horror stories about crime and disease and armed insurgents hiding in the encampments. They followed with campaigns of persistent harassment against people they considered troublemakers, and tried to co-opt more moderate leaders.[23]

The Occupy movement responded, at least initially, by escalating their tactics. In some places—Portland and Oakland are two that I know of—people physically confronted the police to defend the camps. It was a losing battle, but an important one. Later, the camps gone, the Occupiers moved on to launch simultaneous blockades of the major West Coast ports. They said, in effect, *You wanna see disruption? We'll show you some disruption!*

conclusions

THIS DISCUSSION HAS several implications for social movements, including but not limited to Occupy. One is that social movements pose a threat largely through their potential for disruption. The cops' job is to neutralize that threat—through managerial means if possible, through direct coercion if necessary. Questions about violence or sabotage or black blocs are in that sense secondary to the question of disruption or non-confrontation.

It's important to realize that the police change their tactics, and they largely do so in response to changes in the movements they're confronting. The cops adapt to meet new challenges, which means that social movements have to innovate in order to regain the advantage. We can't just do the same thing over and over again. We have to change the game if we want to win it.

Occupy Wall Street found and exploited—by accident, I suspect—a flaw in the Strategic Incapacitation approach, and revealed that it had many of

---

23 Dave Lindorff, "Police State Tactics," *CounterPunch*, November 16, 2011; George Ciccariello-Maher, "The Coming War on the Occupy Movement," *CounterPunch*, November 17, 2011; Shawn Gaynor, "The Cop Group Coordinating the Occupy Crackdowns," *San Francisco Bay Guardian Online* (SFBG. com), November 18, 2011; and Mike King, "Occupy Oakland and State Repression," *CounterPunch*, January 31, 2012.

the same problems as Escalated Force. The movement's use of nonviolent civil disobedience triggered a police response that was discrediting to the state and won sympathy for the demonstrators. It also, not incidentally, set the stage for more disruptive and more militant action later on.

The larger point to remember is that the violence used against the Occupy movement is in no way exceptional. It is simply part of the normal operation of the police force. It is not just a matter of the excesses of ill-disciplined or over-zealous officers. It is a core function of the institution.

The violence police use against activists is only an extension of the violence they use routinely. Aside from the question of scale, there's nothing unusual about it, and it is not particularly worse than normal policing. Usually, the cops work in ones or twos, spread out over a large geographic area. Occasionally, they work in large groups concentrated in a small area.[24] But the work is the same: the cops are using surveillance and violence to manage troublesome populations and hence to preserve the system of white supremacy and capitalism.

For all of these reasons, it is clear that any movement that looks to challenge the existing social order—to challenge the fact of gross inequality—will inevitably face repression at the hands of the police. From this, then, I conclude that any movement interested in pushing our society in the direction of greater equality needs to, as an inherent part of its work, position itself in opposition to the police.

It is not enough to complain when the police attack our demos, if we are not also objecting when the police attack entire neighborhoods. Not only is it unprincipled to treat protest groups as a special case, it is also short-sighted. Ordinary policing—the kind that happens in neighborhood streets, away from crowds and television cameras—is *also* political. It is political in the sense that it targets already powerless people. And it is political in the sense that it helps to keep them powerless—it limits their movement, it monitors their associations, it leads them disproportionately into court and then prison, and thus it disrupts their lives, limits their future prospects, and destabilizes their communities. As I hope I've made clear, none of that is accidental. It is, in fact, an inherent aspect of our system of extreme inequality.

Therefore, the struggle for equality and opposition to policing are mutually inextricable. Just as any effort to address inequality has to be prepared to confront the question of police violence—and for precisely the same reason—any answer to police brutality will have to address the more fundamental problems of inequality.

---

24 Rodney Stark, *Police Riots: Collective Violence and Law Enforcement* (Belmont, California: Focus Books, 1972) 84.

Timothy Krausel
March 24, 2012
Occupy Wall Street, Union Square

Rachel Herzing and Isaac Ontiveros

REFLECTIONS FROM THE FIGHT AGAINST POLICING

IN SEPTEMBER OF 2011, OCCUPY WALL STREET CAPTURED THE IMAGINA-
tion of people around the world and spawned political activity of a breadth
and volume unseen in generations. Occupy's approach left those who opposed it bewildered and disoriented—no single leaders, no one set of demands, a value on spontaneous direct action—and at a loss for concrete
targets to shut it down. The broad appeal of Occupy drew supporters from
a range of ages, backgrounds, and concerns who share disaffection and frustration with the current state of politics and economics in the US.

As Occupy took hold and spread, and as encampments were established, city
leaders began to panic and started to unleash police forces against the protesters.
In some cases, cops surveilled the camps and stood by to "control" situations;
in others, cops delivered eviction notices, tore down tents, or clashed with protesters in the streets. Even just a handful of examples clearly demonstrate the
lengths to which law enforcement has gone to suppress these demonstrations.

High levels of surveillance were a mainstay of the efforts to police and
suppress Occupy. From 24-hour physical police presence to handheld video
surveillance by cops, and the Sky Watch surveillance tower used by the
NYPD, continuous monitoring was a primary means not just of information gathering for law enforcement, but also of intimidating protesters.

Police were used to carry out eviction orders in numerous cities, intimidating protesters in all cases, and making arrests and using force and weapons in many. For instance, 1400 cops swarmed the Occupy Los Angeles
encampment and raided it, arresting about 300 people, tearing down tents,
and beating some protesters with batons. In Phoenix, cops outfitted in riot
gear peppersprayed residents to evict them, while in Oakland, a violent,
early morning raid of the Occupy encampment resulted in cops tearing
down tents and physically assaulting campers as well as dozens of arrests.

Demonstrators have repeatedly been assaulted with tear gas, pepperspray and "non-lethal" projectiles during marches and protests. In Seattle, police used pepperspray and concussion grenades to break up a protest at the port; in Portland, protester Liz Nichols was sprayed from just inches away with pepperspray as she faced a line of cops. The incident was caught on film and the image went viral. Perhaps the most famous use of pepperspray on Occupy protesters happened at the University of California Davis, when students sitting with linked arms were sprayed repeatedly at close range, directly in their faces, by campus cops.

In Oakland, protesters have faced what are reported to be the most violent police responses from any department since Occupy began. In October, following the eviction described above, police repeatedly used tear gas, flash bang grenades, and rubber bullets on protesters in addition to their old standby, the baton. In a dramatic turn, Iraq war veteran and protester, Scott Olsen, was hit in the head at close range with a tear gas canister shot by a cop and suffered a skull fracture. As others tried to attend to him, a cop hurled a flash bang grenade into the group. After repeatedly subjecting protesters to physical violence and intimidation, police force reached a new high in January 2012, when hundreds of protesters were repeatedly kettled, or surrounded without exit, by police and arrested for failures to disperse that the kettling would not allow. Following that incident, Oakland Mayor Jean Quan, who has come under fire for her encouragement of the OPD's use of force, sought stay away orders against select protesters, requiring them to stay 100 yards away from City Hall, which has been the central meeting and gathering place for Occupy Oakland.

In preparation for May Day celebrations, the beleaguered Oakland Police Department, fresh off a report required by the terms of its federal consent decree outlining its dismal record in dealing with Occupy, announced a shift in its policing policy regarding crowd control following a consultation with national security firm, Frazier LLC. In practice, the policy meant a change from a previous model: lines and lines of cops standing off with demonstrators and if demonstrators would not disperse, firing tear gas, wooden dowels, bean bags, rubber bullets or other so-called non-lethal projectiles into the crowds. This was a new model: small groups of cops actively pursuing targeted individuals by chasing them down the street, sometimes wielding batons or other weapons, and isolating them from other protesters. In essence, this is what has been called "snatch and grab" tactics.

Apart from independent municipal responses to Occupy protests in their cities, police departments called for and responded to calls for mutual aid, sharing weapons, tactics, and officers from across jurisdictions in raiding camps, suppressing demonstrations, and monitoring Occupy's activities. Over 16 different law enforcement agencies participated in the October

25 raid of Occupy Oakland, for example, although some local police departments began to question whether or not they would support Oakland Police Department's requests for future mutual aid given the OPD's hyper-aggressive tactics. Similarly, according to an interview Jean Quan gave to the BBC, mayors from across the country also joined in discussions to share strategies for shutting Occupy down.

One remarkable feature of the policing of Occupy is the role this repressive policing had in generating a spike in anti-policing sentiment. People's relationships to policing from within Occupy were certainly as varied as the movement itself, but some who had previously been neutral or supportive in their attitudes toward policing began to express fear, suspicion, and resentment toward the police and their tactics. Occupy protesters also became much more adept at resisting police repression. They stood together against intimidation tactics, they photographed and videoed police activities, and documented incidences of violence. For instance, a Facebook page was created and dedicated solely to police violence targeted toward Occupy, and organizers started a coloring book project on police brutality with contributions from high-profile activist artists. Additionally, each instance of police violence generated even more protests in response and increased solidarity among protesters around the globe, effectively making policing a central focus of how the political and economic problems that Occupy highlighted were secured and maintained.

What may be most remarkable about the policing of Occupy, however, is the stark illustration it provided of how policing works to oppose challenges to capitalism. Rather than being exceptional, the use of policing to suppress dissent made visible its central role in maintaining the economic, political, and social status quo. Filling the streets with riot gear-clad and armed columns of cops to intimidate dissenting voices—political or otherwise—is nothing new. Subjecting protesters and others understood as threats to state power to monitoring through various types of surveillance is commonplace. Arresting and charging dissenters, people of color, and the poor with excessive charges are normal. Subjecting protesters and anyone who resists police containment to clouds of pepperspray and tear gas, rubber bullets, and beatings is standard operating procedure.

For the organizations and activists who have been fighting policing for decades, the spotlight that Occupy shone on the violence of policing and the value of resisting that violence offered new opportunities to engage broader groups of people and erode the power policing has over our lives. At the same time, the challenge was to demonstrate the ways in which this is not an exceptional moment in the history of US policing, but merely a heightened one.

A fundamental means through which policing is effective is the naturalization of its logic, ideology, and practice: it is seen as given—constant, perhaps changing over time, but nonetheless inarguable, and everlasting. This is not at all unlike the repressive institutions and the ideologies policing supports and is supported by; this is how hegemony works. And part of how it works is that it works *on* us. It is important to understand that policing is not natural or neutral. It did not arise separately from the dominant social and economic orders.

Some of the first police in the US were deputized citizens who were given police power in order to hunt runaway slaves. Police forces like the US Marshals find their origins here. In the days after the Revolutionary War, the military's war-making capacity (personnel, funding, arsenal, and technological development) was largely focused domestically, facilitating the extermination of this land's Indigenous people and settlement westward. Central to this genocidal program was a policing function—the management and protection by force of geography, movement, interrelationship, and the use and distribution of resources, along with individual and group punishment and killing. Here we might note how this is very much a description of military occupation. Perhaps the question is less "What is the difference between military occupation and policing," than "Are the two that different at all?" As US policing and militarism has developed over the course of the past 235 years, their techniques, technicians, and technologies have served particular and distinct functions, but the intertwining, collaboration, and one-for-the-other nature of policing and militarism is a large part of their growth. The on-the-ground articulation of policing and militarism has been united not only by an ideological mission of expanding and protecting US economic and political interests, but also by the sharing, exchange, and mutual development of personnel, technology, weaponry, theory, strategy, tactics, and geographic areas of operation.

As US settlement continued to be imposed westward and as towns and cities were established, police (whether in the form of deputized citizenry, municipal forces, county sheriffs, etc.) were explicitly put in place to uphold the law and order the state used to link itself together geographically, socially, and culturally. Interwoven with the development of capitalism as a hegemonic economic order has been the development of a social order based primarily on white supremacy and patriarchy. As has been noted extensively, these oppressions do not exist independently of one another but are mutually supportive and thread together a system that not only controls land, resources, and people, but also ideas, culture, laws, and education. Given that these systems are inherently unstable and unequal, and based on exploitation and, in the case of capitalism, on the extraction of labor and resources, these systems need to be imposed, retooled, and regenerated. They require participation. And as we know, participation is developed from the complex interrelationship between manufactured consent on one hand and coercion on the other. One of the fundamental roles of the state is to codify order. Police play a crucial role in building, protecting, and extending that order. Policing played a central role in enforcing the law and maintaining the economic and social systems that exterminated Indigenous populations or relegated them to reservations that contained, exploited, or killed formerly enslaved people after emancipation and kept workers in line.

Police protect and preserve the social and economic order by force. They do this by protecting property and ensuring the smooth process of production on the day to day; patrolling and enforcing the social order; and monitoring, allowing, and disallowing who goes where, with whom, and when. Policing apparatuses such as the FBI have been used to monitor, disrupt, infiltrate, and neutralize these threats posed by labor organizations, dispossessed and marginalized ethnic minorities, immigrant communities, and youth, for instance. The FBI's Counterintelligence Program (COINTELPRO) of the 1950s, '60s, and '70s is just one example. Homeland Security is another. ICE is yet another. Police play a managerial role in communities on the day-to-day as well as the role of triggermen in operations that seek to neutralize the political aspirations of those same communities.

The state takes its self-preservation and the preservation of the economic and social orders to which it is in service seriously. In more and more crises, it assesses and perceives threats to itself and employs and deploys policing apparatuses and agencies on the local, state, and federal level. These forces are not always coordinated centrally or consciously. Sometimes they are. There might not be a wizard behind a curtain pulling levers, there may not be a centralized plan—but there is a common ideology, methodology, practice, and purpose in operation. Billions of dollars are spent on communications and surveillance technologies that are shared by police organizations on the federal, state, and local levels. Think tanks, colleges, and non-governmental organizations are also employed in the theoretical development of policing. Corporations secure enormous contracts and utilize policing hardware across the globe. States trade information, resources, and training, like the continuous collaboration between Israel and the US, for instance. From post-Katrina New Orleans to the occupation of Iraq or Palestine, or the UN intervention in Haiti, police have become more and more militarized while military forces have taken on more and more policing roles. And all the while, laws and policies—from the Street Terrorism and Enforcement Program (STEP) to the USA PATRIOT Act—broaden the legal powers of police agencies.

In 2011, millions of people came into the streets to protest and act against oppressive social and economic orders. People rose up against the ravages of capitalism and the related violence of racial oppression, gender oppression, and imperialism. These recent uprisings have happened across the globe—some appear to be new, while others are continuations of decades-long organizing. Questions such as "Why are these uprising taking place now?" help us get to others like "What connects them?" Trying to answer either can help us better understand our historical moment.

The role of policing, however, remains clear throughout. From Cairo to Madrid to Oakland, people in the streets calling for change are consistently met with police violence. But in our current moment, part of what people are trying to change and struggle against include the role, nature, and very existence of policing. That is to say, policing is not a separate issue from the struggle to upend violent inequities that have so much of humanity in a chokehold. Along with demands for economic equity and opportunity, jobs, enfranchisement, and regime change, a significant number of demands coming from the different national struggles of the Arab Spring also called for specific and thorough changes in policing. These demands share a close relationship to Palestinian demands against the policing and imprisonment functions of Israeli occupation. Occupy Oakland, along with its demands to end the police repression of Occupy activists, also made specific demands against the use of gang injunctions, curfews, and loitering ordinances in that city.

In fact, it is hard to think of any uprising, whether mass and spontaneous or organization-based and programmatic, that hasn't incorporated anti-policing demands. And many of these anti-policing articulations go beyond merely demanding that police stop cracking down on the activities of specific movements or organizations, instead extending further toward upending the deeper roles and institutions of policing themselves. Civil rights movements have always done battle with and made demands against policing. An initial demand of the 1963 March on Washington was against police brutality. In this same period, more militant chapters of the NAACP took up arms against the police as part of broader anti-segregation strategies. National liberation and anti-imperialist movements have nearly always sought the wholesale expulsion of police and military occupiers playing policing roles. In many cases, particularly for Indigenous peoples' struggles, these same movements have built new ways of dealing with harm, violence, and security into their liberation struggles, dislodging the colonial nature and logic of policing. The Black Panther Party began its work largely in response to police murder in the Black community, and moved on to integrate its demands for substantial changes in police, judicial, economic, and social structure with the social programs it initiated in Black communities across the US. One of the initial targets of the Zapatistas was police headquarters in San Cristóbol. In turn, Zapatista communities have gone to great lengths to rethink concepts of justice and law and order.

Understanding the nature, history, dynamics, and articulations of policing and its relationship to capitalism helps us better understand the context in which policing is used as well as its potential impacts. The policing of Occupy during 2011–2012 provided us with a particularly useful set of responses that allow us to think carefully about how to better equip ourselves to fight back against policing not just of mass mobilizations or political protests, but of the more mundane articulations of policing as well. While Occupy was exceptional in its ability to activate large numbers of people, the policing responses to it were not at all exceptional. Rather, Occupy provided police forces with means through which to refine and expand their techniques and technologies in real time and on real targets. Resisting the urge to exceptionalize the police response to Occupy also prevents us from imagining that the type of policing some people experience for the first time in response to mass protests will not continue to be employed in the containment and control of the enduring targets of law enforcement—people of color, poor people, youth, etc.

Using the lessons learned from Occupy further allows us to expand and extend our ability to activate people in the fight against policing. As a result of direct, violent contact with police during their participation in Occupy-related activities, more people than ever are poised and motivated to oppose policing. The communications and media infrastructure built up through Occupy provides new means of sharing information about policing tactics and the ways of resisting them, as well as mobilizing people more quickly and effectively. Using those lessons in tandem with lessons drawn from earlier historical struggles provides additional breadth and depth to our current context. We are also better positioned

We must remind ourselves that policing is not a natural feature of our landscape. And it is not a necessary evil. From cats in trees to serious violence, engaging the police is not our only option.

than ever to demonstrate how the demands poor people and people of color have been making against police power for decades are in everyone's best interests to move strongly toward.

To move in a direction in which policing might become obsolete, denaturalizing policing is essential. We must break apart the structures, forces, and practices that influence us to accept seeing law enforcement at all scales (private and public, local state, regional, and federal) as commonplace and permanent fixtures. We must remind ourselves that policing is not a natural feature of our landscape. And it is not a necessary evil. From cats in trees to serious violence, engaging the police is not our only option. A brief survey of several projects aimed at eroding policing power help remind us that not only is opposing police repression possible, but that everyday, ordinary people are taking steps in that direction. And while these examples are full of contradictions and we do not necessarily endorse them, we feel it is useful to remind ourselves of what is possible.

Historic moments in queer liberation history such as the Stonewall rebellion of 1969 highlight the militancy of queer and gender non-conforming people in resisting police violence. Formations including the Gay Liberation Front sought to provide organizational and ideological cohesion, and situated queer struggle within the context of anti-imperialism and similar liberation movements of the day. Organizations such as San Francisco's Vanguard also made alliances with progressive church organizations that in turn helped create political and social networks for queer and trans people in the city. Part of the group's project was to create a network of safe spaces in which queer and gender-nonconforming people could take refuge from and undermine heterosexist policing. Organizations such as Community United against Violence have continued the radical organizing legacies of queer and trans activism through activities such as their Safety Labs. They use safety labs to put special emphasis on outfitting their members with tools for using community-based methods for addressing harm and violence. By employing tools and techniques to respond to and resolve harm without engaging the state, they are not only reducing vulnerable community members' contact with police, but also building self-determination.

In response to heightened repression as a result of the powerful, large-scale resistance to apartheid in the mid-1980s in South Africa, street committees were established that took over local governance, defending communities against state repression, and working toward making the apartheid state untenable. Elected by neighbors during public meetings, street committees engaged in everything from cleaning up streets to addressing conflicts and disputes within townships. People's courts were also established through the street committees to address disputes between neighbors and served as an extension of popular courts that had been in place since the 1970s. A variety of iterations of street committees exist even today across South Africa with a range of connections to and relationships with police forces.

Primeiro Comando da Capital (PCC), a social organization rooted in the prisons of São Paulo, grew out of prisoners' desires to defend themselves against violence enacted by the prison administration. Most notably, the PCC responded to the 1992 massacre at Carandirú Penitentiary during which police killed 111 prisoners. Well known for its violent responses, the Brazilian state understands the PCC as a criminal organization. However, by creating a formal (if authoritarian) structure and organization, the PCC not only built up a social, political, and armed force capable of challenging the prison administration and eventually winning the closure of Carandirú prison in 2002 and engaging the Brazilian state militarily, but also addressing issues of safety and harm inside and outside the Brazilian prison system, which has led to substantial drops in violence and HIV infection rates, and garnered them widespread community support.

Spring 2012 marked the 20th anniversary of the LA Rebellion, during which thousands of Los Angeles residents rose up against the violence of policing, racism, and capitalism. A less recognized date is the 20th anniversary of the Watts Truce, also celebrated in 2012. The truce was hashed out by members of the Bloods and Crips street gangs in the Watts district of Los Angeles. On the eve of the LA Rebellion, leadership and rank-and-file members of various cliques, in collaboration with community organizations and residents held formal peace negotiations that contributed to a substantial drop in street violence in Los Angeles. The solidification of the truce also increased engagement in political education and community organizing, and helped to generate clear demands for economic changes by truce participants. The Watts truce also served as a model for other communities in Los Angeles and elsewhere to organize truces. Further, March 2012 saw a historic truce between MS 13 and Calle 18 gangs in El Salvador, which has led to a 50–70% decline in the country's murder rate. Organizations and individuals who played roles in the Watts Truce and other similar truces from that era are supporting truce efforts in El Salvador by sharing best practices and strategies.

Community Restorative Justice Ireland (CRJI) was started by former political prisoners in the north of Ireland around 1998 and currently operates in 14 Republican communities. Formed as a means shifting from violent, physical actions (including beatings, shootings, and banishments) in response to harmful behavior, to peaceful, inclusive, democratic responses, CRJI uses intensive community education and mediation to address harm and disputes. CRJI deals mostly with neighbor disputes but also works in schools and helps people make the transition from prison back to their communities. While not operating totally without influence from the police service, CRJI offers a first line of intervention before police are called in. Because of the enduring distrust of and political hostility toward police among Republican communities, CRJI cannot work directly with police if it wants to be credible within the community.

Fueled by the 2001 Critical Resistance/INCITE! Statement on Gender Violence and the Prison Industrial Complex, a series of projects and sets of practices developed to address the serious harms inflicted by sexual assault and other forms of gender-based violence without augmenting harm by involving policing or other elements of the prison industrial complex. Since that time, both pre-existing groups and organizations, and ones developed in the wake of that statement, joined Critical Resistance and INCITE! in this effort to develop community-based approaches to violence that do not rely on state intervention. Examples include Communities against Rape and Abuse, Community United against Violence, Young Women's Empowerment Project, Generation 5, The Revolution Starts at Home, and Creative Interventions. In 2012, Creative Interventions released the *Creative Interventions Toolkit: An Invitation and Practical Guide for Everyone to Stop Violence*, a community resource for people interested in intervening in situations of harm without engaging the prison industrial complex.

Confronted with persistent surveillance, harassment, and repression at the hands of law enforcement, projects developed during the late 1990s and early 2000s in the US with the express purpose of building up neighborhood capacity to resolve conflict and address harm without calling law enforcement. For instance, two "harm free zones" in New York and Durham, North Carolina, respectively, were launched as pilot projects to build neighborhood self-determination and erode police standing. Employing a combination of mediation, conflict resolution, de-escalation, and community education and community-building tools, the harm free zone projects brought individuals and organizations together to shift neighborhood logic away from calling the cops when a conflict arises, and towards calling on neighbors and community resources. The work of the "harm free zones" in both cities saw the convergence of people from a variety of ages and social and political experiences. Building the zones also created space for diverse organizations to work with one another, including schools, youth media organizations, anti-violence advocates, and anti-prison industrial complex organizations.

Tangentyere Council is an Aboriginal community-controlled resource in the town of Alice Springs, in Central Australia, delivering services and programs to 20 autonomous town camps in the region. Just one example of many Aboriginal community-based efforts to intervene in situations of harm before they draw attention or response by police forces, the Night Patrols were developed to act as a buffer between the Aboriginal residents living in the town camps and local police forces. Night Patrol is a form of community monitoring designed to deal with instances of alcohol-related trouble involving town campers, before they require police intervention. Night patrols walk through camps, keep an eye on things, and negotiate between people or groups fighting with each other. They use negotiation rather than sanctions to resolve conflicts. Night Patrols also help connect people to clinics, remove people from physical danger, provide space for people to sober up, and provide consultation.

When local residents object to policing practices, they sometimes push police forces out entirely. In a recent example, people in the indigenous town of Cherán, Mexico took over all local government, including policing, in response to residents being killed by loggers they believed to be affiliated with a drug cartel, and established community patrols. Earlier in the year, protesters across Egypt set fire to police stations and pushed out local police forces in response to intense police attacks on the protests. In Alexandria, Egypt, police were pushed out of town for nearly 30 days.

In states such as Arizona, Georgia, and Alabama where overtly racist anti-immigration legislation is being pushed, members and allies of immigrant communities, are fighting this legislation and its enforcement by forming *Comités de Defensa del Barrio* (Barrio Defense Committees). The CDBs come out of immigrant organizers' experiences within the social movements of their home countries as well as the legacies the Black Panther Party for Self Defense, the Brown Berets, and the American Indian Movement. Contemporary CDBs are neighborhood networks that prepare contingency plans in anticipation of raids, conduct "know your rights" trainings, and monitor and report on the activity of local police.

The Malcolm X Grassroots Movement reported that between January 1 and June 30, 2012, 120 Black people were killed by police, security guards, and "self-appointed law enforcers;" i.e., roughly one Black person was killed by law enforcement every 36 hours. In summer 2012, sustained protests in Los Angeles over the killing of a young Latino resident were met with police violence that including letting police dogs loose on a crowd of demonstrators. From Occupy to the Arab Spring, this historical moment may well offer some of the ripest opportunities to organize against crushing inequity and violence on a global scale. While there has been an ebb in the nature of popular uprising between late 2011 and mid-2012, rather than see this as a dying off or a retreat, we should imagine it still simmering with potential. To do that we must take a long view of policing, one that keeps in focus the purpose and practice of law enforcement, that denaturalizes it, and understands its elimination as not just necessary, but possible.

CrimethInc.

CrimethInc. Ex-Workers' Collective

BOUNTY HUNTERS AND CHILD PREDATORS
INSIDE THE FBI ENTRAPMENT STRATEGY

PERHAPS, GENTLE READER, YOU'VE NEVER BEEN PART OF A SOCIAL BODY TARgeted by the US government. Imagine undercover agents infiltrating your community with the intention of setting people up to be framed for illegal activity. Most of your friends and family would have the sense to keep themselves out of trouble, of course—but can you be absolutely sure *everyone* would?

What if someone fell in love with the agent and was desperate to impress him or her, and the agent took advantage of this? Every community has people in it that may sometimes be gullible or vulnerable, who may not display the best judgment at all times. And what if the agent provocateur is a person everyone trusts and looks up to? Government agents aren't always outsiders—the FBI often recruit or blackmail long-time participants, or even well-known leaders.

Perhaps you're still saying to yourself, "It would never happen—all of *us* are law-abiding citizens." Sure you are, every last one of you. The US has 2.3 million people in prison, and over 5 million more on probation and parole—if there isn't a single person in your whole community who has ever broken a law, you're exceptional, and probably exceptionally privileged. Anyway, it doesn't matter—your unfortunate friend or neighbor doesn't even have to *do* anything illegal to get framed by the government. He just has to end up in a situation in which it's possible to make it appear that he could have *considered* doing something illegal.

Often the evidence is so tenuous that it takes the government multiple attempts to obtain a conviction. In an entrapment case resulting from the protests against the 2008 Republican National Convention, defendant David McKay received a hung jury at trial, only to be coerced into pleading guilty afterward behind closed doors. In another entrapment case, it took two hung juries before a third jury finally convicted some of the defendants—prompting a law professor quoted by the *New York Times* to say, "It goes to show that if you try it enough times, you'll eventually find a jury that will convict on very little evidence."

Agents provocateurs pick on the most vulnerable people they can find: the lonely, the trusting, the mentally or emotionally unstable, people who lack close friendships or life experience. This is easier than messing with shrewd, well-connected organizers. The point is not to catch those who are actually involved in ongoing resistance, so much as to discredit resistance movements by framing somebody, anybody, as a dangerous terrorist. If this means destroying the life of a person who never would have actually harmed anyone, so be it—honest, compassionate people don't become infiltrators in the first place.

This is not to blame the victims of entrapment. We all have moments of weakness. The guilt lies on those who prey on others' weakness for their own gain.

the latest trend in repression

NOT SO LONG ago, it seemed that the FBI focused on pursuing accomplished anarchists: Marie Mason and Daniel McGowan were both arrested after lengthy careers involving everything from supporting survivors of domestic violence to ecologically-minded arson. It isn't surprising that the security apparatus of the state targeted them: they were threatening the inequalities and injustices the state is founded upon.

However, starting with the entrapment case of Eric McDavid—framed for a single conspiracy charge by an infiltrator who used his attraction to her to manipulate him into discussing illegal actions[1]—the FBI appeared to switch strategies, focusing on younger targets who hadn't actually carried out any actions.

They stepped up this new strategy during the 2008 Republican National Convention, at which FBI informants Brandon Darby and Andrew Darst set up David McKay, Bradley Crowder, and Matthew DePalma on charges of possessing Molotov cocktails in two separate incidents.[2] It's important to note that the only Molotov cocktails that figured in the RNC protests *at*

---

1   Afterwards, *Elle Magazine* quoted regretful jurors as saying "the FBI was an embarrassment" and "I hope he gets a new trial." He is serving a 20-year sentence and has not been granted a new trial.

2   DePalma was approached by Darst, a federal infiltrator posing as a member of the RNC Welcoming Committee, a group planning protests against the Republican National Convention. Darst persuaded DePalma to assist him in manufacturing explosives, recorded conversations with him in a wired apartment, and drove him around doing research and purchasing supplies; DePalma ultimately pleaded guilty to felony charges for possession of "unregistered firearms." The tragic story of Darby's entrapment of McKay and Crowder has been widely publicized, including in the PBS documentary *Better This World*.

any point were the ones used to entrap these young men: the FBI were not responding to a threat, but inventing one.

At the end of April 2012, the FBI shifted into high gear with this approach. Immediately before May Day, five young men associated with the Occupy movement were set up on terrorism charges in Cleveland after an FBI infiltrator apparently guided them into planning to bomb a bridge, in what would have been the only such bombing carried out by anarchists in living memory. During the protests against the NATO summit in Chicago, three young men were arrested and charged with terrorist conspiracy once again involving the only Molotov cocktails within hundreds of miles, set up by at least two FBI informants.

None of the targets of these entrapment cases seem to be longtime anarchist organizers. None of the crimes they're being charged with are representative of the tactics that anarchists have actually used over the past decade. All of the cases rest on the efforts of FBI informants to manufacture conspiracies. All of the arrests have taken place immediately before mass mobilizations, enabling the authorities to frame a narrative justifying their crackdowns on protest as thwarting terrorism. And in all of these cases, the defendants have been described as anarchists in the legal paperwork filed against them, setting precedents for criminalizing anarchism.

why entrapment? why now?

WHY IS THE FBI focusing on entrapping inexperienced young people rather than seasoned anarchists? Isn't that just plain bad sportsmanship? And why are they intensifying this now?

For one thing, experienced activists are harder to catch. Unlike anarchists, FBI agents work for money, not necessarily out of passion or conviction. Their reports often read like second-rate homework assignments even as they wreck people's lives. Agents get funding and promotions based on successful cases, so they have an incentive to set people up; but why go after challenging targets? Why not pick the most marginal, the most vulnerable, the most isolated? If the goal is simply to frame *somebody*, it doesn't really matter who the target is.

Likewise, the tactics anarchists have actually been using are likely to be more popular with the general public than the tactics infiltrators push them towards. Smashing bank windows, for example, may be illegal, but it is increasingly understood as a meaningful political statement; it would be difficult to build a convincing terrorism case around broken glass.

Well-known activists also have much broader support networks. The FBI threatened Daniel McGowan[3] with a mandatory life sentence plus 335 years

---

3   Daniel McGowan, a hardworking anarchist organizer and ecological activist,

in prison; widespread support enabled him to obtain a good lawyer, and the prosecution had to settle for a plea bargain for a seven-year sentence or else admit to engaging in illegal wiretapping. Going after disconnected young people dramatically decreases the resources that will be mobilized to support them. If the point is to set precedents that criminalize anarchism while producing the minimum blowback, then it is easier to manufacture "terror" cases by means of agents provocateurs than to investigate actual anarchist activity.

Above all, this kind of proactive threat-creation enables FBI agents to prepare make-to-order media events. If a protest is coming up at which the authorities anticipate using brutal force, it helps to be able to spin the story in advance as a necessary, measured response to violent criminals. This also sows the seeds of distrust among activists, and intimidates newcomers and fence-sitters out of having anything to do with anarchists. The long-range project, presumably choreographed by FBI leadership rather than rank-and-file agents, is not just to frame a few unfortunate arrestees, but thus to hamstring the entire anti-capitalist movement.

how to destroy a movement

FBI REPRESSION OFTEN does not begin in earnest until a movement has begun to fracture and subside, diminishing the targets' support base. The life cycle of movements passes ever faster in our hyper-mediatized era; the Occupy phenomenon that peaked in November 2011 had slowed down by April 2012, emboldening the authorities to consolidate control and take revenge.

As anarchist values and practices become increasingly central to protest movements, the authorities are anxious to incapacitate and delegitimize anarchists. Yet in this context, it's still inconvenient to admit to targeting people for anarchism alone—that could spread the wrong narrative, rallying outrage against transparently political persecution. Likewise, they dare not initiate repression without a narrative portraying the targets as alien to the rest of the movement, even if that repression is calculated to destroy the movement itself.

Fortunately for the FBI, a few advocates of "nonviolence" within the Occupy movement were happy to provide this narrative, disavowing everyone who didn't affirm their narrow tactical framework. Journalists like Chris Hedges, author of "The Cancer in Occupy," took this further by framing the "black bloc" as a *kind* of people rather than a tactic. Hedges led the charge to consign those who actively defended themselves against state repression to this fabricated political category—in effect, designating them as legitimate targets. It's no coincidence that entrapment cases followed soon after.

---

was arrested as a part of the FBI's Operation Backfire targeting environmentally motivated direct action. http://www.supportdaniel.org

The authorities swiftly took up this narrative. In a subsequent Fox News article advancing the FBI agenda, the authorities parroted Chris Hedges' talking points—"they use the Occupy Movement as a front, but have their own violent agenda"—in order to frame the black bloc as a "home-grown terror group." The article also described the Cleveland arrestees as "Black Bloc anarchists" without evidence that any of them had ever participated in a black bloc.

The goal here was clearly to associate a *form of activity*—acting anonymously, defending oneself against police attacks—with a *kind of people*: terrorists, evildoers, monsters. This is a high priority for the authorities: they were able to crush the Occupy movement much more quickly, at least relative to its numbers, in cities where people did not act anonymously and defend themselves—hence Occupy Oakland's longevity compared to other Occupy groups. The aim of the FBI and corporate media, with the collusion of Chris Hedges and others, is to ensure that when people see a masked crowd that refuses to kowtow to coercive authority, they don't think, "Good for them for standing up for themselves," but rather, "Oh no—a bunch of terrorist bombers."

what comes next

WE CAN EXPECT more and more of these unsportsmanlike entrapments in the years to come. In the aforementioned Fox News article—"The Men in Black

"The individuals we charged are not peaceful protesters, they are domestic terrorists. The charges we bring today are not indicative of a protest movement that has been targeted."
—*Illinois state attorney Anita Alvarez, quoted in* The New York Times *on May 20, 2012 about the arrestees charged with conspiracy during the NATO protests*

To recapitulate the FBI strategy:

- Divide and conquer the movement by isolating the most combative participants.

- Stage-manage entrapments of vulnerable targets at the periphery.

- Use these arrests to delegitimize all but the most docile, and to justify ever-increasing police violence.

with a Violent Agenda"—the authorities explicitly announced that there are to be more "sting operations" at the 2012 Republican National Convention in Tampa.

For decades now, movements have defended themselves against surveillance and infiltration by practicing careful security culture. This has minimized the effectiveness of police operations against experienced activists, but it can't always protect those who are new to anarchism or activism, who haven't had time to internalize complex habits and practices—and these are exactly the people that the FBI entrapment strategy targets.

In a time of widespread social ferment, even the most collectively-oriented security culture is not sufficient to thwart the FBI: we can't hope to reach and protect every single desperate, angry, and vulnerable person in our society. Infiltrators need only find one impressionable young person, however peripheral, to advance their strategy. These are inhuman bounty hunters: they don't balk at taking advantage of any weakness, any need, any mental health issue.

If we are to protect the next generation of young people from these predators, our only hope is to mobilize a popular reaction against entrapment tactics. Only a blowback against the FBI themselves can halt this strategy.

Withdrawing, hiding, and behaving won't stop them from entrapping people. Retreating will only embolden them: we can only protect ourselves by increasing our power to fight back.

appendix:
protecting ourselves, protecting each other

NEVER UNDERTAKE OR discuss illegal activity with people you haven't known and trusted for a long time. Don't trust people just because other people trust them or because they are in influential positions. Don't let others talk you into tactics you're not comfortable with or ready for. Be aware that anything you say may come back to haunt you, even if you don't mean it. Always listen to your instincts; if someone seems pushy or too eager to help you with something, take some time to think about the situation. Reflect on the motivations of those around you—do they make sense? Get to know your comrades' families and friends.

These practices are sensible, but insufficient; we can't only think of security individualistically. Even if 99 out of 100 are able to avoid getting framed, when agents provocateurs manage to entrap the 100th one we all still end up paying the price. We need a security culture that can protect others as well, including vulnerable and marginal participants in radical spaces who may be particularly appetizing targets to federal bounty hunters. In addition to looking out for yourself, keep an eye on others who may put themselves at risk.

For example, imagine that you attend a presentation, and one person in the audience keeps asking crazy questions and demanding that people escalate their tactics. It's possible that this person is an agent provocateur; it's also possible that he's not an agent, but a hothead that might make a very attractive target for agents. Such individuals are typically shunned, which only makes them more vulnerable to agents: "Screw these squares—stick with me and we'll really *do* something!" Someone who has nothing to lose should approach this person in a low-stress environment and emphasize the importance of proper security culture, describing the risks that one exposes himself and others to by speaking so carelessly and urging him to be cautious about trusting anyone who solicits his participation in illegal activity. A ten-minute conversation like this might save years of heartache and prisoner support later on.

WHY WASN'T THE STING OPERATION BEFORE MAY DAY 2012 SET IN OAKLAND? SURELY THERE ARE PLENTY OF ANARCHISTS PLOTTING ILLEGAL ACTIVITY THERE, AND EVEN A FEW IMPRUDENT ENOUGH TO BE SET UP IN A TERROR PLOT?

BUT THERE'S ALSO A POWERFUL MOVEMENT IN OAKLAND THAT WOULD SUPPORT ARRESTEES. THE LAST THING THE FBI WANTS IS TO RISK LOSING A CASE—THE POINT IS TO SET PRECEDENTS FRAMING ANARCHISTS AS TERRORISTS, STARTING WHEREVER IT'S EASIEST. THE ONLY WAY TO BLOCK THE ENTRAPMENT STRATEGY WOULD BE TO SPREAD A COMBATIVE MOVEMENT ALL AROUND THE COUNTRY.

PROPOSAL FOR PRINCIPLE OF SOLIDARITY AGAINST POLICE REPRESSION

PASSED BY THE OCCUPY OAKLAND GENERAL ASSEMBLY ON FEBRUARY 26, 2012

GIVEN THE CURRENT CLIMATE OF POLICE REPRESSION AGAINST Occupy Oakland, and given that a key tactic of this repression is to foment and exploit divisions among us, we hereby collectively agree to stand in solidarity with one another, across all potential divisions.

We enact this principle of solidarity with one another by recognizing our individual and collective responsibility not to incriminate our fellow Occupiers, and hereby agree that:

1. We will not talk to the police about our comrades (This includes all levels of local, state and federal law enforcement, jail staff, Immigration & Customs Enforcement, Internal Affairs, and the Citizens Police Review Board.).

2. We will not post potentially incriminating information about our comrades on the Internet and social media (This includes any forms of information posted on Facebook, Twitter, blogs, email, etc.).

3. We will not post potentially incriminating video footage or photos of our comrades (This includes being attentive to the fact that even minor and unintended incidences can be used as the basis for criminal prosecution.).

We also enact this principle of solidarity through the support and care we provide for one another in the face of repression. We hereby agree to express this solidarity by showing up for court support, doing jail runs and jail visits, writing letters, contributing to bail and/or commissary funds, and generally offering whatever support we are able to.

In the Face of Police Repression—the Principle of Solidarity.

Coco Curranski
October 26, 2011
Oakland Solidarity March in NYC

Michael Andrews

TAKING THE STREETS

It is in the sudden moment of collective engagement that the city becomes elevated, it is then that *it belongs to you*. Platitudes rendered anodyne in aspirational ad campaigns become splinters in the spectacle—"It is your time, seize the moment." Historical time is suspended, allowing us to break out of a slow abandonment. In that moment of rupture there is an explosive escape from solitary malaise. The street becomes the territory of the collective. In that instant, rubble-strewn avenues open and a multitude of futures beckon.

—Laura Oldfield Ford, "Transmissions from a Discarded Future"

Occupy Oakland had been raided by police the previous day. The attack was outlandishly disproportionate: hundreds of riot cops, tear gas, rubber bullets, concussion grenades, and when it was all over, an Iraq War veteran was in the hospital. It was by far the most brutal police assault that any of the occupations had suffered to date. At Occupy Wall Street, we were shocked and angry. We wanted desperately to help our fellow occupiers in Oakland. That night, our General Assembly approved a large donation: 100 tents and $20,000 for legal and medical expenses to Occupy Oakland. The decision was almost as vital for OWS as it was for our Bay Area comrades; OWS had been losing momentum and fragmenting, but coming to consensus about this important gesture of solidarity galvanized us. Spirits were high when the General Assembly ended and we gathered in Zuccotti Park for our planned march in support of Occupy Oakland.

October 26, 2011

WHEN I RETURN TO ZUCCOTTI PARK AFTER USING THE BATHROOM, THE march has already departed. I ask an occupier standing around if he knows which direction the march went. He doesn't, so I text two friends who are on the march. One responds right away—they are a few blocks north. I leave the square and immediately bump into my friend Natasha, who is also looking for the march. We jog north together. A few blocks later we turn down a street where the march has just passed; a police car with lights flashing is parked in the middle of the road and a dozen cops in riot gear stand along the curb. They face the curb to prevent marchers from entering the street, which is strange, since the marchers are long gone. Only a few stragglers remain, shouting obscenities at the cops from the sidewalk. I look further down the street and see the march—a churning mass of bodies with signs and banners—crossing through the next intersection. Natasha and I run to catch up.

We reach the march at the far side of the intersection, just as the last marchers squeeze themselves onto the sidewalk that encircles City Hall and the adjacent park. I look toward the front and see that the column of people stretches past the curve in the sidewalk and all the way to City Hall. There must be a thousand of us or more—large for a march called earlier the same day. Natasha and I quickly find our friends near the end of the column. Everyone exchanges hugs. The people around us are in a buoyant mood, chanting "New York is Oakland! Oakland is New York!" and "Whose streets? Our streets!" As we shuffle down the sidewalk, the police walk in a tight-knit line in the road alongside us, shoving anyone who tries to step into the street. The officers doing the shoving are rank-and-file "blue shirts." Behind them, sauntering in the middle of the road, are a handful of higher-ranking "white shirts." They bark orders at the blue shirts and occasionally yell at marchers through bull horns. We march around City Hall Park once without incident and then turn to march around again. I say to a friend next to me, "I really hope we aren't going to march in a circle all night." The second time around a few people try to run up the steps of city hall but are pushed back by police. Shortly thereafter, the march lingers at a plaza next to City Hall. Without warning several police officers unravel a roll of orange netting, stretch it across the plaza and try to wrap it around a large group of marchers, including me. Everyone scatters. The cops fumble with the net; are they apprehensive about corralling us or just inept? I dash toward the curb, away from anything they might trap me against, like a fence or a wall. I see a large contingent of marchers regrouping on the northern corner of the plaza. Instead of turning to march around City Hall again, they cross the street and head uptown. Everyone else quickly follows in small groups, leaving the cops with an empty net.

I've lost my friends in the commotion so I follow the flow of marchers going uptown. We turn onto a short block devoid of cars. I see, halfway down the block, hundreds of people skipping and cheering in the middle of the street. The scuffle with the police has unleashed something. Before, the march was subdued and orderly. Now it is rollicking. I run to catch up with the exuberant crowd. When I get close I see that a cop has grabbed a young man—its the first arrest of the march. Several more cops converge around the young man to help wrestle him to the ground. Hundreds of marchers then converge around the cops, outnumbering them ten to one and shouting "Shame! Shame! Shame!" Cameras flash and smartphones come out to record video of the arrest. Some people try to grab the young man to pull him free—to "de-arrest" him—but a ring of officers shoves them back while three cops pin the young man against the asphalt and put his hands in zip-tie cuffs. Protesters and media continue to gather around the arrest. A heaving melee has formed by now. I peel off from the crowd and turn the corner onto Broadway. I see a friend of mine, who I didn't know was on the march, mount a short metal pole and shout at the crowd, "Take the streets! There's enough of us to take the streets!" He wants everyone to flood into Broadway, the busiest street in Manhattan, but his voice is drowned out by police sirens and the human roar of the melee.

As more police cars arrive, I look up Broadway and see an incredible sight: dozens of occupiers running towards me in a veritable stampede. They barrel down the sidewalk and through the street on their way to rejoin us. They must've gotten separated from the main march and continued walking uptown, unaware that an arrest was happening behind them. Luckily, someone called them back. They push themselves into the melee and amplify the chant of "Shame! Shame! Shame!" The entire intersection is in chaos. Traffic is blocked and I see several protesters being dragged by police to a paddy wagon across the street. Then, a few feet in front of me, two cops start to unroll more orange netting. They hold one end against the corner of a building and stretch the net across the sidewalk and into the street. Everyone who converged around the arrest is now trapped between the net and a wall of cops. I'm on the outside. The people inside push against the net and yell at the police to let them go. Someone slides under the net and gets free. Another person tries to climb over but is shoved back by a cop. There is a tremendous struggle. A few people near me grab a loose section of the net and start pulling. People inside the net start pulling too. The colossal tug of war overwhelms the cops. A moment later, the net is ours. Marchers wrench it away from the cops and take off running, holding the net aloft and cheering. The people who were trapped behind the net flood onto Broadway.

Seizing the net has further transformed the march. Everyone takes the street now, scrambling up Broadway in a fluid mass, heedless of traffic. Nothing creates a sense of collective empowerment on a march like withstanding a confrontation with the police. The net is stretched across two lanes of traffic and lifted over cars as they pass. We chant louder and more synchronized than before: "Whose streets? *OUR STREETS!* Whose streets? *OUR STREETS!*" People cheer and whistle and skip between passing cars. The whole thing now feels more like a roving street party than a protest.

As we make our way up Broadway, traffic thins so we fan out across the road. The police don't seem to pursue us; they must be tied up making arrests back at the intersection. At this hour, downtown Manhattan, which is dominated by municipal buildings, is empty. The stillness provides a strange counterpoint to our noisy revelry. Some of us chant and blow horns while others slap OWS stickers onto street signs. I see two guys on the opposite side of the street carrying the orange netting. They bring it to my side, roll it up and dump it into a trash can on the sidewalk next to me. I feel an impulse to retrieve it—what a trophy!—but decide it's too heavy to carry.

As we reach the heart of Chinatown, traffic grows heavier. Surprisingly, drivers don't seem to mind as hundreds of us weave through rush-hour gridlock, hooting and shouting. We get far more honks of support than honks of irritation. (It's easy to tell the difference: the former are short and lively, the latter are long and droning.) Since the beginning of the occupation, we've gone on dozens of marches through Manhattan. By now, New York City drivers know that when they see a mass of chanting protesters, it's OWS. If they don't honk in support, most at least slow down and wait patiently for us to pass, which is nothing short of astonishing—New Yorkers aren't known for their patience. This is even more remarkable considering that we usually march *against* traffic, a deliberate tactic to make it harder for police cars to catch up to us.

A few blocks later we cross Canal Street and enter SoHo, one of New York's famous shopping district. The police are nowhere in sight. Shoppers jam the sidewalks, and a few marchers hand them flyers, which most of them accept with curiosity. I see one marcher invite a trio of young black women, shopping bags in hand, to join the march. After a moment's hesitation they hop into the street and pump their fists to the rhythm of the chanting. We pass a Starbucks and there is a barista in the window dancing ecstatically. We have brought traffic to a standstill but most motorists seem unperturbed. The driver of a big hauling truck honks his horn in support. It sounds like the horn of an ocean liner, deep and bellowing. We erupt in cheers, which echo off the surrounding buildings. Several of us reach up and high-five the driver as we pass his truck.

The usual dull atmosphere of SoHo has been temporarily transformed. I walk past a cab stuck in traffic whose driver is cheering and honking for us. His passenger in the back seat, an expensively dressed young man, looks visibly annoyed as the driver holds his arm out the window to get twenty or thirty high fives from the passing marchers. Hearing the honking and cheering, shoppers in the boutiques and high-end chain stores pause to watch us. They seem bewildered by the sight of hundreds of chanting revelers streaming through the traffic-clogged streets. This is one aim of a wildcat march: to disrupt the normal, deadening flow of city life.

We are approaching Broadway and Houston, a major intersection. Two police vans arrive from a side street and try to block the intersection so we can't pass through, but this proves ineffective. We simply walk around them. We continue marching and then see flashing lights approaching from ahead. Two people at the front of the march raise their arms and sweep them to the left, signaling for us to turn. We stream into a narrow street near NYU. The police don't follow and there are no cars coming, so we use the relative calm to regroup. We slow down and swap stories about the exhilarating jaunt through SoHo. People are jubilant. Someone at the front of the march does a cartwheel. Others chant, "New York is Oakland! Oakland is New York!" I run twenty yards ahead and turn around to get a panoramic view of the march. We are smaller than when we started but there are still a few hundred of us. Behind me a police cruiser races through the nearest intersection but does not stop.

As we amble down the street, the scenery changes from quiet university buildings to bustling bars and restaurants. We have entered Greenwich Village. The sidewalks teem with people chatting, smoking, or waiting in line to get into clubs. They seem to instantly recognize who we are. Many give us peace signs and pump their fists. Others stare wide-eyed and confused. We chant "Join us! Join us!" but nobody obliges. I watch a taxi turn into our street a few blocks ahead and then, seeing us, immediately turn off. At the front of the march a dapper man with close-cropped hair is leading us. He looks like he just came from a cocktail party. He peers down a side street and sees something he likes, then motions excitedly for us to turn. We do.

The street is narrow so we fill the roadway and spill onto the sidewalks. Ahead, I see flood lights and movie cameras. There are empty director's chairs on one side of the street and an enormous projection screen on the other. I quickly realize that we are marching through a movie set. Amazingly, the actors and crew don't mind. They step aside and give us thumbs up as we pass.

We've spread out into a long, loose procession now, and I'm towards the end. We turn down an alley. Suddenly, everyone around me starts running. I start running too—it's a reflex—but when I look around, I don't see any police. It takes me a second to realize that people are running for the fun of it. And it *is* fun. I feel a rush of energy as dozens of comrades bound alongside me. The only time I've ever run through the streets of New York was when I was in a hurry to get to work.

After a short sprint we reach Sixth Avenue, a major thoroughfare, and stop in the middle of the street. Our numbers have dwindled but we still have enough people to fill the roadway. Cars honk and drive around us as we unhurriedly discuss where to go next. We abandoned our planned route long ago, which is the best kind of march; it becomes a collective exploration of the city rather than something mapped out and predetermined. Some people want to march up Sixth Avenue while others want to return to Zuccotti Park. The cops are nowhere to be seen. After a few minutes of inconclusive deliberations, a group of marchers starts walking down a residential street in the general direction of Zuccotti Park. Little by little, everyone else follows. For my part, I'm starving so I step away to get pizza.

When I leave the pizza place ten minutes later I have no idea where the march is. I wander around the neighborhood and finally see the march several blocks away, going south on Sixth Avenue. As I run to catch up, I pass a dozen police cars parked along the curb; a dozen officers lean against the cars and chat casually with each other, even as protesters frolic through the street just a few blocks away. I wonder to myself if the NYPD have been instructed to go easy tonight after the absurd display of excessive force in Oakland yesterday.

When I reach the march I'm surprised to notice that we have the street entirely to ourselves. There is no traffic on this stretch of Sixth Avenue. We spread out across the entire roadway, still energetic after marching for an hour and a half. Then, when we reach the intersection of Sixth and Canal Street, two police cars pull up on our right. A few brave marchers stand directly in front of the police cars to block them. Fifty feet ahead I see several officers spilling out a police van and a group of scooter cops forming a cordon to block the street. The gloves have come off. Seeing the scooter cops, we scatter. I run to the right, but when I notice that most people have run to the left, I reverse course. I scamper across Sixth Avenue in a wide arc, barely avoiding the scooter cops. I look behind me and see a girl in her twenties being arrested in the middle of street. She's on her knees in front of a police van with her arms behind her; one cop puts her hands in zip-ties cuffs while another presses her face against the grill of the van. I'm shocked but I don't run to help her. After several wildcat marches I've learned that you don't try to de-arrest someone who's securely in custody. You'll never manage to free the person and you'll get arrested yourself. Still, I'm surprised at myself for not slowing down or calling for help.

When I reach the opposite side of the street there is a bottleneck on the sidewalk where marchers are skirting around the cordon of scooter cops. I slip through the bottleneck and hop back into the street, behind the cordon now. The scooter cops don't get off their bikes to arrest people even as we pour through the opening in the sidewalk, so the cordon is completely ineffective. It's remarkable how lumbering and impotent the NYPD can be in the face of an improvised, energetic march. Besides the girl I saw, nobody seems to have been arrested. We quickly regroup in the street and then leave the scene in several small groups. I'm shaken but also invigorated by the encounter with the police.

We run a few blocks and then slow down to catch our breath. But before long, we hear the familiar buzzing of scooters behind us. We dash down a side street that is closed to traffic because of road work. There are wooden barricade and concrete pylons in the street. Some marchers knock over the barricades, and throw bags of trash into the street to slow down the scooter cops. Others promptly pick up the barricades. I see one guy ask another for help lifting a huge planter that was knocked into the street by another marcher. During these marches there is a constant low-level struggle between protesters who want to indiscriminately smash things and others who are afraid of the bad image this presents to the public.

At the end of the block we stop and gather in the intersection. We're back on Broadway now, where there is no traffic. About 200 of us are left. We again deliberate about where to go next. Some want to march back uptown while others chant, "Zuccotti! Zuccotti!" The latter is far more popular so we set off downtown in a loose-knit swarm.

As we stroll through the avenues of lower Manhattan, there is a swagger in our step. We have been marching for nearly two hours on a beautiful night in New York City. We have outmaneuvered the cops, won over bystanders and—most importantly—we have learned that when we're in the streets together, there is no reason to be afraid. At their best, wildcat marches transform people: from strangers to comrades, from moderates to radicals, from people who reflexively defer to police authority to those who challenge it.

I run ahead half a block to survey our route. From a side street another group of scooter cops pulls into the intersection and forms a cordon. I run past them before they can grab me, then I turn around to watch them confront the marchers. Most of the marchers take to the sidewalk to evade the cordon, but a few—feeling perhaps *too* fearless—try to jump over it. One falls and is immediately smothered by cops. Marchers surround the cops, who are again outnumbered. Some marchers grab the guy who fell and try to pull him free. The police tug back. There is a fierce struggle, and then I see the young man emerge from the pile of bodies. He runs away frantically, followed by the people who freed him, all cheering wildly. When they catch up to me I cheer and run with them.

For the rest of the march the police keep their distance. When we finally reach Zuccotti Park we are greeted by chants of "Welcome home! Welcome home!" Everyone hugs each other, tired but exhilarated. A friend tells me that his girlfriend ended up two miles away in Union Square with another large contingent of marchers. "Huh?," I say. He tells me that this other contingent broke away from the march at some point and took a different route than our contingent. I'm astonished. It means there were two wildcat marches through Manhattan that night. Fifteen minutes later the second march returns to Zuccotti Park from Union Square. They get the same rousing welcome that we got.

Margaret Killjoy
November 2, 2011
Oakland General Strike

Jonathan Matthew Smucker

RADICALS AND THE 99%
CORE AND MASS MOVEMENT

OCCUPY WALL STREET AUDACIOUSLY CLAIMED TO BE A MOVEMENT OF "THE 99%," challenging the extreme consolidation of wealth and political power by the top one percent. Our opponents, however, claim that the 99% movement is little more than a handful of fringe radicals who are out of touch with mainstream America.

They're not 100% wrong about us being radicals. Radicals played pivotal roles in initiating Occupy Wall Street. And radicals continue to pour an enormous amount of time, energy, creativity, and strategic thinking into this burgeoning movement.

What our opponents are wrong about is the equation of *radical* with *fringe*. The word *radical* literally means going to the *root* of something. Establishment forces use the label *radical* interchangeably with the disparaging label *extremist*—as a means to "otherize" the movement. But clearly the radicals did something right here. We flipped the script by framing the top 1% as the real extremists—as the people who are truly out of touch. By striking at the root of the problem and naming the primary culprit in our economic and democratic crises—by creating a defiant symbol on Wall Street's doorstep—a new generation of young radicals has struck a chord with mainstream America. A movement that started as an audacious act by a committed core of radicals quickly and dramatically broadened its appeal.

Radicals will likely continue to play a crucial role in this movement. Throughout history the radicals have tended to be among those who give the most of their time and energy to movements for change. They tend to make up a large part of the movement's core. As such, their contributions are absolutely indispensable.

However, successful movements need a lot more than a radical core. For every core participant who gives nearly everything of herself or himself, a strong movement needs a hundred more people in the next "tier" of participation—folks who are contributing *something*, while balancing other commitments in their lives. If we are to effectively challenge the most powerful institutions in the world (e.g. capitalism), we will need the active involvement of hundreds of thousands if not millions of people—folks who are willing to give *something*. If the core fails to involve a big enough next tier of participants, it will certainly fail to maintain effective engagement with the broader society. These "next tier" participants are not even the base, but rather the *start of the base* needed to accomplish our big-picture aims.

If the kinds of changes we imagine are ever to be realized, it will be through the active participation of large numbers of teachers, nurses, factory workers, barbers, artists, service workers, students, military service members and veterans, religious communities, civic organizations, unions, and even some allies within the existing power establishment. These participants come as they are, and the core must welcome them as such. A broad-based movement cannot afford to have a high bar for entry. The smallest of contributions must be encouraged and affirmed. If we are to keep building a popular movement, we must accommodate a continuum of levels of involvement, as well as levels of political analysis.

Occupy Wall Street got an impressive start in a very short amount of time. And our opponents took notice and kicked into a high gear counter-offensive. They will continue to do what they can to foment division between the radicalized core and the broader movement—because they know well that the dynamic-but-challenging relationship between core and broader base is one of the biggest strengths *and* biggest vulnerabilities of our movement. The successful interplay between these tiers of movement participants is of critical importance. Unfortunately, our opponents sometimes know this better than we do.

story of the righteous few

Too often, radicals play into our opponents' divide-and-conquer strategies, by relishing in our radical identity more than we value connecting with a broader base. Too often we get stuck in a *story of the righteous few*.

Radicals tend to *become radicals* because we become disillusioned with aspects of the dominant culture. When you feel like you're up against the culture, it's easy then to develop an inclination to separate yourself from that culture. When we begin to become aware of the destructive impacts of capitalism, racism, sexism, and whatever other social systems we encounter that we see perpetuating oppression, we don't want to be part of it. We feel a moral repugnance and a desire to not cooperate with injustice.

However, this desire to separate ourselves from injustice can develop into a general mentality of separation from society more generally. In other words, when we see the dominant culture as a perpetrator of injustice, and we see society as the storehouse of the dominant culture, then our desire to separate ourselves from injustice can easily develop into a mentality of separating our-selves from the mainstream of society. With the mainstream seen as bad, we begin to look for ways to distinguish ourselves and our groups from any-thing mainstream. We begin to notice, highlight, exaggerate, and develop distinctions between ourselves and the mainstream, because these distinctions reinforce our radical identity. The distinguishing features go far beyond non-participation in those aspects of the dominant culture that we find offensive.

Radicals may start to adorn themselves with distinguishing features to express separation from society, and also to flag other radicals. In his book *All the Power*, author and community organizer Mark Andersen describes in tribal terms how this phenomenon plays out in punk subcultures:

> The punk subculture has many of the hallmarks of a tribe … piercings, tattoos, more. These markers, also including hairstyle, dress, music form, even slang, help to demark the boundaries of the group, to set it off from the larger populace. In this way, appearance can even be a form of dissent, a strikingly visual way to say, "I am not a part of your corrupt world."

Surely there were similar dynamics in play among radicals at Liberty Square and at other occupations across the country. The big danger is that radical subcultures caught in this pattern of emphasizing how different they are may, over time, start to even prize their own marginalization. If society is unjust, then our justice-oriented identity may be reaffirmed when we are rejected by society (or more accurately, by portions of society). If society is bad, then marginalization in society may be seen as good. We may tell each other stories of how we were ostracized in this or that group, how we're the outcast in our family, how we were the only revolutionary in a group of lib-eral reformists, etc. We may start to swim in our own marginalization. This is the *story of the righteous few*.

In the story of the righteous few, success itself becomes suspect. If a group or individual is embraced by a significant enough portion of society, it must be because they are not truly revolutionary or because their message has been "watered down." It seriously messes with radicals' heads when some of our ideas start to become popular! We are so accustomed to being the most radical kid on the block, and suddenly people we've never met are coming out of the woodwork, marching in the streets with us, and spouting some of the lines we've been saying for years. Frankly, it can lead to a bit of an identity crisis.

Here we see the importance of checking our narratives for faulty compo-nents. If we allow the story of the righteous few to hold a place in our narra-tive about social change, then our efforts are likely to be seriously hindered by a general mentality to separate and distinguish ourselves from society and to retreat from success. To organize effectively, this mentality has to turn 180 degrees. We have to orient ourselves to connect with others, to notice commonalities, to "weave ourselves into the fabric of society" (quoting OWS participant Beka Economopoulos), and to embrace being embraced by society. For many radicals, this can be a big shift in our conceptualizations of ourselves and of our society.

The good news is that we are presently deep into the process of making that profound paradigmatic shift. The framing of *the 99%* asserts an alignment of our vision with the interests of a supermajority of Americans. It encourages us to think of most everyone as a potential ally.

The importance of this paradigm shift cannot be overstated. Over the past four decades radical social justice movements tended to feel like we were up against the whole culture. We began clustering into increasingly insular circles, looking to each other for support and connection, as if to hold onto our sanity in a world gone mad. We often felt entirely powerless in the face of so-called "free trade" agreements, austerity, raging wars of aggression, attacks on the gains made by earlier social justice movements (e.g. Civil Rights and feminism), ecological devastation, and many other setbacks.

That's part of what makes this moment so significant. OWS and the 99% movement have the potential to pull us out of a *counter-cultural* mentality and set us up to claim and contest the culture—*our* culture—rather than denounce, abandon, and distinguish ourselves from it. *We are the 99%. We are the true moral majority.*

But we have a long road ahead. The meme of "the 99%" can help to shift our thinking, but no meme is good enough to do all the work for us, without a conscious effort. While we continue to challenge the dominant storyline, we must also self-reflectively challenge some components of the narratives we tell ourselves about our relationship as radicals to the broader society. If we want to win, we have to scrap the chapter of the righteous few, and replace it with a story about everyday people—about huge swaths of society—stepping into movement together.

The underlying economic conditions are politicizing more and more people by the day, creating greater potential for the emergence of a broader-based movement than we've seen in decades. And this moment needs the full participation and influence of radicals. Without radicals, this wave would lose its fire and settle too soon for too little.

It must be pointed out that some establishment forces in the emerging precarious alignment—and all alignments are precarious!—will try to throw radicals under the bus first chance they get. But really it's on us to make sure no one gets that chance. The way to do that is for radicals to get really good at making friends with a lot of people—to be the life of the party. It must be abundantly clear to tentative allies and opponents alike that it would be difficult to isolate us; that there would be a backlash if they attacked radicals. One thing *not* to do is shrink away from engagement with broader constituencies and unwieldy alignments, even including those who might betray us if they perceive they can get away with it. Such a retreat would make our fears self-fulfilling; would enable those who would screw us; would seal our fate as righteous martyrs whom the world was not ready for. Radicals have to ask ourselves if our radical identity confines us to be eternally rejected, ostracized, and crucified. That's the story of the righteous few. The powerful are always ready to tell that story, and we must determine to not be a predictable character in their script. Serious radicals must decouple radicalism from such a martyr mentality. Serious radicals must aim to succeed. Fighting an advantaged opponent without a real intention and strategy for success is not so much fighting as it is coping. The tendency of the outgunned resister to run headlong, kamikaze-style, into enemy lines is the tendency of someone who wants to be righteous—not of someone who seeks to actually change the world. We must ask ourselves if our intention is to bring about meaningful change, or if it is to act out righteous narratives (either as individuals or in small enlightened groups).

It must be abundantly clear to tentative allies and opponents alike that it would be difficult to isolate us; that there would be a backlash if they attacked radicals. One thing not to do is shrink away from engagement with broader constituencies and unwieldy alignments, even including those who might betray us if they perceive they can get away with it.

our identity paradox

PART OF THIS challenge can be framed in terms of the interaction between the radical and the mainstream, and part of it in terms of the interaction between the movement's core and its broader base. (These two frames of interaction—radical/mainstream, core/broader base—overlap, but not completely.)

Fomenting a strong core—i.e. very active participants—is as essential for Occupy as it is for any social movement. There can be no serious social movement—the kind that challenges the powerful and privileged—without a correspondingly serious group identity that encourages a core of members to contribute an exceptional level of commitment, sacrifice, and heroics over the course of prolonged struggle. This kind of group identity has quickly, clearly, and strikingly emerged among core participants in OWS and occupations across the country and around the world. And that's a good thing.

However, this strong group identity is also something of a double-edged sword. The stronger the identity and cohesion of the core, the more likely we are to become alienated from other groups and from the broader society.

We have to navigate something of a *political identity paradox*: our situation requires a strong internal identity in order to foster the level of commitment needed for protracted struggle; but this same cohesion tends over time to isolate the group, and isolated groups are hard-pressed to build the kind of broad-based power needed to achieve the big changes they imagine.

Strong bonding *within* a group tends to create distinctions *between* groups—that's true to an extent for all kinds of groups. However, it tends to have particular consequences for groups involved in oppositional political struggle. Consider a sports team that defines its group identity partly in distinction from rival teams. The team is likely to play all the harder against rivals as a result of the distinction. No problem there. A group engaged in challenging entrenched power, on the other hand—as the Occupy movement is doing—has not only to foster a strong internal identity; it also has to win allies beyond the bounds of that identity, if it is to build the collective power it needs to accomplish its goals. To extend the sports metaphor, if a movement group wants to score any goals, it has to see and value other groups as players on the same team, moving the ball in the same general direction.

Add to this challenge that dynamics of oppositional struggle can quickly escalate this tendency toward isolation. Oppositional struggle can trigger an oppositional psychology amongst core participants, which can do a real number on a group. Movements that meet the kind of brutal resistance that the Civil Rights movement endured, for example, have quite a balancing act to perform. On the one hand, participants need to turn to each other more than ever for strength and support. They feel a compelling cohesiveness to their group identity in these moments of escalated conflict. On the other hand, they need to keep outwardly oriented, to stay connected to a broad and growing base. This is difficult to do even when core members are fully oriented to the task, let alone when they are unprepared, which is so often the case.

Take, for example, Students for a Democratic Society (the original SDS that fell apart in dramatic fashion in 1969). At the center of the epic implosion of this massive student organization—underneath the rational arguments and accusations that leaders were slinging at each other—there was this *political identity paradox*. Key leaders had become encapsulated in their oppositional identity (or, rather, a few factionalizing identities) and they became more and more out of touch. They lost the ability and even the inclination to relate to their broader membership—a *huge* number of students at the moment of the implosion—let alone to the broader society. Some of the most committed would-be leaders of that generation came to see more value in holing up with a few comrades to make bombs than in organizing masses of students to take coordinated action. This is the tendency toward isolation taken to the extreme. Dedicated radicals cut themselves off, like lone guerrilla fighters in enemy territory. It might have felt glorious, but it was a suicide mission.

The political identity paradox speaks to the need for OWS to develop both strong *bonding* and strong *bridging*. Without strong *intra-group* bonding, core participants will lack the level of commitment required for our serious struggle, and the support needed to hearten us in the face of state repression. But without strong *beyond-group* bridging, we would become too insular and isolated to be able to forge the broad alliances necessary for achieving big changes. Recurring manifestations of self-referential tactics, rituals, and rhetoric in OWS demonstrate this insular tendency.

We have to perform an extraordinary balancing act between the conflicting imperatives of building a strong sense of identity within our core and connecting with allies and potential allies beyond the core. This balancing act will be more and more critical as the Occupy movement matures, as the core further develops a distinct culture, and as our opponents attempt to drive wedges between the movement's most active participants and the broader society.

Ten or twenty years from now, will we look back on Occupy Wall Street and see it as a blip, as a righteous stand that was predictably short-lived? Or will we see this as the moment when America rediscovered collective action—when a broad-based movement for social and economic justice was (re)born? Will we see it as little more than an interesting twist—a peculiar spike—in the otherwise predictable story of the righteous few? Or will we see it as a catalyst of a new moral majority that went on to change the course of history? Our long-term success depends on our skill in navigating the space between radical and mainstream, and between core and broader base; on our ability to foster strong internal solidarity, while also maintaining our orientation to connect with the broader society.

Ilias Bartolini
October 16, 2011
Occupy London

Nathan Schneider

NO REVOLUTION WITHOUT RELIGION

THERE WAS A FLASH OF WISDOM IN OCCUPY WALL STREET'S CONTROVERSIAL and otherwise unsuccessful attempt to occupy a plot of land owned by Trinity Church on December 17 of last year: if the movement was going to last much longer, it would have to occupy, and be supported by, faith. By "faith," let me be clear, I mean religion—the more organized the better. "Hey, church," one could almost hear the Occupiers saying, as they mounted the giant ladder over the fence and dropped down on the other side, "act like a church." And, this being just a month after the eviction from Zuccotti Park, "We need you."

The Occupy movement has been largely a white, urban phenomenon, and one with a bit of a tendency toward vanguardism, which makes it not entirely surprising that it's often blind to the fact that there is no force more potentially revolutionary in US history or in the country today than religion. But the movement remains oblivious to this at its own peril. You who are blind, see.

On the other side of the Atlantic, left intellectuals have been starting to discover what they have to learn from religion about revolution. Slavoj Žižek, Alain Badiou, and Giorgio Agamben have all written about the apostle Paul in recent years: he stood at the intersection of Judaism and Christianity and was the architect of an underground movement that eventually subsumed the Roman Empire. During the early days of Liberty Square, actually, I felt like I was witnessing a glimpse of how Paul described his early church: the holding of all things in common, a single-minded asceticism, and local cells miraculously spreading throughout the known world. Living in societies far less religious than ours, thinkers on the European left are realizing that the loss of religious imagination can mean losing the capacity to imagine and take steps toward a radically different kind of society.

It's hard to think of a place where religion's revolutionary potential has been more fully realized than the United States—both for good and for evil.

Many activists nowadays assume the completely non-empirical notion that religion in this country today is a wholly-owned subsidiary of the Republican Party. But this impression is the result of a very temporary and partial—if singularly effective—alliance forged at the onset of the Reagan era. It's an alliance that need not last. American religion is nothing if not finicky with regard to politics, and highly troublesome to those in power.

While communities of faith have tended of late to be co-opted by the 1%, in the past they were engines that helped drive (as well as suppress) the early labor movement and women's suffrage, together with just about every other political movement with any major impact on American history. And how could it not? About 14 million people belong to labor unions in the United States; closer to 120 million attend religious services regularly. Most of them, at least some of the time, are told in those services to do good, seek justice, and rescue the oppressed. Whether it's on behalf of affordable housing or the those on death row, or for an end to AIDS and human trafficking, religion represents an enormous proportion of how people in this country organize. One need only think of the civil rights movement, arguably the last mass resistance movement in the US to win decisive political gains. In it, churches were often the basic units of organizing. Clergy locked arms with activists at the front lines, and together they won.

Freedom fighters in countries around the world already know this phenomenon. When the People Power Revolution brought down Ferdinand Marcos in the Philippines, nuns knelt in prayer before the army's tanks, preventing them from attacking defectors. Burma's Buddhist monks are the country's revolutionary vanguard, and it was after the color of their robes that the startling but unsuccessful Saffron Revolution of 2007 is named. Archbishop Óscar Romero of El Salvador became so dangerous after taking up the cause of the poor that he had to be assassinated while saying mass; his memory has galvanized the cause of liberation throughout Latin America ever since.

Religious communities possess tremendous quantities of real estate, no small amount of it unused. Such spaces could become available to the movement, and by means more diplomatic than the failed, forced occupations of church property tried in New York and San Francisco. Far preferable, I would think, are Occupiers' successes in defending from closure an historic church in Atlanta and a Catholic homeless center in Providence. What might happen if Occupiers spent half as much time building solidarity with religious groups as with the often-disappointing unions?

The power of religion, however, is always ambivalent, and it can be on the wrong side as often as it's on the right one. The tryst between civil rights and churches, certainly, was no straightforward affair. Southern clergy, both black and white, had learned to benefit from segregation, and a new civil rights organizer in town could represent a threat to their privileges. Saul Alinsky claimed that he never got anywhere appealing to clergy by the precepts of their faith. "Instead," he wrote, "I approach them on the basis of their own self-interest, the welfare of their Church, even its physical property." An eminent religion reporter I know says he deals with them like he used to deal with the mob.

If a revolution fails to co-opt religion for its own side early on, too, religion can turn around and co-opt the revolution. This is what happened, for instance, after the Iranian Revolution of 1979, and it happened again in Egypt following the populist euphoria in Tahrir Square. In both places, a broad-based uprising that cut across all sorts of divisions in those societies created an opening, which well-organized and conservative religious networks were able to charge into without serious challenge from the fledgling movement. The movement failed to take seriously enough the revolutionary, even Promethean capacity of the religious organizations in their midst—resulting in a different kind of revolution from the one for which many had hoped.

About 14 million people belong to labor unions in the United States; closer to 120 million attend religious services regularly.

YOU MIGHT NOT know it, because the stories are rarely told in this way, but religious people and symbols and institutions have played important roles in Occupy Wall Street since the beginning. The first thing I noticed as I biked into the Financial District on the morning of September 17, actually, was a group of "Protest Chaplains" from Boston, in their inaugural action. Standing at the corner of Wall Street and Broadway, facing Trinity Church, they were dressed in white robes, singing hymns and carrying a cardboard cross. Throughout the day, they were a favorite of reporters—a little more approachable than the average crusty protester, a little less weird than the LaRouchePAC choir.

The day's first substantial assembly took place at Bowling Green, on the steps of the National Museum of the American Indian, where people gathered to hear an impromptu sermon of Reverend Billy, the quasi-preacher performance artist. It was there that the decision was made to march a few blocks north to Zuccotti Park.

In the harrowing early days of the occupation, facing constant police intimidation, prayer walks and meditation circles were commonplace for those who wanted or needed them. Once, I remember, a few of us spontaneously decided to take a silent walk to a nearby church to pray, and on the way discovered that each of us was carrying a rosary. For me, at least, this was unusual; I had only begun keeping one with me on the night of September 16, feeling the need for special protection for my new friends. Evidently I wasn't the only one.

Such ad hoc religion soon became more organized. For the holy day of Yom Kippur, hundreds of Jews held a Kol Nidre service across the street from Liberty Square. The following Sunday, Christians and others marched from Judson Church in the Village to Liberty, carrying a golden calf inscribed with the words "GREED" and "FALSE IDOL," and a photo of it appeared on the front page of *The Washington Post*. The clergy-driven Occupy Faith network became an interface between the leaderless movement and the needs of professional religious leaders. Around the country, they've worked to serve the physical, psychological, and spiritual needs of Occupiers, while also launching campaigns of their own, including an ambitious Truth Commission.

It was through a religious ritual, in fact, that the tents first went up at Liberty Square in mid-October. From the beginning, police had prevented anything resembling a tent from being erected. But Occupy Judaism coordinated with people in the Direct Action Working Group to raise a special tent in the park for Sukkot, the Festival of Booths. When the police came to take it down, a crowd gathered around and explained what it was. The cops, spooked by the thought of disturbing a religious observance, backed down, and the Sukkah stood.

"Tonight we're all Jews," cried a voice in the people's mic as it began to rain. "Build yourself a sukkah!" The park became a tent city, and so it would remain.

When eviction finally came, it was to churches—not unions, not nonprofits—around New York that Occupiers fled and took refuge. There they stayed, and met, and ate through the winter. This was a messy arrangement, and eventually having sanctuaries full of homeless activists overtaxed the congregations' resources. But at the moment when so much of the city turned its back on the movement, a coalition of religious communities took Occupiers in.

The possibilities are so much greater. For a movement that has still failed to bring eviction-defense and anti-foreclosure actions to a mass scale, religious communities are ideal platforms for doing so; equip them with the right tools and strategies, and when some of their own are threatened by the banks, their fellow faithful will rally to save their homes—not merely on the basis of political ideology, but with the far more powerful motivation of looking out for one's own. Opposing predatory greed also has special resonance in religious traditions, from the debt-forgiving Jubilee of the Hebrew scriptures, to the radical aid for those in need taught and practiced by Jesus Christ, to the ban on usury in Islamic (and medieval Christian) law. An act may be civil disobedience by temporal standards, but to a higher law, resisting oppression should be a basic requirement.

While most religious communities don't come anywhere near the Occupy standard for horizontality and transparency—nor does Occupy, for that matter—they're not as bad as an outsider might think. The flock often finds plenty of ways of nudging the shepherd—from the power of the pocketbook, to steering committees and boards, to the threat of simply picking up and going elsewhere. That's why, as with unions, Occupy isn't going to get anywhere with religious communities until it wins over the rank-and-file. Then, leaders will have to show support for the movement, or else.

When eviction finally came, it was to churches—not unions, not nonprofits—around New York that Occupiers fled and took refuge. There they stayed, and met, and ate through the winter. This was a messy arrangement, and eventually having sanctuaries full of homeless activists overtaxed the congregations' resources. But at the moment when so much of the city turned its back on the movement, a coalition of religious communities took Occupiers in.

As I STOOD waiting for the action against Trinity Church to begin on December 17, I struck up a conversation with a man in a Roman collar and a black beret, Fr. Paul Mayer—a formerly married Catholic priest and veteran of every major American social justice movement since he marched with Martin Luther King, Jr., in the 1960s. Trinity is an Episcopal church; I asked him what he thought we Catholics would do if OWS were making a demand like this of us.

"We'd be worse," he replied.

I didn't know it at the time, but, together with Episcopal Bishop George Packard and Sr. Susan Wilcox, a Catholic nun, Mayer was about to lead the charge over the fence, down onto Trinity property, and promptly into police custody. The following night, out of jail, he and Wilcox joined me and a lapsed cradle Catholic, a theologian, and a sociology student for the first meeting of Occupy Catholics at a bar near Zuccotti Park. Already, a few of us had been finding one another on Twitter and Facebook, testing out memes and slogans. Without us even asking, a comrade in Baltimore sent us block-cut logos she'd made for us to use: a single candle burning, and a bird with a halo occupying a nest. Another, in Virginia, composed prayers for Occupy days of action.

We came together in person with a common but still not-quite-clarified desire to create a group of Catholics involved with the movement, as well as to take what the movement was teaching us and bring it to our church. Maybe, someday, we could help Catholic churches respond better to Occupiers than Trinity did, and vice versa. The connection between Occupy and our faith was so obvious that we couldn't ignore it. We needed this movement, and we knew that the movement no less needed us.

For my own part, since the occupation began, going to church was harder than ever. It wasn't because I believed less, but because I believed more. Rather than just the priest's sermon, I wanted to hear from the old Caribbean women sitting around me, and from the children, and from the blind man in front. I wanted to know what they thought of the gospel reading. I'd sit in the pews and fantasize about mic-checking the liturgy, about setting the gospel free. Occupy Catholics was a group of people who'd been having similar fantasies. Some hadn't been going to church for years, but when they got involved with Occupy, it reminded them of the social justice tradition they'd learned from nuns growing up. In Occupy Catholics, they found a community that was welcoming in ways Catholic churches themselves had failed to be.

We began by reaching out to laypeople, online and through the social justice ministries of nearby churches. We held a General Assembly at Maryhouse Catholic Worker, part of the organization Dorothy Day cofounded with Christian anarchist principles to serve the poor and struggle for justice and peace. For months our group continued slowly growing, planning, and praying about how to encourage our church, the biggest landowner in New York City, to join Occupy's call for a more righteous society. We brought buckets, water, and packages full of new socks to Federal Hall on Wall Street and washed the feet of tired Occupiers. We arranged for a Catholic school building where Occupy organizers could sleep. When the Vatican started cracking down on American nuns for paying too much attention to the poor and for the "radical feminist themes" in their theology, we picketed the bishops and launched the #radicalfeministthemes hashtag. As the trial of those arrested on December 17 approached, we helped organize solidarity actions, and when it finally came, Occupy Catholics members were sitting in the courtroom.

On Good Friday, the most solemn day of the Christian year, we stood in front of St. Patrick's Cathedral and sang, "Were you there when they crucified the poor?" against the bishops' silence on a budget in Congress poised to slash services upon which the 99% depends. "We love our church," we cried with the people's mic, "and right now the church needs to speak." So we did, and within weeks the bishops echoed these concerns for themselves. When we returned to St. Patrick's again a few months later, we held a General Assembly out front on the sidewalk. That night, we slept there, surrounded by our handmade signs, our Occupy allies, and a wall of police barricades.

Molly Crabapple
& John Leavitt

Rose Bookbinder and Michael Belt

OWS & LABOR ATTEMPTING THE POSSIBLE
BUILDING A MOVEMENT BY LEARNING TO COLLABORATE THROUGH DIFFERENCE

> [G]rassroots organizations that labor in the shadow of the shadow state should consider this: the purpose of the work is to gain liberation, not to guarantee the organization's longevity. In the short run, it seems the work and the organizations are an identity: the staff and the pamphlets and projects and ideas gain some traction on this slippery ground because they have a bit of weight. That's true. But it is also the case that when it comes to social movements, organizations are only as good as the united fronts they bring into being.
>
> —Ruth Wilson Gilmore, *In the Shadow of the Shadow State*

IT WAS THE FIRST TIME IN DECADES THAT THE NEW YORK CITY CENTRAL Labor Council (NYCCLC) endorsed the "radical" holiday May Day. While the NYCCLC, the umbrella organization representing over 1.3 million NYC union workers, is traditionally known for its conservatism, this surprising decision was led by its more progressive members who felt that the unprecedented coalition of unions, immigrant rights organizations, and Occupy Wall Street (OWS) held the possibility of an historic and promising new path for organized labor. May Day 2012 in NYC, under the banner "Legalize, Organize, Unionize," opened a new door for incredible possibilities of continued coalition building and acts of solidarity that could bring power and unity to the 99%.

Our aim in analyzing the past year's innovative collaborations between OWS and organized labor in NYC is not to post warning signs about the dangers and limits of violating the purity of either project. Rather, we hope to identify possibilities and recognize the value and potential of the hard labor so many committed activists have put into developing common visions and putting solidarity into practice.

As Ruth Wilson Gilmore suggests above, closely held allegiances to distinct organizational identities pose a key challenge to building powerful united fronts. Though Gilmore is specifically addressing the work of grassroots organizations, her insight highlights the importance of asking questions about what it will take to build a movement by unifying organizations as diverse as highly-structured labor unions, precariously-funded community organizations, and the relatively over-exposed and under-experienced project that is Occupy Wall Street. Gilmore argues that united fronts require the development of: shared long-term goals that supersede specific organizational identities (solidarity of purpose); a willingness to see possibilities instead of limits; and the building of relationships with likely allies. In our estimation, the coalition that came together to organize May Day, as well as other examples of labor/OWS collaboration, represent hopeful steps toward building a mass movement with the power to change the future.

may day 2012, nyc: organize, legalize, unionize!

OVERCOMING THE LIMITATIONS of strictly delineated organizational identities requires broader identification with the historical struggles that have brought us to the place we stand today. May Day has taken place every May 1 since 1886, when a wave of mass strikes focused on the fight for an 8-hour day swelled across the heartland of America. The American Federation of Labour (AFL) had adopted a resolution stating "eight hours shall constitute a legal day's labour from and after May 1, 1886." In Chicago, 100,000 workers (one fourth of the city's population) struck. There, during a demonstration, a crowd confronted strike-breakers leaving the nearby McCormick factory, chasing them back inside. At a demonstration on May 4, police opened fire on a crowd, killing four and seriously wounding many. The police then arrested, tried, and sentenced to death eight anarchists, triggering global outcry. Several years later, in honor of their slain comrades, a coalition of workers groups declared May 1 "International Workers Day." Ever since, people around the world have come together on May Day to remember the sacrifices of those who have struggled before us, to defend the gains they made, and to discuss the way forward to a better world for the 99%. But in the late 1950s, during the red scare in the US, there was a suppression of May Day and groups who once celebrated this holiday began to conform to the dictates of Cold War nationalism, ignoring the significance of radical labor struggles by capitulating to recognize the overtly anti-internationalist celebration of "Labor Day." It wasn't until 2006 when immigrant rights groups, in reaction to the notorious Sensenbrenner Bill (national legislation promising the mass expulsion of millions of immigrant workers from the US) declared May Day to be "The Day without the Immigrant." Workers and communities organized across the United States to once again rally for May Day and cities from Los Angeles to NYC and Chicago saw millions in the streets. Sensenbrenner died in Congress (to be reborn in state legislatures in years to come) and the mass marches came to an end. "While many observers declared the immigrant rights movement 'dead,' mistaking mobilizations for movements," says Arizona scholar Zoe Hammer, "immigrant rights organizations across the country have continued to organize communities, develop vision and strategy, and build coalitions, such as the NYC organizations that participated in coordinating the May Day coalition" (personal communication).

Last fall, in the glow of the global spotlight generated by the mass uprisings of the Arab Spring, Occupy Wall Street emerged on the world's media stage, bringing the pressing issue of income disparity back into the national discourse for the first time in over three decades of neoliberal rule, and intervening in the rhetoric of the precious individual by telling the story of the 99%. This significant messaging accomplishment has the potential to become strategically significant. It sets the ideological groundwork for new political formations to emerge and reframe political debates, negotiations, and planning processes in ways that displace the needs of corporations by foregrounding the needs of living human beings, including workers, students, dispossessed communities, and

The rhetoric of the struggle of the 99% against the 1% not only puts a class analysis into play, but also has inspired many to question the fundamentally unequal social relationships that capitalism produces. This feat alone is a success, but rhetoric and ideas without a mass movement behind them have no intrinsic ability to alter the social relations of power.

everyone claiming membership in the 99%. The rhetoric of the struggle of the 99% against the 1% not only puts a class analysis into play, but also has inspired many to question the fundamentally unequal social relationships that capitalism produces. This feat alone is a success, but rhetoric and ideas without a mass movement behind them have no intrinsic ability to alter the social relations of power. May Day 2012 was the continuation and consolidation of many coalitions that had emerged in the short time that Occupy Wall Street has existed. Partnerships that have subsequently taken place between organized labor and OWS have already demonstrated small-scale successes in changing the political landscape in the city as well as in the nation.

a small but significant shift in union strategy

ORGANIZED LABOR IN the United States stands at a meager density of 12.3 percent of the overall workforce,[1] down from its highest point in 1954 at 28.3.[2] Even with the rich history of labor struggle in the United States, the organized attack from the political right, starting with Reagan, coupled with the era of neoliberal globalization, privatization, deregulation, and capital mobility, has meant that labor has been struggling against the erosion of historic gains while simultaneously scrambling to renew its base by recruiting new members. Thus the supportive response from unions in New York at the start of Occupy represented a significant move beyond the trend of prioritizing a primarily defensive set of survival strategies. The turnout for the famed "park defense" of thousands of union workers at 6:00AM to protect occupiers from Bloomberg's attempted "clean up" eviction on November 15, to the massive rallies on October 15 and November 17 demonstrate the commitment of organized labor to the struggle of the 99%.

the differences between union organizing and ows-style direct action

OCCUPY WALL STREET and labor unions share a political vision of workers, families, and communities having the power and ability to participate in shaping their own lives. The struggle against the rule of the 1% is a struggle against the concentration of resources, decision-making practices,

---

1   Stephen Greenhouse, "Most US Union Members Are Working for the Government, New Data Shows," January 22, 2010. *New York Times*. http://www. nytimes.com/2010/01/23/business/23labor.html. Accessed May 29, 2012.

2   Gerald Mayer, "Union Membership Trends in the United States," August 31, 2004. Congressional Research Service http://digitalcommons.ilr.cornell.edu/ key_workplace/174. Accessed June 13, 2012.

and power in the hands of a very small minority of the population. Occupy and unions share the goal of redistributing power and resources downward, to the impacted communities, workers, and individuals that make up the 99%. Where they diverge is in their understanding of power, strategy, and tactics. Our experiences suggest that unions and Occupy have the potential to collaborate using mixed political methodologies that can be mutually beneficial. For example, one way to interpret this year's May Day coalition of labor unions, immigrant rights groups, and Occupy Wall Street could be to draw the conclusion that Labor wanted to collaborate with immigrant rights organizations because of the political momentum built by Occupy. In this view, the energy and visibility produced by OWS opened up political space for groups with diverse approaches to collective action and organizing (such as grassroots immigrant rights organizations and labor unions) to collaborate as allies. For the purpose of this analysis we will narrow the focus to the relations between unions and Occupy.

Labor and Occupy have different histories, different analyses, and, frequently, contradictory organizing models and different understandings of power. It is widely understood that Occupy Wall Street emerged on the foundation of struggle laid by generations of activists and organizations, and yet often the credit for its success has been attributed to the direct action tactics and public spectacle that produced popular support for the movement in an incredibly short period of time. While innovative tactics are important tools for movements, direct action without base-building is ephemeral; it may exert power in a given moment, but it does not build or accumulate the capacity to use it. Building a solid base is the foundation of developing the capacity to shape institutional and organizational purposes and practices. The ability to mobilize constituencies around social conditions and political issues is built through the hard, long-term work of face-to-face conversations between neighbors, workers, family members, organizers, and communities.

The lack of on-the-ground relationships with impacted communities presented obstacles to overcome and, simultaneously, many opportunities for collaboration. The political situation that resulted from Occupy Wall Street's tactics was a moment that could not be passed up for those that struggle for the 99% to have more power in their lives. Yet, collaboration with a movement without a recognizable organizational structure or articulation of demands is intrinsically difficult for labor unions, or any organization that answers to a base. As one Occupy activist, Joe DeManuelle-Hall, states, "OWS is a movement in which its demands and goals are implicit in its actions." The struggle over public space, the right and freedom to assemble, the occupation of foreclosed homes, and the rights and benefits for workers are, in the perception of OWS activists, self-evident social goods that are so universally understood that they need not be articulated but simply practiced.

Organized labor exists within a different historic struggle, though it fights for many similar outcomes. Unions are legally and philosophically-bound to struggle for the interests of their constituents, who, as wage workers, occupy a structurally disadvantaged position in relation to employers on whom they depend for survival. Their goals and demands cannot be left implicit, but rather must be succinctly articulated, which allows them to fight on clear fronts in which workers participate in struggles whose stakes and the gains they know. The limitations placed on the practices of unions are complex and are often times beyond the control of the organizations themselves. Different state capacities, for example the National Labor Relations Board (NLRB), have been struggled over politically and in many cases have now come to serve the interests of capital as opposed to workers. If state capacities are politically neutral sites of struggles in which collective wealth is distributed and determined by communities that exercise political power such as the historic struggles for welfare rights, public housing, and labor law, then one can see that the state currently functions to serve the needs and interests of those in our society who have the most resources and power. Richard Bensinger is the organizing director of the United Auto Workers and outlines the ways in which the state is failing to protect worker's interests: "The gradual erosion of worker protection and the destruction of the right to organize is that NLRB elections are down from nearly 9,000 a year in the mid-1970s to about 2,000 a year, while popular approval of unions has increased."[3] The NLRB has gone from being an ally of labor to an unreliable political pawn in the neoliberal war on organized labor.

The uniqueness of the collaboration between Occupy Wall Street and labor has been that labor offers a conceptualization and practice of collective action that makes material gains in the lives of the 99%. The contribution that organized labor makes to Occupy Wall Street is a framework for understanding, building, and demonstrating power. Political power lies not in moments of spectacle alone, but rather in the ability for a constituency to struggle collectively to participate in decision-making processes that affect their lives. Unions build capacity through organizing workers to struggle for the basic right to bargain collectively, though this act is only one outcome of workers fighting together. Collective action is the foundation of political power, it undermines the neoliberal logic of the individual being the center of political power and instead posits a systemic understanding of our collective social relationships. In this conceptualization, those most vulnerable in

3 "The harsh reality of NLRB union elections," *Solidarity Magazine*, January/ February 2011. http://www.uaw.org/story/%C2%A0harsh-reality-nlrb-union-elections. Accessed June 12, 2012.

our society can band together to fight on shared fronts.

the teamsters & ows vs. sotheby's: building vision, building power

GILMORE CONTINUES TO articulate the complexity of coalitions:

"But to create a powerful front, a front with the capacity to change the landscape, it seems that connecting with *likely* allies would be a better use of time and trouble. Remembering that likely allies have all become constricted by mission statements and hostile laws to think in silos rather than expansively, grassroots organizations can be the voices of history and the future to assemble the disparate and sometimes desperate nonprofits who labor in the shadow of the shadow state."[4]

The start of a (hopefully ongoing) process of assembling disparate, yet likely allies has been launched this year, not only on May Day, but also in several other struggles such as the 99 Pickets and the Sotheby's campaign waged by the International Brotherhood of Teamsters Local 814. The Sotheby's campaign was symbolic, not only of the struggle of OWS, but also the contemporary struggle of organized labor. Forty-two workers were locked out of a multinational corporation with $3.4 billion in

The contribution that organized labor makes to Occupy Wall Street is a framework for understanding, building, and demonstrating power. Political power lies not in moments of spectacle alone, but rather in the ability for a constituency to struggle collectively to participate in decision-making processes that affect their lives.

4 Gilmore, Ruth Wilson. "In the Shadow of the Shadow State," in Incite! Women of Color Against Violence, ed. *The Revolution Will Not Be Funded, Beyond the Nonprofit Industrial Complex.* Cambridge: South End Press, 2007. 41–52.

profits in the first six months of the same year.[5] On the one hand, the David vs. Goliath power imbalance of this struggle symbolizes the plight of the American workforce and changing terrain of neoliberal capitalism; on the other hand, it demonstrates the potential that coalitions between allies have to win material gains for the 99%. Gary Roland explains the uniqueness of this collaboration on Truth-out.org: "No longer did we rely on auction disruptions or picket lines as the sole means of communicating our message. OWS groups like Occupy Museums and Arts & Labor dropped banners on crowded nights at the Museum of Modern Art—which has strong ties with Sotheby's—and held general assemblies underneath. We put up provocative websites and occupied boardrooms with performance art. We created free art fairs and circulated petitions. Most importantly, we realized that in order to continue to tell the story of the 42 workers, we would have to do so in creative ways that the media couldn't resist talking about."

The 42 members of Local 814 were locked out for ten months, truly a struggle of the 99% against the 1%. Jason Ide, President of Teamsters Local 814 said, "I am proud of this settlement, which means pay raises and solid benefits for these 42 workers. But the hallmark of this settlement is that together we persevered in securing workplace justice. This lockout was a misguided attempt by the 1% to crush the hopes and lives of middle-class workers—that was never going to happen on our watch. I want to thank all those who supported us in this effort, from the Joint Council to Occupy Wall Street. This was a collective victory for the 99%." This struggle clearly demonstrates that, in an unspoken collaboration, Occupy Wall Street was able to fight on a shared front with Labor, contributing what the locked out workers could not, and in effect, the common struggle contributed to building power for the workers and for the movement.

Occupy Wall Street has been celebrated for creativity and audacious innovation of tactics, but when struggling against systematic inequality wrought by neoliberal restructuring in this day and age, Labor provides the platform for the energy of Occupy to reinvigorate the labor movement. The collaboration between these two groups was never completely articulated. OWS joined Teamsters' pickets, OWS acted on its own volition to research and target decision-makers and shareholders, disrupting business and galas alike. The disruptions of auctions, restaurants of Sotheby's owners, and the everyday business of the 1% grounded the abstract articulation of injustice into tangible struggles.

---

5   No Author listed. "Sotheby's Breaks Record In First Half 2011 With $3.4 Billion In Sales." http://www.huffingtonpost.com/2011/08/05/sothebys-breaks-record-in_n_918809.html. Accessed June 4, 2012.

99 picket lines

ANOTHER CREATIVE INNOVATION during the planning for May Day was the 99 Picket Lines. The #99PKTS actions connected isolated labor, community, and autonomous groups, allowing struggles with different histories and tactics to come together to highlight present-day fights that characterize contemporary urbanization. Most of the "99 pickets" started from a convergence point at Bryant Park at 8AM on the morning of May 1 and went to locations in Midtown, including: Chase Bank, Standard and Poor's, ABC, Wells Fargo, Fidelity, Lazard, construction sites, and the *New York Times* Building. The 99 Pickets campaign began before May Day, on Tax Day in fact, and continued for the following two weeks. Pickets were used as a mobilizing and coalition-building tool in order to connect with workers, unions, community groups, and autonomous groups who were already engaged in fights, with the aim of connecting them not only to each other, but also to the mass convergence on May Day. The pickets allowed for a diversity of tactics, and allowed for each group and campaign to participate in accordance with their own capacity. Unions, which are under contract, cannot engage in workplace walkouts without running the risk of violating their contracts and in some cases being permanently replaced. 99 Pickets allowed for "symbolic" pickets against employers with union contracts over grievances, as well as non-union employers and corporate targets. The campaign incorporated a range of tactics and struggles, and mobilized different constituencies to share an analysis that our struggles are connected by larger systemic issues.

In the United States, we are often encouraged to believe that our individual situations are the result of our own choices, but Occupy Wall Street has re-introduced and started to popularize the understanding that our situation is the result of economic, social, and cultural circumstances that are systemic. Our struggles, as workers, immigrants, activists, and organizers are deeply connected.

One major purpose of the pickets was to draw attention to the common struggles of workers across the city. Moises Cerezo, a line cook at the Capital Grille Chrysler Center said that at his workplace, "there is racial discrimination, wage theft, an abusive environment, retaliation for organizing, and more, and that's why we fight; but we know that many other workers have a similar struggle against their bosses, against the 1%. That is why we not only have our campaign, but we will stand in solidarity with all workers on May Day." The workers at Capital Grille are organizing with the Restaurant Opportunities Center, a worker center that focuses on organizing and advocating for improved working conditions and raising standards for restaurant workers citywide. Their model relies on leadership from some of the most marginalized workers in the city. These workers were part of a picket leading up to May Day and held another picket that was part of the Immigrant Worker Justice Tour. This tour was organized by the immigrant worker justice working group of OWS, which had formed to highlight the realities of low wage undocumented workers in the city. The tour included the struggles at Hot and Crusty (a restaurant chain in NYC), campaigns challenging the prison industrial complex and immigrant detention, the plight of farm workers, and low wages for service sector workers. These sectors and campaigns, until recently, have not been at the forefront of larger union organizing strategies. Grassroots organizing by worker centers, and organizing around immigrant rights are now the face of new and innovative models.

Mahoma Lopez, a worker at Hot and Crusty Bakery, participated in May Day and the 99 Pickets because he recognizes that "everywhere we look, immigrants and poorly paid people are going through the same struggles. People are being exploited all over this city, and we have a responsibility to help them organize for a better life and dignity at their jobs." 99 Pickets is actively succeeding at collaboration, not only educating workers about the systematic condition of their situation, but building true solidarity amongst these seemingly isolated struggles.

telling a new story of who "we" are—replacing "individuals" with "the 99%"— building power and new practices of solidarity by doing the possible

IN MOVEMENT WORK, we are constantly confronted by limitations and challenges. Under neoliberalism, the state has become increasingly controlled by the 1%. In the last forty years, we have seen an unprecedented attack on organized labor, including a massive build-up of the state's ability to control and regulate how we organize. In the United States, we are often encouraged to believe that our individual situations are the result of our own choices, but Occupy Wall Street has re-introduced and started to popularize the understanding that our situation is the result of economic, social, and cultural circumstances that are systemic. Our struggles, as workers, immigrants, activists, and organizers are deeply connected. As we move forward, we need to continue to think creatively about how we work together, we need to allow different communities to exist within their own historic circumstance, recognizing the limitations placed on them externally and the opportunities that we have to struggle together. Our capacity as organizations is limited, and the more that collaborations between likely allies exist the more likely we are to change the political landscape.

Ruth Wilson Gilmore's analysis is as relevant now as it was when she presented it. We exist in an economic crisis that has altered the political landscape in the United States, shutting down many people's hopes and dreams for a sustainable livelihood while at the same time presenting political allies on the left with moments of opportunity to reevaluate our strategies and move forward in building a truly mass movement that struggles for justice. We often fail to conceptualize the traps that we fall into as a result of the influence of neoliberal austerity. We see our struggles and our limitations as inevitable results of the conditions that we live in, but in recognizing the historical difference between our struggles we can organize through that difference to truly build the capacity of the 99% to organize and implement strategies of our own liberation.

Erik Ruin
"Liberation Banner"
HTTP://WWW.JUSTSEEDS.ORG/ARTISTS/ERIK_RUIN/

John Duda

WHERE WAS THE SOCIAL FORUM IN OCCUPY?

IN THE INITIAL WEEKS OF OCCUPY WALL STREET, AS THAT CURIOUS THRESH-old was being crossed between a tenacious direct action of a few hundred people gathered in New York's financial district and a continent-wide tremor of anticapitalist agitation, there was a difficult process of renegotiation and recomposition in which all sorts of people and organizations—labor unions, celebrities, disgruntled progressives, anarchists, artists, the left-wing of the Democratic establishment, along with the unemployed and precarious, the bitter and the romantically optimistic—found themselves occupying pub-lic space together in a sometimes comic, too often tragic, and occasionally beautiful attempt to reclaim democracy and beat back neoliberalism.

I would count myself among those who allowed themselves a kind of tac-tically useful romantic optimism about the prospects at that moment for a more general contestation of the capitalist status quo; in particular, I had hoped that once the initial shock had worn off, the movement of movements that had been patiently building a base at the community level and working towards something like another possible world would have, as it were, come into the field. Imagine: it's the middle of October 2011, and the fault line that Occupy has unexpectedly opened in the neoliberal consensus is forced open a thousand times wider when, in every city across the country, organizations that have been fighting for years, building bases, and developing grassroots leadership, realize that this is a once-in-a-decade chance to, if not overturn the existing order, than at least to trouble it deeply. Hesitantly at first, but with in-creasing clarity of purpose, these organizations, disciplined, strong, with deep roots in all of those communities hardest hit by a crisis that's lasted for decades longer than anyone pining for the return of Glass-Steagall can imagine, come out into the streets, providing a moral backbone and depth of purpose....

And of course, this is precisely what did not happen, at least not on a nationwide scale. It's curious since a process has been in place since before

2007 to develop exactly the kinds of national networks that would have made such a truly transformative grassroots anticapitalist movement possible: the United States Social Forum (USSF).¹ The failure of the networks of the USSF to meaningfully mobilize during the moment presented by Occupy is especially striking given their shared commitment to systemic critique, horizontal processes of direct democracy and assembly, and popular power expressed through a leaderless plurality of voices and perspectives.

But despite these far from superficial affinities, *the Social Forum was not present in Occupy.*

Let me clarify what I mean—and what I don't mean. I *don't* mean that it's impossible to find any individuals who were both part of the USSF process who also participated in Occupy. We could, for instance, point to veteran organizer Jerome Scott, deeply involved in both Social Fora as a cofounder of Project South, the local anchor host for the first Forum in Atlanta, and subsequently as a member of the National Planning Committee behind the 2010 Forum in Detroit, who was also an active participant in Occupy Atlanta. Examples beyond this particularly salient one could no doubt be multiplied. I also don't mean that we should fault the Social Forum, which as an organization exists in order to create a national gathering every three years, for being caught unaware by Occupy's success: if we're really being honest, we were all caught unaware, for one thing, and for another, the NPC has a specific mission and mandate relating to organizing the Forum, and to expect it to have magically remolded itself in late September into some sort of centralized council of Occupy elders is unrealistic on multiple fronts.²

---

1 The US Social Forum, which took place in 2007 in Atlanta and again in 2010 in Detroit, was inspired by the World Social Forum, a gathering which started in the Brazilian city of Porto Alegre in 2001 with the collaboration of numerous groups from transnational civil society. Importantly, the USSF drew on the lessons learned about the at times disproportionate influence of NGO's in the WSF to articulate a more bottom-up organizing model that very explicitly committed to starting the process within marginalized communities, especially communities of color.

2 Although this is precisely what at least one organization involved in the ongoing USSF process—the Michigan Welfare Rights Organization (MWRO)—envisioned:

> The Occupy Movement is a flash in the pan, albeit a bright one. By itself, it cannot develop into a movement building vehicle unless it is tied to a stable organizational structure that has defined outcomes and best steps that are understood. The SF and the SF process can be viewed as the "Joint Chiefs of Staff" that can gather said visionaries from this movement and from those other fronts of struggle into a moment of deep political discussion followed by regional plans.

And, finally, I don't mean to discount the very real and often essential contributions groups involved with the USSF made to Occupy. Some organizations with ties to the Social Forum and to its model of radical community organizing did mobilize their members. In some cities, a popular front against poverty and oppression coalesced more strongly than in others. Some tactics—most notably the foreclosure resistance scenarios pioneered by Boston's City Life/Vida Urbana—have become key tools in the Occupy toolbox, especially as the occupations themselves have been dismantled or have dismantled themselves.[3]

What I do mean is that we need to account for the failure of a massive movement against capitalism, led by the poor and the oppressed, and built along the lines of affinity and communication that the USSF proclaimed itself to be creating, to materialize in the historical opening Occupy provided. To put it another way, the Social Forum, understood as a network of and model for coordination between organizations committed to building a bottom-up, transformative movement to overturn the American status quo, led by those most impacted—was what was missing in Occupy. The result: the organizations and networks that could claim most authentically to be fighting, in the most principled fashion, for the poor, precarious, and marginalized were one of the least present social movement sectors on the streets last September.

So why did things go down this way? The "easy" answer here is to analyze what happened in the fall of 2011 in terms of privilege. For many long-time organizers, especially from communities of color, the spectacle of thousands of newly-minted white Occupiers incoherently swooning at

---

This statement can be found in the political position papers prepared for the January 2012 NPC meeting of the USSF; the collection offers a uniquely useful index to the way that Social Forum core participating organizations felt about Occupy. They can be found online here: https://support.mayfirst.org/attachment/wiki/ussf_npc_position_paper/NPC_PositionPapers_Dec2011.pdf

3 We could also look at the prehistory of Occupy to see what kind of groups engaged with laying the groundwork for the events of September. NYC had a relatively strong network of radical community organizations that had come together under the Right to the City banner after the first Social Forum in Atlanta, all of whom were deeply concerned with contesting the neoliberal city. When a broad movement started building in the first half of 2011 towards Bloombergville, which would occupy public space in the face of municipal austerity measures, and which, along with the first anti-bank direct actions of the summer, would provide the most clear antecedents for the miracle of Zuccotti, only two groups out of the 10 RTTC-NYC member organizations, Picture the Homeless and Community Voices Heard, would lend organizing muscle and public support to the effort.

Ron Paul's contrariness or insisting that concerns about racism could be addressed after we had tackled the "real" problem of corporate personhood may have been just too much too deal with. However, even as we engage in the very necessary work of coming to terms with and hopefully dismantling the machinery of oppression within movements for social justice, we should remember in doing so to not erase the very real contributions that many people of color made to Occupy. Similarly, we should not overly simplify a very complicated and heterogeneous class situation; while many Occupiers were of course drawn from the ranks of the newly precarious but still relatively privileged strata of society, many were not. We could, for instance, ask in all seriousness whether there were more homeless people involved in the Social Forum or in the Occupations. (My unscientific hunch is the latter, by an order of magnitude.)

Let's, then, for the sake of argument, and in good faith, assume that we've unpacked all the complicated issues around the dynamics of privilege in Occupy[4]—a task other contributors to this volume have done in a far more profound way than I could ever hope to; what *else* can we learn from the failure of the Social Forum—understood as process and network—to manifest in the fall of 2011?

Yet another qualification is necessary here: I very pointedly here do not want to engage in a critique that would oppose the supposed living, breathing, spontaneous, and magical space of anarcho-Occupy to the comparatively stifling and demobilizing world of interest- and identity-based organizing on the left edge of the nonprofit industrial complex, however justified some aspects of that critique might be. To do so would be to largely miss the point; I refuse to give up on the promise of Occupy just because there were serious problems with unexamined privilege, in the same way I refuse to give up on the Social Forum because I'm suspicious of professionalization. I want to take both movements at face value, and reject a polarized dichotomy where the failings of one automatically elevate the other: both

---

4   While accounting for privilege is absolutely necessary, it might be counterproductive to discount what history tells us about revolutions; namely, that struggles often crystallize into moments of historical rupture and transformation precisely due to the actions of relatively privileged sectors of the people; we can multiply example of this from Toussaint L'Ouverture to the students at Strasbourg and the Sorbonne in 1968 all the way up to #OWS. It is these defections, in which privilege is refused or put to work in the service of counterhegemony, which can cause of crisis of legitimacy, opening space for movements from further below. This isn't to say that relative privilege can't also be a source of reaction, or that there are no genuine revolutions led by the most oppressed, just that the category of privilege does not give us any empirical guide to who is likely to initiate a revolutionary process.

Occupy and the Social Forum are fundamentally well-intentioned attempts to build radically democratic, horizontal platforms for anticapitalist action, and if, in September 2011, these impulses were two great tastes that did not go together, this lack of compatibility is something we urgently need to work out. First, because it's obviously a dilemma for movement strategy—if the people who are most affected by neoliberalism and its crisis stay home when a space opens up to challenge this situation in the streets, this challenge is going to be weaker and less effective than it could be. Second, and more importantly, we need to work through this dilemma because it points towards an inadequacy of the way both sides of this equation—Occupy and Social Forum—understand radical democracy. In other words, for all our emphatic assertions to the contrary, perhaps we actually *don't* know what democracy looks like.

Let's recall Elizabeth "Betitia" Martinez's wonderful and very widely read essay, "Where Was the Color in Seattle?," which my title here is intended to invoke and pay respect to. And let's remember that while that piece did of course call people out on their bullshit, it's point wasn't just to condemn the unconscious exclusionary dynamics produced and reproduced by the predominantly white activists behind the 1999 anti-WTO protests, but also to highlight a range of both structural and conjunctural factors which kept people of color in the US away from Seattle. Let's also recall that, especially as summit-hopping's productivity to impair or disrupt elite governance declined with the rise of the post-9/11 security state, many antiglobalization activists turned towards local organizing and specifically towards the leadership that grassroots social justice organizations based in communities of color could offer for a serious, long-term movement against capitalism. It's in this context that the USSF emerged, and was widely celebrated.

But at the same time a puzzling historical enigma presents itself: the two US Social Fora bookend the sharpest moments of the financial and housing crisis, which disproportionately affected the very communities in which the organizations leading the Forum process were based. Yet there was no organized mass outrage over the bailout of the financial industry and no immediate radical response to the foreclosure crisis. The movement of movements manifested at the Forum was certainly not sitting on the sidelines, of course—but in a moment of crisis one of the most solidly intentional antiracist, anticapitalist, and grassroots gatherings and network had no success in producing an effective, generalized, popular response challenging the terms of neoliberalism's solution to the crisis. That task would be left, three years later, to Kalle Lasn and *Adbusters*, to some dorks wearing comic book superhero masks, and to a couple hundred wildly-optimistic activists with some sleeping bags. Even the anti-austerity fight in Wisconsin, which, in the wake of Tunisia and Tahrir Square, helped make #OWS thinkable in the first place had little to no involvement from the USSF networks—and this despite the massive gathering a few hours away that had taken place in Detroit only a year and a half beforehand.[5]

What's the lesson to be learned here? My first conjecture is that while antisystemic movements can and should follow in the footsteps of the USSF and consciously work to prioritize the careful and intentional work that contests and undoes privilege, there's nevertheless a strategic impasse that needs to be negotiated here. Antisystemic movements, while focusing on the long term work of composing a movement that reflects the world we want to see, also need to be able to mobilize effectively in moments of systemic crisis. Cracks in the hegemonic narrative of power—those ephemeral spaces in which the status quo loses its legitimacy and in which it is possible to fundamentally change the rules of the game—are few and far between. These moments are, I would wager, less the result of patiently accumulating organizing work that builds steadily towards a threshold of intensity, but *gifts of history*. To characterize a moment like Occupy in terms of "harvest" time, as some have recently done (as a way of placing emphasis on long-term work of base building and community organizing), is to wildly overestimate the capacity of our movements to effect historical change on our own terms.

In these moments, the demands articulated by many community-based organizations that Occupy needed to state intelligible goals before their members would consider joining the occupations—however valid and justified a response—went precisely against the logic of the situation. To be cynical but not necessarily unrealistic, it might be precisely the calculability of more solid, long-term organizing that renders it incapable of threatening the system; the unintelligibility of Occupy, its opacity, its refusal to constitute itself in such a way that it could even begin to answer the question "What do you want?" was precisely what made it dangerous. The slogan "We are the 99%" from this perspective wasn't a bad generalization, it was a way to invoke uncountability, an unruly mass whose boundaries could not be fixed or delimited. This indeterminacy is the key to the viral composition of a mass movement: if hope is possible, it's because movement and action reveal the order imposed by power to be contingent; in troubling the inevitability of this order's perpetuation, what is disclosed is a future which is unknown, which may yet be rewritten.

This is not to say that the point here is that social movements only work when they make themselves unpredictable: as any serious reflection makes clear, being "unpredictable" or "opaque" in a entirely voluntaristic

---

5 NPC members present at the 2012 Left Forum agreed, in their USSF panel discussion, that there was an inability to mobilize the networks forged in Detroit for the fight in Madison.

way is usually a surefire way to fix one's self firmly in the neutralizing gaze of the state. What is important is to understand the way movement and history reciprocally co-create moments in which another world *becomes* possible.

This logic of the event—to use Alain Badiou's terminology—leaves us, to be sure, unsatisfied if we're looking for concrete advice to help us develop and deepen our revolutionary praxis. If the revolution is made only in those moments where determination gives way to indetermination, where certitude gives way to possibility, and if these moments acquire their power precisely because they remain necessarily incalculable, ciphers from the point of view of normal, non-revolutionary time, then when the moment ends, our practice becomes a matter of waiting for the event to return, for history's needle to skip again.

This brings me to my second conjecture, whose implications are, thankfully, more practical. The flip side of the capacity, actualized in a revolutionary moment, to collectively live outside the history of power, is the development of the capacity in everyday life to manage the process of social reproduction on our own terms. Consider something extremely basic yet extremely important: food. Part of Occupy Wall Street's capacity to *indefinitely* occupy public space stemmed from its capacity to feed whomever happened to be in the park, each and every day. Both the popular kitchen (pioneered, in the US, with projects like Food Not Bombs) and magical pizza from the Internet (pioneered in Madison) are ways of reconstructing the process of social reproduction along the

Being in the struggle for the long haul shouldn't mean refusing to wager on moments of possibility; and being committed to radically horizontal and potentially unpredictable processes of self-organization shouldn't mean being unable to reject replicating the dynamics of oppression within the movement.

lines of the *gift*; that is to say, along something which remains unpredictable and resistant to being taken into account.

I bring the example of food up because of a particularly illustrative dynamic at the last USSF in Detroit; despite taking place in a city where urban agricultural movements for autonomous food security are perhaps more developed than anywhere else in the country, nowhere in or outside of Cobo Hall could one actually eat in anything resembling a non-commodified manner; the organizers, who handled so much else so well, had merely organized a handful of food trucks to park on a nearby plaza. Meanwhile, blocks and blocks away at the semi-autonomous anarchist convergence ("A New World From Below"), hundreds of people ate for free each day, sitting together on the grounds of the Spirit of Hope church. If the Forum's principle of construction was one of accountability—the deliberate and intentional construction of situations which staged the centrality of the most marginalized to the movement—the anarchist convergence's food politics, like that of Occupy, remained outside of all account: everyone simply eats.

These two modes of movement composition are very distinct, especially in their relation to time. Our challenge is not to choose one over the other, but to recognize that despite their fundamental incompatibility they are both equally valid and equally necessary for the anticapitalist project. Being in the struggle for the long haul shouldn't mean refusing to wager on moments of possibility; and being committed to radically horizontal and potentially unpredictable processes of self-organization shouldn't mean being unable to reject replicating the dynamics of oppression within the movement. As the next Social Forum potentially approaches, and as Occupiers continue to try to land another monkeywrench in the gears of history, we should remember that no easy synthesis between these two modes is forthcoming, and our duty is to think and act, as it were, in stereo.

Erik Ruin
"Liberation Banner"

Chris Dixon

Building a Mass Movement?

Learning from the Occupy Sudbury
Experience

Like many longtime radicals, I was skeptical about Occupy Wall Street when it first started. Some of my friends were more far-sighted, but I thought it would be a short-lived action. I was wrong, thankfully. I first began to understand this when I went by Liberty Plaza in New York during the first week of the occupation and saw a thriving encampment with lots of determined, newly politicized people. Even then, it was clear that they had managed to tap a surprisingly large reservoir of public outrage about inequality. As I then traveled to the west coast in fall 2011, I encountered people enthusiastically engaging in or preparing for occupations wherever I went.

But it wasn't until I returned to where I live, in Sudbury, Ontario, that I realized exactly how wrong my initial assessment was. Known for its giant smokestacks and ecologically devastated landscape, Sudbury is a small mining city located about 250 miles north of Toronto. Although it has a distinguished history of militant labor organizing, Sudbury isn't an easy place to build movements these days. The few working-class organizations that have survived the last three decades of neoliberal assault are barely holding on, most people struggle to make ends meet, and there is a pervasive sense of resignation. As in many smaller cities and more rural areas, forms of radical activism from big urban centers don't tend to get very far in Sudbury.

And yet, almost from out of nowhere, a motley crew set up an Occupy Sudbury encampment in October 2011 and kept it going for more than a month. The encampment offered meals and tents to the large local houseless population, held regular General Assemblies, and hosted well-attended educational events. (And even after the encampment ended, Occupy Sudbury has continued to generate new kinds of political activity.) But this experience wasn't without its challenges: responding to immediate human needs while also engaging in protest activities, facilitating genuine participation from people who are traditionally marginalized, reconciling very different political ideas and priorities among occupiers, and developing structures and a culture of direct democracy. Still, it was an instructive experience for all of us who participated and it raised important questions.

For me, the most pressing question is about what it means to build a mass movement with a deep working-class character in North America today. Unlike many self-identified radical efforts, the people at the center of Occupy Sudbury's activities were predominantly poor or working-class; they were unemployed or working low-paid service jobs, and some were community college students. Most were white, though there were a number of consistent Indigenous participants too. Coming from these backgrounds, people brought energy, fresh ideas, deep roots in the community, and impressive resourcefulness. They also didn't have much previous organizing experience, which meant that some people held to astoundingly far-fetched theories, collective decision-making was frequently frustrating, sometimes people acted in racist or sexist ways, and there was a lot of organizational clumsiness.

These aspects of Occupy Sudbury were very difficult. However, they also made me realize the extent to which I—and I think many other people on the left—have become accustomed to *not* working in mass movement contexts. So much left political work happens in radical bubbles in which people share very similar backgrounds and vocabulary and are largely disconnected from broader layers of working-class people in all of their diversity.

The Occupy movement—with all of its messiness and dynamism, contradictions and possibilities—has presented us with the opportunity to step onto a much more vast terrain of struggle. Let's not waste this chance.

OCCUPY WALL STREET COMMUNITY AGREEMENT

Proposed to OWS Spokescouncil by Safer Spaces Operational Working Group

Approved by OWS Spokescouncil 2/22/12

i. statement of intention on entering the space

We enter each OWS space with a commitment to:
- mutual respect and support
- anti-oppression
- conflict resolution
- nonviolence towards each other
- direct democracy

We:

1. support the empowerment of each person to challenge the histories and structures of oppression that marginalize some, and divide us all . These may include ableism, ageism, classism, heterosexism, racism, religious discrimination, sexism, transphobia, xenophobia, and among others.
2. commit to learning about different forms of oppression.
3. understand individual freedoms are not above our collective safety, well-being, and ability to function cooperatively; individual freedom without responsibility to the community is not the OWS way.
4. accept the decision of the community if we are not able to follow the agreements below.

A. Commitment to Accessibility, Consent and Anti-Oppression

We will:

1. do our best to provide physical and language access to OWS spaces, and make resources equally available to all.
2. not use physical or verbal violence or threats.
3. get clear permission before touching other people or using their things.
4. not use substances in our spaces that may attract the police and cause harm to our community.
5. acknowledge that some people in our community are more vulnerable to police or hospital interaction,[1] and accept that calling the police or an ambulance is a decision to be made by the person most affected; this does not apply when someone is in critical condition or unable to give permission.
6. respect each person's expressed name and identities and their choice of whether to share that information. We will do our best not to make assumptions about identity—abilities, age, class, race, ethnicity, gender, sexuality, or among others—based on a person's appearance.
7. be aware of how prejudice and structures of oppression affect our

---

1   Because of age, criminal justice or medical history, documentation status, economic situation, experience of police violence, gender, immigration status, and race.

speech and actions, including the ways power and privilege are related to race, gender, physical ability, immigration status, wealth, and/or sexuality, among other identities.

8. show compassion and respect to each other, especially those who have experienced trauma, abuse, or oppression. We will not:
   - shout people down
   - dismiss oppression
   - engage in other dominating or aggressive behavior.

9. respect diverse styles of speaking, learning, and interacting that may not align with the dominant culture and make space for all to communicate.

10. acknowledge that each person comes to our space with different experiences. So while we may not intend to hurt other people by our words or actions, this can still happen. We agree that it's an act of solidarity to listen and not reply right away when a person or group of people say they feel oppressed by our words or actions.

11. not tolerate police informants who intend to undermine OWS goals, and we will not accuse others of informing or otherwise working for law enforcement agencies to undermine OWS without concrete evidence.

B. Commitment to Conflict Resolution & Accountability

WE WILL:

1. do our best to hold ourselves and each other accountable to these agreements.

2. express concerns about violations based on how they affect us or others, without judgment of intent.

3. participate in a conflict resolution process when asked to by the community, and develop transformative ways to address harm.

4. be guided by decisions of the person harmed while providing all involved the chance to change the cycles of abuse and violence.

5. agree that sometimes a situation is important enough to stop a meeting immediately to address concerns.

6. make every effort to understand and be open as a community to change.

7. put in place an OWS de-escalation process to engage with anyone who disrespects these agreements. We may choose to remove the person(s) from the meeting or other OWS space until the harm has been addressed.

8. remove people who have committed sexual violence or abuse and let the survivor decide the conditions for their return. We understand that they may not be able to return.

9. understand that people who have committed harm in or outside OWS that prevents the participation of others may need to leave until the harm has been addressed.
10. commit to keeping each other informed about known and documented safety issues within the OWS community.
11. work to coordinate with organizations chosen by our community to assist individuals who have committed abuse or violence, or those who want to overcome addiction.
12. begin each meeting with a reminder of these agreements.

COMMONS N
CAPITALIS

Dave Onion
October 6, 2011
Dilworth Plaza, Philadelphia
HTTP://MULTI.LECTICAL.NET

Cindy Milstein

OCCUPY ANARCHISM

prehistory 1

SOME SAY THAT ANARCHISM IS AS OLD AS HUMAN HISTORY; THAT PEOPLE have been living it since they first, say, formed into a circle to deliberate about and then decide (with gestures, grunts, or language—maybe even twinkles) where to hunt and gather. Before it had a name, anarchism was practiced and preached by, for instance, Jesus. Maybe that goes partway to explaining why at Occupy Philly, and no doubt at all Occupies, the Occupiers acted like anarchists with a religious-like zeal from day one, even though most were and still are not anarchists.[1] Indeed, a small but vocal bunch of them were vehemently anti-anarchist, which perhaps illuminates why one Occupier hijacked the thirty-thousand-person-"liked" Occupy Philadelphia Facebook page, and then posted a drawing of Christ with his middle finger raised and the words "Cindy Milstein EVEN JESUS HATES YOU" (hint: I'm a vocal anarchist; hence a convenient straw person).

prehistory 2

MONTHS AFTER THE Philly encampment was history, on a brilliant sunny April 2012 day, I ventured into a windowless basement room to do a talk and discussion on "Occupy Anarchism" at the New York Anarchist Bookfair. As I waited for people to gather, one eager participant told me that he

---

1 The anarchism piece of the Occupy puzzle is, appropriately, a circle—or at least the piece told here. And it's told here as a circuitous first-person narrative, because among the numerous things that Occupy taught me, it's that, first, storytelling is a lost art and painful need in the age of (a)social networking, and second, that there's nothing linear about social transformation. My thanks to Kate Khatib and Sean West Wispy for their invaluable insight and editorial assistance; they improved this essay, although its perspective and any missteps are mine. I also offer my gratitude to (almost-all) Occupy Philly folks for the messily beautiful experiment of trying to collectively cobble together a city from below.

and his OWS friends were also speaking later that afternoon on a similar Occupy-related theme—"The Prehistory of Anarchism." I was tabling at the bookfair, so knew I'd miss their workshop, and thus asked, "When does your prehistory start?" "August!" he quickly responded. "This *past* August?" He looked a little taken aback, then exclaimed, "Yes! Why?"

prehistory 3

IN SPRINGTIME 2004, I was in Paris during the anarchist bookfair and so was able to table for the Institute for Anarchist Studies, of which I'm a collective member. When a member of one of the many French anarchist organizations wandered over to ask about the IAS, I in return inquired about his collective. "How long have you been around?" His brow furled, and he threw back his shoulders, as if I'd served up the most impertinent of questions, and haughtily replied, "We French *invented* anarchism!"

prehistory 4

SEVERAL YEARS BEFORE that, in April 2001, in a different French-speaking place, Québec City, during the Carnival against Capitalism to contest the Summit of the Americas, my affinity group and I were walking near a large catapult, constructed and now pushed by the medieval bloc toward the fence protecting the elites from the rabble. In this cluster of autonomous affinity groups' words, in a letter written afterward to help clear Montréal anarchist Jaggi Singh of false charges related to, as the Canadian Crown called it, this "dangerous weapon," the medieval bloc explained that it built the "prop" to "mock the absurdity of holding the secretive and undemocratic Summit within a walled fortress." As our huge "red" contingent—based on the three-tiered color-coding system put in place through a series of consultas and directly democratic assemblies to indicate varying possibilities of arrest risk and militancy, per the new "diversity of tactics" clause in the *Basis of Unity* for this antiauthoritarian convergence—trooped close to the castle gates and lines of heavily armored security, the catapult lobbed its munitions across the perimeter: stuffed animals, or what infamously became known as "teddy bears." The riot cops sent back their own far-from-cuddly fire: tear gas canisters. Through and despite our stinging eyes, it felt revolutionary.

prehistory 5

THERE'S A LOT more—a whole lot more—that could be filled in about the twentieth-century prehistory, like the poetically bold inspiration of the Zapatistas. Or before that, the rebellions of the 1960s and 1970s, and specifically the new social movements, which opened up space for a contemporary anarchism in North America, reimagined and experimented with through the lens of identity, intersectionality, and countercultural lifeways, among others. This, in turn, built on postwar rethinkings of anarchism in counterpoint to the brutality of actually existing colonialism, communism, and fascism. Late-twentieth-century anarchism was also a challenge to and yet shaped by emergent phenomenon after the fall of the Berlin wall, especially the triumph of capitalism, which then exponentially "globalized" and bulldozed its way into an increasingly hegemonic neoliberal phase.

But alas, I can only toss so many stones into the pond here, creating fluid circles that form overlapping circles between each other. So I'll heft an especially big rock and let a prominent circle spread across the waters of Occupy anarchism: the anticapitalist wing of the alter-globalization movement, and in particular one of its well-formed inner circles, the Anticapitalist Convergence (Convergence des Luttes Anti-Capitalistes, or CLAC), an anarchist organization started in the lead up to the teddy bear–tear gas joust described above and still existing in Montréal. In response to free trade agreements, the CLAC and those in its milieu dreamed up innovative anarchist mobilizations in North America, starting in the late 1990s, a few years before a so-called new anarchism burst on to the scene in the famous form—only because it took place in the United States—of a brick through a Starbucks window in Seattle in 1999.

At the dawn or dusk, depending on your perspective, of the twenty-first century, a renewed anarchism was now definitively far beyond its initial classic period of "no gods, no masters." It subscribed to a fully nonhierarchical sensibility, an array of anti-oppression principles, and the notion of prefigurative politics, even if its practice (like all human practice) continually falls far short of its intended mark. This contemporary anarchism stressed a do-it-ourselves culture and mutual aid, radical ecology, collectively run spaces and projects, more explicitly queer, feminist, and people of color organizing, and various types of self-governance (often an affinity group–spokescouncil version, and frequently linked to consensus).

what comes around...

FOR THIS SUMMER 2012 after Occupy—or in Occupy 2.0, 3.0, or maybe some 3G version—I've stumbled just as serendipitously into the Maple Spring neighborhood of Montréal as I did the Occupy Philly one in late September 2011.[2] The curveball path of these two stopovers on my way to

2   In both cases, I also wrote and am writing blog posts. For my "Dispatches from Occupy Philly" and still-accumulating "Dispatches from Maple Spring," see *Outside the Circle* at cbmilstein.wordpress.com. You'll also find essays related to

settling down again soon isn't germane to this tale. Suffice it to say, though, the utter surprise of the North American uprisings ever since last September 17 made me realize that all bets had to be off. Occupy in the United States and now the Québec student strike—both rare moments of possibility—are at once too perplexing and too promising to be missed. They are, in fact, the stuff of what anarchists dream about, or should, myself included.

So I've been in Montréal now for nearly two months as a participant-observer, and that has taken me to many an illegal night demonstration and neighborhood casserole. It's put me into two and soon another of the monthly "grand manifestations" of hundreds of thousands taking to the streets, also illegal. It's brought me to various assemblies too (again illegal, all thanks to loi spéciale 78, or special law 78, passed just before I arrived by the government in a vain effort to squash this movement by criminalizing a wide range of dissent)—mixes of neighborhood, student, and anticapitalist, including the "congress" of la Coalition large de l'Association pour une Solidarité Syndicale Étudiante (CLASSE), a major student federation, made up of the most radical, strategic, and savvy organizers of this now-longest-running student strike in North American history.

And here's where things come full circle, at least for a brief moment. The CLASSE Congress was held deep within the labyrinth of the Université du Québec à Montréal college complex, the hotbed school for Maple Spring. So I didn't make the connection until I sat down that the daylong assembly was in the same room that CLAC had used for some of its general assemblies years ago, at the height of the alter-globalization movement.

Throughout the student strike, current and former CLAC anarchists in Montréal, "grown up" from their Québec City mobilization (and often college) days, have pitched in by, say, organizing themselves into groups of professors, parents, and book and cultural types (such as publishers, writers/translators, musicians, and designers) in solidarity and active engagement. They've also initiated and facilitated assemblies in their neighborhoods, and coordinated baby blocs for marches. CLAC co-organized anticapitalist blocs with CLASSE at some key moments, and no doubt more collaboration is in the cards as things heat up in August when school is supposed to begin—by law. CLASSE, in turn, has been using a modified version of CLAC's directly democratic decision-making process, which involves proposals, debate, caucusing, and voting along an affinity–spokes model. And even though not anarchist per se, CLASSE circled its "A" on the sign pointing to the congress convergence space—a roundabout way of signaling not only its institutional memory and praxis of antiauthoritarian innovation

this piece: "Something *Did* Start in Québec City" and "Anarchism's Promise for Anticapitalist Resistance."

but also the still-dynamic binding ties that helped to forge the remarkable current student–social strike.

present (im)perfect 1: anarchism

I'VE GIVEN MANY an "intro to anarchism" talk—or as a nihilist once remarked in less kind terms, I have this bad habit of trying to encourage folks to explore and embrace anarchism for themselves. So when Occupy Philly first pitched its secondhand couch, then dumpster-dived folding tables, and finally lots and lots of tents on the cold lifeless-gray concrete surrounding Philadelphia's massive city hall, I signed up at the people's library to do a teach-in on the same topic.

We gathered on the pavement in a circle at the far end of the plaza, by then home to many of us, and after describing anarchism in a nutshell, I was met, as usual, with, "What are some examples of anarchism actually working?" I never seem able to supply a convincing response, so as usual, I started hemming and hawing, raised myself up a bit on one knee out of nervousness, and then it hit me, as the vista of the busy beehive of Occupy Philly came into sharp focus. There, all self-organized, self-managed, and self-governed, was our kids' zone, art and comfort areas, health care facilities, outdoor movie theater, safety station, info booth, food and media tents, canvas and pallet housing, recharging and tech centers, education hub, General Assembly spot, and more. There, anarchist-painted banners reading "Commons Not Capitalism" and "We're Occupied with Direct Democracy," but more than

I was met, as usual, with, "What are some examples of anarchism actually working?" I never seem able to supply a convincing response, so as usual, I started hemming and hawing, raised myself up a bit on one knee out of nervousness, and then it hit me, as the vista of the busy beehive of Occupy Philly came into sharp focus.

words, the social fabric of all types of people enacting collective structures and a gift economy to meet needs and desires, based on an egalitarian ethics as well as generosity of spirit. None of it had been there a week ago.

"There!" I said in astonishment, rising up even further on the other knee, "there! Out there, right here. *That's* anarchism in action!"

present (im)perfect 2: anarchy

SOON AFTER OWS began, someone made a Facebook events page calling for an initial meeting for what would become Occupy Philly, the encampment. People were supposed to meet at the Wooden Shoe, a longtime anarchist bookstore in Philadelphia, but it was apparent within minutes that we'd never fit. Somehow, someone managed to get us space at the Arch Street Methodist Church, about a mile and a half away, and so we all started walking—some five hundred or more people, most new to politics. When we got to the church, it was clear that the Facebook "organizers" hadn't showed up, so a few anarchists volunteered to facilitate, because no one else wanted to do it, or more likely, knew how. It was soon apparent that everyone wanted to occupy, and there were many suggestions of locations, but no real notion of the pros and cons of each spot, or how we'd even decide. An ad hoc working group of fifty people was formed, by one guy simply agreeing to collect emails, and it met a day or two later in another space that someone, somehow, managed to find, and sheer confusion notwithstanding, our temporary committee somehow forged a directly democratic process.

A few days after that, we borrowed the Methodist Church again, and this time a thousand people converged, most new to politics. And with little concept of why or how we would occupy, in less than two hours, using our version of the CLAC/CLASSE decision-making structure, we easily came to agreement in the smoothest, most purposeful, most uplifting assembly I've ever participated in. This group of mostly strangers was obviously of a united mind, almost mystically and definitely euphorically, thereby somehow bringing us skeptical anarchists along. We anarchists "conservatively" wanted more time to first conduct skill shares and organize. But we, too, were propelled to our feet after the votes were counted to cheer wildly with all in the room: the illegal takeover of city hall plaza was set for the day after tomorrow at 9AM.

Two days later, sans permit, plan, or experience, a whole bunch of people "broke ground" for the nonhierarchical city of Occupy Philly within the shadow, quite literally, of the extremely hierarchical one of the City of Philadelphia. It was, for hours, beautiful chaos. From that moment on until the end of our physical home some two months later, I heard the phrase "I've never felt so alive" repeated ad nauseam, largely because of how empowering it felt to constantly turn that chaos into our own makeshift self-creations, only to see them become chaotic again, and so begin the cycle afresh. That phrase was matched only by my own use of the term "messy," because among those many things I learned from Occupy Philly, I discovered this as well: trying to create a new society under the heavy boot and socialization of the old is going to involve us making more mistakes than I thought possible, messy and messier ones, including stepping on way too many toes but also stumbling on sheer genius and glimpses of our own potential humanity—precisely through such anarchic experimentation.

So within hours of making camp, one of the original Facebook events page makers showed up in person to declare that Occupy Philly wasn't going how he'd envisioned, and he set about trying to shut it down—the start of his self-appointment as "police liaison." Within days, the assembly voted to get a permit, because according to way too many a trusting white Occupier, the mayor and cops were being "so friendly," which in turn exacerbated already-present tensions in light of years of police violence against blacks in Philly, and particularly after a racial epithet had been yelled at a person of color only a day or two earlier.[3] That first week, many also seemed to think that facilitators were a secret cabal, directing the occupation, and the mushrooming number of working groups along with the once-daily coordinating council and twice-daily assembly quickly became revolving doors for misfits, mayhem, and misunderstandings.

And yet, within a week, those of us who stuck around all had a crush on Occupy Philly, and people were vigilantly defending our face-to-face democracy against any attempts to turn it into something that even remotely reeked of representation. From the spontaneity of being thrown together willy-nilly with people you'd probably never in a million years want to spend time with, or didn't even much like, we became one big, happy family-cum-community, as in "Yeah, your cousin kinda rambles on too long, but we love them anyway." As a previously nonpolitical Occupier put it in the early days, when someone asks them, "What are you doing at Occupy?" they reply, "We don't know. And that's okay. Nobody knows. This may end in a week. Or maybe, just maybe, we'll be the people who change the world."

present (im)perfect 3: anarchistic
WINDING BACK AROUND to my one and only intro to anarchism teach-in at Occupy Philly, besides realizing that we Occupiers were doing anarchism,

---

3 Ironically perhaps, even though our DIY legal working group followed the General Assembly's directive and applied for a round-the-clock permit from the city, the city bureaucrats signed off on that full day but also notated that our "permitted" time was from 7AM to 7PM daily—meaning our General Assembly always began just as we became illegal each night.

it fully struck me that the "we" by and large wasn't made up of anarchists—even though there were probably more anarchists involved than at most other Occupies. If there was one prevailing common denominator among this hodgepodge of human beings, it was this: most were liberals. That loudly took the form of, as one of my anarchist friends called them, "militant liberals," most of them near-caricatures of patriarchal, heteronormative white males who thought the "founding fathers" had it right. Yet it also encompassed a much wider, calmer range of well-meaning "less-militant" liberals, such as progressives, peace and justice activists, Quakers and interfaith folks, veterans, Democrats, democratic socialists, third-party advocates, college and high school students, single and nuclear-family/GLBT parents, community organizers, antiprison and anticurfew activists, feminists, environmentalists, rank-and-file laborers and the un- and underemployed, people without homes, and (neo)hippies—and probably their dogs too.

Without anarchists, of any adjectival variety, expending months of directly democratic elbow grease toward constructing a visible and visibly anticapitalist convergence, or like "occupy everything" part 1 on mostly California and New York City college campuses a couple years ago, autonomously and invisibly seizing spaces, sans demands, with anonymously penned communiqués urging people to then communize them, Occupy Philly was largely constituted and peopled by liberals. These liberalistas followed swiftly in the OWS footsteps out of neither aspirations nor theory, but increasing necessity, often vaguely referred to as "intuition"—a necessity born of foreclosures, lost jobs, no health care, and onward and downward.

To meander back around again, this time to that first walk from the Wooden Shoe to Arch Methodist Church, one young hippie-clothed woman sauntered up to me and cheerfully shared that she'd intuitively known her whole life that something was wrong. She didn't have words for what was wrong or what she wanted, other than a rather-jumbled monologue about her previous week's experience at OWS that was liberally peppered with the word "love." It had taken some powerful people a long time to mess this world up—she was sure of that. She also knew, after sleeping in Liberty Plaza during its first seven days of life, that there were no easy answers, especially any solutions that could be constrained by demands. Instead, and this she was sure of too, she and others were experimenting with building a new world in the corporate parks of the old.

In Philadelphia—the fifth-largest city in the United States, based on 2011 data, and with an unusually disproportionate amount of profound social suffering, structurally enforced along racialized, gendered, and class-based lines—there was always this white elephant in the occupied city hall plaza. Those many liberals at "base camp," as one of them put it, were overwhelmingly Caucasian US citizens from the downwardly (de)mobilized middle class. That they seemed to be the last to discover that the "American dream" was a nightmare for most created a cornucopia of problems. Yet there they were, some of the last people in the United States that one would expect to want to illegally "occupy everything" that's been stolen from so many "othered" people, and in that open space of possibility, act anarchistically. As one particularly naive liberal Occupier dude observed, as if thunderstruck by his own words, "It doesn't matter how, or if, the mainstream media explains what we're doing. *We* know what we're doing!" In the Occupy Philly commons, our doing was our demand; our demand was in our doing.

Let's go back once more to the circle of my intro to anarchism talk, where I experienced another lightbulb moment of my own. If liberalism, neoliberalism, or other various top-down "-ism" forms of social organization, all inherently limiting freedom to a powerful few, can and do function perfectly well when inhabited by all sorts of people who don't identify as liberal, neoliberal, and so on; and if those types of social organization socialize us to their "values" and practices, and not the other way around; then anarchism too, understood as a wholly different form of social organization, sans hierarchy and striving toward a cornucopia of freedoms, can and should—and as Occupy at its best showed, does—function perfectly well when populated by people who aren't anarchists.

An always-enthusiastic Occupier did this hokey, in my view, group exercise at one of our general assemblies, at least a couple months into our occupation. It involved free-ranging brainstorms on our shared core values, and lots of sheets of paper, colorful pens, and running around, culminating in us then narrowing it all down to our collective top-five picks. I hate such reductionist activities and barely participated, grumpily, unlike the several hundred who just as enthusiastically took part—again, mostly liberals. At the end of this half hour or so, without any anarchists at Occupy Philly ever having put out a laundry list of our principles, the five values at the heart of our encampment could easily have been an ABCs of anarchism.

present (im)perfect 4: anarchists

AND THIS, IN turn, brings me round to "us" anarchists, of all stripes—black/green, black/red, black/brown, black/pink, black/black, and so forth. As I noted just above, at Occupy Philly, we were there in good-size numbers, which shouldn't be surprising given Philly's lengthy anarchist history and its longtime "anarchist neighborhood" of West Philly. And over the course of Occupy Philly's life span, our numbers increased, which again shouldn't come as a surprise, because living, breathing anarchism in action—especially when done by us anarchists, who already had some skills in doing it comparatively well, compared to the liberals—made anarchism itself seem extra appealing, or at least commonsensical.

What was surprising, however, was that we found and/or rediscovered each other. None of us entered the encampment as an affinity group, or coordinated ahead of time to be there en masse. In fact, like anarchists in many US cities, we often don't like each other, don't work well together, have stepped back from organizing, or specifically in Philly, simply have many separate micro-projects/collectives and micro-scenes, and so rarely convene in large groups, except at a yearly bookfair, say, and Philly doesn't have a bookfair.

But none of us, even anarchists long dormant, could resist the pull of Occupy Philly when it first started. We scurried downtown from all corners of the city and set about doing what we anarchists do best: self-organizing. Or in this case, we instantly, unthinkingly (because who the hell thought Occupy Philly would last so long), became do-it-ourselves city technocrats and maybe even bureaucrats on pretty much all the working groups of this pop-up city, because that was what was needed: do-it-ourselves know-how. After all, we had a big, well-stocked toolbox to draw from, collected from our anarchist prehistory.

So our Occupy was abundantly supplied with anarchists, and we joyfully reconnected with each other and our anarchism. We just as joyfully leaped into our labors of love, abandoning our paid work or paid-for schooling, remembering the exhilaration of former convergences, but remarking how this felt extraordinary—revolutionary and historic even. And perhaps most especially, we joyfully watched

> *I was a convenient bogeyman, because I'm both visible and not one to back down, but that the state/police directly, indirectly, or serendipitously via these militant liberals targeted anarchists in an effort to destroy Occupies only underscored for me that anarchism in action was working.*

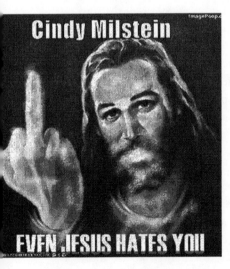

in awe as so many non-anarchists took to our practices so quickly and so ...
well, not so well, but they took to them nonetheless, none the wiser at first
that they were doing anarchism.

Even though it seemed like a dream come true, it was excruciating at times
to be an anarchist among liberals—especially on that early-Occupy night
mentioned above where a huge General Assembly, many of the same folks
who had only a week earlier voted to illegally occupy this same plaza, decided
we suddenly had to have a permit for our own "protection." So we gathered
outdoors for late-night conversations and commiserations in what became
known as the "anarchist guild." It even produced some good literature, workshops, and other projects, but never explicitly as anarchist or by anarchists.

Which brings me to this curiosity: while there were hundreds of anarchists at Occupy Philly throughout its physical-space days, it was hard
for the uninitiated liberal to recognize an anarchist, since most anarchists
in Philly dress like "regular" folk. Even after anarchists verbally identified
themselves as such, or stood up in front of the General Assembly to read
a lovely little statement titled "We Are Anarchists" (explaining that "We're
here with everyone else, practicing power-with not power-over"), or folks
already knew a bunch of us from projects like Decarcerate PA or Food Not
Bombs and collective spaces like LAVA or the A-Space, or it was made clear
that some of the things people loved best about Occupy Philly (such as the
aforementioned couch, to name one) were kicked off and/or sustained by
anarchists—even after all that and more, most of the Occupiers thought
there were few, if any, actual anarchists around.

Thanks to the militant liberals, or rather their militant inner circle of
white, hetero-misogynist, conspiracy-theorist-paranoid macho men (and
this said by someone who rarely thinks in binary or flat identity categories,
much less really believed in them before Occupy Philly), "the" anarchist at
Occupy Philly was me, as in the "EVEN JESUS HATES" example—one of
the less-egregious assaults directed at me, I might add. I was a convenient
bogeyman, because I'm both visible and not one to back down, but that the
state/police directly, indirectly, or serendipitously via these militant liberals
targeted anarchists in an effort to destroy Occupies only underscored for me
that anarchism in action was working. That was my positive spin, most of
the time. But such "red-baiting" also served, I think, to make many a Philly
anarchist cautious about outing themselves as an anarchist, ultimately reducing our contributions and stifling our often-needed voices.

We also inadvertently made ourselves invisible, though, by keeping our
self-imposed technocratic noses to the do-it-ourselves grindstone, thereby
leaving the self-governance way too frequently to the well-meaning liberals,
which in turn made Occupy extra frustrating, to put it mildly, and often
extra unsafe or racist, say, to put it bluntly. (In turn, many anarchists simply

drifted away, back to their other, admittedly far less stressful and far less messy projects.) For instance, two or three of us had basically drafted the directly democratic process for our General Assembly, using methods that worked relatively well in anarchist situations. We had no way of knowing—although in hindsight it seems obvious—that such processes would be wholly inadequate under Occupy conditions, which are precisely the conditions (society at large) that we need to start tinkering with and learning from if we hope to replace states, capitalism, and their ilk. When it didn't work and indeed became a disaster, we didn't step into the decision-making fray to help sort it out. Beyond the "form," we also were wary about offering "content" through proposals, for example, around consent or via collective structures to try to grapple with institutional oppression within our Occupy.

Not that we have all the answers. Or even many of them. Those of us anarchists who showed up at and especially stayed put within Occupy Philly, the encampment, learned more than we ever bartered for. But there were two particularly huge lessons.

First, self-organization really does work, as do all our other principles. The random Occupiers flung together without a road map or boss didn't just stand around looking confused, or tear each other apart (at least initially). They passionately threw themselves headfirst into doing what they love, teaching each other new skills, lending a hand, sharing materials and ideas, trying to protect and care for each other, figuring out how to deal with those tasks none of us really want to do (like, in the case of Occupy Philly, when one of our most considerate general assemblies centered on how to keep the portable toilets clean), and so much more, as other global revolts of late have demonstrated as well.

Second, self-organization ultimately didn't work, and everything we ever thought we knew about ethical social transformation needs to be thoroughly rethought. In our excitement at the outset, at least within Occupy Philly, we misjudged many things, such as the depth of personal and societal damage, and how long it will take to work through—certainly far longer than our occupation—or more to the point, what it will take to undo. We contributed, more than we should have, to letting power dynamics and troublesome individuals spiral increasingly out of anyone's control—partly a result of the genuine dilemma of how, without relying on domination, to ensure and especially "enforce" accountability as well as create safer spaces and consensual boundaries. We didn't have the patience to retool, perhaps time and again, the directly democratic and autonomous structures that we largely brought to the occupation in the first place, even though it soon became apparent that they didn't simply scale-up from, for instance, an anarchist infoshop to daily life within a heterogeneous community with many pressing needs.

To be fair, we also just didn't have time for such reevaluation, much less continually inventing new practices to test out with others. We were all trying to do everything at once, from scratch, without sleep. And more important, there was still the snarling "outside world" barking at our heels, from the many historical and contemporary wrongs in our midst like homelessness and racism to the beat cops stationed on our plaza, from a "good" mayor playing us off against each other to the barrage of bad press, from Homeland Security to capitalism, just to mention a few.

Maybe then, more accurately, there weren't lessons but only a gift. Occupy presented us with the humbling experience of coming face-to-face with the chicken-and-egg question (the vegan version, of course): society and selves need to change before our selves and society can change, yet we can only transform society and our selves through the very process of trying to do so. To an astonishing degree we did—and to an equally astonishing degree, we didn't. It's just a whole hell of a lot messier than we anarchists ever dreamed, even though we also never imagined we'd live to participate in an Occupy, if only for a few months.

what's a poor anarchist to do now?

THE POND OF this essay is, alas, way too small for me to swim into the murky depths of all the problems that Occupy raised for anarchists, anarchism, and those who found they liked living in an anarchistic world populated by all sorts of people, including anarchists. So I'll end with a few circles of hell or maybe heaven, or for us godless anarchists, the constant conundrums we face attempting to do anything in this world.

future (im)perfect 1

"I NEVER THOUGHT it would work. So I never showed up. Okay, so I stopped by for some free pizza a couple times, but it was fucked up from the start. I'm an anarchist. Occupy was some liberal shit."

Or:

"I thought Occupy offered potential, so I showed up, but it got so hard to stay because of the [fill in the blank]. I'm an anarchist. I was already doing rad work that I cared about with folks on the front lines, like prisoners and people without papers, so I've gone back to those struggles. Too bad Occupy never quite figured out a way to reciprocally make those connections."

future (im)perfect 2

"I'M AN ANARCHIST, and Occupy shook up my world; it made me believe again. I'm not sure yet what to do with all I learned, loved, and lost, or what's left of Occupy itself, but maybe I need more processing time, alone and with others. Right now, it feels for naught, but I know that's only my disappointment speaking."

future (im)perfect 3

OCCUPY IS DEAD. Long live Occupy. Or maybe it's just taking a nap. Should we wake it up?

future (im)perfect 4

MAYBE IT'S TIME we kill Occupy once and for all, in our minds and nostalgia, and bring something else to life—and not through wishful thinking, memes, or *Adbusters*, or adding "occupy" to everything. Maybe there's a reason why the more powerful, inspiring, and longer-lasting do-it-ourselves revolts globally of this past year and a half have been attached to springtime, with its renewal, dynamism, and freshness: Arab Spring, Maple Spring. Maybe, in the United States, because we're so behind the curve on rebellion, we needed to start with Occupy Fall—a surprising blaze of autumnal color to reawaken our senses, followed by a raked-up pile of downed crisp leaves to jump in, and yet all too soon blanketed by snow. Practice, with a bittersweet dose of self-reflection, might make for a bit more perfect uprising next time, but only if the next time isn't simply a toothless pantomime of Occupy (or the Arab or Maple springs either).

future (im)perfect 5

ABOUT A MONTH ago in Montréal, I ran into an old friend, who is also a longtime anarchist and CLAC member, at one of the enormous, rambunctious, ungovernable (by the province and police) illegal night demos, which as I write, will be heading tomorrow into consecutive night 78 contra special law 78. The law was intended to have a chilling effect on the student strike; instead, it only heated up Maple Spring, pushing it closer toward a social strike by the people and definitively into a political crisis for the government.

We got to talking intensely about all things Maple Spring, which is what people do night after night on the streets that are ours, and lost in our conversation, we drifted to the back of the huge, snaking mass of people—people of all types and politics, people who never seem at a loss in these near-five-months of student strike for imaginative, flexible, effective strategies that only seem to open up space for more popular participation and solidarity. Not to romanticize what's going on here, but there's a depth that comes from knowing one's prehistory (nearly every seventeen- to twenty-two-year-old striking student I talk to mentions it), having actual practice for several generations in forms of participatory and direct democracy (via institutionalized structures at many of the colleges, and thus the structural basis for carefully organizing this strike), and still believing that society should provide people with social goodness like free education (a legacy, for one, of the promise of the so-called Quiet Revolution here in the 1960s and 1970s).

My friend said that last year, after ten years in Montréal, he was just about to move, because nothing interesting was going on, particularly among the anarchists. "Now," he said, pointing ahead to the thousands of rebellious disobedients in front of us, "The people are leading, and we anarchists are running to catch up"—quite literally, as he and I picked up our pace to join in this historic moment once again.

The date was announced and set very quickly. The place changed venues twice—smaller to larger. People who thought nothing would come of this moment still went. People who had never participated in any kind of moment like this came unprepared.

We all came to build a future. No one really knew what or how. At the first Occupy Baltimore GA, decisions were made that alienated some and fueled others. A site and a day were set for occupying. The second GA dealt with logistics of occupying; media, security, arts, space. We were going to build in McKeldin Square, the middle of downtown Baltimore.

I chose the security group because I feared it would be otherwise made up of action junkies rather than those with a radical perspective of community protection. I wasn't far off: an ex-bouncer who was ready to use his muscles, a man who'd been training for ten years to fight cops, and high school students who had never seen a protest.

We set up our camp. Within a week issues of sexual harassment came up. Accusations were made against the homeless people who lived in McKeldin. People felt there was no working with them, that they were the other. I was approached about an incident of unwanted touching. It was requested that we have an assault policy. As a survivor, I wrote with a holistic viewpoint that recognizes the way in which violence harms the survivor and dehumanizes the perpetrator. The statement gave options to the survivor and would develop a capacity for care--you have choices, you don't have to go to the police, the community will be there for you.

The enactor of violence would still be considered a member of the community, even if they would not be welcome in the camp. They would be given resources to get help. If every person that commits a wrong against another is pushed out, we will never grow. If we don't learn about and live reparative justice and forgiveness, what good is a radical point of view?

But a conservative blog got hold of the policy and it went viral. Local organizations were contacted and all denounced what I had written, saying it encouraged silence; that the encampment was not capable of caring for the needs of its members. The denouncers, ignoring my own experience as a survivor, said that I didn't have proper knowledge or insight on the issue. People, inside Occupy Baltimore and outside of it, were furious that we would provide resources for an enactor of violence.

So I stepped back. I rarely went down to the occupation. Some people supported me and the policy, but most occupiers didn't seem to care. I was disappointed, embarrassed, and I didn't care to have time.

Throughout McKeldin's occupation, there were issues: sexism, genderphobia, homophobia, harassment. Stories of harm and violations of boundaries spread. Many people stopped going. The policy was forgotten, and most of the GAs concerned themselves only with daily maintenance and larger issues were met with a rolling of eyes.

We had come to build a future and we all had a job to do on that construction. My lesson from the dysfunctionality of Occupy is that we need to learn from others and from less-than-ideal experiences to be part of a stronger future. In sharing space and working with people who are not of the same perspective, we begin to prefigure our world.

"The cops are a part of the 99%. They're just doing a job. We should respect them."

"You guys need to stay out of the street. This is a peaceful march."

"We shouldn't go to jail to do a solidarity action. That's going to start trouble. If you're gonna play pussy, you're gonna get fucked."

Those are just a few of the comments I heard during my tenure at Occupy Pittsburgh. There was no thorough understanding of consent, which led to painful interactions. Sexist and homophobic remarks occurred so often that nobody seemed to notice. Jokes about consent were told daily.

An individual was physically sexually harassed. She went to her friends over the matter because she was too ashamed to try to explain the situation to the GA, let alone wait for the group to enact a course of action (something it had proven itself incapable of doing). Her friends asked the individual to leave for two weeks so the survivor would have time to recover. Word of the survivor's identity spread throughout camp and she ended up the butt of jokes and remarks from people who couldn't understand why she was upset—after all nothing they considered serious had happened.

Camp was a decidedly unsafe space, even though the majority of people associated with Occupy Pittsburgh pretended it was. There were drug problems and there were thieves, liars, and authoritarians. There was a constant paradox, "We are the 99%" rang out at most actions, but people formed cliques and actively alienated others. When five people were arrested at an Occupy-organized protest, the Facebook posts about a solidarity action were removed because of the graphic. The action never happened—seemingly occupiers would rather have sat around the camp and complained than honor those who ended up in jail. That was a turning point for me: I was stressed and burnt out, and I couldn't count on them to support me. I left for a month, pondering whether or not I should return.

The anarchists separated themselves from the rest of camp early, and stayed amongst each other at night. They socialized and slept in the same area out of necessity, feeling unsafe and marginalized for their beliefs. Gradually they left due to condemnation and hopelessness. It became increasingly obvious that the camp's fight was not theirs, and whenever something negative happened at a march you could see many posts on Facebook about it being because of "the masked hoodlums."

But I had returned and chose to remain. In hindsight, I was married to what I thought Occupy could be. I thought it could be egalitarian and accepting, non-hierarchical and perhaps worthwhile. It was decided at some point that progressive stack be used, but nobody bothered to abide by it—instead conversations and general assemblies were dominated by white men. In fact, the majority of camp was white and male, with only a handful of womyn and people of color staying even for a night. That led to many voices going unheard, and marginalized communities rarely ever spoke.

Camp was also classist. Though we were all the 99% (as everyone seemed so eager to point out) it seemed apparent that homeless individuals weren't. Entire meetings were devoted to dealing with "the homeless problem" at camp. The only homeless individuals that were allowed to stay were those who had been there since the first day of camp. The rest (according to popular opinion) were only there because they didn't want to stay at a shelter, so obviously they shouldn't be there.

Yes, we were all the 99%, but it only counted if you were a straight white non-anarchist cis male that had a home before camp started. And remember, stay out of the street.

Sophie Whittemore

ORIGINALLY PUBLISHED IN THE RAGING
PELICAN #3

"If I can't keep my white male privilege, I don't want to be part of your revolution."

Sleep away camp suuucked, y'all. Must be all the hormones, that pesky uterus of mine whispering mean somethings in my ear: *"These fuckers would rather ejaculate on the steps of the Federal Reserve..."*

And all the other ladies who felt unsafe, silenced? Our menstrual flows must have synched up, because certainly no person in their rational mind would turn away from Duncan Plaza as it stood, filled with drunk, shirtless men bursting at the seams with The Right Answer.

The right answer seemed to be verbal attacks on banks, congress, dysfunctional schools—caricatures that represent oppressive power to the mainstream. But when a woman points to a strange power dynamic that plays out in her conversation with a man in camp and asks him to check himself, the defensiveness sets in. And sometimes, as happened at a specific General Assembly, in order to be heard, a lady's got to yell. With what quickness the confrontation becomes two-sided in the eyes of the campers! "She shouldn't have yelled at him. We agreed this was a nonviolent space." Well, then. It is too convenient that this space, a space in which a sexual assault or harassment is actually viewed as commonplace (due to its daily occurrence), should suddenly become vehemently defended in terms of nonviolence the moment a fellow is faced with the sneaky "raised volume" tactic that can be so harmful when used to confront patriarchal attitudes.

Over the years, various men have taken "my best interest" on as their area of expertise. There is nothing *less* surprising to me than a group of menfolk who fancy themselves the gatekeepers to the land of revolution also taking on the hefty responsibility of which bills may be posted to said gate. Post no bills that reference race or gender, please!

They are intimidated, you must understand. Be sensitive. You are asking that they let go of their power and that frightens them. Be kind. Remember ladies, make revolution with a smile. The cuter the better. (Please Google "Hot Chicks of Occupy Wall Street.")

"I'm just worried that you may be pushing away the people who are really on your side." This warning from an "ally" after I defected, alienating him with my anger. My side?

How can I describe my side without you thinking I'm running away, tampon tucked between my legs?

I don't give a shit about the Federal Reserve.

Stuff I think would make a real revolution possible: stop raping people.

My side? I want to stand with you! And no, no one delegated secretarial tasks to the ladies of Duncan Plaza, but when our problems are not viewed as primary, then here we are again, like in every lefty movement, playing a supporting role while someone else defines "The Rev." Please understand that your economic status, your debt, your level of unemployment don't mean shit to me when the woman that I love most is struggling to survive a brutal rape. I'm not trying to be dramatic; this is real life for us every day. Show me that this scares you as much as it scares me. Then we can chill together and plot the decline, etc.

Unwoman

I fell in love with the Occupy movement immediately, though I only spent a few hours on a few occasions at Occupy San Francisco, and once in Sacramento after playing a show there, holding signs and chanting with fervor and my big, optimistic smile. I also made 1" buttons at the request of some friends on the Occupy SF media team, and later I made my own buttons that said "I hella (raised fist) Oakland" which I brought to the first day of Occupy Oakland and a few subsequent GAs there.

I wanted to take part in the November 2 General Strike in whatever way I could. I had already committed to perform that night, so I figured I'd take my cello to downtown Oakland and play before that. At the plaza, I joined up with a group of mostly circus performers that had come together for this one event, Artists of the 99%, and we made some quick plans to coordinate my music with their talents. We set up in front of an occupied, shut-down Citibank. I had my cello and a looping amp and I played some upbeat dancey things while my fellow artists danced with some small children.

Just as we were setting up for another number, a man rushed towards us from around the corner and told us there was a group who had just smashed a bunch of bank windows and that we needed to denounce their actions right away. He spoke using the People's Mic, but found that the repeaters faltered when he demanded condemnation.

Now, on the BART ride on the way to the General Strike, I had intervened in some intense intimate partner violence, unrelated to the Strike. "I don't care who started it," I shouted, "Stop hitting each other now!" while the few other passengers on the train said nothing. I'd like to think I know what violence is and isn't, and while I don't condone window smashing, I didn't feel an immediate need to decry it either. Neither did my fellow performers.

So I took a deep breath, then launched into Bach's 3rd cello suite prelude. It was the best answer I could think of. A few bars in, a hundred or so people came around the corner, high on destructive-creative power. I don't know what they thought of me playing Bach there.

Later I played "Written in Red," my setting of Voltairine de Cleyre's last poem, written in 1911 and inspired by the Mexican revolution. I felt the power of the words more viscerally than usual. "Uncurse us the land!"

Since I had a lot of gear, and a gig in SF, I couldn't stay to march on the port, but a couple hours later when I saw pictures my friends were posting I wished I was there. A few weeks later I took part in the planned port shutdown. I wanted the experience of marching: merely lending my literal voice to the movement was not enough, it was too easy and safe (or am I foolish to assume that OPD wouldn't tear-gas a cellist? Probably). So on December 12 I was one of many to march to the already shut-down port, with my partner and a bunch of friends. We heard speeches at the plaza, music from party trucks as we marched, and cheers from Oakland residents we passed. We saw the sunset over train tracks and watched our comrades hang banners. The feeling was electric, empowering. We felt massive and full of loving fight.

Bartosz Brzezinski
February 15, 2012
99 Red Balloons Dance, Occupy Chicago

Michael Premo

UNLOCKING THE RADICAL IMAGINATION

THE RECENT EXPLOSION OF SOCIAL MOVEMENTS THAT HAVE ERUPTED around the world are, perhaps, separated by a diversity of structures, beliefs, and national character. Yet they are united by their insistence on resisting business as usual with large popular uprisings. On a scale not seen in a generation, people are opening their imaginations to new possibilities, taking to the streets, and harnessing our power to continue to build, with renewed excitement, a new society based not on private greed, but on human need and harmony with the Earth. In Europe and the Americas, contemporary popular movements, like Occupy Wall Street, the Spanish *indignados*, and Argentinian *fábricas recuperadas*, have had a prominent anti-capitalist tendency, pushing towards the mainstream a challenge to the myth that capitalism is the best and only way to organize societies.

In common conversation, the word "myth" is often used to dismiss a particular idea or perspective as superstition, fantasy, or pure fallacy. Where we stand on a particular issue or worldview usually determines what stories or prevailing perspectives we designate as myths to be resisted or rejected. I use the term myth here as a fairly neutral way to describe a collection of stories that have been retold again and again about a natural or social circumstance, over time growing into a particular popular narrative (story) that is accepted (or rejected) with a deep reverence otherwise only found in religion or sports.

Throughout human history, stories have been central to our individual expression as well as our shared identity and the cultural understanding that colors how we distinguish right from wrong, shaping the values through which we see the world. These stories come in many forms from the myths that define and shape shared culture to the personal legends we construct to preserve and express the values of our personal lives or family legacy.

Myths are embedded so deeply in our ethos that we often don't realize their impact, or what they mean. Yet they provide emotionally-resonate stories that shape our complex belief systems. A classic example: the Pilgrims landed on Plymouth Rock, found sanctuary for their religious views, and after almost starving, had a nice turkey dinner with the Indians next door. Moral of the story: America is a tolerant safe-haven of religious freedom. The subtext is that their perseverance and dedication in a savage land proved the moral value of hard work and prosperity; a Holy trait of Righteous believers.

This story is significant for a variety of reasons. For one, it completely obscures and erases what actually happened when a band of religious fundamentalists invaded a foreign homeland, committing atrocities (killing both Quakers and Native Americans), and stealing land from people who had no concept of individual land ownership. But the "Thanksgiving story" also provides a firm example of what Max Weber termed the "Protestant ethic," arguing the intrinsic influence of religious thinking on the birth and development of capitalism. And though some Marxists might argue the reverse, that economics had a greater influence on religion, I think it's fair to say they influenced each other. It seems plausible that the economic pursuits of religious men of the era of Reason and Reformation would be influenced by their religion, and those economic pursuits—successes and failures—would then, in turn, reflect back on their religion. And so capitalism, Christianity, and modern nation-states evolved together as symbiotic systems with shared narratives that shape the contemporary belief structure of mainstream America. What's important to consider is the deep piety intertwined into the mythology of our economic system, which, whether we realize it or not, is emotionally rooted in the sensibilities of spiritual reverence.

Like many of the people reading this book, I was one of those kids who, at some point, rejected the Thanksgiving story outright. It was probably some combination of me growing up in a diverse community and my mother exposing me, from an early age, to traditional folk tales and different types of art and culture, compounded by a mean anti-authoritarian streak, that provided me the privilege of an awareness of different realities and contrary perspectives. But all the progressive, feminist child rearing in the world couldn't really change the fact that this myth was communicated to me hundreds of times every year for my entire life—from cartoon specials to paper napkins with pictures of a horn-of-plenty (the funny-looking horn overflowing with food).

Myths are also supported and reinforced in subtle ways. For the majority of people who attend grade school in the United States, the day begins with the ritual of reciting the Pledge of Allegiance, a daily expression of our undying loyalty to the American flag, an unwavering symbol of the indivisible republic. Every single school day for years on end, many of us had to repeat these fateful words: "I pledge allegiance to the flag of the United States of America, and to the republic for which it stands, one nation under

God, indivisible, with liberty and justice for all." Considering that there are 180 school days in the school year, and I recited, or at least had to hear, the Pledge every day until 6th grade, that means that I probably heard this at least 1,080 times by my eleventh birthday. The middle and high schools I went to were kind of off-the-wall schools, and I don't remember hearing the Pledge, but assuming I had heard or recited this every day for the 12 years of compulsory education, that would have been a grand total of 2,160 times.

This is just one, extreme, example of the many ways myths are imprinted in our emotional muscle memory. The final line, "liberty and justice for all," is a cherry on top of the collection of stories that help construct the myth of the American Dream and the narrative of America as a benevolent bastion of freedom and opportunity (and therefore a reinforcement for the Thanksgiving story). While this is reality for some people, it's certainly not a shared reality. The relationship to that myth is very different for the victims of the brutal, protracted attempt to extinguish Native Americans from history, or the Africans brought here as slaves to build the foundation of a global empire as well as women, the working class, and the growing list of causalities and "collateral damage" of American imperialism.

But we know all this, right? We've read the books by our favorite intellectuals. We've seen the documentaries. Maybe we even experience the pain of these hypocrisies personally. In progressive circles it often seems to be common knowledge that consent for these myths is manufactured by those who stand to profit from their continuation. Yet even those who call ourselves "radical" or "progressive" routinely underestimate how deeply, emotionally, and spiritually ingrained these myths are, and all the seemingly inconsequential ways this mythology—these narratives—are pounded into our bodies. Even when we claim to understand this, it is often not apparent in the strategic and tactical decisions of both the resistance and reconstructive work of social justice movements. And it is also absent in our messaging, which instead of persuading, often assaults and repulses the very people we seek to reach. This is perhaps a big reason why movement narratives, our counter myths, so rarely capture popular imaginations on a scale that excites and ignites the masses.

The constant repetition of myths that define cultural identity places parameters on our imaginations and what we believe, emotionally, to be the "way it is" or "business as usual." Any intellectual growth is incomplete without parallel emotional understanding. And we can't underestimate the impact of all the different forms of media that communicate these narratives. Little things as mundane as the familiar pattern of turkeys and a horn-of-plenty on paper plates are quiet reinforcement.

What further complicates the cultural myths that frame our imaginations is the ostensible public acceptance of the notion of protest that acts as a sort of buffer against the entrenched resistance to challenging the established order. Part of the genius of the American "experiment" is how deeply embedded protest is in the national character of the American narrative. The United States was created by a so-called revolution, a rebellion against the Monarchy against, in part, "taxation without representation." No matter where you stand on the nuances of this history, it was a bloody conflict to forge a new society from the high ideals of democracy (during the era of African enslavement). And, as a result, protest is a foundational American "belief" that is a core part of our national values.

The genius lies in the reality that normalizing the narrative of protest as an accepted part of society complicates the efficacy of many forms of protest to meaningfully challenge business as usual—let alone the structural roots of complex systems of domination like capitalism and even white supremacy. How do we challenge the status quo and its underlying power structure when protest itself is too often a part of, and reliant on, the status quo? In the last 30 years we've seen the evolution of a professionalized social justice industry that you could call "business as usual" protest. Even despite this development, it's easy to dismiss or ignore as just "exercising their rights." Furthermore, state-sanctioned protest inherently tends to result in an inability to gain anything more than tacit acknowledgments or occasional reforms, which while important, don't fully address deeply rooted imbalances of power. This is not to undermine or discount any one particular approach on the spectrum of important resistance and reconstructive work contributing to the revolutionary evolution of our society. I mean only to place all these narratives, and counter narratives, in the context of our popular mythology so we can consider the emotional rhythms they dance to in our collective imaginations. Protest and capitalism are two narratives that are both firmly rooted in the American myth that shapes our values—values that we have a deep emotional attachment to.

The occupation of Wall Street on September 17, 2011 sent sparks ricocheting around the country, exciting the popular imagination. People across a diverse set of demographics, geographies, and political tendencies lit up with a sort of excitement not seen on this scale in a generation. Judging by the stacks of letters that came pouring in from every corner of the country, people were deeply moved. As far as the prevailing wisdom of traditional "business as usual" protest culture, the occupation's planning process was half-baked, ragged, and too audacious. Yet it managed to puncture popular myths, challenging the narrative of the infallibility and high wisdom of Wall Street demagogues.

During the phase of the physical occupation there was so much happening on the ground, around the country, and in the media echo chamber that every hour seemed like a week, making it easy to forget that the actual occupation of Liberty Plaza lasted a mere 58 days, just two days shy of two months. But in that very short time the model of Occupations and General Assemblies spread to over a thousand communities adapting in numerous ways to the nuances of local cultural expressions, evolving names like Decolonize, 99% Club, and Occupy [insert any word you can think of].

Practically overnight, the national conversation had transformed from the arcane topic of National Debt to the more deeply resonate realities of income inequality and the crimes of Wall Street. As a result, a mass of people found common cause: from the socially displaced (so-called homeless) and people marginalized for generations to newly affected working and middle class families, from earnest reformers to anti-capitalist insurrectionists. Big money, mainstream progressive organizations had spent months and months and millions of dollars on traditional campaigns hoping to do what we did in just a few weeks.

Occupy didn't create or offer a new alternative system or one particular coherent political critique. The ideas swirling around the eye of the Occupy storm were ideas that have been around for a long time, albeit not necessarily in the mainstream. The core ideas transcended issues and attempted to focus on employing processes grounded in values—mutual aid, cooperation, horizontalism—that could build a force to take shots at the root causes of the many issues that affect us. It was more like old ideas dreamt a little differently and baked together in an open-source social movement (complete with all the complexities and contradictions implicit in that).

For all its shortcomings and achievements, what Occupy Wall Street did, and what made it a popular force, was

Normalizing the narrative of protest as an accepted part of society complicates the efficacy of many forms of protest to meaningfully challenge business as usual.

it unlocked our radical imaginations, opening up the social and emotional space for us to creatively practice our power to meaningfully resist and reconstruct a society that unapologetically privileges the idolatry of profit above all else. This was not just a conversation relegated to the fringes, where self-described revolutionaries berate the so-called enemy and "blind enablers" with tired, self-referential rhetoric and boring propaganda. This was a fairly broad and popular nonviolent creative insurgency against the dominant myths of Western society that crown capitalism as the one true god. It takes fearless creativity and swaggering audacity to attempt to reclaim our imaginations from the gorilla grip of these myths.

Part of the reason for this result was the key role artists and creatives played in the incubation and birth of the movement. From the activist/art magazine *Adbusters* to the participants in the General Assemblies before and after the occupation began, artists were not just the cheap entertainment or the "banner-making" committee; they were integral participants in the process of crafting the essence that would define the heart of Occupy.

The General Assembly, or GA for short, was the main forum for discussion and community decisions before, during, and a short time after the eviction. The NYC GA was cumbersome, unwieldy, and only really found its most functional stride during the first month or so, when its form was anchored and dictated by the physical occupation. But it performed a far more critical role than managing finances, setting administrative purgatives, or any of what the values of capitalist dogma expected of it. Our society lacks a meaningful autonomous political space that is 100% free from the apparatus of State bureaucracy or profit driven agendas. For its part, the GA was as much performance art as it was "decision-making" body. The assembly created a space where people could come together and perform what it *feels* like to participate in political discussions and community-driven decision making in a directly democratic forum, one that its participants perceived to have a level of real consequence. This performance of "alternative" values provided emotional relief and opportunity to many who experienced the GA or the thousands who watched it live-streaming on the Internet.

Adding to the layers of emotional resonance was the "People's Mic," the aural device where a speaker's words are repeated by the crowd as a means of amplification. (The City of New York does not allow electronic amplification without a permit.) It's initiated by shouting "mic check, mic check," until the speaker has gotten enough attention to sufficiently share their announcement. The crowd then repeats the speaker's words, line for line, so everyone can hear. This device quickly spread and evolved. Almost as soon as it was being used as a practical way to share information or conduct large political meetings, it became a direct-action tactic of disruption, a way to distinctly announce that "we are here, demanding to be heard." Yet most importantly, the People's Mic also transcended its practical purpose. In a profit-oriented, hierarchical society obsessed with image, many people without the correct formulas of privilege are routinely silenced or under valued. Using the People's Mic in these large assemblies allowed an individual, especially someone who frequently feels marginalized or thinks that their words fall on deaf ears, to see and feel themselves being heard. Furthermore, its use as a tactic of disruption offered the user the affirmation of group cohesion, providing a fleeting level of connection to a common cause, which is important for a progressive movement fractured by geography and identity and issue politics. This was not 100% unanimous across race and class, but anecdotally, I saw this effect to be somewhat ubiquitous.

We need spaces to come together to resist, rebuild, and re-imagine how we do something as simple as interact with each other. We need a stage to perform our resistance to predominate myths and false idols. For this reason the General Assembly was far more important for emotional learning than it was for exercising intellectual notions of organization. Although in reality, we need forums that serve both these roles.

The challenges we experience performing direct democracy and horizontal organization, without much rehearsal, has less to do with these systems and much more to do with our (in)ability to unlearn the values of a broken system and to re-imagine how a free society should function on the most basic interpersonal level. Performing this re-imagination helps some people to uproot the myths that unconsciously influence their perceptions and contributes to evolving the strategic direction of our resistance and reconstructive work from the symbolic to the real.

Since the occupation of Liberty Plaza, evidence of the popular reawakening of the radical imagination continues to flicker within and beyond the Occupy Movement. One small example of how this concept has shaped specific efforts can be found in the work of New York City-based Organizing for Occupation (O4O), a group of community members, artists, organizers, activists, and lawyers committed to actualizing the human right to housing through direct action.

O4O has a dual strategy of offence and defense, working to prevent evictions, and helping displaced families turn vacant buildings into homes. In New York State, the foreclosure process is long and grueling. It takes an average of three years for foreclosure litigation to find a resolution, with some cases dragging on for much longer. The final, culminating moment of this dehumanizing process is an auction that takes place in Civil Court. To support the organizing we were doing with homeowners, we decided to intervene at the final moment of this emotionally-violent process with something so beautiful and peaceful that the very contrast of our actions against the backdrop of an austere courtroom and callous representatives of Wall Street's tentacles would communicate the hypocrisy of their myths.

O4O member and poet Luke Nephew wrote a beautiful refrain to sing, which we used as the centerpiece of a simple, easily replicated direct action. The way it works is when the auctioneer opens the bidding, a chorus of community members peacefully erupt in song, sometimes with multiple part harmonies, and we don't stop until the auction does or the last singer is arrested and removed for their "disorderly conduct." Using the power of song we bring a presence of calm and beauty to nonviolently obstruct an immoral process. In January 2012, the *New York Times* published an article entitled "Foreclosure Auctions Show Raw Form of Capitalism." The headline suggests how the scenario provides a perfect stage for us to create a performance illustrating the conflict of competing narratives that collide the moment our first note reverberates off the courtroom's vaulted ceiling.

Homeowners who participate in O4O's legal clinic have been deeply moved watching this scene unfold. It's a glimpse of possibility that helps both people who are already part of our community as well as others we are trying to reach to see that we can in fact build the power to resist and rebuild. This serves several tactical and strategic outcomes. The immediate goal is to stop the auction—with memorable flair—as one tactic in an escalating plan. The broader strategic outcome is to move people emotionally and to develop inspired leaders. The music reminds our muscle memory that this is not about principal reduction, legislation, or election cycles, this is about life, and the emotional and imaginative reconstruction of a system that privileges profit over people, where stolen land is commodified and the wounds of hypocritical myths fester as wads of cash try to flash away the cruel inhumanity of a global empire.

Because we live in a society that places a high value on professional intellectuals and devalues the art of creativity (with a few exceptions, notably business innovation), it's often a leap for us to consider the paramount role of imagination and its ability to nourish humanity's progress. The journey up the mountain requires a series of small leaps of imagination, one after another. On this path is the constant obstacle of being so oversaturated by the bombardment of messages we absorb that we take their impact for granted. For exactly that reason, if the myths of a life beyond capitalism are to challenge the myth of capitalism as the best and only way to organize society, we need to employ a level of creativity and imagination that rivals the sophistication of the current system. We don't fully know what that looks like, on a level that moves us spiritually, emotionally, and intellectually, because we haven't invented it yet. The seemingly mundane acts of occupying Wall Street, hearing yourself repeated in a mass political meeting, or singing in a courtroom are insurgent guerrilla strikes trying to uproot the emotional sentries that guard the castles made of myths that protect the status quo.

The most potent forms of resistance and political art affect us emotionally; they sit on the razor's edge of reality, creating within us a crisis of faith within that which we hold to be self-evident. And if our crisis has led us down lonely roads or to a community in exile, this resistance, executed in a way that cuts against the grain and excites us in our hearts, can call us back together so we, united, can relearn how to work together to construct a free society. All the mighty words and deeds of philosophers and freedom fighters will propel us forward, but the emotional logic of capitalism is, perhaps, as great an obstacle as there is, and it is the one for which we're least prepared. The popular myths that deify the false idols of capitalism can be unhinged through the creativity of unbridled imaginations capable of reaching as deeply as the deepest root of our reverence for the values of this logic. The occupation of Wall Street helped unlock our collective radical imagination, invigorating the revolution of consciousness that is helping to liberate the impossible. It's not the first, the only, nor the last. It is, however, a tiny glimpse of the sheer scale of popular resistance required to challenge and reconstruct complex value systems. A healthy and powerful movement ecology must be anchored at the grassroots by leaders of the directly affected and most marginalized, building power and charting our course. But that is only one, albeit critical, piece of the social movement puzzle. America's representative republic, forged in the revolutions of the sixteenth century, is being rendered obsolete, in part by our continued enlightenment and the revolutionary evolution of history. For new forms of participatory democracy, self-governance, and the foundation of a free society to emerge, they will require creativity, imagination, and the participation of radical artists who are, of course, the midwives of revolution.

GENERAL STRIKE

Molly Crabapple
& John Leavitt

MOLLY CRABAPPLE AND JOHN LEAV

MAY

Janelle Treibitz

THE ART OF CULTURAL RESISTANCE

RECENTLY, ON AN OCCUPY LISTSERV, I READ ABOUT THE REVOLUYAHS, A nomadic group of Occupy artists and musicians. They refer to themselves as a "travelling joy committee" and are touring with a boisterous road show to build alternative communities. One activist on the listserv responded to the tour announcement by saying "Well sure, but how are they gonna get corporate money out of politics?"

It is common to hear comments like this in many grassroots organizing settings where activists refuse to prioritize cultural work because they don't see the point. And what is the point? What role do art and culture play in our lives? And what is the role of cultural resistance in a social movement?

Though some Occupy communities have been on the forefront of integrating effective cultural work into their movement activities, many still habitually separate art from activism, reducing the potential of art to mere decoration. Activists may have a healthy understanding that art can capture more mass media, that it can help get our stories out, and that it can bypass people's intellectual filters to hit them on a deeper emotional level. But even then it is generally viewed as just another tool that can be picked up and put down again at will. This perception of art demonstrates a devastating misconception of the power and breadth of culture in our lives. My goal here is to explore three strategies for cultural resistance that allow us either to dismantle or to harness that power. To set the stage, it is first important to have a basic understanding of our modern culture so we can clearly see that when we are not using culture, it is using us.

why culture?

The destiny of the world is determined less by the battles that are lost and won than by the stories it loves and believes in.[1]

—Harold Goddard

---

1 In: Patrick Reinsborough and Doyle Canning, *Re:Imagining Change: How To Use Story-based Strategy to Win Campaigns, Build Movements, and Change the World* (Oakland: PM Press, 2010), 45.

"CULTURE" IS A big term. It refers to the collection of expressions that make a society. In the world, it is dance, music, art, fashion, language, food, etiquette, religion, mythology. In ourselves, it is the stories we believe about who we are, what we can accomplish, our values, worldviews; it is the lens through which we interpret our realities. There are different cultures within a given society, but they often operate within a cultural hierarchy.[2] A dominant culture wields the most power and sets the rules and standards of its society. Dominance is determined more by who holds the power over political and economic institutions than by who holds the majority.

The dominant culture in the United States was built from a foundation of European, English-language, Protestant Christian ancestry with strong white supremacist roots. Before the late nineteenth century, it promoted "thrift, modesty, and moderation," but as the Industrial Revolution took hold, major cultural shifts were put into motion that began changing the culture of the pious spendthrift into one of consumerism. As industrial production grew, droves of workers moved away from community-oriented small town life to alienating urban centers for factory jobs. While union organizing fought to raise wages and decrease the hours in a workday, the growth of mass production lowered costs of luxury items to the price range of workers. Credit was extended to more people, making spending easier and more accessible to a larger population. Psychology gained popularity with an emphasis on the experience and fulfillment of the individual. Psychologists entered the field of advertising, ushering in a new era that used psychological theories (like behaviorism) to influence consumer decisions, creating "'lifestyle branding'—selling products by attracting consumers to a particular way of life rather than the good itself."[3]

Over just a few generations, consumerism became the predominant characteristic in our modern dominant culture; it is the driving force for much of our popular cultural output. We produce movies, tv shows, literature, theater, and advertisements that reinforce its cherished ideas through an endless and constant barrage of stories, images, and sounds. We grow up understanding ourselves and our world through the frameworks these media provide. Even if we are raised into a subculture that rejects the dominant ideas and celebrates other standards, we still have to deal with the cultural ocean around us, and its powerful tide that casts us against the rocks in spite of any countercultural life rafts in which we may try to stay afloat.

---

2   "Hierarchy of Cultures" *SparkNotes,* accessed July 13, 2012, http://www. sparknotes.com/sociology/society-and-culture/section6.rhtml.

3   Richard H. Robbins, *Global Problems and the Culture of Capitalism,* 5th ed. (New Jersey: Prentice Hall, 2011), 17–22.

A people's expressive culture, which is at the heart of its folklore, has a profound significance. It is a powerful statement of what is most deeply felt and of what gives meaning to people's lives. If it flourishes, so too does their way of life.

—David Maybury-Lewis, *Cultural Expression and Grassroots Development*

The impact of the dominant culture in our lives is undeniably hard to ignore. Even the most supportive parents will be hard-pressed to raise a girl without body issues when the culture holds up impossible Western European-based aesthetics as the standards for beauty. It's common for people who are stuck in poverty, though working multiple jobs, to blame themselves when the culture promotes an American Dream myth that says everyone can achieve equally if they just work hard enough. We learn that time is money and money is power, that retail is therapy and that success is measured in acquired luxury goods.

These are the stories that rule our lives, that tell us who we are and who we should want to be, what we can achieve and how we're supposed to fit in to the world around us. These are the stories that maintain our political and economic systems. Though not all of our dominant culture is begging for subversion, so many of its basic tenets, particularly when combined with consumer capitalism, are upholding institutions and systems that make some of our greatest values (like democracy, freedom, and equality) impossible to achieve. On the other hand, within the dominant culture, music, religion, art, food, and community traditions can provide healing, joy, strength, and connection.

As activists, we must understand where culture has power over us and where it has power to support us. We must understand how culture has the strength to heal our wounds and grow our movements. Above all, we must take the time and make the effort to engage it. Cultural resistance is a central function of changing society. How can we shift any system of oppression if we don't shift the culture that loyally believes in it?

strategies for cultural resistance

IF WE UNDERSTAND how culture works as a force in our lives, then we can use that force to our advantage. It's not a matter of simply adding music to an event or using a puppet at a rally, though that is certainly a part of it. We need to focus more broadly on developing larger cultural strategies. In the same way we design goals and strategies for our campaigns, we should be equally intentional about our approach to cultural work. Here I offer three primary strategies for cultural resistance that I identify as necessary to maintain an effective and enduring social movement.

Luther Blissett
February, 2012
Foreclosed School in Bed-Stuy, Brooklyn

To demonstrate each strategy, I use case studies from within the Occupy movement. Though someone could probably write a tome about the culture of our movement overall, I focus the case studies specifically on examples of how creative expression, the arts, have been used. I have had the great privilege of being involved in organizing a series of InterOccupy Arts Conference Calls, through which I learned about many of these efforts.[4] The projects I've highlighted here I've chosen because they were particularly effective or innovative examples of a particular strategy (though they may in fact serve to fulfill multiple strategies). I am sure I am missing equally worthy projects and for that, I apologize. But I encourage all of you readers to find out more about what your Occupy community or other local arts activists have been doing in this realm.

And now, three strategies for cultural resistance:

1. subvert, co-opt or reclaim the dominant culture

To ENACT THIS strategy, we take the icons, images, stories, and traditions of the dominant culture and alter them. (Think of the image of the ballerina on the Wall Street bull that helped incite OWS, the flashmobs using pop

---

4 The InterOccupy Arts Conference Calls are organized in collaboration with ArtIsMyOccupation.org, a project to support artists and cultural workers engaged in the Occupy movement through small grants, publicity, and distribution.

Luther Blissett
December 6, 2012
Moving into foreclosed property in East NY

songs, the religious holiday services highlighting Occupy themes hosted at Occupy camps.) Using this strategy we can begin to take away or transform the power the dominant culture holds over us. We make visible the ways it manipulates our emotions and values, we interrupt it, we mock it, or we embrace its more powerful elements to push our messages.

As movement activists, our relationship to the dominant culture often has to be fluid. It's a force too powerful to ignore completely. Deeply instilled behaviors, beliefs, and power dynamics from the dominant culture tend to show themselves within our movement work whether we like it or not. There are some elements of the dominant culture that hold real personal value for people and thus hold the potential to enrich and advance movements (i.e., religious traditions or popular music), while other elements limit human potential and are worth the effort to disrupt or subvert (i.e., religious traditions or beauty standards). The case studies included here explore both approaches to this cultural strategy.

Occupied Real Estate. Occupied Real Estate is an art activist project coming out of New York City, working around foreclosures, eviction defense, and squatting. They have re-imagined the cultural construct of a real estate agency by creating their own that advertises abandoned properties for occupations, publicizes eviction defense, and promotes tools and tactics for successful squatting. Through a home renovation show on YouTube teaching squatting skills, "real estate" brochures given to auction bidders advertising that the properties up for sale come with "500 protesters," and the creation of eviction defense shields with life-size pictures of the families whose homes are being defended (creating a media spectacle when police smash through the picture-shields), they redefine the culture of "real estate" and its agents, co-opting its traditional imagery and showmanship to elevate their own values and movement tactics.

"For Squat" Signs. In a thematically similar vein, Occupy Minneapolis has been putting up "For Squat" signs on abandoned properties around their city. The signs are an exact imitation of traditional "For Sale" signs. Capitalizing on that easily recognizable image and the loaded symbology of a real estate sale, activists have set up a public challenge to the dominant culture surrounding the sanctity of private property.

Flashmob in Wells Fargo. Using the popular Lady Gaga song, "Telephone," San Francisco Pride At Work/HAVOQ activists organized a flashmob in the lobby of a Wells Fargo bank to highlight the bank's role in the economic and housing crisis, turning it into a YouTube video that advertised an upcoming Occupy day of action against banks. The protesters flooded the bank lobby with costumed dancers, jumping up on counters and doing a choreographed dance routine to rewritten lyrics of the Gaga song (featuring the line "Stop calling, stop calling, can't afford to pay anymore/I left my head and my heart in the class war"). [5]

Tax Dodgers Baseball Team. The Tax Dodgers is a fake baseball team that enacts live street theatre performances in satirical support of tax-dodging corporations. (Their slogan? "We go to bat for the 1%.") A replicable street theater tactic reminiscent of Billionaires for Bush, the team targets real-life, high-profile tax dodgers and shows up to their events and corporate headquarters as their biggest supporters. They organize real baseball games in which they invite community members to form the opposing team—the 99%ers—and then change the rules, pay off the umpires, and rig the game. Taking advantage of the deeply entrenched values attached to the sport, the Tax Dodgers loudly defy them with their corporate, money-focused, rule-breaking, unsportsmanlike team character, creating a humorous media spectacle that effectively re-brands whomever they target as a Tax Dodger. A jersey and cap of the team has just been put on display at the National Baseball Hall of Fame in Cooperstown, NY. [6]

---

5   You can see their flashmob on YouTube at: http://bit.ly/MRrzaQ.

6   For more information on the Tax Dodgers: http://taxdodgers.net.

Luminous Intervention. Formed as an offshoot of Occupy Baltimore, the Green Pants Collective has been re-making spaces throughout Baltimore with large-scale, outdoor projections. They partner with community groups to identify locations and subject matter, supporting local struggles by bringing to light "the hidden histories, practices, and envisioned futures" of Baltimore residents. Projecting onto buildings owned by corporate targets or in branded shopping districts, Green Pants has been able to interrupt business-as-usual, calling attention to invisibilized stories while calling out bad corporate actors, achieving both a form of subversion and reclamation of the dominant narratives operating in public space.[7]

2. build our own movement culture

FOR THIS STRATEGY, we develop our own ways of communicating, our own rituals, our own symbols, our own literature and music. This includes creating spaces for transformation; retraining and healing ourselves from damage done by the dominant culture and legacies of oppression. (Think General Assemblies; tents; Guy Fawkes masks; favorite chants; committees devoted to anti-racism, faith, or healing). Using this strategy we build a sense of community, of unity, of shared values, an alternative worldview, and a commitment to making the struggle for social justice an integrated part of our lives.

A movement culture develops whether we acknowledge it or not. The act of coming together repeatedly inevitably gives rise to some kind of group culture. To make it sustainable and long-term, we must be intentional about how it develops. Building our own movement culture is an act of re-making society as we want to live it. We make it for ourselves, we model it for others. We use it to sustain our communities, our families, and ourselves for a long and ongoing struggle for justice.

Artists, designers, comedians, performers, and other cultural workers have been contributing their skills to build a common language, a community identity, an intentional movement-based subculture that helps people connect, build relationships, create new traditions and art, and make the movement a way of life that reinforces our shared values. Creative expression is just one part of building a movement culture, but it is significant and can straddle many mediums.

The Occupy movement has given rise already to many projects oriented towards this cultural resistance strategy, but in my search for case studies, this is the strategy with the fewest examples. Perhaps this indicates that developing our own movement culture (with a heavy emphasis on building community) is a necessary focus moving forward.

---

7   For more information on Luminous Intervention: http://luminousintervention.org.

IndigNación Newspaper. A spanish-language media project affiliated with Occupy Wall Street. The group publishes a website and printed newspaper with news and analysis about the Occupy movement and other local, national, and international issues and political struggles relevant to the Latino community. The group has also printed posters for mass mobilizations. They use the process of poster and newspaper distribution as an outreach tool to develop relationships with Latino business owners and community members, engaging in conversations about the ideas behind their project and the Occupy movement.[8]

Occupy Town Square. An affinity group of Occupy Wall Street that organizes "mobile, daytime, pop-up occupations" in parks and public spaces around New York City. The occupations aim to reclaim the commons, creating temporary zones where people can re-imagine a society based on mutual aid. The Town Squares feature a kitchen offering free food, a library, teach-ins, political discussions, music, art activities, guerilla installations, and cultural activities. The Town Squares pop up in different neighborhoods, doing local outreach in advance to collaborate with neighborhood groups so that the Town Squares offer community-specific teach-ins, cultural presentations, and language access. The group also collaborates with many artists and art groups (like the OWS People's Puppets who perform puppet shows with community themes and give workshops) to infuse each Town Square with a festive, joyful atmosphere.[9]

Occupy Design. Maintains a website to connect graphic designers to Occupy activists, letting people freely add to and take graphics and posters from the site. They are engaged in "building a visual language for the 99%," creating new symbols and images that represent and give power to Occupy issues and values.[10]

Laughter Against the Machine. A touring stand-up comedy troupe dealing with the main themes of the Occupy movement. By putting Occupy stories on stage and allowing activists to laugh at the powers they are fighting, they legitimize dissenting viewpoints. By allowing activists to laugh at themselves, they help cement a feeling of being part of a broader movement community.[11]

---

8   For more information on *IndigNación*: http://www.indig-nacion.org.

9   For more information on Occupy Town Squares: http://www.facebook.com/occupytownsq.

10 For more information on Occupy Design: http://www.occupydesign.org.

11 For more information on Laughter Against the Machine:

Occupy Comix. Capturing the stories, dreams and struggles of the Occupy movement through comic books, repurposing that artistic genre to help develop an alternative culture made up of our stories and our values.[12]

3. use cultural elements to give power to our outreach, actions, events and other key strategic processes[13]

TO ACTUALIZE THIS strategy we turn actions into creative spectacles, we turn concerts into recruitment tools, we develop our own media to tell our stories, and we sustain participation in our strategy sessions with food or fun meeting rituals. (Think colorful posters, inspiring YouTube videos, brass bands at demonstrations, weekly strategy brunches at OWS.) Using this strategy we not only find different ways for people to participate in our campaigns, but we make our actions more visible, push our stories into the public eye, spread oppositional thought and discourse, grow our movement, and reinforce the first two cultural resistance strategies. [14]

Just as a movement will not achieve lasting success without a compelling movement culture to give it heart, so too will it fizzle without some level of organizing strategy. Strategy, simply put, is a roadmap of how to get from Point A to Point B. It's the plan of action undertaken to reach the goals of a campaign, an action, or an entire movement. To enact our roadmap and build towards our goals, we educate ourselves and others, we share skills and resources, we do outreach and recruitment, and we mobilize for actions and events. In these strategic spaces we can find endless opportunities to use culture. Cultural elements can be used as educational tools within a workshop (showing films, creating skits, etc.), sparking greater levels of engagement and deeper discussion. Visuals, music, and movement can multiply the effect of an action or event, prompting better media coverage and more energy and inspiration from participants. Supportive artists or art events can make a movement and the values for which it stands seem "cool," helping gain new recruits and resources. And good strategic storytelling (whether through performance, newspapers, sermons, actions, etc.) can help shift the popular understanding of, and sentiments toward, an issue.

---

http://laughteragainstthemachine.wordpress.com.

12 For more information on Occupy Comix: http://occupycomix.wordpress.com.

13 Hank Johnston and Bert Klandermans, "The Cultural Analysis of Social Movements," in *Social Movements and Culture,* ed. Hank Johnston and Bert Klandermans (Minneapolis: University of Minnesota Press, 2004), 14.

14 Ibid., 7.

Creative expression in the service of targeted strategy has been common within the Occupy movement, as artists and cultural workers have joined in the planning of direct actions and campaign strategy. Here are a few examples:

May Day Posters. Leading up to the May Day 2012 Occupy actions, Occuprint (a group collecting global Occupy poster art and making it available to activists) worked with Occupy artists across the country to design a series of visually powerful posters calling for the planned General Strike. The collective distributed them to Occupy communities around the country where they were wheatpasted throughout cities.[15]

Occupy Kabaret Street. As a cover action for an illegal building occupation, the Puppet Underground collective in DC organized a cabaret of music and puppet shows that taught about the history of occupations in DC and the history of the chosen building, gathering an audience and media for the surprise banner drop and announcement of the takeover.[16]

Tent of Dreams. In response to new enforcement regulations about sleeping in Occupy K Street's McPherson Square encampment, activists painted a giant tarp with constellations and labeled it as the "Tent of Dreams," draping it over the large central statue of General McPherson to turn it into a gigantic tent. Other compelling visuals were made using the theme of "Let us sleep so we can dream," to create a narrative that would both challenge the police's justification for enforcement and keep the public conversation grounded in the larger social justice issues that drove Occupy activists to stay at the camp.

Working Groups and Affinity Groups. Art and culture working groups and affinity groups have become a mainstay of Occupy communities and approach their movement work from different angles. Occupy Wall Street's Art and Labor group and San Francisco's Artists of the 99% have focused their work around the economic inequalities art workers face, organizing actions targeting art institutions and publishing zines exploring the issues. Other groups like the Occupy Wall Street People's Puppets and the Rude Mechanical Orchestra have focused on supporting or organizing actions and events, and training more activists in artistic skill sets.

---

15 For more information on Occuprint: http://www.occuprint.org.

16 For more information on Puppet Underground: http://www.facebook.com/PuppetUnderground.

Foreclosure Song. Housing activists with Organizing for Occupation in NYC have successfully and repeatedly blocked auctions of foreclosed homes by singing. They turn out sizeable numbers to attend auctions, which they disrupt with their own simple song (sung in harmonies) that asks "Listen Auctioneer, all the people here, we're asking you to hold off the sales right now." It has prevented the auctions from happening, inspired participating activists, and garnered a lot of media on the issue.[17]

> It is important to note that in only a few cases is protest directed explicitly at the culture of capitalism itself. Rather, protesters select as objects of their protest groups or individuals who they hold individually responsible... In other words, rarely do social protest movements specifically attack the system that is the source of their distress; instead they focus on real or symbolic figures who, for them, embody their oppression.
> —Richard H. Robbins, *Global Problems and the Culture of Capitalism*

The stories we live by, the values we hold, our creative expression, how we build community: this is the realm of culture. This is why we cannot rely on factsheets, marches, and manifestos alone. This is why we desperately need to recognize that culture has to be on the front lines of any resistance movement. Because whether we acknowledge it or not, culture is not just a piece of the battle, it is the very ground on which the battle is being fought. We have been so focused on the guns that keep firing at us—the student debt, the bank bailouts, mass incarceration, privatization, neocolonialism, war—that we rarely take a moment to look at the landscape on which we stand. It is time we examine the hills and the holes of our battlefield and make some decisions about what terrain we actually want to be fighting on. Because right now the battle is still centered smack in the middle of the culture of capitalism, complete with individualist ideals and oppressive behaviors. The sooner we recognize this, the sooner we can determine both where we should dig our trenches and where we can find more fertile ground away from the bullets to build something new.

---

17 For more information on Organizing for Occupation: http://www.o4onyc.org.

Sunset Parkerpix
November 17, 2011
"Bat Signal" projection, NYC

Nadine Bloch

SHINE A LIGHT ON IT
CULTURAL RESISTANCE ILLUMINATED

Often such little small cultural experiments open up space and possibility for the bigger changes to happen. The real seeds for revolutionary changes can grow in artistic practices.

—John Jordan

Art is not a mirror held up to reality, but a hammer with which to shape it.

—Bertolt Brecht

The role of the artist is to make the revolution irresistible.

—Toni Cade Bambara

ALL OVER THE WORLD ACTIVISTS ARE THROWING ... LIGHT. IT'S BEEN GOING on for some time now—projections of still images or videos, black and white and color, simple and complex—though as with many tools, the advent and refinement of digital technology and access to computers have made it possible for mass movement actors to take advantage of things movements only dreamed about a decade ago.

One early example of the use of projections in protest came from artists themselves. In 1970, the Ad Hoc Women's Art Committee harnessed the power of projection to cover NYC's Whitney Museum of Art with slides of women's works that had been excluded from the Museum's prestigious show that year. Next year, the inclusion of women artists went up 17%.

In the late 1980s, Greenpeace projected images onto warships secretly carrying nuclear weapons into populated harbors, creating glowing public safety announcements. This was engineered from inflatable boats outfitted with huge theatrical slide projectors.

In 2006, the US Holocaust Museum in Washington, DC projected images from Darfur onto their own external walls just as the country was

Twelve Methodologies of Creative Cultural Resistance

1. **2-D arts:** graphics/images/words: murals, banners, posters, stickers, comics, caricature, logos)

2. **3-D arts:** puppets, props, objects, costumes, mascots, sculpture

3. **Sound/music arts:** drumming, noisemaking, spoken word

4. **Theater arts:** guerrilla, invisible, traditional, identity correction.

5. **Movement arts:** dance, martial arts, walks, marches, circus arts

6. **Media/documentation arts:** video, radio, film, archives, projection, whistle blowing

7. **Literature:** newspapers, leaflets, books, poetry

8. **Delineation of space:** physical spaces/structures which exclude or resist violence/militarization; peace parks/demilitarized zones, peace villages, peace abbies

9. **Cultural institution building**

10. **Crafts & Traditions:** clothing, food

11. **Rituals:** national/spiritual/religious celebrations, funerals, fasts

12. **Language preservation**

about to celebrate Thanksgiving, fashioning a monumental plea to address the genocide in the darkest light.

Fast forward to 2011 and 2012, with now (relatively) inexpensive video projectors and scrappy DVD players easily available, along with tech innovations enabling much more powerful video projection: Flash-mob-style Guerilla Drive-Ins featuring full color video projections focused on exposing the Koch Brothers undue influence on American politics materialized in NY and DC; images were also seen projected on the Supreme Court, the US Chamber of Commerce, and other landmarks and historical sites, highlighting the real history, exposing corruption, and demanding change. The OWS "Bat Signal" set off a round of light throwing and inspired the start of several activist groups dedicated to this form (Luminous Intervention in Baltimore and The Illuminator in NYC are two). In the spring of 2012, an Egyptian group, Kazaboon (Liars), broadcast the lies of their mainstream media armed with actual video footage challenging false assertions of protesters being foreign agents, and exposing Military repression. These videos of actual footage lit up walls of prominent buildings all over the country, with a team of volunteers producing nearly 500 showings in 2 months.

Of course, projections are just one of the immense diversity of artistic methods that have been employed in resistance, from 2-D and 3-D arts to sound/music and theater/movement arts. From literature and crafts to documentation and delineation of space, as well as rituals and language preservation, creative cultural work has immense power in organizing, mobilizing, and grounding actions.

At a very basic level, cultural work is perhaps the most powerful way to combat corporate insistence on homogenization—and to fight the pervasive and demoralizing messages that individuals don't count, and that cultural differences are liabilities. Validating cultural work and connection empowers individuals and communities, emotionally, physically, and psychologically. Integration of arts/culture into one's life is a way to reclaim our agency, a way to effect change—one keffiyeh scarf, one prayer, one song, one projection at a time.

So, where to start? Perhaps with realizing that the solutions are as varied as the individuals involved—real people power builds diverse creative resistance. Ecological systems, in which diversity is the key to sustainability, are clear examples of this. When scholars have evaluated campaigns, they find that tactical innovation is one of the key elements of successful nonviolent campaigns.

Occupy's encampments themselves constitute creative cultural resistance, in the sense of offering an opportunity to experiment with an alternative way of living together (essential culture.) As well, all over the world, delineating space to achieve a specific goal has been a tool of cultural workers—from designations of posted Drug-Free School Zones to areas where truces are honored even during war time, sometimes called Peace Villages.

Encampments are extraordinarily public by nature, and though Occupy was simply one of a long line of historical uses of occupation as a tactic, it has a peculiar common characteristic of this century: the ever increasing public

At a very basic level, cultural work is perhaps the most powerful way to combat corporate insistence on homogenization—and to fight the pervasive and demoralizing messages that individuals don't count, and that cultural differences are liabilities.

Cultural resistance can:

1. Motivate:
- articulate a vision
- provide psychological & emotional support
- overcome fear
- offer a framework for commitment

2. Promote Group Formation:
- build group identity
- create a container for consciousness-raising and self-recognition
- establish group culture and values
- encourage unity

3. Develop Cause Consciousness:
- increase effectiveness of internal and external education and public relations
- expand potential for political discourse
- undermine control of authorities

4. Create Space:
- to self-organize and ID leaders
- to have political discourse
- for opposition that can minimize the risk of oppression
- to practice organizational development and self government

5. Serve as Constructive Programs:
- the cultural work can often be the direct action itself, modeling the future
- encourage tactical innovation through creative and traditional programs
- provide mechanisms for fundraising

nature of our lives and the willingness and/or comfort with exposing one's life whether on Facebook or via Twitter to many more people than ever before. Perhaps the increase in projections is not only due to the accessibility of the technology but also to the understanding of the value of public display and our collective comfort level with it.

Projections, as with most cultural resistance, can serve campaigns and movements in many functional ways. Artists and cultural workers are often visionaries, and as such they provide **motivation** by helping to articulate a vision that helps to build a container for the work, fighting fear and growing a support group. **Group formation** and unity are served by cultural work, which can create visible expressions that define a group publicly. Projections offer a high powered form of **outreach and visibility** for a campaign and the group associated with it; they can also increase the effectiveness of internal and external education, public relations, and expand the potential for political discourse and dialogue—all the while staying out of reach and therefore undermining the control of authorities. Throwing light is also a way for voicing opposition that can minimize the risk of oppression. Organizing a projection or any action is a way to practice organizational development and self government.

Projections, like any intentional creative work, can provide many and diverse entry points for people into the movement—think about art/cultural work as a gateway drug to broader involvement!—and this gets at the heart of the sustainability for our movements, whether camped out in the city center or meeting weekly to plan action. But beleaguered bits of "art" (or culture, or action of any type) external to the rest of our lives and our strategic plans can't alone lead us to "win."

How can projection and creative arts help us "win"—or serve us in regaining agency and building capacity? It is only through intentional incorporation of more inclusive "cultural work"—weaving it in as the radical connecting thread of potential that it can be.

You don't have to literally shine a light on something to make it visible. It can be theoretical light, something done differently, an opening, a new way. Thinking about arts as cultural work, or thinking about cultural work as an art itself, expands the platforms available for delivering more and better meetings, trainings, actions and campaigns. This can translate into work on the ground very directly when we hold the core belief that creativity is supported by acknowledging that each of us has something valuable to contribute. Specifically, whenever possible, use the process and principles of experiential and popular education, harnessing the wisdom of as many people as doable and being open to information and ideas coming from many sources. Equalize participation throughout your work and organization. Don't just give someone a seat at the table, do make sure they are supported in fully participating. Sit in a circle, and mean it. Leave the banking method of education to the bankers—no standing up in front of a room depositing your "knowledge" into others. There's not much that is creative or culturally supportive in that framework.

Since the tents are no longer in the public space, projections can be—and without any of the issues of maintaining a community, nor of property destruction.

Beyond the generic functions of creative cultural work, projections offer some specific gifts to activists post-Occupy encampments. Since the tents are no longer in the public space, projections can be—and without any of the issues of maintaining a community, nor of property destruction (though it is neither legal nor recommended to shine lasers through windows, FYI.) And, as with the Feminist Art action, the Darfur Genocide projection, or the Nuclear Weapons on Board announcements, projections can make the invisible visible—whether the issue is invisible due to culture, simple chemistry and physics, or distance. Issues of class, race, opportunity, and even things relating to our very existence, often are obscured by the dominant corporate culture and shining a literal light can be illuminating in more ways than one!

It's also true now that access to digital technologies means that ever increasing numbers of people can collect, distribute, and modify whatever they want—images, video, etc. The practice of "remix" has changed the look and feel of our art, our media, and our activism. In some ways it has "democratized" the creation of media, art, and documentation practices, and certainly has de-professionalized it.

Projecting images or videos also offers a way to make a bold statement with an element of surprise, and sometimes in locations that would be impossible or very difficult to access for things like banner-drops or graffiti. It can offer a way to build an audience from the ground up (literally), to focus an audience you invite, or a way to usurp an audience gathered for another reason. Images can be projected without preamble or immediate audience —a "stealth" projection that builds an audience over time as word gets out about its existence.

Here are some things to know if you're considering projection: Low powered video projectors that are under 10,000 lumens are exponentially more affordable than those over 10,000 lumens; consider layering two smaller projectors to increase the additive lumens rather than renting or purchasing a larger machine. Using slides or theatrical gobos with high intensity spotlights rather than videos will be considerably less expensive and require less complicated power solutions (batteries will work just fine in most cases.) The higher the lumen capacity, the larger and/or heavier the projector generally, and the greater the power needs—impacting portability. And although the tech is changing so rapidly, the images that work the best are still simple and bold designs. Ambient light and the distance of the projection throw need to be considered; don't completely black out the object you are projecting onto if that object is instrumental in telling the story!

The bottom line? Integrated and intensive use of creative cultural resistance in campaigns can move your campaign light years ahead in building your constituency, expanding the dialogue and connecting people where it counts.

So go ahead, throw some light; whether its actual photons or metaphysical art, using creative cultural resistance techniques can only be illuminating.

recommended resources

"A Force More Powerful," Book and Video Series. Peter Ackerman and Jack DuVall: http://www.aForceMorePowerful.org/index.php

"The Strategic Dimensions of Civil Resistance." Peter Ackerman and Berel Rodal: http://www.david-kilgour.com/2008/pdf/misc/50–3%2010%20Ackerman%20Author%20Proof.pdf

"Singing Revolution," Video: http://www.singingrevolution.com/cgi-local/content.cgi?pg=3&p=19

"The Arts of Protest, Creative Cultural Resistance: A Webinar." Nadine Bloch, for International Center of Nonviolent Conflict: http://www.nonviolent-conflict.org/index.php/learning-and-resources/educational-initiatives/academic-webinar-series/2011-series/1792-the-arts-of-protest-creative-cultural-resistance

Mattilda Bernstein Sycamore
The Tourist Brochures in People's Hearts
A snapshot from Occupy Santa Fe

Apparently we are part of the Whole Foods community, because tonight's General Assembly takes place in the Whole Foods community space. Aside from the hypocrisy of relying on corporate charity in order to get out of the cold, it's a welcome respite from sitting in the dirt or on cement—there's even a bathroom that isn't locked. There are about 40 people in attendance when the meeting starts. It's the typical demographic breakdown, slanted more to the older side than some meetings but not unusually so— about two-thirds of the crowd consists of white people in their 50s and older; there are a maximum of 10 people under 40 (probably closer to five), maybe five people of color. A few youngish people arrive just after the meeting starts.

I present the proposal of the Occupy Canyon Road working group. We've made it as succinct and nonconfrontational as possible, so the General Assembly will approve it and then we can move on to planning specifics. It's a proposal for the direct action a few weeks from now—so far the weekly actions have consisted either of holding signs in a Bank of America parking lot while facing a thoroughfare, or standing outside the Statehouse when it's closed. We want to do something that doesn't just mimic Occupy protests across the country, but actually interrupts business as usual in Santa Fe. The art and tourism industries are our Wall Street, so we propose a march from Canyon Road, the symbolic heart of Santa Fe's art market, to the Plaza, the center of tourism. We propose a loose theme: "Free Art, Occupy Canyon Road." We want to set art free from the confines of big money by creating a confrontational and celebratory spectacle that invites everyone to participate—including artists and gallery owners, as well as people who hate artists and people who hate gallery owners.

The facilitator has implemented a different process than the one we've used so far, although no one explains it. Apparently now the questions about the proposal come first. And so, people want to know whether we will talk about artists who are pushed out of juried exhibits, minimum-wage workers at hotels, and the idea of using public land for artists. Sure, why not?

But then comes the part of the process now known as "concerns." This used to happen after discussion, which makes more sense to me, but apparently now concerns come before discussion. There are a lot of concerns. Turns out that the head of the Canyon Road gallery association is at the meeting—what a coincidence that she showed up at this particular meeting. She gives a speech about how she went to school for art, and after she decided to open a gallery she worked so many eight-dollar-an-hour jobs just to be able to afford her rent; she barely makes ends meet. She only does it to help artists. Twenty galleries on Canyon Road have closed recently; everyone is struggling. By the time she's done with her soliloquy, she literally has tears in her eyes.

I stop myself from asking about her commission, or from reminding her that there are more than 100 galleries on a one-mile strip of a tiny winding street, selling $40,000 lawn ornaments and rare oil paintings of "Indians" from the frontier years, a $65,000 glass sculpture, and Native artifacts in glass cases. If 20 galleries have closed, it's amazing that there isn't a single visible for-rent sign.

Everyone at this meeting seems concerned about the merchants on Canyon Road. I point out that we are not targeting the merchants, but the art market—everyone is welcome to join us, including the merchants who are paying way too much for rent—even Gerald Peters is welcome, I say, throwing out the name of the gallery owner who moved here in the 1960s, made his money in real estate, and now literally owns a bank.

Someone says she doesn't think the gallery owners on Canyon Road are part of the 1%—maybe the 10%. Oh, the limitations of Occupy rhetoric: a gallery owner who might make several hundred thousand dollars a year and own a couple million dollars in property is still part of the 99%, right? We hate the masters but we love the cops that do their bidding. Is Barack Obama part of the 99%? Let's check his tax return.

And then, one comment after another about not wanting to hurt small business people. Several people want us to "bring artists" to the group. I point out that there are people in the working group who actually make art for sale on Canyon Road, and they see the importance of exposing the hypocrisy and limitations of creativity as an industry. Someone else gives a meandering speech that starts and ends: We are a peaceful group. Others nod their heads in agreement.

How is it not peaceful to plan a march down a meandering tourist street? Someone says he supported the idea at first, but now he sees that it's divisive, how does this connect to Wall Street? It connects to Wall Street because this town is run by the art market and the tourism industries, which are subsidiaries of Wall Street. Someone says this isn't New York or Oakland—we don't have those issues here.

This is just after 17 different police departments coordinated their efforts to shut down the Occupy Oakland encampment, using stun grenades, rubber bullets, tear gas, and who knows what else. That same night, at the Occupy Santa Fe encampment, people were saying that the cops were with us, because in Albany, New York they refused to shut down the Occupy site. Probably so they could harass, intimidate, and arrest people of color in another neighborhood.

Are those the issues this guy is talking about? Oakland is a much larger city than Santa Fe, but its art market is miniscule in comparison. I point out that Santa Fe is a town of 70,000 people, and yet the annual value of art sales in Santa Fe is often larger than that of LA, a city with a metropolitan area about 100 times larger. That means the art market in Santa Fe is the second largest in the country, after New York: do people understand the effect of all that money in this small town?

"People are awakening," someone says. I have no idea what this relates to, and the facilitator makes no intervention. People keep talking about awakening, and it sounds so Christian to me—what about those of us who were already awake, as much as we've tried to get some restful sleep over the years? And, if this is an awakening, shouldn't people start by waking up to structural violence? Isn't that what the Occupy movement is supposed to be about?

But, my favorite: "I don't think we really have that 1% here." Where is this person living? Does he not realize that we're in a town with an art market bigger than LA, and yet the city doesn't even fund art supplies for public school students? Does he not notice that rich people have their third, fourth, fifth homes here, and public services are systematically defunded? I can't believe I'm talking to a roomful of people, many of whom have probably lived here decades longer than me, and they're all acting like they don't understand how the power structure in Santa Fe works. A roomful of people who are supposedly trying to engage politically about how the big banks have taken control of everything, and yet they refuse to acknowledge how this process operates in their own backyard, this playground for the rich and famously fond of "openness," "energy," and other small words signifying big colonial gestures.

Probably 20 people speak, and there are more on the stack—it's obvious that we won't reach consensus so I say I'm withdrawing the proposal. "Don't you want to hear friendly amendments," the facilitator asks.

The first supposedly friendly amendment is about talking to the gallery owners and artists on Canyon Road first. Right—maybe we can make a Christmas card list too. Someone says she doesn't feel comfortable attacking the art market or the tourism industry—no kidding. I'm not even sure how we get to the point of withdrawing the proposal without hearing the other fascinating friendly amendments, I just know that when the facilitator says the proposal is withdrawn for further discussion, I say: "This is just a personal statement, but I can't imagine ever bringing back any proposal about Canyon Road to this group."

Up until this moment, I've succeeded at remaining neutral in demeanor, but walking back to my chair I can't help shaking my head and waving my hands and sighing loudly. The woman next to me says: "Don't take it as an affront to your ego." This isn't about my ego, it's about realizing that this group will never be interested in doing the type of activism that means something to me.

Right after making the proposal, I felt like I sounded so clear. One of the other people in the Occupy Canyon Road working group even gave me a look that I think meant: You are on. But, I'm in a room full of hippie disengagement masquerading as truth-telling, oh Santa Fe! At the beginning of

Occupy Santa Fe, I was actually inspired by the fact that the age demographics were so much different than in other cities—maybe I could learn from radicals of an older generation.

There's so much talk in national news about Occupy Wall Street lacking demands, the absence of a coherent strategy, and actually I agree with those who believe that the absence of demands is a strength. As soon as you make demands of an unjust system, you become part of that system.

And yet here in Santa Fe, there's not just the absence of a coherent strategy, but the absence of any confrontational stance whatsoever. This is my moment of truth, and the good thing is that I'm able to express it so clearly right away. When someone comes up to me after the meeting and says "I'm sorry things didn't go the way you wanted them to," I respond that, actually, this isn't about me, but about the fact that this group is only interested in some kind of New Age version of cheerleading. When someone says "we should work on the proposal more, and bring it back to the group," I point out that we already made it as nonconfrontational as possible, and there isn't anywhere else to go.

Oh, how I want to engage with the world in a way that gives me hope. Oh, how I want to connect with people in a collective process of critical challenge to the status quo. Oh, how I want to be involved in something that matters to me, something other than people spouting empty rhetoric about how "this movement is going to get bigger." Whenever someone says that, I look around the room—can't you see that there are 50 people here? Fifty people at an activist meeting, in this tiny town. Three times a week. It's amazing, really.

Except, I'm not sure this is an activist group. There is a process, a process with which I'm engaged. Sometimes there are even conversations that mean something. But overall—right now it feels like nothing. My one friend in the room says to me afterwards: "It seems like the group is about redefining Santa Fe as a peaceful community, and that's something I can get behind, but I want to know that ahead of time—I want people to say that."

Of course, Santa Fe is already defined as a peaceful community—what we need is a group that will unmask the violence. The art market in Santa Fe—and, Santa Fe, by extension—is built on colonial exploitation of Native artists, cultures, identities, symbolism, land. And now it's expanded to incorporate 1960s high-art minimalism, pop art, collage, cartoon art, even a little bit of graffiti here and there—whatever sells. Santa Fe as we see it today was built by East Coast socialites fleeing conformity, looking for something "different," something "primitive" to stimulate their creative juices. Followed by West Coast real estate speculators and Texas oil money. Santa Fe of the tourist brochures, and the tourist brochures in people's hearts.

After the meeting, I'm so wired that I walk further than usual in one direction, turn around to go back home but then keep walking past my house; when I finally get back I'm still so wired that I can't imagine how I'm going to fall asleep. "This movement is going to get bigger," these people keep saying—maybe that's how you create a mass movement: take all the meaning out of it and then everyone will belong.

Jaime Omar Yassin

FARMERS, CLOUD COMMUNITIES, AND ISSUE-DRIVEN OCCUPATIONS

part 1: to plant, you must supplant

ON A DAMP AND OVERCAST EARTH DAY 2012, A SMALL BUT BOISTEROUS group of activists made their way to a rusty gate off of San Pablo Avenue, at the Berkeley-Albany border. Led by a marching band and carrying a shiny red tiller and wheeling trailers full of tools, the group cut the modest chains holding the gate closed, opening a mostly overlooked and forgotten ex-urban continuum of wildlife and unspoiled soil to the world beyond. This was the first breath of life of the Gill Tract Occupation, also known as "Occupy the Farm."

Activists got to work quickly on their food-justice-based occupation, pulling up the tender mustard weeds and tilling the soil in ascending north-ward rows. But only minutes into the labor, just a dozen feet into the first row, the new farmers inadvertently upturned a writhing nest of baby rodents from the earth. The translucent pink forms were smaller than the space between nail and index finger joint, as naked and exposed as a living thing could be. A debate ensued on how to handle the infant creatures; it was clear their mother would most likely not come back for them now, nor could she in the turned earth that had been her nest. The only valid question was where to put them and how to think about what the occupiers had done. There was an essential and somewhat harsh truth in the dirt—to plant something, you must supplant what was there before.

There is a significant tenacious and inventive ex-urban ecosystem that has grown in the confines of the overgrown and blighted Gill Tract over the decades as Berkeley and Albany evolved from suburban communities into an urban archipelago, conjoined by San Pablo Avenue with the nearby and grittier Oakland, and the episode with the rodents was not the last unfortunate encounter with it. The tract itself is the last acreage of farmable high-grade soil in the area, bequeathed to the University of California to benefit agricultural education in the days when the system of public universities was more than simply a REIT (Real-Estate Investment Trust) for the governor's cronies and benefactors. A colony of deer inhabits the southern end of the tract while wild turkey range far beyond the tract itself, out to the sidewalks and asphalt of Solano and San Pablo Avenues. Almost immediately after the activists entered the space, an infant deer was left behind by a frightened mother and a handful of turkey eggs were unfortunately separated from their nest.

Despite the initial unfortunate encounters, farmers soon got the hang of coexistence. A "turkey corridor" was created as a no-go zone. Occupiers were advised to leave deer areas in peace, and the southwest area became a kind of wildlife preserve. Those farmers that stayed to work on the land and learned to live within the limits of this new ecosystem were treated to an ultimately peaceful coexistence with a nesting wild turkey hen that birthed her young during the last days of the farm. The deer made their way back to the area and stayed, despite the quasi-military siege by UC police.

This initial unfortunate collision with the native ecosystem serves as an instructive metaphor for the narrative of the Occupy movement as it transitioned into more focused occupations like the Gill Tract. Though firmly within the Occupy action tradition, the Gill Tract was, from its start, distinct from those that had preceded it. Planned in advance and in relative secret, the occupation was the work of a self-selecting group of organizers who had met through the loose East Bay Occupy and activist network.

Nurtured in secret, the group was relatively horizontal internally, but it actively eschewed the open ideology that created the initial excitement around an ideal popular movement at Zuccotti Park. The Gill Tract Occupation (GTO) was relatively successful where other occupations in the past months had failed. But it shared a similar life arc with its predecessors: a group of activists started out with a set of principles based on broad and only tangentially-related goals. Some activists were protesting the Regents' growing unaccountability to the state and students and its emergence as a real estate broker using public land and funds. Others had long-standing grievances against the UC's relationship with Albany. Still others were advocates of urban farming, trying to create a symbolic kick-start and encourage other people to likewise take control of under-used tracts in their community. And then there were the veterans of the first wave Occupations in San Francisco's Bradley Manning Plaza and Oakland's Oscar Grant Plaza (OGP), now bereft of a camp, and looking for new ways to implement a powerful tactic and creator of community.

These various political interpretations of the same plot of land coalesced into one campaign with a unified goal—pressuring the Regents into using the land productively for farming and simultaneously preventing the university from selling the adjacent property to corporate behemoth Whole Foods. The farmers shared another unifying idea—a rejection of the dialogue-driven democratic-aligned mainstream politics that have impeded change of any kind for decades. Occupation, the unpermitted use of the commons for political goals, was their unanimous answer to such decrepit institutional organizing. Once the act of "unlawful assembly" was ignited, however, the potent intersection of local government propaganda, police repression, community interaction, expanding membership, and blind luck spawned trajectories that no one could foresee. The synergistic outcome is something more, and perhaps less controllable and ultimately directed, than the original group planning the action might have foreseen.

GTO upset the previous scheme of things. The Oakland occupation at OGP had as well, shaking up a helter-skelter ecosystem composed of vast wealth disparities: homelessness juxtaposed with luxury-condo living, hunger side by side with opulent dining, curb-side drug and alcohol abuse in front of high-priced alcoholism and upscale recreational-pharma in Uptown's bars and night clubs. Occupation does displace, it does halt, it can damage; but its intentionality, its open process, its not-profit-driven focus is the obvious alternative to the rapacious and constant transformation that creates blight out of fecund expanses like the Gill Tract.

The Gill Tract Occupation went even further, juxtaposed as it was with the last desperate attempt of Occupy Oakland to reclaim the commons on May Day. While an ever-shrinking but committed May Day Assembly met throughout the week in downtown, some of its previously most active members migrated up the San Pablo corridor, spending increasing amounts of time at GTO. Oakland's Downtown May Day convergence, though as well-attended and chaotically business-halting as one could hope for, given the circumstances, failed miserably at re-establishing a public occupation. In the aftermath, there were serious public questions from Occupy Oakland's most committed proponents about the viability of another Oakland occupation.

That night of May first, and throughout the next day and week, many Occupy Oakland activists joined their comrades at the Gill Tract. While there had never been any intention of over-shadowing its partner to the south, GTO had effectively, and perhaps reluctantly, turned the last shovel full of dirt on the hopes of re-occupying the commons under the rubric of Occupy 1.0.

part 2: intentional and found communities come to life beneath a supermoon

ON ITS FIRST night, the Farm formed a social nucleus in the center of the tract, consisting of a large tent for the dozen or so people who would be staying the night and farming throughout the next day. Tables for an abundance of donated food were situated nearby—a broad, uprooted ganglia of mustard weeds served as barriers, wind protection, organic arm-chairs. As enumerated at that night's first assembly, the camp itself would be the utilitarian servant to the Farm, to exist only so long as it was helpful and productive to the political work of the Farm itself.

During the next days, however, as the cultivated area expanded so did the social milieu that supported it. A kitchen committee formed; the food tables became a food preparation area and moved southward to the entrance of the Farm, housed in an easy-up and then two, and a familiar dish-washing area was added to clean donated cooking and dishware. The kitchen committee—animated by Occupy Oakland food justice advocates—became the heart of the camp, its most consistently staffed and amplified working group.

Next came the "Lady Bug Patch," a children's garden bottom-lined by many of the same Occupiers that had created the "Children's Village" at Oscar Grant Plaza and some new recruits. From there, a culture and a society emerged, fed by those who slept at the camp, and farmed and did other support during the day, and buttressed by daily morning work meetings in which the day's struggles were diagrammed and work was divided.

The farm work itself was an indispensable part of this community-building process in a way that less-concrete political labor may not have been able to duplicate. Farmers worked opposite one another on the rows, sharing tips, knowledge, water, compost, and political insights in the hot spring sun. Some of these people were committed activists, some had never attended a demonstration; some had extensive farming experience, and some had none; some were polyamorous nomads, others were conventional families firmly rooted in the community; some were bottom-liners seeing out their political vision, others had fled to the Farm to escape the harsher, withering political battles of Occupy Oakland.

Though the tract itself was surrounded on two sides by heavy traffic and wasn't far from a freeway, being in the center of the cultivated area, digging into the dirt and nestling the starts, one could really be convinced they were long miles from the city in an idyllic commune. Farmers and visitors did not have to be urged to do work—they took ownership of their tasks and of their product. The farm indeed seemed like a magical place, where a "super-moon," the largest and closest of the year, filled the night sky in its middle age. With all of this, it was not difficult for farmers and their supporters to become emotionally invested in their struggle, in their crops, and in the well-being of their Occupation.

The focus on production, and a solid, identifiable goal, allowed farmers to escape some of the antagonisms generated by locals in other occupations. In the first place, many neighbors had been sick of years of fighting with UC about the eyesore in their community. Early on, I took on the task of clearing weeds on the outside of the fence. I was approached by at least a dozen neighbors over the next few days, each thanking me for taking care of the blighted property. UC uses only a small portion of the available land, leaving the rest fallow and overgrown, hemmed in by a rotting and rusted hulk of a chain-link fence.

Other members of the community had been trying to get UC to share the land for sustainable agricultural projects for years, only to run up against the Regents' preference for enriching corporations over the communities their growing real estate empire abuts. Still others resented the intrusion of UC into their daily lives; one neighbor I talked to was bitter about the large population that UC had inserted into his community and the fact that the Regents pay no property taxes.

It was not surprising then that some of the bottom-liners were, in fact, community residents living just a block or two from the area. But the Farm would have formed in quite a different configuration if it had not been for the intact community that inhabited it from the start. A distinct children's garden, for example, had not been part of the original vision for the Farm, and it's quite likely that it would not have emerged organically. It was, rather, an artifact from Oakland's OGP Occupation, transplanted thematically to provide some protection and visibility for the permaculture garden on the west side of the farm which was slated for the UC's corn research in May.

The "Lady Bug Patch" did some of the same heavy-lifting in community outreach and narrative-writing. The Farm was always envisioned as being family-friendly, but nothing could have

Occupation does displace, it does halt, it can damage; but its intentionality, its open process, its not-profit-driven focus is the obvious alternative to the rapacious and constant transformation that creates blight out of fecund expanses like the Gill Tract.

been as effective in that regard as creating a mini-farm that children and their parents would have undisputed ownership over, one that was highly visible from the elementary school and street.

Organic community buy-in produced a beneficial side-effect at Albany City Hall, just a stone's throw from the last cultivated row on the Farm on San Pablo Avenue. Without lobbying, and with no sacrifice of principles, city council members threw their lot in with activists, at least symbolically, by promising to find a way to prevent the sale of the south tract to Whole Foods.

Albany police had a hands-off policy that made them all but invisible, despite the fact that the police station is right across the street of the northern end of the tract. At least one UC researcher visiting the tract sided with the occupiers, despite the UC's attempts to imply his research would be halted by the activists. His op-ed in a local paper laid out some of the same arguments for taking over the land as many of the most radical anti-Regents activists had in the past years. All of these factors at once produced a vibrant, positive, stable community of the kind that existed unspoiled at Oscar Grant Plaza, only in tragically brief, though wonderful, bursts.

Ironically, the threat of police repression added a potent accelerant to this formation of community. Indeed, there would have been no need for the society provided by the camp at the Farm without it. The sense of community-building and solidarity became even more pronounced as the deadline for UC's cultivation of research corn crops loomed and as the UC Police Department began turning well-known screws.

The siege began with the placement of concrete barriers at the various gates surrounding the tract. This meant that although farmers could still enter and exit the tract with a simple hop over the modest fencing or by entering the ajar-but-guarded west end gate, food, materials and, of course, water for the crops became difficult to get onto the site. A few days later, the University ostensibly barred anyone from entering the tract, though they were allowed to leave as they wished. UCPD became more obnoxious with dispersal orders, at one point making the long trek to the children's garden at the northwest end of the tract, where they threatened parents and children with their daily monotone speech about the possibility of being charged with trespass. Inexorably, the UCPD presence in the Farm became constant and daily.

Despite the ultimate raid that shut down the Farm, none of these measures dampened enthusiasm for the Farm, nor support for it. Indeed, the sense of community only grew stronger. Farmers built a ladder and slide over the San Pablo gate that solved the problem of access. Families used the slide in full view of the police only a few feet away, in a whimsical nod to a new radicalism in the community.

Neighbors who had been bringing water to nourish the crops continued to do so even after the concrete barriers were placed, forming bucket brigades with farmers to pass water from large containers outside to those near the cultivated rows. Food was passed from hand to hand over the sharp tops of the fence. Farmers and supporters hopped back and forth over the fence to do their daily work. These were people of all ages and economic situations, supporting each other communally in full view of, and despite the UCPD and their assurances that anyone that did so would face trespass charges.

As the supermoon waned in the night sky, farmers continued to sleep in the camp in tents and under the stars. They never stopped nurturing the planted crops, they continued to fill the empty rows with new starts— "farming under siege" as one of the bottom-liners put it. Neighbors even offered their driveways and garages for the storage of tools when a raid seemed imminent. The sense of community, built from the focused labor of cultivation and the creation of a societal and community network necessary to support it was one of the unintended side effects of the Farm occupation, and it only grew stronger in the face of repression.

It made farmers bolder and braver in the face of an impending UC raid and created something people felt invested in fighting for. Much more than a farm or a camp, and not dependent on static points in space and time, the Gill Tract Occupation created a politicized cloud society that has outlasted the ephemeral occupation of the Gill Tract.

part 3: an occupy continuum of cloud communities

IN ALL, THE GTO's camp lasted three weeks—coincidentally, about the same amount of time as the OGP camp—before UCPD finally closed down the burgeoning commune. Despite the loss of the social systems that thrived in the camp, and the uncertain fate of the cultivation that it created, the Farm as an ideal and model of Occupation can be seen from many vantage points as a success, and as a possible route for the future of the Occupy movement.

The structure of an Occupation is inherently politicizing. Individuals, some for the first time, experience the joy and hardship of creating an intentional community, of maintaining peace and security without violence or police, of creating a food production and sanitation system, of urban planning. The initial power of the Occupy movement then, was not only in its extra-legal character and its break from electoral politics and the nonprofit industrial complex. The process itself was more than the sum of its parts, it was a role-play of self-actualization that revealed the limitations of capitalism to sustain the bodies and souls of human beings.

The endless donations of food, tents, money, and other resources, for example, illuminate the reality that there is no scarcity of resources in the city of Oakland. The fulfillment of sharing and consensus-driven process of production reveals the emptiness and limitations of traditional top-down, for-profit systems. Discussions about how to create security without calling the police reveal the convenient choices that communities make instead of engaging their most problematic members. The process of sharing in the preparation of food, the disposal of it, the cleaning of the wares used to prepare it, and the planning necessary to continue it reveal the loss of fundamental human relationships, altered by Westernized consumption.

Despite all of these socially-transforming processes, the original occupations were born with a fatal flaw. Perhaps it was fundamentally necessary for the Occupy movement to enter life without demands of any kind to draw in as diverse a grouping of people as possible, to prevent the kind of campaign-based routing into democratic stables that's typical of sudden popular outbursts. But the lack of issue-driven focus eventually caused some support to erode for the Oakland Occupation, as well as those in other cities, a reality reflected in the fact that downtown Oakland is a commercial center without a community, and thus, with no central issue to direct action towards. Though nothing can excuse the city and the police repression that has created the daunting barriers toward rebuilding Occupy 1.0, much of the enthusiasm necessary to combat it has withered in the narrative-vacuum that was necessary for the creation of Oscar Grant Plaza.

GTO, then, can be seen as a viable model of Occupy 2.0—embodied by a series of ongoing issue-driven occupations, created and maintained by a core group of Occupiers but nurturing an ever-growing cloud community of new Occupiers awakened to the political potential of mass mobilization through the process of Occupation.

The repercussions are obvious for a diversity of focused, currently campaign-anchored issues languishing in electoral-based and institutional politics. And the advantages of such Occupations are enormous and obvious. Much like the Gill Tract, the spectacle of issue-driven Occupation creates a weeks-long and layered discourse on what were previously campaign-driven politics. A very public contest for space allows a diverse set of voices on issues like land use and public education, creating a 3-D map of the social, political, and cultural impact of any societal sector.

GTO opened up the issues of genetically-modified crops, of publicly funded research, of the conversion of public lands into private ones for profit by insular state consortiums like the Regents, of the necessity of affordable public education, and of the viability of urban farming, amongst others. This process makes issue-driven Occupation a routine interrogation of the entire system, not just one aspect of it.

If Occupation politicizes and radicalizes, then taking this catalyzing process, and introducing it via practical applications for institutional problems in communities is a meta-outreach; it draws in communities and hurls them into an accelerated program of political education and activism with tangible benefits. The Occupy cloud communities that are thus built are extra-territorial and pan-sector, recycling a bubbling and diverse political community across the imaginable spectrum of social experience into the next Occupation and carrying entire paradigmatic working groups—like the Kitchen Committee and Children's Village—fully formed and amplified along with them.

Issue-driven Occupation can also encourage participants to re-imagine the construction of the societal component they're focused on, be it education, food production, or workplace organizing. Working toward solutions for complex social problems that may, in the current context, have limited scope—such as saving a school, or unionizing a workplace—such activists also teach themselves and each other about the endless possibilities for recreating equitable and affirming processes for their lives, transforming consumerist processes into more human and humane forms.

All of these factors coalesced at the Lakeview Sit-In—which, as of this writing, just completed an historic three-week occupation of a shuttered public school in Oakland's Grand Lake district before being shut down by Oakland School District police. The occupation was bottomlined by teachers, parents, and activists from within and without the Occupy community. Most importantly, however, critical support was provided by intact Occupy Oakland committees, including the dynamic and organic participation of the Kitchen Committee and the intact food and infrastructure committees that had grown up around recent Occupy actions and campaigns—Occupy Oakland's so-called "Barbecue Committee." While initial friction between occupiers and non-occupiers created early problems, education activists focused solely on the school closure moved their issues further into the discursive realm of the anti-austerity fight that is most critical to the Occupy movement. That was a product of the success of the Occupation and the tireless support offered by Oakland's Occupy committees. Occupy Oakland activists participated in every subsequent action around the school closure, and indeed, as of this writing are quite likely planning a solidarity occupation of another shuttered OUSD building.

As communities finally take their issues beyond the realm of electoral and institutional politics, Occupiers will begin to see the radicalization of the mainstream they've hoped for as they've looked out from their tents and easy-ups, waiting for the surrounding communities to embrace their movement. Despite the current proliferation of pronouncements on the death of Occupy, this political tool still contains the possibility of reigniting a new movement as powerful as the original one that spread from New York to Oakland. And we already have everything we need in place to make it happen.

Quinn Norton
October 17, 2011
Occupy LA

Gabriel Hetland

OCCUPYING DEMOCRACY
REALIZING THE RADICAL POTENTIAL OF
PARTICIPATORY BUDGETING IN THE US

IN ADDITION TO FOCUSING THE NATION'S ATTENTION ON ISSUES OF CLASS, inequality, and corporate power, Occupy Wall Street has generated a much-needed discussion about democracy. On the one hand, OWS has exposed the shortcomings of American-style representative democracy, highlighting how relatively free and fair elections and plutocracy (government by the wealthy) are far from incompatible. At the same time, OWS has generated renewed interest in non-representative forms of democracy, with the General Assembly form demonstrating the viability (and challenges) of participatory democratic decision-making structures.

Yet, while OWS has succeeded in changing the nature of American political *discourse*, it remains to be seen whether the movement will be able to produce long-term transformations of American political *institutions*. The key to doing so, I argue, lies in finding ways to connect the seemingly irreconcilable logics of insurgent and institutional politics. OWS is a perfect example of insurgent politics, through which political "challengers" (i.e. non-elites) seeking transformative change use direct action to disrupt the normal functioning of political and economic institutions.[1] Institutional politics refers to the "normal" activity of "constituted" political actors (i.e. political elites and government functionaries) operating within established political institutions that follow a bureaucratic logic.

The challenges of combining insurgent and institutional forms of political action are formidable. As scholars like Robert Michels (1959) and Adam Przeworski (1985) argue, the danger is that insurgent organizations will lose their radical edge upon coming into contact with established political institutions. Michels highlights the danger of "oligarchization" which results from the "necessity of organization" posed by political struggle. Przeworski's argument is similar: the challenge of achieving an electoral majority in

---

1   The notion of insurgent politics is similar to McAdam et al.'s (2003) concept of contentious politics, but maintains the distinction between "institutional" and "non-institutional" politics.

support of socialism or any program of radical change means that radical organizations that engage in institutional politics will inevitably shed their radical goals even if they retain their radical rhetoric. The danger of failing to engage with established political institutions, however, is irrelevance, a "pure" radicalism that is empty because it lacks institutional force.

Is there any way out of the cooptation-versus-irrelevance dilemma? Can the inherently opposed logics of insurgent and institutional politics be combined in a meaningful and sustainable way? Drawing on two cases of participatory budgeting (PB), in the Brazilian city of Porto Alegre and the Venezuelan municipality of Torres, I argue that the answer is yes. In both cases, the key to combining insurgent and institutional politics (while preventing oligarchization) lay in the coming to power of a radical left political party with (1) a commitment to participatory democracy and (2) strong links to social movements, with (1) and (2) strengthened by (3) opposition from local/regional political elites.

Can the lessons of Porto Alegre and Torres be applied in the US? Inspired by Porto Alegre, several cities in the US have experimented with PB in recent years. And the emergence of OWS has renewed hopes for radical change in the US. I argue that the key to realizing these hopes is to find ways to link the insurgent energy of OWS with concrete institutional reforms such as PB. This will also increase the likelihood of realizing the radical potential of such reforms. For this to happen, OWS (and similar movements, like the Spanish *indignados*) must organize politically while maintaining its movement character. This is a tall order, but opens up the possibility of overcoming the cooptation-versus-irrelevance conundrum.

participatory budgeting: a different way to occupy city hall

PARTICIPATORY BUDGETING REFERS to a process through which ordinary citizens exercise control over the municipal budget. This can occur in a variety of ways, but almost always involves popular assemblies where local residents are given the opportunity to deliberate about spending priorities and some mechanism for taking these discussions into account when it comes to decision-making, with the ideal being a binding vote by local residents themselves. The first successful example of PB occurred in the Brazilian city of Porto Alegre when the Workers' Party was elected in 1989. The success of Porto Alegre's PB led to imitations in hundreds of additional Brazilian cities over the course of the 1990s, and PB is now practiced in thousands of cities around the world.

Porto Alegre

In addition to generating popular acclaim around the world, Porto Alegre's PB has given rise to numerous academic studies. In this brief account I will focus on the way in which Porto Alegre's PB allowed the Workers' Party administration to combine institutional and insurgent politics and surmount the cooptation-versus-irrelevance dilemma that has plagued so many attempts to achieve radical change. As Gianpaolo Baiocchi (2005) and other scholars discuss, the origins of Porto Alegre's PB lie with the city's combative neighborhood movement, which was very active during the 1970s and 1980s in the struggle to end Brazil's military dictatorship.[2] With the return to democracy in 1985, Porto Alegre's neighborhood associations issued demands for greater popular participation in governance.

The origins of Porto Alegre's PB are thoroughly civic. But without the election of the Workers' Party in 1989, these demands would probably have gone unrealized. As often occurs when the left takes power, the Workers' Party came to office on a protest vote against the previous populist administration of Alceu Collares. Upon taking office, the party was in an unenviable position, facing high expectations from its base of unions and social movements, along with hostile opposition from other parties and local elites in control of the city's media.

During the party's first year in office it was far from clear that it would be able to reconcile institutional and insurgent political logics. Facing demands to do something upon taking office, the administration engaged in a disastrous attempt to take over the city's bus line. At the same time it confronted militant activism on the part of municipal workers, who were linked to the previous mayor's party. The administration's initial attempt at participatory budgeting also ended in failure, with local residents frustrated at the administration's inability to take the demands issued during the first PB assemblies into account when spending decisions were made.

This situation of crisis is what led to the party's decision to focus on PB in a more serious and innovative way. Doing so paid off, with participation increasing markedly once residents realized that their demands would in fact be taken into account. The PB also helped the administration overcome the gulf between institutional and insurgent politics that had threatened it during the first years. Neighborhood associations and district-level popular councils played a key role in making the PB work, with seasoned community organizers forming an important intermediary layer in-between ordinary residents and municipal functionaries. As Baiocchi reports, these organizers performed crucial, albeit largely informal, tasks within the PB, such as ensuring that discussions were not hijacked for personal reasons. At the same time, the Workers' Party administration was committed to fostering open participation, irrespective of participants' political affiliation, ensuring that the PB enjoyed broad legitimacy.

As Baiocchi's account emphasizes, Porto Alegre's PB was most successful in districts with a strong history of civic activism but without civic

---

2 This account draws on Baiocchi (2005).

associations that were tied to opposing political parties and actively opposed to the success of the PB. The combination of autonomous-but-sympathetic associations and an administration committed to participatory democracy was key to combining insurgent and institutional logics of action. In districts where there was a lack of insurgent history, the PB came to dominate civic life. And in a district where there was a strong history of activism but antagonistic political relations, the relationship between insurgent and institutional politics remained hostile rather than cooperative.

Torres

In October 2004, Julio Chavez (of no relation to Venezuelan president Hugo Chavez) was elected mayor of the largely rural municipality of Torres, Venezuela.[3] The (Julio) Chavez administration's signature reform was the implementation of an ambitious participatory budget in which 100% of the municipality's investment fund is subject to popular control. This occurs by means of community- and parish- (the Venezuelan equivalent of a city district) level popular assemblies. Through these assemblies, ordinary *Torrenses* have gained control over the city's budget. As Julio Chavez is fond of recalling, "The mayor can't even veto these decisions."

As in Porto Alegre, the path to Torres' PB was far from straightforward. At the time he was elected, Julio Chavez had no experience with organized politics. An engineer by training, Chavez had gained a reputation as a rabble-rousing student activist and social movement leader. In 2000 he ran for office in Torres, but won only a few thousand votes. Between 2000 and 2004, however, Chavez traveled throughout the municipality, talking with local farmers, students, and social movement leaders.

In 2004, Chavez's years of organizing paid off. But like the Workers' Party in Porto Alegre, Chavez was elected by a razor-thin margin, winning with just over a third of the vote. He was opposed by the local agrarian elite along with the Chavista regional power structure, headed by Luis Reyes Reyes, the Chavista governor of Lara state (where Torres is located). Over the next several years, Chavez faced unremitting resistance from local city councilors who were allied with the Governor and did everything they could to stop the radical mayor's participatory plans.

The key to the success of these plans was the combination of institutional and insurgent politics. Chavez's election gave him a clear place within the local power structure. But with 8 of 9 city councilors opposed to the mayor (despite belonging to parties rhetorically committed to participatory democracy and popular power), Chavez had to rely on support from movements *outside* City Hall in order to push his agenda through. The

---

3 The following account is based on 5 months of field work in Torres.

institutional resistance Chavez faced was in fact key in preventing his administration from succumbing to the dangers of oligarchization, since it
ensured that the administration stayed tied to social mobilization.

Chavez's first move upon taking office was to convoke a Municipal Constituent Assembly, with local residents meeting in fields and school halls for
several months to rewrite the ordinances guiding their city. At the end of the
process, popular assemblies were held in which the results were discussed
and voted upon. Chavez sought to have the National Electoral Council
certify the process but the CNE refused to do so. City council also tried to
block the process, with Chavez and his supporters responding by physically
occupying City Hall. The same technique was used months later when City
Council refused to approve the PB.

The success of Torres' PB is due to the combination of institutional reform and insurgent mobilization. This, as discussed, was an artifact of the
specific context that existed in Torres. The first necessary condition was the
election of a social movement leader to local office. The second condition
was the existence of continuing links between the local ruling party and social movements. In the absence of such links, the dangers of oligarchization
and ossification that Michels and Przeworski discuss might have occurred.
The reason this was prevented was because the local ruling party was fiercely
opposed by regional and national elites. This forced the party to rely on
links to its bases. These links, and the insurgent origins of Torres' PB, have
proven particularly crucial in recent years. In 2007, Julio Chavez joined
the PSUV, bringing new challenges as the party has sought to control and
bureaucratize the municipality's innovative participatory projects (which
include, but go beyond PB). Thus far, popular mobilization has enabled the
municipality to resist these efforts and maintain its status as a nationally and
internationally recognized model of participatory governance.

occupy and the challenges of implementing
radical change in the us

THE CHALLENGES OF implementing radical change in the US are formidable. First, there is the firm grip that the Democratic and Republican parties exercise over US politics, despite a number of recent efforts to establish
third parties (e.g. the Green Party, the Labor Party, the New Party). The
differences between the Democrats and Republicans can be hard to discern
due to the tremendous influence that finance capital exercises over both parties (albeit this influence is greater in the case of Republicans). The already
pervasive and insidious political clout of Wall Street has been exponentially
magnified by the Supreme Court's decision in *Citizens United*, which opens
the floodgates to unlimited corporate political spending. Finally, there is

the decades-long rightward shift of American politics. This shift shows no signs of abating and has resulted in such absurdities as the claim that Barack Obama, a devout supporter of free market capitalism, is a "socialist"!

Given all this, the emergence of the Occupy movement in September 2011 came as a breath of fresh air. The movement's ability to shift the national political conversation away from austerity and towards inequality is an accomplishment in itself. So too is the fact that it has managed to generate renewed interest in participatory democracy in a country where the words "democracy" and "elections" are viewed as synonymous. The test of OWS' mettle, however, is whether it can enhance democratic control over political and economic decision-making in the US.

The experiences of Porto Alegre and Torres demonstrate that the idea of establishing participatory democratic control over state decision-making is not a utopian fantasy. The similarities between the two cases point to a workable model for achieving this: the election of a radical left political party with a commitment to participatory democracy and strong links to a mobilized citizenry. The obvious question is whether this model could work in the US?

The first obvious hurdle is the lack of a viable radical left party in the US. The existence of participatory budgeting in three US cities—Chicago, New York, and Vallejo, California—without a radical left party in power demonstrates that participatory reforms can be achieved within the confines of the "actually-existing-democracy" of the US (i.e. the two-party system). In all three cases, progressive Democratic politicians spearheaded the efforts to establish PB. So long as struggles to establish viable third parties remain (largely) unsuccessful, it seems likely that progressive Democrats will continue to play a key role in efforts to bring PB to US cities. It should, however, be noted that one of the four New York City councilors who initiated PB in fall 2011 is a Republican, demonstrating the idea's bipartisan appeal.

Might it be possible to initiate PB without relying on parties or political leaders? While this scenario has not yet been achieved, Occupy activists in Baltimore and Oakland (and perhaps other cities) are working to do just this through efforts to amend their cities' charters. The effort to bring PB to Oakland has been led by the Community Democracy Project (CDP), a small group of committed activists who met at Occupy Oakland in October 2011. (In full disclosure I have been a member of CDP since November 2011.) CDP's plan is to establish PB on a citywide scale through a ballot initiative. This effort enjoys support from various political leaders, including a number of Green Party activists. But like many Occupy activists, CDP's leaders are quite wary of political parties, and the group is politically independent. A key difference is that, unlike anarchists—who have played an important role within the Occupy movement in Oakland and elsewhere—CDP and other groups promoting PB seek to transform rather than abolish existing political institutions.

The fact that PB has already been achieved in several US cities, and the existence of active campaigns to bring PB to additional cities are encouraging signs regarding the prospects for progressive institutional change in the US. It is important, however, to recognize the limitations of existing US-based PB experiments when compared to PB in Porto Alegre and Torres. The key challenge of PB in Chicago and New York is its limited scale, with PB restricted to the relatively small discretionary funds of select city councilors. As several participants at a March 2012 conference on PB in New York put it, "this is money that no one cares about." This critique was not meant to dismiss the significance of the city's PB experiment, but to highlight the lack of participatory control over the city's general fund, which business and other powerful interests definitely do "care about."

The important point is that PB is not a magic bullet. Its political impact depends upon the political context—local and national—within which it is implemented. In both Porto Alegre and Torres, PB has touched upon money that "matters" to powerful interests and been tied to a broader agenda of radical social(ist) transformation. This has not been the case, thus far, in the US. The key difference is that radical left parties, connected to strong social movements, played the lead role in Porto Alegre and Torres, helping to connect insurgent and institutional forms of politics. In the US, progressive Democrats—with help from academics, NGOs, and community-based organizations—have played the lead in fostering more limited PB experiments. The connection between insurgent and institutional politics has, thus far, been largely missing in the US cases of PB.

The above analysis suggests that in order to change this, US activists must look for ways to connect the insurgent energy of the Occupy movement with institutional reforms such as PB. Alliances with progressive Democrats offer possibilities for achieving progressive institutional change, as the PB reforms in Chicago, New York and Vallejo demonstrate. But in order to achieve more radical change, these reforms must be deepened and connected to a broader transformative agenda. Porto Alegre and Torres suggest that it may be difficult to do this in the absence of a radical left party.

Occupy has shattered the myth that Americans are quiescent and apathetic. It has drawn attention to the growing divide between the haves (the 1%) and the have-nots (the 99%). And it provides a reminder that the only democracy worth the name must provide a way for the have-nots to participate in political and economic decision-making. The insurgent energy of the Occupy Wall Street movement is impressive. To move forward it has to engage within institutional politics, which means organizing politically while retaining its movement character. This will not be easy. But a glance "south of the border" suggests that it is not impossible.

STATEMENT OF AUTONOMY

Passed by the General Assembly at Occupy Wall Street on November 10, 2011, and passed revision by the General Assembly at Occupy Wall Street, March 3, 2012

Occupy Wall Street is a people's movement. It is party-less, leaderless, by the people and for the people. It is not a business, a political party, an advertising campaign or a brand. It is not for sale.

We welcome all, who, in good faith, petition for a redress of grievances through nonviolence. We provide a forum for peaceful assembly of individuals to engage in participatory democracy. We welcome dissent.

Any statement or declaration not released through the General Assembly and made public online at www.nycga.net should be considered independent of Occupy Wall Street.

We wish to clarify that Occupy Wall Street is not and never has been affiliated with any established political party, candidate or organization. Our only affiliation is with the people.

The people who are working together to create this movement are its sole and mutual caretakers. If you have chosen to devote resources to building this movement, especially your time and labor, then it is yours.

Any organization is welcome to support us with the knowledge that doing so will mean questioning your own institutional frameworks of work and hierarchy and integrating our principles into your modes of action.

Speak with us, not for us.

Occupy Wall Street values collective resources, dignity, integrity and autonomy above money. We have not made endorsements. All donations are accepted anonymously and are transparently allocated via consensus by the General Assembly or the Operational Spokescouncil.

We acknowledge the existence of professional activists who work to make our world a better place. If you are representing, or being compensated by an independent source while participating in our process, please disclose your affiliation at the outset. Those seeking to capitalize on this movement or undermine it by appropriating its message or symbols are not a part of Occupy Wall Street.

We stand in solidarity. We are Occupy Wall Street.

Mark Bray
Something That Takes Time
Resisting the Media Narrative

"So, has Occupy Wall Street actually managed to accomplish *anything*?" The journalist's microphone extended out for a response as drummers pounded to my right, the line for lunch was forming down to the clothing station, a contingent of transit workers with signs spread out on Broadway, and a Muslim prayer service started on the steps. I paused to take in the energy of the thousands of bodies navigating past each other on this forgotten slab of concrete and couldn't help but smirk at the reporter as he awaited my comment. "Well, in less than a month we've sparked the most dynamic American social movement in decades with hundreds of occupations springing up across the country and the world. I'd say that would qualify as *something*."

As a member of the OWS Press Team I've fielded a wide variety of questions about economics, politics, toilets, sleeping bags, tents, and many other subjects. Increasingly, however, as journalists asked more and more questions about gauging the success of the movement, I started to gain an insight into discourses that have systematically marginalized non-electoral politics. In my experience, the media battle over the legitimacy of social movements and direct action (and therefore of Occupy) has been waged around two simple questions: (1) what counts as *something* politically? and (2) how long should it take for *something* to happen? Regarding the first question, it is plainly evident that we have managed to initiate an unprecedented national conversation about economic justice and democracy, revive a long-dormant tradition of civic participation, and rejuvenate the American left. More "concretely," we've prevented foreclosures across the country and directly assisted successful labor campaigns. Nevertheless, in the eyes of the media (and much of the country) this is, at best, a cute narrative that often provides fertile ground for plucking engaging human-interest stories about students in debt and unemployed dads but it doesn't count as *something*. For them, *something* is measured strictly in elections and legislation. To counter this perspective, I've taken every opportunity to point out to journalists that the most profound social changes in American history have been stimulated by the direct action of movements such as the labor movement and civil rights movement rather than by the independent decisions of politicians. We must redefine direct action as a tangible *something* that changes lives and challenges structures of oppression, and electioneering as an elitist, alienating process that accomplishes *nothing* more than reinforcing the upper class.

The second question about time raises one of the main challenges in this process of redefinition. It took decades before the early labor movement and civil rights movement started to gain the momentum and mass support for which they are remembered. However, with the expansion of the 24-hour cable news cycle and the development of social media, assumptions about the time frame of social change have drastically shortened. The initial expectation was for Occupy to be born fully-grown, with a narrow set of policy demands, ready to affect legislation or put together a slate of candidates within a month. Chronologically, we have been evaluated based on the standards of political parties; standards designed for us to fail, standards that we must reject. This ahistorical conception of time makes it nearly impossible to even imagine a movement designed to revolutionize society over the course of decades. Therefore, we must insist on Occupy as a process and an ethos of direct democracy and direct action whose success or failure must be gauged in years rather than weeks. Who knows, maybe ultimately Occupy's greatest legacy will be its political progeny.

David Shankbone
November 15, 2011
Zuccotti Park after the OWS eviction, NYC

Frances Fox Piven

IS OCCUPY OVER?

WHEN OCCUPY EMERGED IN THE FALL OF 2011, SYMPATHETIC OBSERVERS thought here at last was the movement we had been waiting for. For decades we had watched in wonder as inequalities in the United States grew to historically unprecedented levels, as the public sector was cannibalized by business, and as corporate assertions of power became ever more brazen. Here, finally, was evidence of popular moral outrage, and maybe the birth of a protest movement. But the happy moment did not last. After a couple of months, local officials ordered their police forces to clear most of the small occupations. Many erstwhile sympathizers fell silent. The tents were gone, along with the general assemblies and the protest theater, and "We are the 99%" simply melded into everyday language. The movement had erupted, and now we wondered, was it over?

I think not. The notion that Occupy is over is too much influenced by the misleading metaphors we rely on to describe social movements. For example, when movement actions attract public attention we refer to the events as "explosions," and we say these explosion are lit by "sparks." The metaphor tells us that the dynamics of movements are like the dynamics of combustion. But what does that mean in terms of the complex social relations that undergird movement actions? And what does it mean to say that movements are lit by sparks, except perhaps to evade the question of just what it is that sets off the movement?[1] Reliance on these metaphors leads us to think of movements in ways that are historically misleading. Movements are only superficially like Fourth of July fireworks—they are not accidental, only partly spontaneous, and they do not explode only to quickly fall to earth like the flares set off by rockets. None of this is right. Movements are in fact complex, they have deep and tangled causes eluded by the spark and explosion metaphor, they include organized and spontaneous elements, and their life trajectory generally unfolds not in a moment but over several decades.

---

1 See Reed.

American history has been marked by periodic convulsions caused by mass protest movements, and we can learn quite a lot by paying attention to the dynamics of these past movement periods. Indeed, the creation of the American republic, the legal emancipation of the slaves, the winning of some labor rights in the twentieth century, and then women's rights, the dismantling of Jim Crow, the achievement of some gay and lesbian rights, all of these were reforms in which movements played a pivotal role. It is not too much to say that the democratic and humanitarian aspects of American institutions were the achievement of protest movements. To be sure, these movements all produced moments of explosive drama, as masses of people faced off against the authorities in one setting or another, farmers against the Redcoats, John Brown at Harpers Ferry, sit-down strikers in Flint, Michigan, the Stonewall riot that signaled the beginning of the gay and lesbian movement. But those explosive moments emerged from movements that unfolded over many years. To reduce the larger movements to these moments of dramatic conflict turns us away from the deeper dynamics that produced and sustained the uprisings and also produced its victories.

Great protest movements arise from the depths of society. They are fueled by deep stresses in the lives of people, stresses that are rooted in institutional arrangements, and in the social divisions these arrangements create. Of course, sometimes the strains are worsened by the temporary conditions of market collapse or bad harvests or war, but even then, the conflicts that emerge reflect more longstanding experiences and the animosities and understandings experience generates. The protest movements that fed into the revolutionary war with England drew their energy and anger from the extractions imposed by England on its colonies, and also from the rapidly emerging class divisions in the colonies themselves. It was a mark of the genius, in a way, of revolutionists among the colonial elites that they were able to blend these grievances together under the banner of democratic rights, thus bringing the dual agitations of the rich and poor together to fight a war for independence from England.

Similarly, the abolitionist movement that led to civil war had complex and intertwined roots in the egalitarian ideology that lingered from the revolutionary period, in the reformism sparked by the Protestant revival movement that began in the 1820s, and in the deepening sectional economic conflicts between the slave-based south and the "free labor" north. As early as 1774, the annual meeting of the Philadelphia Quakers authorized expulsion of anyone involved in buying or transferring slave property.[2]

---

2   David Brion Davis, "The Quaker Ethic and the Antislavery International," in *The Antislavery Debate: Capitalism and Abolitionism as a Problem in Historical Interpretation*, ed. Thomas Bender (Berkeley: University of California Press), 1992.

True, as revolutionary era ideas faded and slavery became ever more profitable, abolitionist fervor faded. But it reemerged in the 1830s, producing schisms in the Protestant churches, retaliatory fury and vigilantism from the south, and then the daring development of the Underground Railroad—an underground route with capital, stations, and conductors[3]—that succeeded in bleeding tens of thousands of slaves—slave property that is— from the south, deepening the divisions that ultimately led to secession and Civil War.

An adequate history of the labor movement or the women's movement or the civil rights movement or the gay and lesbian movement would reveal similarly deep roots in institutional arrangements, and a similarly long time span during which the people who were to become the troops of the great protest movements found their footing and tested their ideas and protest strategies. Strikes and riots by workers began long before the labor movement's great victories during the sit-down strikes of the 1930s, and continued thereafter as well. And the early Civil Rights movement can also be seen as a reemergence of black abolitionism and the currents of resistance among slaves that, given the draconian controls imposed by the slavocracy, usually did not take the form of outright revolt but tended toward the more covert forms of evasion, sabotage, or running away.

However, these movements were not shaped only by controlling institutional arrangements and the stresses and tensions these created. They were also shaped by the people who reacted against these conditions. Very importantly, they were shaped by the activist cadres who produced the emancipatory ideas that came to distinguish the movements, and who also invented or rediscovered and propagated the defiant collective action strategies that gave movements from the lower reaches of society some power.

The strains and hardships of daily life certainly help to give rise to protest movements, particularly when these are worsened by the sudden deprivations of economic collapse. But hardship by itself does not lead people to rise up against the authorities. More likely, they will blame God or blame themselves. Before people come together in the collective defiance we call a protest movement, popular ideas about who is to blame have to change, and popular ideas about what can be done about the hardships and uncertainties people confront have to change. This does not mean they have to become communists or socialists or anarchists. It simply means that people have to recognize the role of elites in creating or tolerating the conditions that cause hardship and insecurity, and they have to see the injustice of those conditions. The two kinds of shifts go together, simply because conditions

---

3   John Hope Franklin, *From Slavery to Freedom: A History of Negro Americans*, New York: Vintage, 1969: 253–60.

that are seen as inevitable and immutable can hardly be seen as unjust. And finally, there is another ideological task for movement cadres. They have to show not only that the hardships and fears people suffer are unjust and not inevitable, but that people in motion can do something about them.

We can call this the first great task of an emerging protest movement, to communicate the message that things as they stand are not only intolerable, something that people feel often enough, but that they can be changed, and that the people themselves can force the change. All the great movements in American history accomplished this. Revolutionary agitators denounced the taxes imposed by the Crown as unjust, rallied against the impressment of Americans into the British navy and against attempts by the parliament to require the colonies to billet English soldiers. For colonial elites, these grievances were clear-cut economic disputes. For the masses of ordinary people who rallied to free impressed seamen or to dump English tea, something else was going on. Revolutionary-era mobs were fired up by the new passion for democracy, a passion that helped to bring ordinary farmers into the revolutionary army where demands spread even for the democratic election of militia officers. Gordon Woods comments on the period that "politics was nothing more than a perpetual battle between the passions of the rulers, whether one or a few, and the united interest of the people."[4]

Similar periods of ideological fervor regarding the monumental questions of the justice of existing arrangements accompanied subsequent movements. For the abolitionists, ideas about the imperative of a "new birth of freedom" were often rooted in uncompromising theological interpretation, as well as in the lingering influence of radical democracy. One might say of the abolitionists that they were preoccupied with words, with the words of scripture, and their own uncompromising call for immediate and unconditional emancipation. "I will be as harsh as truth, and as uncompromising as justice. I do not wish to think, speak, or write, with moderation…. I am in earnest—I will not equivocate—I will not excuse—I will not retreat a single inch—*and I will be heard*."[5]

The Wobblies (as the members of the IWW are called) were also agitators who developed ideas that helped propel the many-sided labor movement that unfolded unevenly over the next few decades. Their rhetoric was prescient, expressed in speeches, in songs (many derived from Protestant hymns), and in bold, even fantastical exemplary actions like the free speech movement that they carried to the small towns of the west. The Wobblies

---

4   Gordon Woods, *The Creation of the American Republic, 1776–1787,* New York: W. W. Norton, 1968: 18.

5   Quoted in Franklin, *From Slavery to Freedom,* 244.

spoke not only to questions of injustice, but also to the potential power of an aroused working class, to worker power as the motor that had built society, and therefore the motor that could change it. One of their dazzling arguments was precisely about this. The meaning of what they said and what they sang was that the entire society depended on them and that therefore they had power: "It is we who plowed the prairies, built the cities where they trade." Similarly, civil rights leaders gave their movement grandeur and hope and the blessings of God by cloaking it in the Jesus story, calling on their followers to bow their heads in the face of southern white violence, and even to love their assailants. Perhaps we should call this phase of movement development the *communicative* phase, in which a movement delineates its sense of the injustice of current arrangements, announces who is responsible for those arrangements, and also points to itself and its constituencies as the agents who can change them.

Much about Occupy seems to follow the pattern of earlier American movements. It is clearly fueled by deep changes in American and world capitalism, including steeply rising inequality, high unemployment especially among the young, rising indebtedness that is not only stripping millions of homeowners of their lifetime savings, but is especially menacing to students and former students who accumulated huge student loans. Unemployment, declining economic mobility, and rising poverty all signaled broken promises to the young people who had staked so much on education. And this was occurring in

The great movements of the American past did much more than communicate their point of view. They mobbed the houses of the rich, helped steal the slave property of the south, shut down the mines and factories and even occupied them, rioted in the biggest cities. Again and again they enacted, in other words, what Paul Mason calls "the power of mayhem."

the context of a wild increase in other predatory "rent-seeking" modes of profiteering, and growing evidence of political corruption.

But all this did not gain public attention just because it happened. It took movement agitation to begin to make a coherent narrative out of these events and to communicate that narrative dramatically. In other words, movements not only respond to events, but they change our understanding of events by their responses. I don't think there can be any argument but that Occupy performed this movement-building task brilliantly. They pointed to financial and corporate elites as the villains and the movement's targets. And they named their main grievance, extreme inequality. The symbolism of the occupations and the slogans fitted together, and the clear meaning reached not only most Americans but spread across the globe where protesters against austerity policies everywhere began to claim the Occupy label.

Cascading events also contributed to the force of the Occupy message, exposing the perpetrators of the financial crisis, the manipulations and thefts that caused the near-collapse, manipulations that continued in one form or another as financial leaders denounced any effort to rein them in with new regulations or increased taxes as "job killers." Scandal helped Occupy's message to gain traction. By midsummer of 2012, the *New York Times* carried a story on the first page of its business section titled "The Spreading Scourge of Corporate Corruption," showing plummeting public confidence in banks.[6] It seems reasonable to think Occupy made a major contribution to this shift in public attitudes.[7]

What about power? The great movements of the American past did much more than communicate their point of view. They mobbed the houses of the rich, helped steal the slave property of the south, shut down the mines and factories and even occupied them, rioted in the biggest cities. Again and again they enacted, in other words, what Paul Mason calls "the power of mayhem."

Occupy has still not found its power strategy. The "occupation" of Wall Street was much more about communicating a message than exercising power. After all, Zuccotti Park was four blocks north of Wall Street, and

---

6   Eduardo Porter, "The Spreading Scourge of Corporate Corruption," July 11, 2012.

7   Maybe something like this happened all over the world, as a result of the policies and practices promoted by the multinational financial and governmental elites who make globalization happen, as Paul Mason argues in *Why Its Kicking Off Everywhere*. Certainly the protest movements that erupted elsewhere, from the Spanish *indignados* to the UK Uncut protests to the risings of the Arab spring to the mobs in the streets of Athens show a strong kinship with Occupy. So, Mason may be right, we may be in the midst of a global youth revolt. I am highlighting another set of parallels here, though the similarities of Occupy to earlier American protests.

the bankers went about their business quite as they always had. However I would put it differently than Mason. I think they have not yet discovered the manifold forms of power inherent in their contributions to social cooperation. People go to work each day and so the factories run, the stores in the mall can open, the subways and buses transport people, the women in executive positions can go to their offices because the nannies have arrived, young people sit in orderly rows in classrooms, traffic moves because people stay on sidewalks and obey the traffic lights.

I think that the growth of the movement we call Occupy depends on its ability to reach beyond its largely young and student constituency and to sweep in diverse groups of workers and students and the poor. The movement is trying to do that now. Evicted from the squares and parks it occupied, it has moved to connect with community and worker struggles, to demonstrate against banks, to block evictions resulting from foreclosures, and so on. This is promising. All the great movements of the past recruited large and diverse constituencies. Howard Zinn describes the abolitionists as "that mixed crew of editors, orators, run-away slaves, free Negro militants, and gun-toting preachers known as the abolitionists."[8] Or, although we think of the great uprising of labor in the 1930s as composed of industrial and mineworkers, women workers in the five and dime stores and projectionists in local movie houses staged their own sit-downs too.

But numbers alone will not give this protest movement the leverage it needs to halt or slow down or turn around a predatory financialized capitalism with global reach. More likely it will have to discover or rediscover the strategies of disruption that gave earlier movements some power. I think that is what movement activists are now trying to do. Like the anonymous strategists of past movements they are trying to identify the leverage that people who are usually on the bottom side of cooperative relationships might have over the people on the top side, and what has to be done to make that leverage actionable. How can debtors exert power over lenders, or mortgaged householders exert power over mortgage holders? These questions are broadly similar to questions that have sometimes been answered in the past, when tenants did sometimes exert power over landlords, workers over bosses, urban mobs over rulers, and so on. When they did it was because they found ways to tap the multi-sided dependencies in which landlords, bosses, and rulers were also enmeshed. So, is Occupy over? I think it is still being invented as a multi-faceted mass protest movement that just might change our world.

---

8   Howard Zinn, "Abolitionists, Freedom-Riders, and the Tactics of Agitation," in *The Antislavery Vanguard: New Essays on the Abolitionists,* ed. Martin Duberman, Princeton NJ: Princeton University Press, 1965: 417.

Clayton Conn
November 6, 2011
Tar Sands Action, Washington DC

Lisa Fithian

STRATEGIC DIRECTIONS FOR THE OCCUPY MOVEMENT[1]

THE OCCUPY WALL STREET MOVEMENT, BORN OUT OF THE ARAB SPRING, the Wisconsin Wave, the May 12 Wall Street mobilization, and the May 15 Movement of *indignados* in Spain, is creating that better world we always talk about. Just as the Zapatista Movement and the 1999 Seattle Shutdown of the World Trade Organization exploded into a growing global justice movement during the past decade, these new political movements are setting the stage for the decade ahead.

They are building off of movements before them and using the self-organization, mutual aid, direct action, and non-cooperation which flourished in the streets of Tunisia, Cairo, Athens, Barcelona, Montréal, and elsewhere. This movement is a popular uprising and everyone has a seat at our table. It is a people-powered movement that has spread across the world.

Frances Fox Piven talks about the history and cycles of movements, reminding us that this country was born in revolution and that we have had a long and rich tradition of resistance to oppressive powers and structures. Whether it was the Boston Tea Party or insurgent farmers, labor organizing, or the black freedom movement, all these movements made progress but eventually receded and lost ground. Critical elements of social movements include lots of propaganda and direct action to keep the pressure on.

We face significant organizing ahead. How do we build the power we need to take down this system and replace it with a new one? Will it happen overnight? Over time? Is it happening right now? I believe it is. At the same time we struggle against the current system, we are building alternative networks and organizations to replace it. If we were to map all the intentional communities, housing cooperatives, community gardens, community agriculture projects, infoshops, community bookstores, bike coops, and community clinics, we would begin to see that there is a whole other world out there, just hidden from view by the social and media distractions around us.

---

1 Adapted from a talk at Left Forum on March 17, 2012.

Given that this change is happening now and over time, what kind of strategies might be of use for the Occupy movement to grow? I humbly offer the following suggestions:

develop an analysis of the system we live in

IT IS IMPORTANT to understand that Capitalism requires poverty, which in turn drives competition for wages. People will work under almost any conditions in order to have a job. Unions take wages out of competition through contracts, which is why they are under attack. The system we are socialized into is designed at every level to keep people from accessing their power to build a healthy world. It is the medical system we are born into, the educational system, the media, the prison-industrial complex, the lack of affordable housing and resulting homelessness, the agricultural complex that gives us processed, GMO foods, the energy systems that destroy communities through extraction of natural resources like coal, uranium, oil, gas, mineral and more, the military security state, etc. I could go on and on. The point is that we have all been raised to give up our power to an external authority or system by cooperating with its means of command and control.

Each of the pillars of this system has their own mechanisms to keep us entwined in it. Debt is a big one. For decades the neo-conservatives have moved a free market and neoliberal ideology, exported jobs, de-industrialized our economy, privatized the commons, and taken over the local and state elected offices that are now driving regressive legislation that is building a hateful, addictive, and destructive culture.

Capitalism uses oppression to keep the majority divided. Capitalism breeds hate, judgment, comparison, and competition. Capitalism breeds fear of the other and fear of the consequences of not going along. Capitalism requires militarism—to enforce, coerce, or impose its will whether it is the military, the police or the new security industry. Capitalism sucks. But there is another way and it is blooming every day!

practice healthy and liberating community

WE HAVE ALL internalized oppressive systems. We are born and socialized into this oppressive culture in such a way that it is impossible for us not to embody it. Our task is to be conscious of how we manifest this oppression and then develop healthier practices.

We carry within ourselves ideas and understandings that we have inherited from generations of capitalism, imperialism, racism, homophobia, and patriarchy and we participate in all of these forms of oppression on a daily basis. We did not create them, but we are responsible for how we engage them. From the personal to the institutional, we must deconstruct oppression and practice liberation. To make fundamental or radical change, we need to reclaim our power, practice living alternatively, and organize our communities to fight for justice—no matter how big or small the cause.

The Occupy movement unleashed enormous potential for community building through the encampments. But, as we are young tender souls, not fully conscious of our actions most of the time, and buried in the cynicism of our era, many did not believe, many did not step forward quickly with their gifts, and many who did step forward did so carrying an old mindset of how things should be done.

We hit the wall of racism, sexism, homophobia, class, and privilege. We have struggled with issues of access and resources and who is in and who is not. We came through a hard winter of internal work and reflection, and while many of our challenges have not yet been resolved, people have stayed in, made new and powerful friendships, and we all have held open this space with a willingness to address these hard, systemic issues of power and privilege. We are learning that this is life work.

To strengthen this movement, we need to be vigilant in deepening our practice of healthy communities. It may require developing a new language, like the language of Nonviolent Communication, which has been growing in many of the Occupies. The first step in Nonviolent Communication is deepening our power of observation and noticing what is going on. The second is discerning how you are feeling about this observation. Third is understanding what you need as a result of this observation, and finally, what request can you make of the group, your partner, organization, etc. that will meet your need. These simple and elegant steps take work. We are not socialized to communicate like this. Those in power don't want us in touch with our emotions or needs—they would rather have us cover them all with addictions or distractions.

Another powerful tip is one that I learned from Juniper, a member of my collective: understanding the herd instincts of the mammalian brain. Essentially this means understanding that through the ages mammals have gathered in packs, herds, prides, and tribes and that our survival is interdependent with the group. Every time we walk into a group—just like everyone who walks into Occupy—the first question is "Do I belong or not? Will I be accepted or rejected?" This is fundamental and it is key that people feel like they can show up, without having to hide who they are, and be accepted.

One last piece of this practice is understanding the Strategic Use of Privilege. Those of us with whatever privilege we have (an unearned benefit derived from one's race, gender, or class) must use that privilege to raise all boats. We must work to ensure that if we are straight and a homophobic comment is made, we speak about gay rights. If we are older or educated, we must help break down complex language so everyone can understand. If we are male (socialized to take the space), we must understand our role is to hold the space for those who have been marginalized to participate. If we are white (socialized to feel entitled, smart, deserving, in control), we must hold the space for the anger and frustration and despair of those who have been treated as less than human over the course of generations. We must also work to be strong allies, bringing resources, solidarity, and support to those who have less. This is not for the purpose of charity but for the purpose of enabling communities to take effective action on their own behalf.

build grassroots organization and networks

ORGANIZATION IS NECESSARY for building power. Within the Occupy movement, we can see many individuals acting on their own agency as well as staff and members of unions, community-based organizations, student groups, and other nonprofit and online organizations. The vast majority of the 99% however is not in any organized structure or group. The General Assembly model is inspiring at times but also promotes the rugged individualism of this culture ... with no accountability to boot! Networks are the way of the future. Locally-based but connected over geography, time, and action.

When I came of age politically in horizontal movements, we used working groups, coordinating councils, affinity groups, clusters, and action spokescouncils. We used consensus as our decision-making process and we used many of the same hand signals Occupy uses today. One major difference, though, is the fact that in the past, we frequently started with a common set of values and goals. Within Occupy, on the other hand, we have clearly shattered the notion that there are clear demands. We are not interested in demanding anything from a corrupt system of power. We are much more interested in engaging in self-organizing and direct democracy, direct action, and mutual aid to remedy the problems this system of power has created. We demand from ourselves sustainable, renewable, and replicable environmental and economic practices, until we have enough power to fully manifest that world. No movement has ever won significant justice without a willingness to put their bodies on the line through direct action (including civil resistance and civil disobedience) to achieve justice. This kind of movement organization that supports and practices direct democracy and direct action as a means to create change is one of the most empowering and transformative models of organization we can have.

target the 1%

WE NEED TO know who they are, where they work, where they live. We can use the Pillar of Power tool to hone our strategic framework to understand the core institutions of support and then we can target and learn about the most important. We are more effective once we know which leaders to target within specific industries. We need to know the CEOs, the board of directors, the executive management, the shareholders, and the major investors. We need to build databases that will allow us to map them and build lists to call them or email them. We need to know their buildings, factories, worksites: where the doors are, the lobbies, what floor are they on, where is the parking, public transportation, the nearest parks, open spaces? What do they care about? Who are the most powerful? What are the interconnections within and between industries? Who are their lobbyists? Who are their lawyers? What industry groups do they participate in? What other boards are they on? What conference and events are they attending? What are their political roles or relationships? Who do they donate money to? What are their quirks, idiosyncrasies? Do you have their photos? We need to look for opportunities for engagement. Find their calendars of events and then surround those events with things we create like street theater, teach-ins, mobile tactics, picket lines, occupations, sit-ins, and beyond.

We need to see that all of the institutions/systems/industries we engage are pillars that support and uphold the American Empire. We don't all need to do the same thing, but if we are chipping away at them, eventually our actions will add up, things will shift, and the empire may fall.

We need to create our own calendar, and develop a plan that escalates over time. This allows more and more people

If we can successfully build more self-organized, cooperative groups, over time we create the foundation for federating these different groups. We might have affinity groups and actions, spokescouncils or neighborhood councils or worker coops that all come together into city-wide, then bio-regional, and then national councils. It may not work, but what the heck, what we have sure ain't working and at least this way embodies so many of the values we hold dear.

to gain access to the empowering and meaningful experience of concrete organizing against Empire.

take space/take risks

WE NEED TO take space—physical space, visual space, intellectual space, emotional space, mental space, and so on. Occupation give us space to build relationships, experience, and skills. It opens space for our creativity. It allows us room to challenge the notion of ownership and privatization and explore issues like what is in the collective interest, or establishing our own sort of commons—literally and figuratively. Taking space goes to the heart of the 1% strategy of owning and controlling everything … little by little they keep taking more.

Again, we need to understand the dynamics of power and recognize that we have been cooperating with these systems of oppression—mostly unconsciously. Only then can we understand that taking back space is about liberation through non-cooperation. Our challenge is to make sure it is liberation for all. When we escalate and take risks, we need to make sure we have sufficient support structures, solid logistics, multiple points of entry, and varying levels of risk for participants. On any given day, at any given action, we all have different situations that allow for different levels of participation. We need to honor all that we can do and gently keep pushing for more.

What space do we occupy? Inside? Outside? Well just like yin and yang, just like the sun and the moon, just like two sides of a coin, there is space inside and outside. Instead of competing or preaching the virtues of engaging one space over the other, do both and work to ensure we are truly in alignment on the outcomes. Ensure that those with more privilege, and thus more access (and often less consciousness), work strategically with the broader and more marginalized communities and assume this community's interests as their own.

We also need to know that taking space and holding onto just one place is not enough either. We must grow beyond and reclaim/establish many spaces. We can already see this happening. We grow like the mycelium under this earth, spreading in vast interconnected networks that can be an unstoppable force.

escalate/compress/crisis

UNDERSTAND THAT MOVEMENTS often have life cycles of 10 to 15 years, and know that other movements will grow out of this, just as has happened in the past. We need to balance between the long haul and the immediacy of finding appropriate and urgent action. You can build some serious culture over a decade or more, and we must nurture that path and keep it integrated throughout our direct action resistance. That being said, we must create a crisis for the 1% and it needs to be done again and again, with moments of escalation and compression to pressurize the situation to the point of change. In between actions, we need to leave time for rest, reflection, deepening, and growing.

We know there are clear moments ahead—we are not going to win immediately. The question of change becomes one of magnitude and ends. I continue to be an advocate for what I call a week of action (or rage) that is fundamentally a leadership action training program: concerted, concentrated, and creative activity with a broad public reach and a targeted and broad corporate engagement. We can look at events the 1% host or participate in as opportunities for engagement, or we can create our own events in their spaces. We can employ a broad range of tactics to keep them off balance and we can make what they are doing have a consequence.

federate system change—begin again

It's ONE THING to take on the State. It's another thing to build a lasting form of self-organization and governance, and in this moment I am interested in how small self-organized groups work collaboratively at larger and larger scales. Again, we are still young, our GAs and spokes have been so painful, and many have failed or collapsed. We know there is lots of room for improvement. We must be patient with ourselves and be willing to succeed and fail. Either way, we must persevere and evolve.

What would it look like if we started to secure more and more spaces to work and organize out of, building massive networks that supported local communities? Places where people can learn, contribute, or just get something they may need?

If we can successfully build more self-organized, cooperative groups, over time we create the foundation for federating these different groups. We might have affinity groups and actions, spokescouncils or neighborhood councils or worker coops that all come together into city-wide, then bioregional, and then national councils. It may not work, but what the heck, what we have sure ain't working and at least this way embodies so many of the values we hold dear.

I am sure there are many other important pieces of work I have not addressed here, but we have this. In fact we have our whole lives to practice building a better world. Just as the seasons have cycles, movements have cycles and people have cycles. We will have our highs and our lows and our lives are now forever changed. Let's dream big. Let's vision boldly. Let our hearts beat strong. Let our prejudices go. My life is bound to you and all living things, we must do this together and we must do this now.

OccupyMaine
Reclaims
Democracy

Margaret Killjoy
February 11, 2012
Occupy Maine Encampment in Portland

George Caffentzis

IN THE DESERT OF CITIES:
NOTES ON THE OCCUPY MOVEMENT IN THE US

The Coptic hermits who left the world as though escaping from a wreck, did not merely intend to save themselves. They knew that they were helpless to do any good for others as long as they floundered about in the wreckage. But once they got a foothold on solid ground, things were different. Then they had not only the power but even the obligation to pull the whole world to safety after them.

—Thomas Merton, *The Wisdom of the Desert*

No person shall sit, lie or sleep in or upon any street, sidewalk or other public way.

—L.A.M.C. Sec. 41 18 (D)

the occupy movement's limits and possibilities
internally and externally

THE GOVERNMENTAL REPRESSION OF THE "OCCUPY MOVEMENT" IN THE US has as its icons photos of New York City police officers' harsh treatment of the Occupy Wall Street participants who practiced nonviolence in the face of tremendous provocation: from the arrest of over 700 people in one action on the Brooklyn Bridge to the wrecking of the kitchen, library, and the inhabited tents filled with personal effects on the Zuccotti Park site. Similar police violence occurred in most of the occupations in the larger cities like Boston, Oakland, San Francisco, and Denver as well as New York City.

In the wake of the repression—justified under a ragtag series of minor, largely municipal (or, as Foucault would say, "biopolitical") regulations: health and sanitary rulings, park closing hour regulations, restrictions on overnight presence in a public space, and regulations like L.A.M.C. Sec. 41 18 (D), which were devised to drive homeless people from the streets—there was outrage, for after all why should one be beaten to a pulp or be pepper-sprayed in the eyes by police officers for the crime of over-night camping in a public park, an offence that would normally deserve the equivalent of a parking ticket? Why should so-called "free speech" constitutional rights not trump these local ordinances? After all, there is no 9PM closure inscribed in the First Amendment. And indeed, these Clearances have generated thousands of lawsuits against municipal governments that will fill the court dockets around the country for a long time to come.

We know, on the testimony of Oakland's mayor, Jean Quan, to the BBC, that the assaults against the occupy sites were not the result of cops' spontaneous sadism given free rein. They were coordinated and discussed by mayors from eighteen other cities. There is also good evidence of the involvement of Department of Homeland Security and FBI personnel co-ordinating the assaults.

It is also clear that these attacks were never repulsed by the type of self-defense that was (and is) practiced in Tahrir Square in over a year of deadly struggle in the face of live bullets and tear gas. In fact, and this is some-thing I heard in the New York City, Oakland, and San Francisco Occupy sites, many occupiers were either ambiguous about or almost relieved by the clearances while many others were bitter about the lack of resolve of the occupiers to defend their new community in formation. In the midst of this crisis, some even went as far as to say that the clearances came just in time to "save" the situation because there was so much discord in the encampments that they were on the verge of decomposition, while still others were angry about the lack of resolve of their fellow occupiers to hold the site.

Though, of course, the violence of the state is a significant barrier to the growth of the movement and constitutes an external limit, it is even more urgent to discuss the movement's internal limits as we take new steps in expanding its scope. For, in actual fact, these internal limits are based upon the movement's success in bringing together many class strata that had rare-ly encountered each other body to body politically. The political problem/challenge of the Occupy movement that was recognized with some chagrin was that the Occupy sites actually arose out of their success in doing a re-markable job of attracting many new strata of the 99% (or what used to be called the working class) to the occupy site.

In this essay I will discuss the paradoxical success of the Occupy move-ment, its relationship to some past movements, and what its challenges are.

the occupy movement's class composition: get a job!

IN ORDER TO understand any class phenomenon in a capitalist society, we must understand how it is composed, for there is rarely any movement that is perfectly homogenous with a unified strategy and program. The Occupy movement claims to be a piece of the 99% and occupiers chant, "We are the 99%!" It is a great slogan because it is majoritarian, it refuses marginalization, and it calls on those who reject re-presentation to present themselves bodily here, to join us now. But the slogan holds two dangers. First, if we are as common as "leaves of grass" (the 99%), we might think we know already who we are and what are the limits of our powers. However, the most common is—like the dark matter that constitutes 90% of the universe, according to physicists—often the least known. There is much to learn about our powers and the opening that the Occupy movement has created.

Second, but even more important, the slogan can tempt us to neglect the striations, the divisions, the hierarchies within the 99% that have such great power to stop movements in their tracks, in fact, much more power than the 1% can raise. True, no one can easily forget in this day and age sexism, racism, ableism, ageism, and the ever-growing list of other forms of intra-class conflict. From the very beginning of the movement, there were critiques and concerns about the racial and gender composition of the occupiers, for example. Was it a young, white male movement? How many people of color, how few trans and queer people, how many women were speaking at the GA? So, the insightful Max Rameau of Take Back the Land sees the Occupy movement's composition as one part of a larger entity that includes another complementary movement (the Liberate movement) differentiated by race: "Far from homogeneous, this budding movement is evolving towards parallel, but interrelated campaign tracks: #Occupy and Liberate.... #Occupy has mobilized mainly, though not exclusively, disaffected young and impacted working- and middle-class whites. Liberate is mainly low- and middle-income people of color."

I want to note another important division between those occupiers who had a job that required keeping regular work hours and a family in a home and those who were either unemployed, or without a family or homeless. This division permeated the most mundane decisions of the Occupy sites. For example, in a recent General Assembly (GA) at the Occupy Maine site there was a discussion concerning the scheduling of the hours of the GA, should it be at 6PM or 4PM? What's the difference? It was soon revealed. The original time for the GA was 6PM in order to give people with jobs time to come to the meeting. But it turned out that the local homeless shelter that served a hot dinner to the homeless population opened its doors at 6PM and closed them at 7PM (and the kitchen at the Occupy Maine site was not too reliable). It was noted in the discussion that increasingly there was a shift from one type of worker who was waged to another who was not.

The power of the encampments is that it brought together much of the working class, both the waged and the unwaged, from the homeless to the long-term unemployed to the former university student facing an unpayable student loan with the worker on a job who can only find a political opportunity for resistance in a transformed space outside the factory, dock, office, or school.

The double-sided nature of the Occupy sites speaks to both sides of the working class: (a) as a vehicle for the protest of workers with a job but who are powerless to express their resistance on and against the job; and (b) the site of reproduction of both the labor power and the refusal of labor of the irregularly employed people who are attracted to the Occupy site. The immediate interest that the unions took in allying themselves with the Occupy movement is a sign of the problem the unions (and workers with jobs) face. Thus, in the "general strike" in Oakland, the people who could not officially say they were striking were the *reason d'etre* of the strike itself: the truckers and the dockworkers! Similarly, the state workers in Wisconsin could not strike to protest Governor Walker's destruction of their union rights, so they had to depend on the people (many without jobs) who had occupied the state house for weeks for active resistance to Walker's schemes.

It is this two-sided aspect of Occupy sites—one as a political siege of the machinery of finance (as in the original Occupy Wall Street site) or the state (in the case of Wisconsin, a prescient Occupy moment) and the other, an attempt to create a self-enclosed site of a reproductive commons operating on the basis of sharing money and labor—that made the experience of the first phase of the Occupy movement so complex, verging on the contradictory, since these two types of workers had very different needs. But it was in the boldness to take on and bring together these two sides of the working class division that made the Occupy experience such an extraordinary source of political knowledge.

One epistemological maxim in politics is: "By the insults hurled at them, ye shall know them." Applying this maxim to the Occupy movement, the typical taunt from its opponents was "Get a Job!" since the idea of the Occupy protests is that the occupiers would be hermit-like in protesting 'round-the-clock (the way the hermits carry on prayer and meditation) and so it would be impossible to reconcile their life with having a regular "job." The taunt was taken ironically by the occupiers, because, on the one side, many in the movement have a job, but can do little to protect it except with the help of those without one! As Chris Carlsson so powerfully pointed out in his *Nowtopia*, in this period waged work does not provide a viable identity for struggle for most workers. It now turns out that even struggling about a job must increasingly be done outside the job as well. But on the other side, those occupiers without regular jobs, through their participation in the Occupy protest, *got* a "job" in the sense that the full-time political job of protesting the injustices of the inegalitarian structure of contemporary society became theirs, if they were willing and able to do it.

These two aspects of the Occupy sites are both the source of conflict and the promise of a "recomposition" of the working class now that the home is becoming an increasingly precarious condition of living and the tent is becoming a site of immediate communication within the class. The answer to the question, "Will the job/no job conflict defeat the recomposition or become its stimulus?" will determine whether the Occupy effort will continue to not only challenge the rule of capitalists (the 1%) but also to help to transform the nature of the working class (the 99%) or not in the coming months.

rejection of representative politics and a call for body politics

AN IMPORTANT ASPECT of the Occupy movement is its rejection of representative politics for a body politics in earnest. You simply have to bodily be at the center of the circulation of cities to practice this politics. Its opposite, representative politics, is being rejected by millions of people. Let's remember where representative politics comes from, i.e., re-presentation. Your re-presentative presents you in order for you to be *absent* from the political debates and decisions. So actually what appears to be a politics of presence is really one of absence.

Now for many of us busy, overworked folk this appears to be a good deal. After all, sitting through long debates and getting trained to go over

Sitting through long debates and getting trained to go over government accounts is time-consuming and tedious. But in periods of crisis when you no longer trust who is presenting you again in your absence and when you no longer trust the whole apparatus of representation, the need to make your presence felt physically returns, i.e., to go back to basics and originally present yourself as a body in motion at a historic juncture ready to swerve the relations of power in your favor.

government accounts is time-consuming and tedious. But in periods of crisis when you no longer trust who is presenting you again in your absence and when you no longer trust the whole apparatus of representation, the need to make your presence felt physically returns, i.e., to go back to basics and originally present yourself as a body in motion at a historic juncture ready to swerve the relations of power in your favor. The occupying mass of bodies that we have seen from Tunisia, Egypt, Syria, Yemen, Greece, and Spain are made up of those who, for good reason, no longer trust any form of representation, whether electoral or not.

You might remember a time when the notion of the power of the street and of the public gathering was ridiculed by political theorists like Paul Virilio. The politics of lightening speed or the virtual and the ethereal was all the rage in the postmodern cosmos, but the experiences of the last year have shown that speed is not enough for political effect, momentum (mass times velocity) is necessary as well. Though Twitter and Facebook were important, in the final analysis, the bodies and the site or place ("the squares") were still politically decisive, even *sine qua non*s for any revolutionary transformation. The siege was considered the most archaic arrangement of forces, but now it has been revived. "Occupy," not in the imperialist, but in the spatio-temporal sense of the word, is beginning to have a political meaning again.

This round-the-clock bodily presence makes the Occupy movement self-reproducing, in Silvia Federici's sense. In other words, before the rise of the Occupy movement, there was an unfulfilled desire "to put an end to the separation between the personal and the political, and political activism and the reproduction of everyday life," in her words. This erasure of these separations is exactly what the Occupy sites provided as a political experience in response to the concept of politics as a performance that one does as an event at a particular place and time (whether it be "violent" or "nonviolent" is irrelevant in this regard) and then returns to the quotidian life. Much of the excitement of the Occupy movement was the creation of a new living *topos* in the center of the city that had been previously deserted and that was being used to transform the quotidian, a place that was generative of political action and at the same time a living space for hundreds in the desert of cities.

in the desert of cities

FOR THERE IS an ascetic element in the Occupy movement. By facing all the weathers in the open, the occupiers showed that they were willing to suffer to say their piece to Wall Street. This aspect was especially emphasized for me in the Occupy Maine camp, where the occupiers were offered an easy out by the Portland City Council, which ordered their encampment be dismantled in late December, but the occupiers did not take the invitation and decided to fight the order in the courts and stay on in their tents in the face of a Maine winter! Whenever it rained, snowed, or the temperature fell below freezing at night, I would think of my comrades in their tents and share at a distance a sense of discomfort; as if their suffering was a verification of the worth of the political message that is being expressed. Similar stories of ascetic suffering could be told of the other Occupy sites.

In a society where shoppers are crushed by their fellows in a frenzied quest for the purchase of an iPhone, this asceticism is a potent living expression of disgust over the willingness of so many of the 99% to destroy themselves at the behest of a capitalism that is increasingly making the cities deserts of "an immense collection of commodities." The sharing of the Occupy site is not only that of food and shelter, but of shared pain, discomfort and commitment. Sleeping in the rain and snow, finding places to wash, to urinate and defecate, dealing with frostbite (at least in the northern areas), devoting 24 hours a day to political activities marked those who stayed at the Occupy site from the ones who came intermittently during the day. The ever-renewed discomfort and commitment remained as a badge of honor and a sign of legitimacy.

This might sound strange, but all this experience was reminiscent of the ascetics of the desert, whether Hebrew, Christian, or Muslim. I was especially moved to compare the occupiers with the Desert Fathers and Mothers in the fourth century, who, at the moment

The truly subversive intent of the Occupy site is to transform public space into a commons. A public space is ultimately a space owned and opened/closed by the state…. A common space, in contrast, is opened by those who occupy it, i.e., those who live on it and share it according to their own rules. The worldwide movement of occupiers (through their practice) is demanding common spaces where they can live on in order to give body to their political thoughts.

when Christianity became the established religion of the Roman Empire, walked out of their comfortable homes in the cities of the Nile, gave away their wealth to the poor, and started to live in the Egyptian desert, suffering much, but learning much and through their very pain cast doubt on the new turn of the faithful to state power. As Thomas Merton wrote of the Desert Fathers and Mothers in the epigraph to this essay, they found in their bodily privations the solitude and self-recognition that made it possible "to pull the whole world to safety after them," if the world was interested in being saved!

The Occupy method transfers a similar ascetic passion to the political level. It calls for a twenty-four hour political life that gives the Occupiers a moral authority that appealed to the 99% in comparison to the anxious self-satisfaction of the Wall Streeters looking down from their office towers wondering whether Occupy Wall Street will affect their bonuses!

conclusion: public versus common

THE TRANSFORMATION OF the public space run for the convenience of the state into a common space that is organized by the commoners who live and work in it is another and final aspect of the Occupy movement that I will address. This transformation is often expressed by the question: which trumps which, "free speech" rights or municipal biopolitical ordinances (regulation of sanitation, food preparation, etc.)? After all, what happens if integral to exercising free speech in Los Angeles a person "shall sit, lie or sleep in or upon any street, sidewalk or other public way" and therefore violates L.A.M.C. Sec. 41 18 (D)? This conundrum, however, describes the situation in the language of the state, i.e., in the form of constitutional rights taking precedence over municipal ordinances or not.

The truly subversive intent of the Occupy site is to transform public space into a commons. A public space is ultimately a space owned and opened/closed by the state, it is a *res-publica*, a public thing. A common space, in contrast, is opened by those who occupy it, i.e., those who live on it and share it according to their own rules. The worldwide movement of occupiers (through their practice) is demanding common spaces where they can live on, in order to give body to their political thoughts. That is why the first acts of the Occupations involve housework: where are we to sleep, eat, urinate, defecate, clean up, etc.? This is not trivial, for in discovering the power of bodies that present themselves instead of being represented by others, their continued presence multiplies that power and momentum. This is what the government and Wall Street especially hate about the occupations and why there has been so much violence unleashed against them: they prefigure another way to organize society and to create a new commons. The parliaments and council chambers are temples of absence, while the Tahrir Squares of the world are places where a general will is embodied and in action.

Indeed, the twenty-first-century Occupiers, instead of going to the Egyptian desert, have gone instead to a more desolate desert at the center of their Cairos to save the world!

bibliography

Chris Carlsson, *Nowtopia: How Pirate Programmers, Outlaw Bicyclists, and Vacant-Lot Gardeners are Inventing the Future Today*. Oakland: AK Press, 2008.

Silvia Federici, "Feminism and the Politics of the Commons in an Era of Primitive Accumulation," in *Uses of a Whirlwind: Movement, Movements, and Contemporary Radical Currents in the United States*, edited by Team Colors Collective. Oakland: AK Press, 2010.

Christina Heatherton (ed.), *Downtown Blues: A Skid Row Reader*, Los Angeles: Los Angeles Community Action Network, 2011.

Thomas Merton, *The Wisdom of the Desert*, New York: New Directions, 1960.

Richard Rodriguez, "The God of the Desert: Jerusalem and the Ecology of Monotheism," *Harpers*, Vol. 316, No. 1892 (Jan. 2008), pp. 35–46.

Paul Virilio, *Speed and Politics*, New York: Semiotext(e), 1986.

Clayton Conn
October 31, 2010
Stop the Youth Jail, Baltimore MD

Team Colors Collective

MESSY HEARTS MADE OF THUNDER
OCCUPY, STRUGGLE, AND RADICAL COMMUNITY ORGANIZING

> By class I understand an historical phenomenon, unifying a number of disparate and seemingly unconnected events, both in the raw material of experience and in consciousness. I emphasize that it is an historical phenomenon. I do not see class as a "structure," nor even as a "category," but as something which in fact happens (and can be shown to have happened) in human relationships.
>
> —E.P. Thompson, *The Making of the English Working Class*

WHERE DOES THE OCCUPY MOVEMENT GO FROM HERE? ITS EMERGENCE IN the fall of 2011 was extraordinary after a decade of fleeting struggles and collective impasse; its rapid dissemination across a wide swath of places in the months that followed was equally unexpected. Yet even amidst the endless surprises, Occupy also carries the sediment of past and recent struggles, from poor people's urban movements and anti-police brutality struggles to the Arab Spring and precarity movements in Europe; it furthers encounters between organizers working on housing rights, student strikes, and prison abolition; and it offers a space for everyday resistance—simmering in homes, schools, streets, and workplaces—to arise into an outraged chorus that spans multitudes. Occupy is one of many loosely networked anchors in a sea of global revolt against the capitalist crisis, imposed austerity, state violence, and bankrupt avenues of acceptable politics.

The protests have been heartening for many of us, but they cannot be sustained through sheer determination. Police brutality, tactical dead-ends, and attempted cooptation by the professional left are challenging Occupy; unfortunately, many of the responses to these threats have tended towards closing off those relations that are the movement's greatest strength. We in Team Colors want to offer a few thoughts on movement building and why radical community organizing can be a motor for Occupy when its tenacity and will are exhausted. We can learn a great deal from historic struggles here in the US and the rich field of practices they deployed, as well as how they responded to pitfalls and threats that are similar to those Occupy faces today. We don't presume to know where Occupy is going—if anything it is "making the path by walking"—but we argue that attention to the current terrain of political possibility and the struggles that have shaped it can offer important guidance.

occupy & movement

IMMEDIATELY FOLLOWING THE occupation of Zuccotti Park, just a few blocks from Wall Street, on September 17, 2011 the movement spread to many dozens of encampments around the US. Seemingly, the war finally came home, as movements across the planet have been through periodic cycles of struggle since the counter-globalization movement. As Occupy disseminated and developed, a radical shift out of the previous period seemed underway among movement participants as well as the general population; in the winter of 2012, however, Occupy no longer occupies public space so prominently and it is unclear if it has moved beyond the limitations of the previous counter-globalization and anti-Iraq-war cycle of protest.

This tenuous moment shares a few parallels with the Students for a Democratic Society (SDS), which broke into three major factions following its final convention in Chicago in 1969. One went on to form the clandestine Weather Underground, another shifted into party building activities that would ultimately fail, and another would attempt to organize in factories and communities. Of course, no such convention has yet to take place within Occupy, and many of its separate factions remain within its framework; more importantly for our purposes here, there are few current mechanisms within Occupy to develop movement-wide strategy. While there have been a number of highly organized radical and community-based organizations drawing upon larger Occupy resources and deploying them in on-the-ground struggles, this has not become generalized.

The parallels with 1969 are perhaps most notable in terms of the arguments in common circulation currently: the masses are bought off and unable to participate in radical politics; certain populations (homeless, drug addicts and alcoholics, mentally ill, the poor, and others) are drawing resources and attention from the real struggle; certain types of militant protest are not acceptable. Occupy, as with SDS before it, has also tended towards blindness to the class position of its members and the complexity of poor and working-class communities (the unifying "99%" slogan notwithstanding). This is not simply to portray Occupy as an overwhelmingly white, middle-class, and student-aged movement, but to illustrate that there are certainly sectors of this movement that are actively portraying it as such, and attempting to remove other elements from the movement.

As one example, in the New York biweekly newspaper, *The Indypendent*, Nicholas Powers wrote a full-page story that noted, "Every utopia has extreme behavior that is a symptom of its value.... Into Liberty Park have come homeless street youth, drug addicts and alcoholics." Powers conflates homelessness with "extreme behavior" and apparently sees it as voluntary. He negatively refers to "drug addicts" and "alcoholics" with no further explanation; the reader is expected to agree: *those people are problems.* Such sentiments can be found in other Occupations, most notably Portland and Eugene, Oregon, where vocal sectors of the occupation called upon the authorities to remove "dangerous and unsafe elements." On November 6, the Portland Occupy Media Volunteers released a statement summarizing an emergency meeting held the night before: "Ideas that were discussed included obtaining a permit for the space to allow exclusion of dangerous or unsafe elements, involving the police immediately to address situations as they arise, and even stopping services that the camp provides to those who do not involve themselves in the process or the movement." In their eyes, this "extreme behavior" is "distract[ing] from the message of the movement and the effort of our volunteers. Occupy Portland will never support dangerous, violent or destructive behavior. [...] Volunteers will be meeting... to discuss further steps to take, including coordination with the City and the Portland Police to address these issues." This position is unfortunately common. In short, those who have faced the brunt of the attacks on the social safety net are to blame for diverting the movement's energy toward ostensibly more important and relevant work, and delaying the growth of the struggle. That many of those being blamed are people of color and many of those doing the blaming are white is not lost on us.

Similar sentiments and practices towards poor and homeless Occupiers are hidden behind recent discussions of appropriate tactics within the Occupy movement, specifically regarding the legitimacy of Black Bloc tactics. While the Black Bloc can be found around the country, it has been most active in Oakland and Portland. In a volatile and well-circulated article, left-democratic commentator Chris Hedges called the Black Bloc a "cancer" and called for its removal from the Occupy movement. Hedges' analysis ignores the contemporary history of Black Blocs in the US as an import from the 1980s Autonomen of Germany and the 1970s Autonomia Movement in Italy, and specifically their important role in the most recent anti-police brutality protests as well as producing economic sabotage during otherwise symbolic summit protests. But even more, the current formation of the Black Bloc on the West Coast find its immediate precedents in the anti-police brutality marches of 2009–2011. Particularly in Oakland, it was the engaged and militant action of the bloc in concert with other formations that led to the indictment of a murderous police officer. Without such action in Oakland and elsewhere, it is doubtful that the state would even consider punishing one of its functionaries for killing a civilian. Yet this cycle of protest is at risk of erasure, now that particular sectors of Occupy have begun claiming that the "police are part of the 99%." While a complex issue, such pronouncements undermine the struggles against the daily realities of police violence and signal a possible shift of Occupy's radical politics into more acceptable and liberal channels. As George Orwell stated in his monumental *Homage to Catalonia*, "I have no particular love for the idealized 'worker' … but when I see an actual flesh-and-blood worker in conflict with his natural enemy, the policeman, I do not have to ask myself which side I am on." While we in Team Colors have no great love for the Black Bloc and its idealized configurations of activist identities, we think a historically-situated defense of the bloc's actions is necessary, if only to re-focus the anxieties brewing within Occupy that villainize poor people and militant action as a rationale for liberal and reformist politics.

radical community organizing

THERE ARE MANY motors of organizing, and each generates very different relations and political possibilities. One of the more popular forms in the US is centered on changing consciousness: educating and developing individuals into activists that focus on particular issues. This approach is useful for forming affinities and knowledges, but often tends towards insularity (making activism one's identity instead of a vehicle towards other possible politics) and stark failure (such as the mass demonstrations against the 2003 Iraq invasion, which evinced that de-legitimizing the state or particular tactics of the state does not mean changing either). Another form comes out of the Alinsky school, which focuses on activating people's interests *en masse* to achieve small reforms that tend towards greater equality. The victories of this organizing cannot be discounted (especially in the midst of crisis), but they tend towards nonprofit cooptation and a delimited range of politics that leaves state and capital arrangements intact (even if more "equal"). Both of these motors attempt to mobilize money, resources, and people, but they do not necessarily build movements; their tendency is to limit possible strategies and tactics. Occupy and related radical movements should be on guard for how particular forms of organizing function—where they close off political possibilities, are readily co-opted by the state, and how particular discourses seek to tame militancy.

Radical community organizing, though diffuse, takes a much more generative tack. Unlike other motors that assume people must be "brought into" organizing, this approach works from the understanding that people are *always already* to deal with, negotiate, and struggle against the political problems of their everyday lives. Radical community organizing is thus not orchestrated by professional activists, but by communities that create autonomous initiatives intended to circulate and amplify such everyday resistance into potent political weapons. It is not the amount of money or number of people that defines the strength of this, but rather the density of human relationships, the cross-pollination across many movements and communities, the wealth of political strategies and activity, and the openness of dialogue and communication. Instead of delimiting the "who" and "what" of a movement, radical community organizing aspires toward "permanent encounter" with ever more people and problems, thus leading towards sharper analyses, greater circulation and production of knowledge, stronger mutual aid and support networks, and more powerful direct actions. Radical community organizing fuels movement-building through *political recomposition* in relation to the technical composition of state and capital forces; the struggle between both changes the terrain of the possible. We believe that Occupy can only move beyond the "stuckness" of the current moment—still dominated by spectacular actions—by grounding itself in long-term initiatives for survival and revolution.

Unlike other motors that assume people must be "brought into" organizing, [radical community organizing] works from the understanding that people are always already to deal with, negotiate, and struggle against the political problems of their everyday lives.

principles, examples, pitfalls, and their
resonance today

PART OF THE reasoning behind arguments that modify Occupy's radicalism and militant tactics is the trap of acceptability—the notion that a massive sector of the American population will only support action if particular radical bits such as property destruction and confrontational protest are scrubbed out. This "imaginary middle" is invoked to justify a rightward shift in politics, appeals to the middle-class, and the de-emphasis of issues of particular importance to poor peoples, people of color, and queer and gender-nonconforming peoples, as well as to prevent militancy. More insidiously, subtle rightward shifts and a lack of grounding in substantive community organizing can lead to cooptation and recuperation within existing institutions of reform and state control. Against these tendencies, we propose that radical movements need to make substantial changes in people's lives, build relationships, and ground themselves in everyday needs and desires. Several historical struggles illustrate the principles of maintaining vigilance against excluding poor people, the homeless, the mentally ill, people of color, and other marginalized sections of the population; extending the reach and depth of struggle rather than closing inward; and looking at the content of our lives rather than just our discourses.

The "survival pending revolution" programs of the Black Panther Party sought to address the generations of neglect and outright violence perpetrated against the black population. Rather than launching a campaign to demand that the state create breakfast programs for school children, distribute clothes and shoes, and provide legal aid and basic medical care, the Panthers created their own programs. Not simply apt at providing services, these programs also served as the basis for political education and further organizing. A decade after the Panthers collapsed amidst brutal government repression, the AIDS Coalition to Unleash Power (ACT-UP) organized an entire ecology of initiatives to address the AIDS crisis and its extraordinary death toll. ACT-UP developed original research on AIDS treatment, drugs, and transmission, and also deployed direct action to attack government inaction and force the FDA to release affordable AIDS drugs. Additionally, and in a similar fashion to the Black Panther programs, ACT-UP held daily meetings for people with AIDS, educated LGBTQ and straight communities about safe sex, and created space for these communities to build relationships in a time of crisis and death. This particular work drew from the feminist consciousness-raising efforts of the 1970s, which were initiated to address the isolation women felt in their lives around issues of unpaid housework, rape, abuse, incest, abortion, and women's health. Consciousness-raising groups built dense relationships among women and when pushed toward their logical end can develop mandates for action and strategies for liberation.

Most importantly, the silence that surrounded many women's lives and experiences was addressed through directly supportive relationships that grounded a political consciousness internally rather than from an external source.

Each of these historical examples contains crucial principles: survival is in fact pending revolution, direct action should develop from the needs in everyday life, community mandates for action should emerge from dialogs within working-class and oppressed populations. Such principles live on in numerous current initiatives that can be amplified and replicated to further the course of the Occupy movement in particular and radical movements in general. During a period of union decline, workers' centers have arisen in immigrant and day labor communities. Due to the need to set wages and working conditions, seek unpaid wages from unscrupulous employers, address healthcare concerns, and establish legal residency, workers have organized bottom-up organizations based in popular education models that develop campaigns and set demands. As an auxiliary to these struggles, the Seattle Solidarity Network (SeaSol) and similar projects have formed a base of squads that are deployed to support striking workers, prevent evictions, and fight employers and debt collectors. SeaSol's work with specific campaigns effectively develops relationships that strengthen these initiatives and improves outcomes. As one final example, New York's Rock Dove Collective—initially begun as a referral service for activists to access low-cost healthcare—has recently expanded into a solidarity role as well. Partnering with

Occupy and related radical movements should be on guard for how particular forms of organizing function— where they close off political possibilities, are readily co-opted by the state, and how particular discourses seek to tame militancy.

a worker co-op, immigrant organizations, and organizations of color, Rock Dove provides referrals to healthcare services that would not otherwise be available to those without insurance; they have also begun to set up a roaming clinic to service these communities as well as their activist "base." Herein we recognize that healthcare is fundamental as well as part of a movement's ability to reproduce itself. While SeaSol and Rock Dove are small initiatives, and members have been active in the larger Occupy movement, for our purposes it is important to note the possibility for amplifying and replicating these forms of organizing.

These contemporary initiatives illustrate additional organizing principles: campaign development and need-based demands, the need for active solidarity with other struggles, and creating movements around self-reproduction. Radical organizing that launches attacks against capital and the state must also be coupled with challenging the vestiges of racism, patriarchy, and class-power. Particular caucuses within Occupy, such as Decolonize and queer committees, are already pushing this organizing forward. Furthermore, sectors of the movements are beginning to partner with existing organizations squatting foreclosed homes, acting in direct solidarity with striking workers and poor people's movements, and conducting self-education programs; these should certainly be replicated and expanded.

together, together, together, together

WHAT IS MOST apparent about Occupy is its resonance. Since its emergence it has been infectious and its cogent critiques and revisionings increasingly saturate the political terrain. Occupy clearly has begun to launch nationwide days of action; yet reaching for actual movement building, reproduction, and political recomposition—becoming a class both in *and* of itself—necessitates a richer understanding of who is struggling and how. We have attempted to illustrate some of these dimensions here, and how they contribute to what E.P. Thompson identified as a class project, "something which in fact happens in human relationships." Hence the focus of organizing turns to how these relationships function currently and how they can be strengthened, expanded, and used to further class struggle.

"We are the 99%" articulates a potential rather than a reality; it emerges into this potential through the motor of radical community organizing, specifically, those encounters that build new relationships in refusal *a priori* of who is or is not "resisting," who is or is not "political." "We" is not "new" so much as an ever-shifting historical condensation of resistance; it is the same legacy as the free breakfast programs, the AIDS activism, the organizing of undocumented laborers, and a multitude of other struggles that have shaped the present-day terrain. Finally, "We" is not the dream of unity, but rather "a world where many worlds fit," as per the Zapatistas; it entails processes of *organizing together* through experimentation, creativity, and new knowledges to meet new problems and challenges.

Where Occupy goes from here not only turns on these different potentials, but on how its participants seriously engage with what is politically possible right now, how the movement will be organized, how it can be sustained and reproduced, and where it is situated in a longer historical legacy of struggle. Not small questions for a movement still so young, as messy as it is thunderous; yet they are crucial in a time of extraordinary crisis, "stuckness," and upheaval. For a movement that is only beginning to realize the potentials and dangers of its own emergence, such reflection is needed now more than ever.

the OAKLAND COMMUNE

ONE HUMAN

DEATH to CAPITALISM

occupy everything!

general strike!

Margaret Killjoy
November 2, 2011
Oscar Grant Plaza, Oakland

OCCUPY OAKLAND IS DEAD. LONG LIVE THE OAKLAND COMMUNE.
MAY 1, DECOMPOSITION, AND THE COMING ANTAGONISMS

the commune

For those of us in Oakland, "Occupy Wall Street" was always a strange fit. While much of the country sat eerily quiet in the years before the Hot Fall of 2011, a unique rebelliousness that regularly erupted in militant antagonisms with the police was already taking root in the streets of the Bay. From numerous anti-police riots triggered by the execution of Oscar Grant on New Year's Day 2009, to the wave of anti-austerity student occupations in late 2009 and early 2010, to the native protest encampment at Glen Cove in 2011, to the sequence of Anonymous BART disruptions in the month before Occupy Wall Street kicked off, our greater metropolitan area re-emerged in recent years as a primary hub of struggle in this country. The intersection at 14th and Broadway in downtown Oakland was, more often than not, "ground zero" for these conflicts.

If we had chosen to follow the specific trajectory prescribed by *Adbusters* and the Zuccotti-based organizers of Occupy Wall Street, we would have staked out our local Occupy camp somewhere in the heart of the capitol of West Coast capital, as a beachhead in the enemy territory of San Francisco's financial district. Some did this early on, following in the footsteps of the growing list of other encampments scattered across the country like a colorful but confused archipelago of anti-financial indignation. According to this logic, it would make no sense for the epicenter of the movement to emerge in a medium sized, proletarian city on the other side of the bay.

We intentionally chose a different path based on a longer trajectory and rooted in a set of shared experiences that emerged directly from recent struggles. Vague populist slogans about the 99%, savvy use of social net-working, shady figures running around in Guy Fawkes masks, none of this played any kind of significant role in bringing us to the forefront of the Occupy movement. In the rebel town of Oakland, we built a camp that was not so much the emergence of a new social movement, but the un-precedented convergence of preexisting local movements and antagonistic tendencies all looking for a fight with capital and the state while learning to take care of each other and our city in the most radical ways possible.

This is what we began to call The Oakland Commune; that dense net-work of new found affinity and rebelliousness that sliced through seemingly impenetrable social barriers like never before. Our "war machine and our care machine" as one comrade put it. No cops, no politicians, plenty of "au-tonomous actions;" the Commune materialized for one month in liberated Oscar Grant Plaza at the corner of 14th & Broadway. Here we fed each other, lived together and began to learn how to actually care for one another while launching unmediated assaults on our enemies: local government, the down-town business elite, and transnational capital. These attacks culminated with the General Strike of November 2 and subsequent West Coast Port Blockade.

In their repeated attacks on Occupy Oakland, the local decolonize ten-dency is in some ways correct.[1] Occupy Wall Street and the movement of the 99% become very problematic when applied to a city such as Oakland and reek of white liberal politics imposed from afar on a diverse population al-ready living under brutal police occupation. What our decolonizing comrades fail to grasp (intentionally or not) is that the rebellion which unfolded in front of City Hall in Oscar Grant Plaza does not trace its roots back to September 17, 2011 when thousands of 99%ers marched through Wall Street and set up camp in Lower Manhattan. The Oakland Commune was born much earlier on January 7, 2009 when those youngsters climbed on top of an OPD cruiser and started kicking in the windshield to the cheers of the crowd. Thus the name of the Commune's temporarily reclaimed space where anti-capitalist processes of decolonization were unleashed: Oscar Grant Plaza.

Why then did it take nearly three years for the Commune to finally come out into the open and begin to unveil its true potential? Maybe it needed time to grow quietly, celebrating the small victories and nursing itself back to health after bitter defeats such as the depressing end of the

---

1 The decolonize tendency emerged in Oakland and elsewhere as a people of color and indigenous-led initiative within the Occupy movement to confront the deep colonialist roots of contemporary oppression and exploitation. Decolonize Oakland publicly split with Occupy on December 5, 2011 after failing to pass a proposal in the Occupy Oakland General Assembly to change the name of the local movement to Decolonize Oakland. For more information on this split see the "Escalating Identity" pamphlet: http://escalatingidentity.wordpress.com/.

student movement on March 4, 2010. Or maybe it needed to see its own reflection in Tahrir, Plaza del Sol, and Syntagma before having the confidence to brazenly declare war on the entire capitalist order. One thing is for sure. Regardless of Occupy Wall Street's shortcomings and the reformist tendencies that latched on to the movement of the 99%, the fact that some kind of open revolt was rapidly spreading like a virus across the rest of the country is what gave us the political space in Oakland to realize our rebel dreams. This point cannot be overemphasized. We are strongest when we are not alone. We will be isolated and crushed if Oakland is contained as some militant outlier while the rest of the country sits quiet and our comrades in other cities are content consuming riot porn emerging from our streets while cheering us on and occasionally coming to visit, hoping to get their small piece of the action.

the movement

FOR A WHOLE generation of young people in this country, these past six months have been the first taste of what it means to struggle as part of a multiplying and complex social movement that continually expands the realm of possibilities and pushes participants through radicalization processes that normally take years. The closest recent equivalent is probably the first (and most vibrant) wave of North American anti-globalization mobilizations from late 1999 through the first half of 2001. This movement also brought a wide range of tendencies together under a reformist banner of "Fair Trade" and "Global Justice" while simultaneously pointing towards a systemic critique of global capitalism and a militant street politics of disruption.

The similarities end there and this break with the past is what Occupy got right. Looking back over those heady days at the turn of the millennia (or the waves of summit hopping that followed), the moments of actually living in struggle and experiencing rupture in front of one's eyes were few and far between. They usually unfolded during a mass mobilization in the middle of one "National Security Event" or another in some city on the other side of the country (or world!). The affinities developed during that time were invaluable, but cannot compare to the seeds of resistance that were sown simultaneously in hundreds of urban areas this past fall.

It makes no sense to overly fetishize the tactic of occupations, no more than it does to limit resistance exclusively to blockades or clandestine attacks. Yet the widespread emergence of public occupations qualitatively changed what it means *to resist*. For contemporary American social movements, it is something new to liberate space that is normally policed to keep the city functioning smoothly as a wealth generating machine and transform it into a node of struggle and rebellion. To do this day after day, rooted in the city where you live and strengthening connections with neighbors and comrades, is a first taste of what it truly means to have a life worth living. For those few months in the fall, American cities took on new geographies of the movement's making and rebels began to sketch out maps of coming insurrections and revolts.

This was the climate that the Oakland Commune blossomed within. In those places and moments where Occupy Wall Street embodied these characteristics as opposed to the reformist tendencies of the 99%'s nonviolent campaign to fix capitalism, the movement itself was a beautiful thing. Little communes came to life in cities and towns near and far. Those days have now passed but the consequences of millions having felt that solidarity, power, and freedom will have long lasting and extreme consequences.

We shouldn't be surprised that the movement is now decomposing and that we are now, more or less, alone, passing that empty park or plaza on the way to work (or looking for work) which seemed only yesterday so loud and colorful and full of possibilities.

All of the large social movements in this country following the anti-globalization period have heated up quickly, bringing in millions before being crushed or co-opted equally as quickly. The anti-war movement brought millions out in mass marches in the months before bombs began falling over Baghdad but was quickly co-opted into an "Anybody but Bush" campaign just in time for the 2004 election cycle. The immigrant rights movement exploded during the spring of 2006, successfully stopping the repressive and racist HR4437 legislation by organizing the largest protest in US history (and arguably the closest thing we have ever seen to a nation-wide general strike) on May 1 of that year.[2] The movement was quickly scared off the streets by a brutal wave of ICE raids and deportations that continue to this day. Closer to home, the anti-austerity movement that swept through California campuses in late 2009 escalated rapidly during the fall through combative building occupations across the state. But by March 4, 2010, the movement had been successfully split apart by repressing the militant tendencies and trapping the more moderate ones in an impotent campaign to lobby elected officials in Sacramento. Such is the rapid cycle of mobilization

---

2   The demonstrations on May 1, 2006, called *El Gran Paro Estadounidense*, or The Great American Boycott, were the climax of a nationwide series of mobilizations that had begun two months earlier with large marches in Chicago and Los Angeles as well as spontaneous high school walkouts in California and beyond. Millions took to the streets across the country that May 1, with an estimated two million marching in Los Angeles alone. Entire business districts in immigrant neighborhoods or where immigrants made up the majority of workers shut down for the day in what some called "A Day Without an Immigrant."

and decomposition for social movements in late capitalist America.

the decomposition

So WHAT THEN killed Occupy? The 99%ers and reactionary liberals will quickly point to those of us in Oakland and our counterparts in other cites who wave the black flag as having alienated the masses with our "Black Bloc Tactics" and extremist views on the police and the economy. Many militants will just as quickly blame the sinister forces of cooptation, whether they be the trade union bureaucrats, the 99% Spring nonviolence training seminars, or the array of pacifying social justice nonprofits. Both of these positions fundamentally miss the underlying dynamic that has been the determining factor in the outcome thus far: all of the camps were evicted by the cops. Every single one.

All of those liberated spaces where rebellious relationships, ideas, and actions could proliferate were bulldozed like so many shantytowns across the world that stand in the way of airports, highways, and Olympic arenas. The sad reality is that we are not getting those camps back. Not after power saw the contagious militancy spreading from Oakland and other points of conflict on the Occupy map and realized what a threat all those tents and cardboard signs and discussions late into the night could potentially become.

No matter how different Occupy Oakland was from the rest of Occupy Wall Street, its life and death were intimately connected with the health of the broader movement. Once the camps were evicted, the other major defining feature

The underlying dynamic that has been the determining factor in the outcome thus far: all of the camps were evicted by the cops. Every single one.

of Occupy, the general assemblies, were left without an anchor and have since floated into irrelevance as hollow decision-making bodies that represent no one and are more concerned with their own reproduction than anything else. There have been a wide range of attempts here in Oakland at illuminating a path forward into the next phase of the movement. These include foreclosure defense, the port blockades, linking up with rank and file labor to fight bosses in a variety of sectors, clandestine squatting, and even neighborhood BBQs. All of these are interesting directions and have potential. Yet without being connected to the vortex of a communal occupation, they become isolated activist campaigns. None of them can replace the essential role of weaving together a rebel social fabric of affinity and camaraderie that only the camps have been able to play thus far.

May 1 confirmed the end of the national Occupy Wall Street movement because it was the best opportunity the movement had to reestablish the occupations, and yet it couldn't. Nowhere was this more clear than in Oakland as the sun set after a day of marches, pickets, and clashes. Rumors had been circulating for weeks that tents would start going up and the camp would reemerge in the evening of that long day. The hundreds of riot police backed by armored personnel carriers and SWAT teams carrying assault rifles made no secret of their intention to sweep the plaza clear after all the "good protesters" scurried home, making any reoccupation physically impossible. It was the same on January 28 when plans for a large public building occupation were shattered in a shower of flash bang grenades and 400 arrests, just as it was on March 17 in Zuccotti Park when dreams of a new Wall Street camp were clubbed and peppersprayed to death by the NYPD. Any hopes of a spring offensive leading to a new round of space reclamations and liberated zones has come and gone. And with that, Occupy Wall Street and Occupy Oakland are now dead.

the future

IF ONE HAD already come to terms with Occupy's passing, May 1 could actually be viewed as an impressive success. No other 24-hour period in recent memory has unleashed such a diverse array of militancy in cities across the country. From the all day street fighting in Oakland, to the shield bloc in LA, to the courageous attempt at a Wildcat March in New York, to the surprise attack on the Mission police station in San Francisco, to the anti-capitalist march in New Orleans, to the spectacular trashing of Seattle banks and corporate chains by black flag wielding comrades, the large crowds which took to the streets on May 1 were no longer afraid of militant confrontations with police and seemed relatively comfortable with property destruction. This is an important turning point which suggests that the tone and tactics of the next sequence will be quite different from those of last fall.

Yet the consistent rhythm and resonance of resistance that the camps made possible has not returned. We are once again wading through a depressing sea of everyday normality waiting for the next spectacular day of action to come and go in much the same way as comrades did a decade ago in the anti-globalization movement or the anti-war movement. In the Bay Area, the call to strike was picked up by nurses and ferry workers who picketed their respective workplaces on May 1 along with the longshoremen who walked off the job for the day. This display of solidarity is impressive considering the overall lack of momentum in the movement right now. Still, it was not enough of an interruption in capital's daily flows to escalate out of a day of action and into a general strike like we saw on November 2.

And thus we continue on through this quieter period of uncertainty. We still occasionally catch glimpses of the Commune in those special moments when friends and comrades successfully break the rules and start self-organizing to take care of one another while simultaneously launching attacks against those who profit from mass immiseration. We saw this off and on during the actions of May 1, or in the two occupations of the building at 888 Turk Street in San Francisco, or most recently on the occupied farmland that was temporarily liberated from the University of California before being evicted by UCPD riot police a few days ago. But with the inertia of the fall camps nearly depleted, the fierce but delicate life of our Commune relies more and more on the vibrancy of the rebel social relationships which have always been its foundation.

The task ahead of us in Oakland and beyond is to search out and nurture new means of finding each other. We are quickly reaching the point where the dead weight of Occupy threatens to drag down the Commune into the dustbin of history. We need to breathe new life into our network of rebellious relationships that does not rely on the Occupy Oakland General Assembly or the array of movement protagonists who have emerged to represent the struggle. This is by no means an argument against assemblies or for a retreat back into the small countercultural ghettos that keep us isolated and irrelevant. On the contrary, we need more public assemblies that take different forms and experiment with themes, styles of decision making (or lack there of), and levels of affinity. We need new ways to reclaim space and regularize a contagious rebel spirit rooted in our specific urban contexts while breaking a losing cycle of attempted occupations followed by state repression that the movement has now fallen into. Most of all, we need desperately to stay connected with comrades old and new and not let these relationships completely decompose. This will determine the health of the Commune and ultimately its ability to effectively wage war on our enemies in the struggles to come.

Andra Mlhali
October 1, 2011
Occupy Wall Street on the Brooklyn Bridge

Yotam Marom

ROME WASN'T SACKED IN A DAY
ON REFORM, REVOLUTION, AND WINNING

reform vs. revolution

THE QUESTION OF WHETHER MOVEMENTS SHOULD FIGHT FOR REFORM OR revolution is not a new one. It pops up in any time period where people think it's possible to win one or the other, or both. Thanks to Occupy, the question is on the table again, in this new political climate.

A friend once told me—if you're struggling to choose between two different options, and you just can't make up your mind, don't bother: just have both. I think he might have meant it in terms of something smaller, like which flavor ice cream to order, but I think we can use that thinking about reform and revolution as well—and many revolutionaries of old have come up with similar answers (André Gorz is a good place to start if you are looking for further reading).

It's a mistake to position revolution and reform against one another. The two do not stand in conflict, and there is no need to choose between them. Reform on its own is not enough, and thinking narrowly about reform can hurt the movement in the long-run, so we need revolution, but you can't have a revolution without winning reforms along the way. You need both. In fact, the question itself is too narrow. It's not about reforms or revolution as two abstract options, it's about *winning*, and the question is not *whether* we should win things, but *what* things we should try to win, and *how*.

we need transformation

WHEN THE ARGENTINES began occupying and reclaiming their factories in the wake of the economic crisis of 2001, they had a slogan in response to those who told them they should take their concerns to the ballot: our dreams, they said, do not fit in your ballot boxes. Though the slogans have been different, it is clear the Occupy Movement has been driven by this same impulse. The direct action we have taken, the occupations we carried out, the things we said and wrote and painted revealed a deep understanding that there is something fundamentally wrong with society as it is, and an unrelenting belief that another world is possible.

We can make important improvements within the system, but ultimately we can't solve our crises by making cosmetic changes or tweaking things here and there. We are dealing with a system of oppression in which capitalism, authoritarianism, patriarchy, and white supremacy produce and reproduce one another in all aspects of social life—in ways as subtle as the ads we see in public bathrooms or the lessons we are taught in school, and as overt as the foreclosure crisis and indefinite detention at Guantanamo Bay. It is a system that rests on exploitation, domination, and coercion in fundamental ways, in which oppression and injustice are not anomalies, but in the very DNA of the institutions that dominate our lives.

Austerity—the gutting of vital social services so that the wealthy can get tax cuts while profiting from privatization—is a natural extension of neoliberalism, which is a natural evolution of capitalism. Mass incarceration and stop-and-frisk are policies that grow from a system that is white supremacist at its roots, one built on the backs of enslaved people and in the wake of genocide. Sexual assault against women is part of the normalized culture of our society, and LGBTQ youth face homelessness in astronomical proportions because the system we face is patriarchal in its core. We experience hierarchy everywhere from the school to the workplace to the prison to the home because authoritarianism is part of the fabric of this society, and it is taught to us everywhere we go. War abroad, the hoarding of natural resources by the Global North at the expense of the Global South, massive climate change that threatens the whole planet, and the commodification of everything from humans to air are outgrowths of this system as well.

The things we deal with in our day-to-day lives are outgrowths of these systemic realities. An economy with greater regulations, publicly-funded elections, decent healthcare, quality public education—these are immensely important wins to fight for, necessary on the road to something better, but winning these things alone doesn't unravel those greater systems of oppression. And even though we zoom out to understand different forms of oppression more clearly, we can't deal with those things apart from the whole—capitalism doesn't limit itself to the stock market, it is in the foundations of governments, it is burrowed deeply in our culture, it follows us into our bedrooms. The same is true for white supremacy, for patriarchy, for authoritarianism: these systems are intimately intertwined with one another to form a system of oppression that is deeply embedded in all areas of social life.

Only a real social transformation—one that understands our oppression as linked and at the very roots of the institutions that serve as the frameworks of our social life—can change that, and we shouldn't settle for anything less. If we fight for reforms without a deep commitment to building a movement that can strike at the roots of oppression and win real liberation, we risk putting ourselves in the position to trade in long-term power for short-term wins. We must constantly remember that, even when we fight for the things we need in the here and now, it is always on the road to something much bigger. We will always demand more, because we demand it all.

We want a political and economic system that we all actually control together, one that is equitable and humane, one that allows people to manage their own lives but encourages them to act in solidarity with one another, one that is participatory and democratic to its core. We want a world where people have the right to their own identities, communities, and cultures, and control over the institutions needed to live them out. We want a world with institutions that take care of us, our partners, our youth, our elderly, and our families in ways that are nurturing, liberating, healthy, and actively consensual. We want a world in which community is not a hamper on individual freedom, but rather an expression of its fullest potential.

We need a real social transformation—a revolution of values and the institutions we use to live them out.

Those notions are based on immature premises, proven wrong time and time again, that the worse things get, the more likely we are to rise up—that reform, because it makes peoples' lives better, is counter-revolutionary.

rome was not sacked in a day

THEY SAY ROME wasn't built in a day. Well, it wasn't sacked in a day either.

In school, history is taught around dates and figures. We learn that revolutions are led by gallant individuals, and fought on certain days. We see images of revolutionary flags billowing on liberated mountaintops, of magnificent leaders applauded by masses of people, of moments of struggle when old orders collapse and new ones take their place.

But we rarely read about the decades of hard organizing that led up to those moments, the fight for small gains all along the way, the many working people of all colors and genders and sexual orientations who fought for survival day in day out making the movement a reality, the countless smaller uprisings that won smaller victories, the many that were crushed along the way. And we learn very little, too, about the struggle that takes place after momentary victories—the incredible work of transforming ourselves and those around us, of building institutions that facilitate a free society, of fighting again and again to keep what we've won, of the beautiful struggle of resisting, reclaiming, and reconstructing over and over again.

We have to come to terms with that history, although it might not be as appealing. We've got to outgrow the idea that the revolution is an event to be measured in moments and actions, and that it's just around the corner—that all we need are oppressive conditions and a match to light the flame. Those notions are based on immature premises, proven wrong time and time again, that the worse things get, the more likely we are to rise up—that reform, because it makes peoples' lives better, is counter-revolutionary. We have to confront that thinking, because it's popular, it's sexy, it comes up over and over throughout history, and because it is cruel, empirically false, and incredibly divisive to the movement.

On a very basic level, that kind of thinking is heartless. A theory that compels us to oppose measures that would materially improve people's lives in the service of some abstract goal cannot possibly be driven by the compassion, love, and idealism that must be at the center of any worthwhile revolution. The consequences of theories like this are disproportionately felt by those already most oppressed and most marginalized, and often proposed and defended by those with great privilege.

But even more to the point, it's empirically untrue. The theory itself—that deep crisis on its own leads to revolution if it is met with a spark—is bankrupt. If all it took was conditions being terrible and a vanguard marching in the streets to wake everyone up, we wouldn't need to be having this conversation. It's already bad enough—just how awful does it have to get? The truth is it's harder to fight back under worse conditions, not easier. The many working people all across this country struggling around the clock to support their families, straddled with debt, or facing foreclosure can attest to how hard it is to scrape together the time to be a revolutionary while constantly facing crisis. So can political organizers living in police states like Egypt, or under military occupations like Afghanistan, or close to starvation in places like Haiti where people eat cakes made of mud to survive. Desperation doesn't mean it is any easier to be a revolutionary; it just means more suffering.

There is no magical tipping point, no low point so low that it automatically compels us to fight, no spark so compelling that it spontaneously wakes us all up. We fight because of our concrete experiences of oppression as well as the little bittersweet tastes of freedom we have pieced together, because of our education and the culture around us or the unexplained ways in which we have learned to reject them, because of hard organizing people have done for decades to prepare us, because of a whole host of other factors we don't even understand. In many cases, actually, we rise up not when we are absolutely desperate, but when we have won a little bit—enough to realize our collective strength.

Revolution is not an event, but a process. There is nothing inevitable about it, and our freedom is not historically determined. To win it, we have to build movements able to fight for it, movements that struggle over long periods of time to knock down the institutions of the status quo and replace them with the institutions of a free society. That means growing, practicing, learning, teaching, and winning things that put the movement in an increasingly better position to win more; it means fighting back to protect ourselves while pushing forward to create new possibilities.

If all it took was conditions being terrible and a vanguard marching in the streets to wake everyone up, we wouldn't need to be having this conversation. It's already bad enough—just how awful does it have to get? The truth is it's harder to fight back under worse conditions, not easier.

fighting back and pushing forward

IT'S NOT ABOUT reform or revolution, it's about winning things that meet our needs now while improving our position to struggle in the long-run, and it's about fighting in ways that grow and deepen the movement as we go. We need to choose struggles that allow us to fight back and push forward at the same time, to defend ourselves and win things we truly need while building power for the struggle beyond.

An example of a strategic battle like this might be fighting against tuition increases at public universities, and for free higher education. Fighting for free universities gives us the opportunity to draw connections between injustices faced in our daily lives—such as tuition increases, mass student debt, the policing of college campuses, the de-education of people of color, the concentration of wealth and power in the hands of the already wealthy in the form of tax breaks and privatization—to the deep-seated systems of oppression that cause them. But just as importantly, winning a struggle for free higher education grows the movement, because it means students don't have to work two jobs just to stay in school; it means they would have the time and energy to breathe, to organize, to fight back, to push further—to join the movement.

Beyond this, we need to look not only at what we ought to be struggling for, but how we ought to struggle. We should use methods that are practical and related directly to the things we are trying to win, with a wide range of options on the table. But we need to always remember to choose tactics that achieve the long-term goal of growing and deepening the movement and put us in a better position to fight for liberation—tactics that open up space for the movement to grow, that deepen our resolve and understanding of the system and its alternatives, that teach new skills so people can self-manage and struggle further, that allow us to practice our visions of freedom and make it feel good to be in the movement. Sometimes it means being in the streets, sometimes it means walkouts and strikes or other forms of civil disobedience, and sometimes it means flyering and one-on-ones, teach-ins and mass meetings, or a whole host of other tactics. Every context has its own solutions, and we have to be flexible, but we need to remember our principles and our goals—to win now while creating more opportunities for winning beyond the immediate struggles, to fight back while pushing forward.

winning

ULTIMATELY, THE KEY is power—recognizing and contesting it in our enemies, building it for ourselves, taking it from those who oppress and exploit, using it to transform ourselves and the values and institutions of our society. Winning matters. We are in a battle over the massive human potential wasted, squandered, and buried under systems of oppression, capable of so much. We are in a battle over our futures, the futures of our families and communities. We are in a battle for our lives.

We have to recognize that the institutions of the status quo and the individuals who control them have real power over us—power that can't simply be willed away, that has to be challenged and overcome, taken and used in the service of freedom. We must take our opponents seriously and confront them, by standing in the face of power to challenge and replace it. We have to fight to win things in the present, not only because we want our communities to survive and flourish, but because that's how we build another kind of power: people power. Winning things in the here and now is how we open up space for further struggle, grow the movement, begin to develop institutions of a free society, and chip away at the status quo. We fight back while pushing forward, struggle today to win the things that put us in the position to win even more tomorrow. We do this by struggling around the daily injustices people suffer while always remembering our visions of freedom beyond.

And as we fight, we must never give up the power we are building for the comfort we might gain through battles along the way. We must assert that we will never be satisfied by anything this system can give us, that there is always another victory to be won, that our struggle over concrete and present things is always on the road to something greater. We must remember that reform plus reform plus reform does not equal revolution, that real transformation necessitates moments of confrontation, that we must build power to stand up and sit down at those key times and places when crumbling systems are dealt their death blows and doors to new possibilities of freedom are forced open.

It is there—in those difficult battles over the reality of our lives, those long and visionary struggles for freedom beyond what is possible now, those incredible confrontations that clear the rubble away for the new world we are creating—that protest becomes resistance, practice becomes creation, and rebellion becomes revolution. And we are already winning. We have pried open a little space to breathe, to fight, and to imagine a world being born. Yes, it has already begun. Every day, little by little, we are remembering how to dream again.

Seth Tobocman

David Graeber

AFTERWORD
(OR, WHY THIS WHOLE BOOK SHOULD BE READ AS A PREFACE)

NO MOVEMENT EVER CHANGED THE WORLD IN JUST THREE MONTHS. THE fact that Occupy is now being criticized for *failing* to do so is a testimony to just how much we really did accomplish.

Contaminationism—the faith that the experience of direct democracy is infectious, that anyone exposed to it will never be the same, that exposing any significant number of people to it would inevitably lead to the creation of a new political culture—was the core principle of the global justice movement. In North America, for a brief moment after Seattle '99, it actually seemed like we might achieve it. Activist culture certainly changed. By 2001, the old world of steering committees, sectarian purges, and marching around with signs had been largely recast as old, comical, Stalinist throwbacks and a new, open-ended, pragmatic anarchism was emerging as the spiritual center of the revolutionary left.

The problem was that it turned out to be extremely difficult to break out of the activist ghetto; and when 9/11 changed the terms of engagement, and made any sort of direct-action-oriented politics far more difficult, everything reversed itself—or seemed to, at least. It's taken us a decade to fully realize that this wasn't really true. A groundwork had been built. Freedom was potentially infectious. We just had to wait for our moment.

The occupation of Zuccotti Park, on September 17, 2011, ten years and six days after the attack on the Towers, might be conceived as the anti-9/11. Zuccotti—soon to be renamed Liberty Plaza—was only a minute's walk from Ground Zero. In the years immediately following 9/11, New York activists simply assumed that any sort of action in the area would be inconceivable, yet remarkably, in the endless torrent of commentary that soon poured out about the meaning of the occupation, almost no one found reason to even *mention* that Ground Zero was only two blocks away. In global terms, what we did there was simply reproduce a miniature version of the great occupied squares—Tahrir, Syntagma, Plaça de Catalunya—that had marked the revolutionary ferment of 2011. In American terms, we created a symbol that largely undid everything that both sides of the War on Terror had attempted to create: a world where politics was reduced to a matter of violent demagogues, would-be superheroes and supervillains, commando teams, conspiracies, torture chambers, religious absolutism, and improvised explosive devices. Liberty Park was a potent antidote to all of this because, with its free food, free books, music, and General Assemblies, it was an exercise in the politics of mutual aid, solidarity, and caring. A simple, unauthorized act of love. This did, indeed, begin to change people's conceptions of what politics could be about.

Hardly surprising, then, that state was so desperate to suppress it. Nothing scares the rulers of America more than the threat of actual democracy. The attack came on two planes: one, sheer physical assault, in complete contempt of America's much-vaunted pretensions of rights to democratic assembly; second, a symbolic campaign to replace images of free music, art, and libraries with Hobbesian images of violence, excrement, and sexual assault. This was only to be expected. What surprised many of us was the almost instant betrayal, once the repression began, on the part of our liberal allies. There is a kind of tacit understanding between liberals and radical social movements in America: we make you relevant, you keep us out of jail. We came through with our part of the bargain. They utterly failed in theirs.

It's all the more surprising since civil liberties is normally a bread-and-butter issue for groups like MoveOn and Rebuild the Dream, or networks like MSNBC. True, historically, liberals have had a notorious tendency to look the other way during campaigns of government violence against radical social movements: think of the Red Scare, or the repression of the Wobblies or the Panthers. But generally speaking, those were either working-class movements, or people of color. When arguably milder repression was directed against middle-class white people, for example during the McCarthy era, liberals eventually, if grudgingly, rose up in righteous indignation. In a way, the repression of Occupy might just mark a turning point, since this was outright, militarized violence directed against a movement that contained a very large proportion—perhaps a majority—of middle-class white people. The liberal classes had already come to terms with the contempt for international law and flagrant unilateral use of US military power that had characterized the War on Terror, once a Democratic administration took it up. Now, they made it clear that they were, effectively, throwing their support behind the use of militarized police violence internally, against even the most peaceful civil disobedience, as long as it served their political interests in some way. And, the moment it became clear Occupy was not going to "join the political process" and become a left-wing version of the Tea Party, it seems they decided that the camps would have to go.

It's important that readers understand that Occupy did not disappear after the attacks on the camps: it's just that the media attention, so mysteriously frenetic in the first two months, halted just as mysteriously as it began. True (and I am speaking here from my own experience in New York), the movement was thrown into confusion and squabbles at first, and it took us a long time to figure out that the right to freedom of assembly really had been definitively repealed, and that the media would simply passively accept new standards whereby it was considered perfectly normal and un-newsworthy that if any large number of Occupiers attempted to pull off even a completely legal street action, at least one or two would end up in the hospital from police attacks.

Still, the camps were always primarily an advertisement, a defiant experiment in libertarian communism that was never going to be allowed to last for very long. It's kind of amazing we got away for it as long as we did. Real social movements take years, even decades. The problem is how to continue in a way that maintains our original principles: the refusal to engage with a "political process" that we consider to be fundamentally illegitimate and corrupt. From the vantage point of New York, as I write this Afterword in the middle of August 2012, I'd say that we have, indeed, laid the groundwork for long-term mass resistance to financial capitalism. We are in the process of acquiring a permanent space, we already have, to give just one example, eight different occupied farms, and experienced crews of medics, lawyers, media activists, housing activists,

Liberty Park was a potent antidote to the War on Terror because, with its free food, free books, music, and General Assemblies, it was an exercise in the politics of mutual aid, solidarity, and caring. A simple, unauthorized act of love. This did, indeed, begin to change people's conceptions of what politics could be about.

artists, writers, magazines, facilitators, and close allies in unions and community groups. We have hundreds of activists with extensive street experience and thousands who will show up in support for a major action. Still,
for most of the summer, we've been talking less about major actions, and
more about how to dig in for the long haul.

In part, we came to realize that while the contamination theory does
work, it takes a very long time to build a genuinely democratic culture. The
General Assemblies were each and all tiny miracles; we were all astounded
that it was possible for such diverse groups of people to come together and
reasonably work out matters of common concern. But without camps to
organize, they almost invariably fell apart. All sorts of divisions, all sorts of
toxic behavior we thought we'd overcome suddenly flooded back upon us.
But should this be surprising? We are all the products of a society that is not
only profoundly undemocratic, but is also full of institutions designed to
teach us habits that would make any sort of democratic society impossible.
We weren't really going to overcome all that in just a matter of months. The
key is to take advantage of the fact that millions have now been exposed to
the basic tenets of horizontality, and to create what might be called *democratic capacity*, so as to ensure that the next time the system begins to fall
apart (as it inevitably will; most honest economists predict another crash in
a maximum of three years) we will be the ones in a position to provide a
viable alternative.

Yet it isn't just a matter of lying in wait—a movement can only grow if
there are campaigns and victories, and a larger analysis of how those campaigns and victories contribute to its long-term goals. This means sitting
down to a real analysis of why Occupy exploded the way it did in the first
place: what is our real social base? These conversations have blossomed over
the summer, and a conclusion that many of us have come to is that as
a movement against the depredations of financial capitalism, we have to
think about the social role of debt. It was largely heavily-indebted students,
or recent graduates, who first flocked to Liberty Park. What was surprising
was that their plight struck such a chord—in particular among unionized
workers who would not, historically, have been the people most likely to
identify with their cause. While there are all sorts of specific reasons this
has changed, they all ultimately hearken back to the role of finance capital itself: the fact that most of Wall Street's profits are no longer extracted
from industry and commerce at all, but from speculation and "financial
services," which—though capitalists would have us believe that it is all a
matter of producing money out of thin air through various sorts of magic
tricks—turns out to be simply a shakedown operation: outright imperialism overseas, and colluding with the government at home to ensure that the
vast majority of Americans fall into debt, and then extracting the money

directly. It's impossible to know what percentage of the average household's income is now simply appropriated in one way or another by the financial services sector, since the figures are unavailable, but some place it as high as 20%, and many saddled with student debt—often for the cost of obtaining certificates to make employment possible—are currently paying 40% or even half. Three quarters of Americans are now debtors (the ones who are not cluster at the very top and very bottom of the income spectrum), and maybe a quarter are already defaulters (at least 1 in 7 are current being pursued by a debt collector). Above all, we concluded, Occupy is a campaign against financial terrorism: against the fear, violence, and deprivation that policies intentionally designed to create debt have wrought across America.

How do we fight against a phenomenon like debt, which is designed to shame and isolate its victims? One can try to create a new, alternative community. This is what we did in the camps, but now it is much more difficult. Still, when we began to hold "debtor's assemblies" over the course of the summer, they always ended up larger, and more lively than anything else we tried to do. People literally couldn't stop talking about the subject. Gradually, the outlines of a new campaign emerged, one we are calling Strike Debt. We've discussed everything from buying up debt from the same brokers who sell it to debt collectors, at 5 cents on the dollar (and then cancelling, and setting fire to the stuff), to creating a free Defaulter's Manual, to a whole host of actions revolving around the Invisible Army of defaulters who, though they cannot show their faces, are in the process of, effectively, withdrawing their consent from capitalism. All of these are just initial projects. They are meant as ideas to build upon, to expand, to inspire other projects with similar themes. Debt seems the most realistic way to tie all the threads that continue to be vital in the movement—home defenses, farms, rent strikes, student debt campaigns inspired by Montreal—together, ultimately culminating in a nationwide series of bona fide debt strikes. Considering the endless securitization of American debt, the results of any such strike would be multiplied endlessly and create a serious strategic threat to global capital.

There is of course a huge temptation when dealing with such concrete, real-world issues to compromise on our initial attitude of pure defiance to the existing political order, to pursue legislation, or even just to make concrete demands. It seems to me (and most OWS folks in New York, I think, have come to the same conclusion) that this would be a mistake. It was always that defiance—that refusal to grant the system legitimacy—that struck a chord in the collective imagination, precisely because, in the eyes of most of the American public, the existing political system is basically seen as illegitimate. A recent survey indicated that a larger percentage of the American public would like to see the country switch over to a Soviet-style communist economic system (roughly 10% [!!]), than approved of Congress (roughly 8.5%). And, wielding the power of delegitimation can produce very concrete, real-world results. Perhaps the greatest example in recent years was the rebellion in Argentina in 2001-02, where the slogan was *que se vayan todos* (roughly translated: "they can all go to hell")—a profound and general rejection of the entire political establishment and dominant institutions, accompanied by the creation of popular assemblies, occupied factories, experiments in horizontality and autonomy on every level and in every form. The famous result: the installation of an extremely moderate, even timid, Social Democratic party that, in order to re-establish some tiny modicum of legitimacy in the eyes of the public for the very idea of government, was forced to do something genuinely radical: to default on Argentina's loans. The result was a cascade of events that ultimately undid the rule of the IMF in Latin America and changed the political economy of the entire world. And, it was accomplished by a movement that never made a single legislative proposition, that was successful, in fact, precisely because it refused to do so.

What might a contemporary parallel be? In reality, the situation in the US today is not entirely different. "Structural adjustment" has come home to the Imperial heartland; once again, it's all justified in a language of debt, but everyone knows the debts cannot really be paid. I'd like to end, then, with an essay that I recently contributed to *Tidal*, the journal of the Occupy Theory working group, which was an attempt to strike this kind of balance. It contains the closest I've come to offering my own idea for a "demand." But it's offered with the knowledge that some sort of dramatic change in the existing debt regime is going to have to happen. While we can't, and would never want to, write the legislation or make the executive decisions, it is absolutely crucial that, as a social movement, we provide the moral framework, and the political context, in which these events are going to take place:

after the jubilee

IF YOU LOOK just at how things look on paper, the entire world is awash in debt. All governments are in debt. Corporate debt is at historic highs. And so is what economists like to call "household debt"—both in the sense of how many people are in the red, and the sheer quantity of what they owe. There's a consensus among economists that this is a terrible problem, even if, as usual, economists can't agree as to why. The mainstream, conventional view is that the "debt overhang" from all three is so vast it is stifling other economic activity. We have to reduce all of them, they say, largely by either raising taxes on ordinary people, or cutting their services. (Only on ordinary people, mind you—mainstream economists are of course paid to come up with reasons why one should never do either of these things to the rich.) More level heads point out that national debt, especially for countries like the US, is nothing like personal debt, since the US government could eliminate its entire debt overnight if it simply instructed the Federal Reserve to print the money and hand it over to the government.

No doubt, readers will object: "but if you just print trillions of dollars, wouldn't that cause severe inflation?" Well, yes, in theory, it should. But it seems the theory here is flawed, since that's exactly what the government is doing: they've been printing trillions of dollars, and so far, it hasn't had any notable inflationary effect.

The US government's policy, both under Bush and under Obama (on such matters there's been almost zero difference in policy between the two), has been to print money and give it to the banks. Actually, this is the way the US financial system has always worked, but since 2008, it has been intensified with reckless abandon. The Federal Reserve has whisked trillions of dollars into existence by waving its magic wand, and then lent it at almost negligible interest rates to large financial institutions like Bank of America or Goldman Sachs. The supposed purpose was first to save them from bankruptcy, then to get them lending and jump-start the economy. But there seems good reason to believe there's another purpose, as well: to flood the economy with so much money that it would, in fact, create inflation, as a way

This is the real burden of debt we're passing on to future generations: the burden of having to work ever harder, while at the same time, consuming more energy, eroding the earth's ecosystems, and ultimately accelerating catastrophic climate change at just the moment we desperately need some way to reverse it. Seen in this light, a debt cancellation might be the last chance we have to save the planet.

of reducing debts. (After all, if you owe $1,000.00 and the value of the dollar falls by half, the value of your debt has just been reduced by half as well.)

The problem is it didn't work. Either to get the economy moving, or to increase inflation. First of all, banks did not invest the money. Mainly, they either lent it back to the government again, or deposited it in the Federal Reserve, which paid them a higher interest rate for just keeping it there than they were charging those same banks to borrow it. So in effect, the government has been printing money and giving it to the banks and the banks have just sat on it. This is perhaps not too surprising, since the Federal Reserve itself is governed by the very bankers that it is giving money to. Still, while a policy of allowing bankers to print money and give it to themselves can work quite well if your aim is restoring the fortunes of the 1%—and it has done quite nicely at this—and though it has also allowed the rich to pay off their own debts and sent a good deal of new money sloshing around in the political system to reward politicians for allowing them to do so, even the Fed now admits it has done very little to get employers hiring, or even to create any significant inflation.

THE CONCLUSION TO all of this is so obvious that even the people on the top are increasingly beginning to recognize it—at least, that minority of them who actually do care about the long-term viability of the system (rather than simply being concerned with their own personal short-term enrichment). There will have to be some kind of mass debt cancellation. And not just the debts of the rich, which can always be erased in one way or another if they become inconvenient, but the debts of ordinary citizens as well. In Europe, even professional economists are beginning to talk of "jubilees," and the Fed itself recently issued a white paper recommending mass cancellation of mortgage debt.

The very fact that such people are contemplating this shows that they know the system is in trouble. Up until now, the very idea of debt cancellation was the ultimate taboo. Again: not for those on top themselves. Donald Trump, for instance, has walked away from billions of debt and none of his friends find this at all a problem, but all of them absolutely insist that for the little people, the rules must be different.

One might well question why. Why should the rich care so much that the debt of the poor should never be forgiven? Is it simple sadism? Do rich people somehow get a kick out of knowing that at any moment there are at least a few hardworking mothers being kicked out of their homes and having to pawn their children's toys to pay for the costs of some catastrophic illness? This seems implausible. If you know anything about extremely rich people you know they almost never think about poor people at all—except perhaps as occasional objects of charity.

No, the real answer seems to be ideological. To put the matter crudely, a ruling class whose main claim to wealth is no longer the ability to make anything, or even really sell anything, but increasingly on a series of credit scams propped up by government support, has to rely very heavily on every mechanism that might tend to legitimize the system. This is why the last 30 years of "financialization" have been accompanied by an ideological offensive unparalleled in human history, arguing that current economic arrangements—which they have rather whimsically dubbed "the free market" even though it functions almost entirely through the government giving money to the rich—is not just the best economic system, but the only economic system that could possibly exist, except possibly for Soviet-style communism. Much more energy has been put into creating mechanisms to convince people that the system is morally justified, and the only viable economic system, than has been put into actually creating a viable economic system (as its near collapse in 2008 clearly showed.) The last thing the 1% wants, as the world economy continues to teeter from crisis to crisis, is to give up on one of their most powerful moral weapons: the idea that decent people always pay their debts.

So: SOME KIND of mass debt cancellation is on the way. Almost everyone is willing to admit this now. It's the only way to resolve the sovereign debt crisis in Europe. It's the only way to resolve the ongoing mortgage crisis in America. The real battle is over the form that it will take. Even apart from obvious questions, like how much debt will be cancelled (just certain mortgage debt? Or a grand jubilee for all personal debt up to say, $100,000?), and of course, for whom, there are two absolutely critical factors to look at here:

1) Will they admit they are doing it? That is, will the debt cancellation be presented *as* a debt cancellation, as an honest acknowledgement that money is really just a political arrangement now, and, therefore, the beginning of a process of finally beginning to bring such arrangements under democratic control, or will it will be dressed up as something else?

2) What will come afterwards? That is, will the cancellation just be a way of preserving the system and its extreme inequalities, perhaps in an even more savage form, or will it be a way to begin to move beyond it.

The two are obviously linked. To get a sense of what the most conservative option would be like, one might consult a recent report of the Boston Consulting Group, a mainstream economic think tank. They begin by agreeing that since there's no way to grow or inflate our way out of debt, cancellation is inevitable. Why postpone it? However, their solution is to frame the whole thing as a one-time tax on wealth to pay off, say, 60% of all outstanding debt, and then declare that the price for such sacrifices by the rich will be even more austerity for everybody else. Others suggest having the government print money, buying mortgages, and giving them to homeowners. No one dares to suggest that the government could just as easily declare those same debts unenforceable (if you want to pay back your loan you're free to do so but the government will no longer recognize its legal standing in court if you decide not to). That would open windows those running the system are desperate to keep locked.

So what would a radical alternative really look like? There have been some intriguing suggestions: democratization of the Fed, a full employment program to pull wages upwards, some sort of basic income scheme. Some are quite radical, but almost all involve both expanding government, and increasing the overall number of jobs and hours worked.

This is a real problem because feeding the global work machine, increasing production, productivity, and employment levels, is really the last thing we need to be doing right now if we want to save the planet from ecological catastrophe.

But this, I think, points us towards a solution. Because in fact, the ecological crisis and the debt crisis have everything to do with another.

Here it might help to understand that debts are, basically, promises of future productivity. Think of it this way: Imagine everyone on earth produces a trillion dollars worth of goods and services a year. And imagine they consume about the same—since of course that's what generally happens, we consume most of what we produce, minus a little wastage. Yet 1% of them somehow contrive to convince 99% of them that they still, collectively, owe them a trillion dollars. Well, aside from the fact that someone is obviously being seriously overcharged here, there's clearly no way these debts can be repaid at their current value unless everyone produces even more the next year. In fact, if the interest payments are set at, say, 5% a year, they'll have to produce 5% more just to break even.

This is the real burden of debt we're passing on to future generations: the burden of having to work ever harder, while at the same time, consuming more energy, eroding the earth's ecosystems, and ultimately accelerating catastrophic climate change at just the moment we desperately need some way to reverse it. Seen in this light, a debt cancellation might be the last chance we have to save the planet. The problem is that conservatives don't care, and liberals are still caught up in impossible dreams of returning to the Keynesian economic policies of the '50s and '60s, which based broad prosperity on continual economic expansion. We're going to have to come up with an entirely different kind of economic policy.

So, if a post-jubilee society can't promise the workers of the world an endless expansion of new consumer goods, what can it do? I think the answer is obvious. It could offer security in basic needs—guarantees of food, housing, and health care that can ensure that our children don't have to face the fear, shame, and anxiety that defines most of our lives today. And above all, it can offer them less work. Remember that in the 1870s, the idea of an 8-hour day seemed just as unrealistic and utopian as, say, demanding a 4-hour day would seem today. Yet the labor movement managed to achieve it. So why not demand a 4-hour day? Or a guaranteed five months of paid vacation? It is very clear that Americans—those who do have jobs—are absurdly overworked. It's also clear that a very large proportion of that work is completely unnecessary. And every hour saved from work is an hour that we can give to our friends, families, communities.

This is not the place to come up with a detailed economic program of how it could be done or how such a system could work—these are matters to be worked out democratically (myself, I'd like to see wage labor eliminated entirely. But maybe that's just me). Anyway, social change doesn't begin by someone mapping out a program. It begins with visions and principles. Our rulers have made it clear they no longer know what it would be like to even have either. But in a way even that doesn't matter. Real, lasting change always comes from below. In 2001, the world saw the first stirrings of a global uprising against the current empire of debt. It has already begun to alter the global terms of debate. The prospect of mass debt cancellation provides us with a unique opportunity to turn that democratic impulse towards a fundamental transformation of values, and towards a genuinely viable accommodation with the earth.

It's not clear if there's ever been a political moment with so much at stake.

about the authors in this collection:

Michael Andrews has participated in Occupy Wall Street since its inception. He is a writer and editor living in Brooklyn. Find him online at http://www.michael-andrews.net.

Michael Belt is a labor organizer and activist based in New York City. Michael attended Prescott College where he received his bachelors degree in Participatory Community Development. Before moving to New York, Michael was an adjunct instructor teaching Border Studies, community activism and critical theory in Arizona. He is also the founder of the Praxis Youth Action Conference, AN ANNUAL youth organizers conference IN ARIZONA. Michael has been active with the Immigrant Workers Justice Working Group of Occupy Wall Street, the Labor Outreach Committee, the Mayday Planning Committee and the 99 Picket Lines Working Group.

Nadine Bloch is an innovative artist, nonviolent practitioner, political organizer, direct-action trainer, and puppetista, who combines the principles and strategies of nonviolent civil disobedience with creative use of the arts in cultural resistance and public protest. She has worked with diverse organizations, including Nonviolence International, Greenpeace, The Ruckus Society, The Labor Heritage Foundation, Health GAP, Housing Works and the Bread & Puppet Theater.

Rose Bookbinder has been an organizer and activist for the last 10 years. Her work has been primarily focused in union organizing campaigns in Massachusetts, New York, Connecticut and Puerto Rico. She has also worked with day laborers and immigrants doing legal advocacy and workers' rights trainings and organizing with Workers Centers in Westchester and the Hudson Valley of NY. She sits on the board of the Rosenberg Fund for Children, which provides money to children of targeted activists and on the Steering Committee of Western Mass Jobs with Justice. Rose has been active with the Immigrant Workers Justice Working Group of Occupy Wall Street, the Labor Outreach Committee, the Mayday, O15, N17, and D12 Direct Action Planning Committees and the 99 Picket Lines Working Group.

Mark Bray is a member of the Occupy Wall Street Press Team. For 12 years, he has been a political organizer involved in the anti-globalization movement, the anti-war movement, labor organizing, and student and immigrant rights organizing. He is also a PhD student in European History at Rutgers University. His research focuses on anarchism, human rights, terrorism and state repression in late nineteenth century Spain.

Emily Brissette has been involved in Occupy Oakland, particularly in anti-repression work, and has written on the debate in the movement around violence for *CounterPunch*. She is a doctoral candidate in Sociology at UC Berkeley, where she explores the role of deeply engrained cultural assumptions about the nature of state in the movements against the Vietnam and Iraq wars.

George Caffentzis is a Professor of Philosophy at the University of Southern Maine in Portland, Maine. He is a founding member of the Midnight Notes Collective. He is the author of many books and articles on money, machines and capitalism. His e-book, *No Blood for Oil!* can be downloaded gratis at www.radicalpolytics.org.

George Ciccariello-Maher teaches political theory at Drexel University in Philadelphia. Exiled from Oakland, he was active in organizing around the 2009 murder of Oscar Grant and wrote frequently about the ensuing struggles for *CounterPunch*. His first book, *We Cre-*

ated Him: A People's History of Venezuela's Bolivarian Revolution, is forthcoming from Duke University Press. He is a co-founder and Editorial Council member for *Reclamations* (http://reclamationsjournal.org), a journal of the radical Bay Area student milieu.

Joshua Clover is the author of two books of poetry and two of cultural criticism; he studies poetry and political economy. He has taken part in university struggles in the UC system, and in the Oakland Commune.

Annie Cockrell writes here about her participation in Occupy Wall Street.

Andrew Cornell is a writer, organizer, and educator who teaches American Studies at Williams College in Massachusetts. He is the author of *Oppose and Propose! Lessons from Movement for a New Society* and he is completing a history of the US anarchist movement in the mid-20th century.

Molly Crabapple is a New York artist and the creator of the global drawing movement Dr. Sketchy's Anti- Art School. She has created subversive, Victorian inspired art for clients including *The New York Times*, Red Bull, *The Wall Street Journal*, CNN, Marvel Comics, DC Comics, and South by Southwest Interactive, as well as Occupy Wall Street. She can be found online at http://mollycrabapple.com.

The **CrimethInc. Ex-Workers' Collective** is a top-secret anarchist think tank dedicated to the abolition of capitalism, hierarchy, and tedium and the transformation of life into a joyous game played for the highest stakes. http://crimethinc.com.

Croatoan is a group of people who were brought together by the Occupy Oakland encampment and who were active in its subcommittees and general assemblies.

Paul Dalton is an anarchist and AIDS activist living in Oakland, CA. He enjoys cats, coffee, crosswords, finding a cure, and destroying capitalism. Contact: paulsdalton@yahoo.com.

Chris Dixon is a longtime anti-authoritarian organizer who recently received his PhD from the University of California at Santa Cruz. He lives in Sudbury, Ontario, where he is involved with anti-war and Indigenous solidarity organizing. Dixon serves on the board of the Institute for Anarchist Studies and the advisory board for the journal *Upping the Anti*. He is currently completing a book based on interviews with anti-authoritarian organizers involved in broader-based movements.

John Duda was a participant in Occupy Baltimore. He is completing a study of the idea of self-organization in radical politics, works on postcapitalist political economy at the Democracy Collaborative, and is a founding collective member of Red Emma's Bookstore Coffeehouse.

Brendan Maslauskas Dunn was active with Port Militarization Resistance for the better part of five years and in shutting down the Port of Olympia in 2007. He helped with the outing of John Towery II who was sent by the US Army to infiltrate, disrupt and spy on Port Militarization Resistance, SDS, other activist groups and anarchists in Olympia and Tacoma, WA. After the eviction of Zuccotti Park in November 2011, he returned to his hometown of Utica, NY and helped to organize Occupy Utica.

Lisa Fithian is a long-time organizer focused on strategic, creative direct actions to disrupt those who oppress communities and steal the wealth of the planet. Lisa has been organizing mass shutdowns since the mid-80s and continues supporting new generations and the occupy movement in growing their power to win victories while radically restructuring local and global economies.

Gabriella writes here about her work with Occupy Santa Cruz, and the internal work we must do as movement actors.

David Graeber teaches anthropology at Goldsmiths College, University of London. He is the author of the bestselling *Debt: The First 5,000 Years*, and *Direct Action: An Ethnography*, among other works. His work has recently appeared in *The Nation*, *Mute*, *The Guardian*, *Al-Jazeera*, and countless other publications. Widely credited with coining the "99 Percent" meme, he was one of the first New Yorkers to take up the *Adbusters* call to Occupy Wall Street, and continues to be an active participant in the Occupy movement.

Ryan Harvey is a member of the Riot-Folk musician's collective and is an organizer with the Civilian-Soldier Alliance. He writes on war, social movements, and music on his blog http://www.voiceshakes.wordpress.com. He lives in Baltimore, MD.

Rachel Herzing and **Isaac Ontiveros** are members of Critical Resistance, a national grass-roots organization working to abolish the prison industrial complex.

Gabriel Hetland is a doctoral candidate in sociology at the University of California, Berkeley. His research focuses on participatory budgeting in Venezuela and Bolivia. Since November, he has been a core member of the Community Democracy Project in Oakland.

Marisa Holmes has been organizing with Occupy Wall Street since its inception in August, 2011. She is an independent filmmaker, activist, and educator based in Brooklyn, NY. For the past seven years she has been involved in the international student movement, anti-war movement, independent media projects, and intentional communities. She is currently an MFA student in Integrated Media at Hunter College, where she utilizes new media for social change.

Kate Khatib is a writer, designer, and activist based in Baltimore, Maryland. She is a founding member of the Red Emma's collective, and a collective member at AK Press. She currently teaches politics the Maryland Institute College of Art, and is completing a book-length treatise on surrealism and the politics of history. Find her online at http://www.manifestor.org.

Margaret Killjoy is a nomadic anarchist, author, photographer, and editor. He was involved with and inspired by Occupy Santa Cruz in the autumn of 2011. His other books include *Mythmakers & Lawbreakers: Anarchist Writers on Fiction*, *What Lies Beneath the Clock Tower*, and *A Steampunk's Guide to the Apocalypse*. He can be found online at http://birdsbeforethestorm.net.

Mike King has been an active member of Occupy Oakland, helping to organize the November 2nd and December 12th Port Shutdowns. He has been involved with the Labor Solidarity Committee, Occupy AC-Transit, and the Oakland Assembly of the Unemployed, and has written pieces for *CounterPunch*. Mike was involved in the Oscar Grant movement and is currently a part of the Justice for Alan Blueford Coalition. He is currently finishing a dissertation in Sociology at UC Santa Cruz and writing a book on the policing and social control tactics and strategies used against Occupy Oakland.

Koala Largess is a long-term organizer who worked in Washington, DC with the homeless population until moving to Baltimore in 2005. They have been a member of the Industrial

Workers of the World, for five years, and they have participated in different projects and organizations including a newly formed Animal Rights group, the Red Clover Collective, the Velocipede Bicycle Project, the United Workers Association, and an Occupy-based direct action group known as Schools Not Jails. They are an anarchist who believes in bicycles, mutual aid, and interdependence.

Yvonne Yen Liu is a senior researcher at the Applied Research Center, a racial justice think and action tank, which publishes Colorlines.com. In addition to contributing regularly to Colorlines.com, Yvonne has been published in *Yes! Magazine, In These Times*, and Alternet. She serves on the board of Smart Meme and the advisory committee for the Food Chain Workers Alliance. She cofounded NYC Summer, a youth of color organizing school, and served on the boards of WBAI 99.5 FM and Seven Stories Institute.

Josh MacPhee is a designer, artist, activist, and archivist. He is a member of both the Justseeds Artists' Cooperative and Occuprint collective. He is the co-author of *Signs of Change: Social Movement Cultures 1960s to Now*, co-editor of *Signal: A Journal of International Political Graphics and Culture*, and he recently helped open the Interference Archive, a public collection of cultural materials produced by social movements (http://www.interferencearchive.org).

Manissa McCleave Maharawal is a writer, activist and Graduate Student in the Anthropology Department at the CUNY Graduate Center in New York.

Yotam Marom is a political organizer, activist, educator, musician, and writer based in New York City. He has been active in the Occupy Wall Street movement since its planning stages, as well as precursors such as the May 12 demonstrations and Bloombergville, a two-week occupation to resist the city's budget cuts of 2011. Yotam is a founding member of the Organization for a Free Society, and has experience in student activism, anti-austerity struggles, democratic education, and communal living. His writing about Occupy has been featured in publications such as *The Nation, n+1, Organizing Upgrade, Z Magazine*, and *AlterNet*, and can be found at http://www.yotammarom.com.

Mike McGuire is a builder and organizer with a background in labor, Latin America, global justice, direct action, and creative protest. He has been working within the Occupy movement since its birth on September 17, 2011 in Zuccotti Park.

Cindy Milstein is a board member of the Institute for Anarchist Studies—focusing her efforts on the Lexicon pamphlet series, IAS/AK Anarchist Interventions book series, and anarchist theory tracks—and author of *Anarchism and Its Aspirations* (IAS/AK Press, 2010) and, in collaboration with Erik Ruin, *Paths toward Utopia: Graphic Explorations of Everyday Anarchism*. She has been involved in various social movements and community organizing from below, and numerous collective projects, such as Occupy Philly, Station 40 in San Francisco, and Black Sheep Books in Montpelier, VT. She can be reached at cbmilstein@yahoo.com.

Occupy Research is an open, shared space for distributed research focused around the Occupy Movement | http://www.occupyreserach.net. **DataCenter** is a national social justice organization that provides strategic research support for social movements | http://www.datacenter.org.

Joel Olson was a tireless advocate for the abolition of whiteness and a long-time activist. A member of both Love and Rage Federation and Bring the Ruckus, he taught at Northern

Arizona University and was at work on a book exploring extremism before his sudden passing in March 2012.

Morrigan Phillips is a community social worker and organizer in Boston, MA. She works with Suvivors Inc./Mass.Welfare Rights Union and has been involved with Occupy Boston as a non-violent direct action trainer and member of the Health Justice working group. Morrigan can be found on twitter at @mbotastic.

Frances Fox Piven is Distinguished Professor of Sociology and Political Science at the CUNY Graduate Center. Her scholarship and activism have centered on social movements, electoral politics, and welfare policy. She is the author of *Poor People's Movements* and *Challenging Authority*, among a great wealth of other works.

Vijay Prashad is the George and Martha Kellner Chair of South Asian History, and professor and director of international studies at Trinity College in Hartford, Connecticut. He is the author or editor of over a dozen books, including *The Darker Nations: A People's History of the Third World* and *Arab Spring, Libyan Winter*.

Michael Premo is an artist, activist, organizer and cultural worker dedicated to human rights. He is co-producer of the *Housing is a Human Right* storytelling project. He has collaborated with the Hip-Hop Theater Festival, The Foundry Theatre, The Civilians and StoryCorps, among many others. He serves on the board of directors for the Network of Ensemble Theaters. Currently, he is a member of Organizing for Occupation, a group dedicated to actualizing the human right to housing through nonviolent direct action. Michael's radio stories have been broadcast internationally and his photography has appeared in publications that include *Left Turn, The Village Voice, The New York Times,* and *Het Parool.*

Max Rameau is a Haitian-born Pan-African theorist and organizer, living in Washington, DC. Max has organized in Miami, FL and DC around a range of issues, including immigrant rights, especially for Haitian immigrants, LGBTQ rights and police brutality, among others. Max helped found the land-based Take Back the Land in 2006, and in October of that year, the organization seized control of a vacant lot in the Liberty City section of Miami, and built the Umoja Village, a full urban shantytown.

Research & Destroy is a collective of antistate/communist antagonists that formed in the Bay Area in 2009.

Nathan Schneider is an editor of WagingNonviolence.org, for which he began covering the planning of Occupy Wall Street in August of 2011. His writing about the Occupy movement has appeared in *The Occupied Wall Street Journal, Harper's, The Nation, The New York Times, Tidal,* the *Boston Review*, and elsewhere.

Jonathan Matthew Smucker is a grassroots organizer, trainer, writer, and director of Beyond the Choir. He has worked with School of the Americas Watch, Lancaster Coalition for Peace & Justice, War Resisters League, MoveOn.org, and Beyond the Choir; and in partnership with Iraq Veterans Against the War, smartMeme, Ruckus Society, AK Press, and many local efforts. His writing has been published by *Alternet, Yes! Magazine, Huffington Post, The Nation, n+1, Cognitive Policy Works,* and in the book *Beautiful Trouble: A Toolbox for Revolution.* On October 12, 2011, he went to Occupy Wall Street, where he has worked with the press working group, the movement building working group, Occupy Homes, and Occupy Faith. He blogs at http://beyondthechoir.org and http://devoketheapocalypse.com.

Lester Spence is an associate professor of Political Science and Africana Studies at Johns Hopkins University, where he specializes in black politics, racial politics, urban politics, public opinion, and American political thought. He is the author of *Stare in the Darkness: The Limits of Hip-Hop and Black Politics*, and is a frequent contributor to both academic journals and mainstream media outlets. A co-founder of the Baltimore Mixtape Project (an attempt to generate locally produced progressive hip-hop), he has been engaged in activist politics for over 25 years up to and including Occupy Baltimore.

Janaina Stronzake is a farm worker and part of the National Coordination of the MST. She is also a historian, with master's degrees in Contemporary History (Universidad Autonoma de Madrid) and International Development and Cooperation (Universidad de Pais Vasco).

Mattilda Bernstein Sycamore (http://mattildabernsteinsycamore.com) is the author of two novels, *So Many Ways to Sleep Badly* and *Pulling Taffy*, and the editor of five nonfiction anthologies, most recently *Why Are Faggots So Afraid of Faggots?: Flaming Challenges to Masculinity, Objectification, and the Desire to Conform*. At the end of 2010, Sycamore fled San Francisco in an act of desperation, and moved to Santa Fe. This move lasted a little over a year, and then Mattilda fled again, this time for Seattle. Sycamore's next book (part memoir, part social history, and part elegy) is *The End of San Francisco*, which City Lights will be publishing in April 2013. Watch out!

Team Colors is a collective engaged in militant research to provide strategic analysis for the intervention into everyday life. Recently the collective edited the collection *Uses of a Whirlwind: Movement, Movements, and Contemporary Radical Currents in the United States* and authored the short book *Winds From Below and other interventions)*. Collective members have been involved in various organizing efforts together for over a decade. http://www.warmachines.info

Janelle Treibitz is a puppeteer and organizer with the DC-based Puppet Underground collective. She collaborates with local organizations, neighborhood groups and grassroots campaigns, supporting their efforts to incorporate cultural strategies into their work. She has also worked for many years with the Bread and Puppet Theater in Vermont.

Unwoman (aka Erica Mulkey) is a Bay Area-based cellist-singer-songwriter best known for performing at steampunk conventions. She can be found online at http://unwoman.com.

Immanuel Wallerstein is a sociologist and world systems analyst based at Yale University. He is the author a multiple works including *The Modern World System*, *World Systems Analysis*, and *The Decline of American Power*.

Sophie Whittemore is a Southern anarcha-feminist residing in New Orleans, LA.

Kristian Williams is the author of *Hurt: Notes on Torture, American Methods: Torture and the Logic of Domination*, and *Our Enemies in Blue: Police and Power in America*. His work on policing and torture has also appeared in *Counterpunch, New Politics, In These Times,* and in the collection *Confrontations*. His is the co-editor of a new book on counterinsurgency and resistance, *Life During Wartime*, forthcoming in 2013 from AK Press.

Jaime Omar Yassin is an Oakland-based author and activist. Find his writings online at http://hyphenatedrepublic.wordpress.com.

Support AK Press!

AK Press is one of the world's largest and most productive anarchist publishing houses. We're entirely worker-run and democratically

managed. We operate without a corporate structure—no boss, no managers, no bullshit. We publish close to twenty books every year, and distribute thousands of other titles published by other like-minded independent presses from around the globe.

The Friends of AK program is a way that you can directly contribute to the continued existence of AK Press, and ensure that we're able to keep publishing great books just like this one! Friends pay a minimum of $25 per month, for a minimum three month period, into our publishing account. In return, Friends automatically receive (for the duration of their membership), as they appear, one free copy of every new AK Press title. They're also entitled to a 20% discount on everything featured in the AK Press Distribution catalog and on the website, and a 50% discount on AK Press-published products, on any and every order. You can choose between a traditional print book subscription or an e-book subscription, or sign up for our combination plan and get both!

There's great stuff in the works—so sign up now to become a Friend of AK Press, and let the presses roll!

Won't you be our friend? Email friendsofak@akpress.org for more info, or visit the Friends of AK Press website: www.akpress.org/programs/friendsofak